LAW WITHOUT JUSTICE

LAW WITHOUT JUSTICE

Why Criminal Law Doesn't Give People What They Deserve

PAUL H. ROBINSON AND MICHAEL T. CAHILL

OXFORD
UNIVERSITY PRESS

2006

OXFORD
UNIVERSITY PRESS

Oxford University Press, Inc., publishes works that further
Oxford University's objective of excellence
in research, scholarship, and education.

Oxford   New York
Auckland   Cape Town   Dar es Salaam   Hong Kong   Karachi
Kuala Lumpur   Madrid   Melbourne   Mexico City   Nairobi
New Delhi   Shanghai   Taipei   Toronto

With offices in
Argentina   Austria   Brazil   Chile   Czech Republic   France   Greece
Guatemala   Hungary   Italy   Japan   Poland   Portugal   Singapore
South Korea   Switzerland   Thailand   Turkey   Ukraine   Vietnam

Published by Oxford University Press, Inc.
198 Madison Avenue, New York, New York 10016

www.oup.com

Oxford is a registered trademark of Oxford University Press

Library of Congress Cataloging-in-Publication Data
Robinson, Paul H., 1948–
Law without justice : why criminal law doesn't give people what they deserve /
Paul H. Robinson, Michael T. Cahill.
    p. cm.
Includes bibliographical references.
ISBN-13 978-0-19-516015-4
ISBN 0-19-516015-0
1. Criminal justice, Administration of—United States. 2. Judicial error—United
States. 3. Law reform—United States. I. Cahill, Michael T. II. Title.
KF9223.R62 2005
345.73—dc22   2005004637

9 8 7 6 5 4 3 2 1

Printed in the United States of America
on acid-free paper

To Atticus Charles, Harper Kane,
Ian McAlpine, and Sarah McAlpine
and
To Patricia and Lee Cahill

ACKNOWLEDGMENTS

Paul Robinson thanks the participants of faculty workshops at Northwestern University School of Law and University of Minnesota Law School, and the Fordham University School of Law Advanced Criminal Law Seminar. The first presentation of these materials was as the Sackler Professorship Lecture at Tel Aviv University in December 2000. Research into the case facts and the collection of the many photographs was done through the unstinting efforts of several generations of research assistants, including, most ably, Michael Areinoff, Joseph Wheatley, Lindsay Suttenberg, and Steven Valdes, of the University of Pennsylvania Law School, and Alex Paul, Megan Bell, and Stephen Haedicke of the Northwestern University School of Law.

Michael Cahill thanks Brooklyn Law School and Dean Joan Wexler for supporting this project through the Dean's Summer Research Stipend program. He joins Paul in thanking the law faculties at Northwestern, University of Minnesota, and Fordham—at Fordham, Deborah Denno specifically—for offering the opportunity to discuss this project and for their feedback. Similar thanks are due to Chicago-Kent College of Law and Florida State University College of Law, and to the faculty participants in workshops at those schools. Various colleagues at Brooklyn and at Chicago-Kent provided useful comments about the project, either in conversation or after reading parts of the manuscript. Susan Herman in particular offered valuable perspective regarding materials in chapter 7. Larry Heuer of the Columbia University psychology department offered very helpful information about the social-science literature and pointed to fruitful research avenues. At Brooklyn Law School, Mark Ellis (class of 2005), Christopher Prior (class of 2007), and David Kim, Ben Wass, and Barak Wrobel (all of the class of 2006) provided capable research assistance.

The authors also received helpful comments from three anonymous reviewers arranged by Oxford University Press. At OUP, Dedi Felman and Michele Bové provided excellent editorial assistance and expertly prepared the book for publication.

CONTENTS

Introduction   3
   Objectives and Organization   6
   The Relevance of the Project   10

Chapter 1: Doing Justice and the Distractions from It   13
   Why Focus on Doing Justice?   15
   A Further Word on What We Mean by "Doing Justice"   18
   *The Utility of Desert: The Practical Costs
      of Deviations from Doing Justice*   21

PART I: PROMOTING JUSTICE IN A COMPLEX WORLD

Chapter 2: Fear of Manipulation and Abuse   27
   Is a Federal Prison Guard a "Peace Officer"?   28
   *Rejecting a Defense for Reasonable Mistake of Law
      (or for Necessity or Immaturity)*   31
   "Whoosh, Whoosh, Push"   35
   Improperly Narrowing or Rejecting Legitimate Excuses   41
   Sodomized and Taunted, the Pot Boils Over   44
   Relying upon a Purely Objective Standard   46
   Preventing Over-Individualization of an Objective Standard   49

Chapter 3: Advancing Reliability   52
  Too Late for Justice   53
  Statutes of Limitation   58
  Howard Aftermath   62
  Mistakes of Youth   62
  Strict Liability   65
  Excluding Coerced Confessions and Uncounseled Lineups   69

Chapter 4: Making the Most of Limited Resources   72
  A Bargain on Contract Killings?   74
  Plea Bargaining and Witness Immunity   79
  Gravano Aftermath   84

PART II: SACRIFICING JUSTICE TO
  PROMOTE OTHER INTERESTS

Chapter 5: Living by Rules   89
  Three Hundred Bodies in the Backyard   90
  Legality   96
  Marsh Aftermath   99
  Cannibalism at Sea   101
  Denying Legitimate Excuses (for the Sake of Clarity)   109
  Dudley Aftermath   110
  Setting Boundaries: Legality and Changing Norms   111

Chapter 6: Controlling Crime and Criminals   117
  Fleeing as Murder   119
  Deterrence   124
  Rehabilitation   130
  TV Violence   132
  Incapacitation   133

Chapter 7: Controlling Police and Prosecutors   137
  Released to Kill   139
  Exclusionary Rules   149
  Speedy Trial   155
  Eyler Aftermath   157
  Pictures in the Heating Duct   159
  Double Jeopardy   166
  Ignatow Aftermath   169

Incompetency   170
A Winged Car Powered by Cocaine   172
Entrapment   180
Moral Credibility "versus" Legitimacy: Evaluating the Tradeoffs   183

Chapter 8: Promoting Interests Unrelated to Criminal Justice   186
Criminal Camping   187
Criminalization of Regulatory Violations   190
Lindsey Aftermath   192
Corporate Criminality   192
The Diplomatic Rapist   195
Diplomatic and Official Immunity   199

PART III: REGAINING MORAL CREDIBILITY

Chapter 9: Criminal Justice Reforms   205
Shifting Evidentiary Burdens   205
Revamping the Verdict System   210
Using Alternative Punishment Methods   212

Chapter 10: Employing Civil Rather Than Criminal Processes   218
Using Administrative, Instead of Criminal,
     Sanctions for Regulatory Violations   218
Controlling Police and Prosecutor Misconduct
     without Letting the Criminal Go Free   222
Distinguishing Dangerousness from Blameworthiness   225

Conclusion: Doing Justice in a Complex World   229

Notes   233

Index   313

LAW WITHOUT JUSTICE

I N LAW AS in life, we want people to get what they deserve. Indeed, many (probably most) people, both legal experts and ordinary citizens, think that is a fundamental reason (and perhaps *the* reason) that we have a legal system at all: to help give people what they deserve when life has not. If one person wrongs another, the law makes the wrongdoer pay. On the other hand, if someone has done nothing wrong, we expect the law to leave that person alone, as she does not deserve to be sanctioned or punished.

This basic notion holds particularly true for criminal law, in part because the stakes are higher on all sides. When a person literally gets away with murder, we are outraged. Why? Because we are concerned about the message this sends to other would-be murderers, who will now think they can kill without fear? Perhaps in part, but surely our outrage is more deeply related to the particulars: *this* murderer has committed an evil act and deserves to be punished, yet has evaded punishment. Similarly, when we hear that an innocent person has been incarcerated, we are outraged. Why? Because we fear that this indicates a general corruption in the system and that the government may come for us next? A little, perhaps, but surely the main reason is that we sympathize with the individual, who has not received the treatment she deserves. In both cases, we feel that justice has not been done, and this offends and angers us. Isn't justice supposed to be the system's goal?

Surprisingly often, it isn't. To take just one brief example—we discuss the underlying rule in more detail in chapter 6—consider the case of Leandro

Andrade.[1] In November 1995, Andrade went to two K-Mart stores and stole nine videotapes worth a total of about $154. Because he had earlier convictions for burglary, minor thefts, and drug offenses involving marijuana—though he had already served his time for those offenses—Andrade was sentenced under California's "three strikes" law to two consecutive sentences of twenty-five years to life, meaning he will serve a minimum of fifty years in prison for his videotape thefts. Currently, California is spending about $26,000 per year for the incarceration of Andrade and each of its other prisoners.[2] But it is also paying another heavy price: the price of sacrificing justice by treating minor offenses as if they were far more serious than significant, violent felonies.

Indeed, even the supporters of three-strikes laws do not pretend that those laws are about imposing just punishment for specified crimes, but claim instead that they are needed to achieve deterrence and to "lock up the bad guys" so they are kept off the street. Members of the public, whose views regarding the crime rate and the need to control criminal activity are notoriously inaccurate and overblown,[3] tend to support three-strikes and similar laws.[4] But often they do so while laboring under a misunderstanding about how these laws work, assuming, for example, that the laws will only apply to seriously violent criminals or other offenders for whom the long punishments might seem sensible in desert-related terms.[5] Exploiting these misconceptions, many modern criminal laws follow the trend of being "tough on crime" even when doing so will require, for some or all cases, imposing punishments that patently exceed the amount deserved. That modern focus—one might even call it a fixation—is, in our view, not only misguided but counterproductive. In any case, that focus leads to rules that cause tangible injustices and do so regularly and routinely.

Of course, in practically any real-world system of justice, there will be some results that seem unfair or unjust. Probably no criminal-justice system could punish every wrongdoer, and only wrongdoers, and manage to give each of them precisely the punishment he deserves. And cases in which our system has gone wrong, either by failing to punish a known wrongdoer or by imposing too much punishment on a relatively blameless person, are a common feature of news reports. These individual stories may be newsworthy, but the general fact that the system isn't perfect is hardly news to anyone. Many of the factors that contribute to the system's inability to achieve justice are obvious and well known: limitations on resources for investigating crimes and prosecuting offenders, inevitable human error due to participants' imperfect knowledge and talents, the system's necessary reliance on the fallible observation and memory of witnesses, and the potential influence of bias and corruption, to name just a few. We realize that such things are bound to happen at least occasionally. Sometimes evidence is not found, or is lost; witnesses forget, or lie, or disappear, or are never identified; lawyers make mistakes, or are simply out-lawyered by other lawyers.

Even so, when these failures occur and become known, we are all disappointed. The public laments and criticizes the results,[6] whether they lead to wrongful convictions, overly harsh punishments, or undeserved acquittals. In addition, the people who shape and run the criminal-justice system themselves view such outcomes as unfortunate, hope they are no more than individual aberrations, and make efforts to avoid their recurrence. Some of these errors may reflect widespread and significant problems with the criminal-justice system. For example, one can only be troubled by the numerous and well-publicized recent cases involving convicted criminals, including some who were sentenced to death, who were later proved to be innocent. Less well-publicized, but perhaps more pervasive, are problems involving indigent defendants' lack of access to effective representation. Even so, however significant these problems, at least everyone agrees that they are problems. Although there may be a lack of resources or a failure of political will that prevents resolution of the problems, nobody disputes that conviction of an innocent person is an abhorrent result that the system would not generate deliberately.

Yet there are other cases, like the Andrade case, that exemplify a categorically different group of deviations from justice—deviations that are not irregular or unpredictable, but reflect instances where the criminal law *chooses* to depart from the goal of punishing people according to what they deserve. In these instances, a result departs from the demands of desert *because* the system works as it is designed to work, not because it fails to do so. In other words, it is sometimes the case that a known killer avoids punishment, or a person known to be blameless is sent to prison, not because there has been a tragic error in implementing the law, but because the law actually demands this result. In these cases, there is a visible gap between the law and justice—a gap, moreover, that has been created by the law itself, deliberately and with full awareness of the failure of justice or the injustice that will result.

Given our general and deep commitment to doing justice, such cases seem not just odd or unusual, but disturbing and offensive. Why would the criminal law deliberately sacrifice justice? Why would there be rules *designed* to give people something other than what they deserve?

This book tries to answer those questions. We detail the various legal rules that operate to inhibit, rather than advance, the goal of doing justice, and we give specific, real-life examples of the failures of justice that result from having those rules. We seek to explain why these law-justice gaps exist, when they are acceptable—or, surprising as it may sound, even desirable—and what can be done to narrow or eliminate these gaps when they are *not* acceptable. In doing so, we also survey the various goals and rationales that underlie the gap-creating rules. These objectives are numerous and complex; without parsing and examining them carefully, it can be hard to sort out the various tradeoffs, both principled and practical, involved in adopting a given legal rule, much less weigh the costs and benefits of those trade-offs. Our project, then, is to take just one goal—doing justice, by which we mean giving each criminal offender the punishment she deserves, no more, no less—and to use it as a baseline of comparison to draw out other goals and explore how those goals relate to and conflict with the goal of doing justice.

Some might argue that our project, which takes seriously the potential justifications for rules that sacrifice desert and tries to assess those justifications in a measured, rational fashion, gives those rules (and the people who make them) too much credit. Such a cynic might say that criminal-law rules often do not result from any legitimate, deliberative weighing of competing interests, but from a purely political process that often ignores or distorts valid moral or policy-related considerations. Many laws are enacted as knee-jerk reactions to individual, highly emotionally charged cases or to perceived crises demanding extreme measures. In such a system, we should hardly be surprised that the goal of doing justice, or any other policy goal for that matter, is often sacrificed for no good reason or positive result.

We generally agree with these arguments about what one observer has called the "pathological politics of criminal law."[7] Indeed, we have ourselves made similar complaints elsewhere.[8] We have seen how political processes can lead to the enactment of bad laws or the rejection of good ones, and it is entirely possible that much of the analysis we provide in this book will be roundly ignored by political actors. But surely that is no reason not to offer what analysis we can. Hopefully, by drawing out the best, most-plausible purposes and rationales for existing rules and holding those rules up to scrutiny based on their purposes, we can clarify the debate and, if nothing else, identify the rules for which no explanation exists other than political maneuvering or grandstanding.

OBJECTIVES AND ORGANIZATION

The book has three objectives, which guide its organization.

Identifying Deviations

We set our first task as simply pointing out just how often criminal law deliberately sacrifices justice. Accordingly, chapters 2–8 survey and describe various specific doctrines that lead to violations of desert—that is, results that deviate from what the defendant deserves—thereby providing what we think is a nearly comprehensive guide to such "deviation rules." Throughout, we provide detailed studies of actual cases that show the deviation rules in operation, in the belief that such concrete examples best illustrate the law-justice gap in ways that will touch readers' own intuitions of justice and thereby make clear the extent of the sacrifice that the law has chosen to make.

Some readers may feel that the cases we present seem "extreme" or unusual. And those readers are right. The cases are extreme; they are outrageous. One might feel that outrages of this magnitude are not common and that we are therefore somehow stacking the deck by using such cases as examples. We respond initially that no one, including us, knows how common these injustices really are. One of our themes is that embarrassingly little homework has been done to determine the real-world frequency or effects of deviation rules, either before adoption or while they are in force. In taking on this project, we set ourselves the goal of uncovering as much of this evidence as possible.

Further, and perhaps more important, even if these extreme cases are not common, this hardly leads to the conclusion that the rules generating the cases are unproblematic. Indeed, we consider such a conclusion dangerous. Is a legal rule that gives a defendant ten times more punishment than he deserves, but only in rare and extreme cases, more or less objectionable than a rule that gives ten times as many defendants "only" twice the punishment they deserve? We think both rules are seriously objectionable. And each of our illustrative cases highlights a rule that both generates extreme results and may regularly produce more modest perversions of justice.

We should also point out that a willingness to derogate or downplay the importance of extreme cases as long as they are not too common reveals a lack of understanding of the role of social norms and the law's reputation. It may take only one extreme case to damage the law's moral credibility with the community it seeks to influence. (The "Utility of Desert" section in chapter 1 discusses the psychological literature on building and undercutting reputations.) Remember, these extreme cases do *not* reflect legal mistakes or errors. Each is an instance where the governing legal rule is deliberately and thoughtfully applied to give the outrageous result and will be applied again on similar facts in the future. It is the deliberateness of these deviations that is so destructive to the criminal law's moral authority with the community. We seek to make clear the costs of eroding that authority and to reverse the counterproductive current tendency to ignore its force.

Categorizing Deviations and Critiquing Rationales

Our project is more than a discussion and critique of specific doctrines, however. We seek not just to identify the rules that deviate from desert but to categorize those rules according to their underlying purposes and justifications. These explorations of underlying principles are useful not only because of the insight they provide into why specific rules exist, but also because they shed light on the broader conflicting goals and purposes that exist within the criminal-justice system and that the system must constantly seek to balance and reconcile.

This second task shapes the organizational structure of the book. We have identified seven kinds of reasons—each the subject of a separate chapter, in chapters 2–8—that are used to justify departures from desert, each of which is the source of one or more criminal-law rules that cause such departures in the real world. The justifications for deviating from desert fall into two major categories: *practical constraints* and *competing interests*.

The first category, practical constraints, contains rules that depart from the abstract demands of justice but do so in order ultimately to advance the interests of justice. These rules are thought to produce a just result in the majority of cases, although they may fail to obtain that result, or may even prevent that result, in certain instances due to the compromises necessary to implement a system of criminal justice in the real world. Frequently, the accuracy of these rules, in terms of whether they are more just than not, will be debatable, but the important thing is that the terms of the debate are clear. The advocates as well as the opponents of these rules support the principle of desert-based punishment; they simply differ in their opinions of how to achieve that result given the practical constraints. These rationales are the subject of chapters 2, 3, and 4.

The second category, competing interests, is the subject of chapters 5–8. It contains rules that deviate from desert both in effect and in spirit. These rules truly create a gap between desert and legal liability. They cannot be, and are not, justified in terms of the desire to achieve desert. Instead, they reflect a decision, whether conscious or inadvertent, to sacrifice the interests of justice to advance some other goal. Some of these goals, we will argue, are better promoted through other mechanisms that do not distort the criminal-justice system's potential to do justice.

Once we have examined the purposes of the rules that generate departures from desert, we are able to explore the question of whether these rules are warranted given their clear violation of desert. Our assessment takes place at an empirical as well as a normative level. We do not examine each competing rule only in relation to desert, but also in relation to its own stated goal (or goals—some rules we discuss, such as the felony-murder doctrine, have multiple justifications and thus appear in multiple chapters). We find that rules supported by nondesert justifications are often unsupportable even on their own terms. Some rules simply do not, or no longer, live up to their underlying objectives. Other rules may serve their intended purpose (or may not; frequently their efficacy is untested or uncertain as an empirical matter) but could be replaced by other rules that would serve the purpose as well and would not deflect the distribution of liability and punishment from desert. For still other rules, the motivating reasons cannot be advanced in any way other than by deviating from desert, so that the rules must be tolerated—although there may be ways to mitigate or minimize the extent of the deviations.

Proposing Reforms

In chapters 9 and 10, we discuss reforms that may help to eliminate, or at least reduce, the current system's deviations from the principle of desert. We find that some current doctrines do effectively promote important interests, but can and should be replaced or supplemented by other rules that promote those interests as or more effectively without producing deviations from desert. We argue for two general types of reform.

The first group of reforms would occur within the criminal-justice system. Specifically, we argue that shifting the burden of persuasion to the defendant is a more rational response to potential abuses than the formal deviation doctrines, which rely on fears of manipulation. We also maintain that a more detailed verdict system, which could effectively condemn a defendant's conduct while exculpating the defendant, for example, would avoid the need for some deviation doctrines and might mitigate the distortion caused by others. Finally, we argue that a system incorporating alternative sanctions to incarceration, but also measuring each sanction according to a common metric of "units of punishment," might better achieve various crime-control goals without compromising the goal of desert.

The second set of reforms deals with changes that can be made outside the criminal-justice system to deal with problems that currently are treated within the system. In some cases, civil law offers a better mechanism for advancing the interests now advanced by a criminal-law doctrine of deviation. We suggest, for example, that civil damages or administrative sanctions are a better (i.e., potentially more effective, as well as more just) means of dealing with official violations of rights than the current method of excluding reliable evidence in criminal proceedings. We also advocate the development of a distinct civil system, as exists in other countries, to impose liability for minor administrative violations and corporate wrongdoing, which are presently (and inappropriately) dealt with by American criminal law. Finally, we contend that an open system of post–criminal-term civil commitment would provide a more honest and effective means of providing protection from dangerous offenders than the current system, which uses criminal liability as a method of achieving cloaked preventive detention.

Only a few of these reform proposals are novel. Some of them have been widely discussed and debated in the academic literature for years. We are not asserting that we have devised all-new solutions to the issues and tensions we identify in chapters 2–8. Rather, we discuss the previously offered proposals because we wish to point out their relation to the project of promoting desert, and because, where appropriate, we wish to discuss how these proposals might best be tailored to maximize their potential to achieve both desert and any other relevant goal.

THE RELEVANCE OF THE PROJECT

We think this book is significant and timely because of the growing recognition of the important practical implications of criminal law's central focus on doing justice. Many lawmakers and academics have become comfortable trading off justice to advance other interests—the interests we catalog and critique in chapters 2–8. As we discuss in chapter 1, however, it is becoming increasingly clear that doing justice is the most sound basis for distributing criminal liability, for both practical and moral reasons. The major competing perspective—the utilitarian deterrence or law-and-economics view—held sway over criminal-law formulation for some time but is now the subject of much controversy, at least in its application as a guide to the formulation of criminal law.

Yet despite the ascendance of desert, no one has taken the next step to sort out just what desert's priority means for evaluating our current criminal law, which has been a product of mixed (if not deterrence-dominated) influences for the past several decades. This book seeks to take that step: to catalog just how other interests, like deterrence, have led current American criminal law astray from desert, to explain how and why this has happened, and to lay out how we can eliminate, or at least minimize, departures from desert.

Accordingly, central to the book's message is its organization, which may strike some readers as unusual, but which directly relates to the contribution we seek to make. We do not organize our chapters based on the typical distinctions between offenses and defenses, between culpability rules and conduct rules, between rules establishing liability and rules determining the amount of liability, or between substance and procedure. Instead, we examine together rules that share a common underlying purpose. By doing so, we hope to highlight some of the shared themes and concerns that cut across the usual legal categories. For this reason, we hope the book will be appealing and useful even for a reader who entirely rejects its preference for desert, for the book points out the tradeoffs and competing values that drive criminal-law doctrine and the way those values are instantiated into doctrines of all sorts. Identifying and exploring those general undercurrents, their relation to each other, and the means of their implementation should be relevant to anyone interested in the criminal-justice system, regardless of priorities.

We know of no other work that takes on the task of identifying and critiquing the criminal-law doctrines that deviate from justice. Thus, we think the book makes a useful contribution simply by bringing together the scattered debates to highlight deviation from desert as an important topic in its own right and to set the terms of the conversation about that topic. But more to the point, it seems astonishing to us, given the importance of the issue, that such a book has not been previously written.

We think the explanation for this odd absence lies in the intersection of two developments of the past several decades. First, the system's willingness to barter justice for other interests has reached new extremes in, for example, the use of three-strikes statutes that turn the criminal-justice system into a system of cloaked preventive detention and in the creation of an entirely new department of offenses, "regulatory" crimes. This is recent history, and we have only reached our present point through increments, any one of which may not have been enough to trigger alarm.

Second, over the same period, we have begun to appreciate the importance of social influences (as opposed to coercive legal sanctions) in shaping conduct and thereby to appreciate the criminal-justice system's practical need to concern itself with its reputation for doing justice. In short, we have grown increasingly aware that the first trend, in its extreme efforts to convert criminal justice into a general behavioral-control system, risks *reducing* the system's long-term effectiveness in controlling crime by undermining its effectiveness as a moral force. We discuss further in chapter 1 the potential for a desert-based system to equal, and perhaps surpass, an explicitly deterrence-based system in achieving compliance with criminal law.

CHAPTER 1

Doing Justice and the Distractions from It

WHAT IF THERE were a law that prevented punishing someone we know to be a murderer or a rapist? Not merely a lack of evidence or some other regrettable problem impeding our ability to prosecute that particular case, but a *law*, a categorical rule, saying that we must let the person go, though we all agree he has committed a crime. Or what if there were a law that punished people as criminals, perhaps even sending them to prison, when they were known to be blameless? Again, not because of some tragic mistake or faulty perception of the facts, but because the law *required* us to punish someone we all agree is without fault.

Both of these kinds of laws exist. In fact, there are numerous such laws. They are the subject of this book. Our claim is that each of these laws presents a problem, in one or both of two senses. We believe that many of them—although, perhaps surprisingly at first blush, not all of them—are problems in the sense of something that is wrong and must be corrected. But at the very least, each one of them poses a problem in the sense of a question or riddle that demands an answer. Why do these laws exist? Why would the law create rules so contrary to our sense of what justice demands?

Let us be clear about what we mean by *justice* in this context. We believe that criminal law should seek to give defendants the amount of punishment they deserve—no more and no less. We suspect that most people would agree with this principle. In this book, we list and explain various criminal law rules that fail to uphold that basic principle. They deliberately and systematically ensure that defendants will get something other than what they deserve: either too little punishment or too much. (For the interested reader, we describe what we mean by justice, or *desert,* in further detail below.)[1]

But the reader might ask, how do we, the two of us, know what level of punishment everybody deserves? The amount of punishment a given individual deserves seems like a value judgment about which reasonable people might disagree. How can we be sure that the rules we discuss are violating the principle of desert, rather than just violating *our* particular, and perhaps idiosyncratic, views of what desert means? We have two reasons for confidence in our position that each of the rules we discuss offends the notion that criminal defendants should get what they deserve.

First, although attitudes toward desert do reflect value judgments, it turns out that they are widely shared value judgments. People can and do agree—not always, but usually, and more often than one might think—about what constitutes deserved punishment in specific cases. It is not that a given case has some magical connection with a specific punishment. Rather, people's intuitions of justice are quite specific about the *relative* blameworthiness of different cases. Given a finite range of possible punishments, people will typically agree on a rank ordering of cases, putting each case at a similar point along the range, along with other cases of similar blameworthiness. A growing literature documents that public intuitions regarding the principles of deserved punishment are widely and deeply shared.[2] One of us has cowritten an entire book collecting empirical studies of public intuitions about desert, to which we refer the interested (or dubious) reader.[3]

Second, and probably more important for present purposes, we are certain that these rules violate desert because the rules do not even pretend to advance desert. Even their advocates would have to admit that these rules impede the goal of desert. As we shall discuss, each of these rules ultimately depends on some other basis for its justification. (Of course, the political rhetoric surrounding many of these rules may use "justicespeak," claiming that the rules are needed to "achieve justice" or to "give criminals what they deserve." It is also common for politicians to use "deterrencespeak," claiming that various proposals—sometimes even on opposite sides of an issue—will curb crime, when no such deterrent benefit can be proved or is even plausible.[4] But this talk is just talk. Advocates on *both* sides of numerous issues may try to use justicespeak in support of their position until pressed with the facts of specific, predictable cases in which injustice will result, at which point they will not contest the injustice of the result, but switch to some other justification for the rule in question.)

There are surely other controversial laws and rules that many people think are questionable in terms of the punishments they assign. For example, people may argue about whether the death penalty imposes punishment beyond what any person, even a mass murderer, deserves. (Notice that this example is not contrary to what we just said about people's general agreement as to *relative* punishments. Everyone would agree that a mass murderer deserves to be punished with the severest of penalties; there is merely disagreement as to what the severest absolute penalties should be.) Such debates, though interesting and important, are not within this book's scope. We have limited ourselves to discussing rules that violate broadly shared sensibilities of justice and do so openly and transparently—and as shall become clear, even with that limitation, we have plenty to discuss.

To summarize, we value the goal of doing justice, and we think most people and our society as a whole value that goal also. And nearly all the time, nearly all of us would be in rough agreement about what it means to give a particular defendant what she deserves. Yet, strangely, the criminal-justice system employs numerous rules that undermine our ability to do that— even while recognizing that the rules will have that effect.

Why is this so? Can the system eliminate those rules or make them narrower? Should it always try to do so, or are some of the rules there for a good reason? We wrote this book because we think these are important questions, because we think others share our concern, and because we think that, with some close attention and examination, some answers may begin to emerge. *Law Without Justice* represents a first step toward those answers.

This chapter explains and defends our basic position about the meaning and significance of pursuing justice, or *desert*, as we will also refer to it. Chapters 2–8 survey the various criminal-law rules that depart from the desert goal, categorizing them based on their underlying purposes. We explain why, give examples of how the rules lead to unjust results, and consider whether these results are avoidable or worth the cost of sacrificing justice. Chapters 9 and 10 develop and discuss some proposed reforms, signaled in chapters 2–8, that we think might help to narrow and in some cases close the gaps between law and justice.

WHY FOCUS ON DOING JUSTICE?

Why do we care so much about giving defendants what they deserve, to the extent that we organize this entire book around that central principle? As we note above, the rules that violate desert are justified on other, nondesert grounds, indicating that desert is not the only goal of the criminal-justice system. So why treat the goal of achieving desert as *the* central goal serving as the basis of comparison with other goals, thereby apparently privileging desert relative to those other goals?

The Centrality of Justice

We have several reasons for considering desert to be most fundamental. First, many of the other goals we identify—such as upholding the legality principle, which we discuss in chapter 5, or ensuring procedural fairness, which we discuss in chapter 7—might be extremely important for purposes of *implementing* the substantive purposes and principles of criminal law, but they are not freestanding justifications for *having* a criminal-justice system in the first place. Accordingly, it would seem odd, and in some cases would prove impossible, to treat one of those goals as *the* goal to use as a basis for comparison and evaluation.

In fact, only one broad goal that we discuss might compete with desert as a fundamental basis for the existence of a criminal-law system: what is known as the *utilitarian* crime-control goal. (We discuss this goal in greater detail in chapter 6.) Whereas the desert principle is essentially backward-looking, seeking to impose deserved punishment (or no punishment, where none is deserved) for past conduct, the utilitarian goal is forward-looking, seeking to use the criminal-justice system to control people's future behavior. Specifically, its goal is to minimize the amount of seriously undesirable, and therefore criminal, behavior in society. A purely utilitarian system would pursue this goal without regard to any competing sense of justice or fairness. Accordingly, a dedicated utilitarian would be willing to punish even an innocent person if doing so would have crime-control benefits outweighing the costs of punishment, or would be willing to let a killer go unpunished if punishment would achieve no crime-control benefit.

We choose to base our analysis on the desert goal rather than on the crime-control goal for a few different reasons. First, as we have stated, in prioritizing desert, we are like most other people. According to most people's intuitions and the considered positions of many academics, doing justice—in the sense of imposing deserved, and only deserved, punishment—is the fundamental purpose for having a distinct regime of criminal law rather than, say, relying on tort liability (or some other civil- or private-law mechanism) to redress wrongful behavior. Most people (aside from some academics) do not instinctively or spontaneously think that criminal law is fundamentally "about" behavior modification; they think it is about punishing wrongdoers.

Second, although our current project focuses on the handful of rules that do not track the desert goal, the overall contours of criminal-law doctrine make clear that the commonly shared intuition is essentially accurate as a descriptive matter. That is, criminal law does typically try to "do justice," just as people want it to do. As a general matter, and across cultures, the rules imposed by criminal-law regimes tend to reflect what one would expect from a system whose central concern is just punishment—certainly much more so than they reflect what one would expect from a system whose fundamental purpose was achieving crime control, even at the cost of justice. On those occasions where it chooses not to reflect that emphasis, one is tempted to ask why, as we do in this book.

Then again, if one gave more thought to the matter, one might expect an overtly crime-control-based system to resemble what we actually see. As one of us has argued elsewhere, *a desert-based system may more effectively reduce crime than would a system that sacrificed desert, even if it did so precisely for the sake of achieving crime reduction.*[5] To put the argument in stark terms, what would happen if the criminal-justice system openly began to punish the innocent for the sake of deterring future crime, or freed murderers who were highly unlikely to ever kill again? People would be outraged; they would lose all respect for the system. Why? Because they want the system to do justice, and they will only grant it legitimacy—and, accordingly, only respect its dictates—to the extent that it pursues justice.

Partly because of the growing support for this point, we have a third reason for favoring desert as a basis for comparison: we think the only major competing model, the utilitarian program, is deeply flawed—even in terms of its ability to achieve its own stated goals. Therefore, even if you do not share the common intuition that desert is and should be the fundamental purpose of criminal law, but rather believe that criminal law should focus on behavior modification and on promoting safety, you should nonetheless value desert as a practical means of achieving those ends.

This point bears emphasis. The standard critique of the utilitarian crime-control project comes from the so-called retributivist school of thought. *Retributivist* thinkers support imposing deserved punishment because they consider punishing wrongdoers to be an absolute good, and even a moral duty, regardless of any future benefits it may bring. But our critique of the crime-control project does not fundamentally or essentially depend on adherence to a retributivist view (although people who have such a view might certainly be sympathetic to our position). Therefore one can accept our view without necessarily adopting any specific retributivist agenda or agreeing with the idea of retributivism generally.

Rather, a critical component of our project is the desire to make clear that the utilitarian crime-control agenda is counterproductive on its own terms. The literature of the last decade increasingly makes clear that those commentators who value deterring crime, for example, over achieving justice have been sloppy in their own analysis of how to deter crime. In other words, the system's willingness to sacrifice justice also has dramatic consequences even for, and perhaps particularly for, its ability to reduce crime. We have no desire, then, to deprecate (or at least depreciate) the utilitarian goals of criminal law nor to trivialize the significance of those goals. We support the goal of reducing crime as much as anybody does. (For the interested reader, we return to this point in more detail and offer more support for it in the "Utility of Desert" section below.)

The Neutrality of Justice (for Our Purposes)

Just as we have no quarrel with the underlying goals of the utilitarian crime-control agenda, we wish to make emphatically clear that we do *not* seek in this book to demonstrate that *any* of the competing goals we identify is illegitimate or unimportant, nor to assert that desert is somehow more important than another goal. On the contrary, we think that these other goals are extremely important—for example, as we have just noted, one reason we think pursuing desert is important is that we believe doing so advances the utilitarian goals of effective crime control.

But the more significant point is that, for the purposes of this book, we *assume* the validity of the other goals and make no claim as to whether, or when, desert should outweigh or trump them. The very fact that there are long-standing legal rules reflecting a willingness to prioritize these competing interests over the goal of just punishment indicates their significance. Instead of disputing the substantive merits of these interests, we address an empirical issue whose resolution may obviate, as a practical matter, the deeper philosophical debate about whether these other commitments should trump desert. We ask: is there an alternative rule that manages to advance *both* principles, thereby rendering the sacrifice of either unnecessary? Where it is possible to achieve the competing goal without deviating from desert—and we maintain that this is often the case—the unfortunate tradeoff can be avoided altogether. Thus our decision to make desert the "primary" goal in our discussion, by making it the goal to which other goals are compared, should not be read to mean that we give primacy to desert in terms of its relative importance vis-à-vis those other goals, at least in the abstract.

A FURTHER WORD ON WHAT WE MEAN BY "DOING JUSTICE"

In succeeding chapters, we focus on various rules that depart from the goal of doing justice and analyze the reasons for having those rules. But before we do so, one more bit of clarification may be helpful as to what we mean by the terms *justice* and *desert*. *Justice* is used in this book to mean assigning criminal liability and punishment according to the principle of desert, so that each offender receives the punishment deserved, no more, no less. But the concept of *desert* has at least two distinct meanings.

Desert could be seen as the distribution of liability and punishment that follows the community's shared principles of justice—the moral intuitions of the people whom the law governs. On this view, we could find out what justice demands just by asking people what they think it demands, and then do what they say. We might call this the *bottom-up* take on desert, building from the individual sensibilities of people toward a more general sense of what justice means. One of us has argued elsewhere that this notion of desert is a sensible distributive principle from a utilitarian viewpoint, because it gives the criminal law a moral authority with the community that has potentially great crime-control benefit.[6] In other words, rules that follow people's intuitive sense of justice are good because they can promote compliance with the law, thereby achieving certain practical benefits. Let us call supporters of the bottom-up theory, then, the *desert pragmatists* (a more technical term would be *desert utilitarians*).

Alternatively, desert could be seen as the distribution of liability and punishment dictated by abstract principles of moral right and goodness—what a philosopher or legal academic might call the *deontological*, or *retributivist*, sense of the term. This is the *top-down* view, claiming that we need to start with some fundamental set of abstract moral principles, from which we derive more particular rules about what constitutes justice in individual cases. Adherents of the top-down view do not cite any practical benefits, but support desert on the ground that imposing deserved punishment, as defined by moral principles, is simply the right (or even morally required) thing to do. Supporters of the top-down theory, then, might be called *desert moralists* (here the technical term would be *retributivists*).

As it happens, there is broad overlap between the specific rules that flow from the bottom-up (desert pragmatist) and from the top-down (desert moralist) conceptions of desert, though there are differences as well.[7] For example, the two conceptions might take different views as to the significance of resulting harm—that is, as to whether an attempted crime should be punished less seriously than a completed one. Desert pragmatists, who follow widely shared community views of justice, would have a clear position on this issue, for there is strong and broad lay support for taking account of resulting harm in assessing deserved liability and punishment (e.g., for punishing attempted murders less than completed murders).[8] Desert moralists, on the other hand, take differing positions as to whether the occurrence of a harmful result should matter in assessing punishment.[9] Some think so, but others say that where similarly culpable persons engage in similarly wrong-ful behavior, it is only a matter of luck that one, say, shoots and kills while the other shoots and misses, and luck should not influence moral evaluation.

In other words, each of these conceptions of desert would cite at least some (though probably not very many) of the rules arising from the other conception as deviations from its own sense of desert. For a desert moralist, any pragmatic rules that violate the moralist's moral theories would be like any other deviations from (the moralist's sense of) desert that sacrifice jus-tice in favor of some practical goal. A desert moralist would view these rules in the same way a desert moralist (as well as a desert pragmatist) would view any other rules that willingly sacrifice desert to obtain, say, additional crime control or cost savings. So the moralist might say, "Even if most people agree that attempts are less serious than completed crimes, it's morally wrong to treat them that way, and the pragmatists are doing that only to appease the popular will and promote compliance with law."

The desert pragmatists, by contrast, would see the moralist-based devia-tions as a unique form of deviation. Unlike other deviations that would vio-late the desert pragmatist's view for the sake of achieving some other prac-tical goal (such as cost savings), these deviations would be rooted only in an effort to fulfill a (misguided) abstract, absolutist moral mission. The prag-matists would say, "Some moralists want to punish attempts the same as completed crimes, and for what? Not to accomplish anything in the real world, but only to satisfy the dictates of their own grand moral philosophy."

The disagreements between the two notions of desert are not entirely in-significant, but they are ancillary to our project here. The focus of this book is the gap between justice, under *either* of these conceptions, and existing law. The differences between the two conceptions of desert have been dis-cussed elsewhere.[10] We focus, for the most part, on their many similarities. As will become apparent, the gaps that are clearly objectionable to both views of desert are so numerous and deep that in most instances they render in-consequential the moralist-pragmatist desert differences. In one or two in-stances, we may discuss a rule that violates one conception of desert but not the other, or violates one more obviously or severely than the other. Where that occurs, we will point it out.

Some (traditional utilitarian) writers would argue that the notion of specific "deviations" from desert makes little sense because desert only sets outer limits on punishment and not demands for specific sentences.[11] But retribu-tivists rarely consider the demands of desert to be so vague or flexible. Von Hirsch, for example, notes that desert includes an ordinal ranking of cases: offenders of lesser blameworthiness should be punished less than offenders of greater blameworthiness.[12] As noted previously, given the finite range over which the amount of punishment can vary and the large number of dis-tinctions commonly recognized between degrees of blameworthiness,[13] the punishment deserved in any given case falls into a narrow range. That range is set not by some special connection between a certain degree of blame-worthiness and a certain amount of punishment, but by the need to distin-guish each case from the large number of other cases of distinguishable blameworthiness. (Note that desert constraints apply only to the *amount* of punishment and not to the *method* of punishment. Thus, nondesert preven-tive concerns may properly guide the selection of a sentencing method with-out offending desert.)[14]

THE UTILITY OF DESERT: THE PRACTICAL COSTS OF DEVIATIONS FROM DOING JUSTICE

We have stated that most people find desert to be a proper goal for criminal law and have affirmative (if abstract) reasons for doing so: punishing ac-cording to the demands of desert is just, fair, and morally right. Further, one might promote desert simply out of a democratic sense: if most people think the system should pursue desert, then it should. Yet even beyond whatever positive theoretical or ethical justifications supporters may advance in favor of desert, the goal of desert may also be defended on the ground that the fail-ure to pursue desert carries concomitant and serious costs, including very practical costs.

From the retributivists' perspective, the cost of deviation from desert is obvious: doing justice is a value in itself, and every instance of deviation from it injures that value. But as we briefly noted above, deviation from desert has utilitarian costs as well. The most striking theme of recent empirical work is the influence of complex social forces on crime control. While the old school dismissed lay intuitions as uneducated and irrelevant, it is increasingly under-stood that good utilitarians must pay close attention to them. There is often greater power in the influence of social forces than in the criminal law's threat of official punishment, and it is criminal law's reputation for doing jus-tice that will determine its ability to harness those social forces in shaping behavior. Thus a thorough utilitarian, if willing to take account of all factors that can influence crime control, also will see deviations from desert as im-posing a substantial cost.

Let us first summarize the utilitarian reasons for supporting a desert dis-tribution that have been offered elsewhere.[15] The power to gain compliance with society's rules of prescribed conduct lies not in the threat or reality of official criminal sanction, but in the power of the intertwined forces of social and individual moral control. The law is not extrinsic or irrelevant to these social and personal forces. Criminal law, in particular, plays a central role in creating and maintaining the social consensus necessary for sustaining moral norms. In a society as diverse as ours, the criminal law may be the only society-wide mechanism that transcends cultural and ethnic differences. Thus, the criminal law's most important real-world effect may be its ability to assist in building, shaping, and maintaining these norms and moral principles, and thereby to contribute to and harness the compliance-producing power of interpersonal relationships and personal morality.

The criminal law can have a second effect in gaining compliance with its commands. If it earns a reputation as a reliable statement of what the community, upon thoughtful reflection, would perceive as condemnable, people are more likely to defer to its commands as morally authoritative and appropriate to follow in those borderline cases where the propriety of certain conduct is unsettled or ambiguous in the mind of the actor. The importance of this role should not be underestimated; in a society with the complex interdependencies characteristic of ours, an apparently harmless action can have destructive consequences. When the action is criminalized by the legal system, one would want the citizen to "respect the law" in such an instance even though he does not immediately intuit why that action is banned. Such deference will be facilitated if citizens are disposed to believe that the law is an accurate guide to appropriate prudential and moral behavior.

The extent of the criminal law's effectiveness in both of these respects—in facilitating and communicating societal consensus on what is and is not condemnable, and in gaining compliance in borderline cases through deference to its moral authority—depends greatly on the degree of moral credibility the criminal law possesses for the citizens it governs. Thus, the criminal law's moral credibility is essential to effective crime control and is enhanced if the rules of criminal liability are perceived as doing justice— that is, if they assign liability and punishment in ways that the community perceives as consistent with its own understanding of appropriate liability and punishment. Conversely, the system's moral credibility, and therefore its crime-control effectiveness, is undermined by a distribution of liability that deviates from community perceptions of just desert.

Some may argue that the deviations from desert we discuss in this book do not occur so regularly as to create serious problems for compliance with the criminal law. Moreover, only the small portion of the population that deals routinely with the criminal law may be aware of the rule-based deviations from desert. We respond that even if the deviation rules are unknown, the results become apparent to a variety of people either through direct involvement in the process or in media portrayals. And if a deviation is known to be the predictable result of a systematic rule, the rules of "attributional perception" are such that observers are likely to lose respect for the system that condones such repeated and predictable deviations.[16] If the cause of a deviation remains opaque, with no specific law to blame, the observer will simply grow suspicious of the system as a whole.[17]

We do not suggest that the costs of deviation will always be decisive. Rather, we recognize that tradeoffs will be necessary, and we seek to formulate some rules to govern how those tradeoffs will be made. It is important, however, to recognize that those tradeoffs exist and that they are all too often ignored at present. Where implementation of desert is complex, so that a seemingly deviating rule can be justified as a practical method of *advancing* desert, as we discuss in chapters 2–4, we must evaluate the empirical underpinnings of that rule and weigh any potential "demoralization costs" from the apparent deviation. Where desert and another goal conflict, as we discuss in chapters 5–8, we must weigh the costs and benefits of pursuing the other goal by deviating from desert against the costs and benefits of pursuing the goal by other means, or of sacrificing the goal in that instance.

Thus, the analyses in this book apply if one believes that desert has *any* value, for *any* reason—whether based on retributivism, on desert utilitarianism, or simply on a robust sense of democracy seeking to give voice to the broad and deep popular sense that criminal law is, and should be, about punishing blameworthiness. (We trust that few readers will take the contrary position of utter indifference to desert, taking no preference between two otherwise equal, alternative legal regimes, one of which promotes desert better than the other.) Our premise is merely that, if desert matters, we should pursue legal rules that promote desert to the greatest extent possible, subject to unavoidable constraints.

I

PROMOTING JUSTICE
IN A COMPLEX WORLD

THE FIRST CATEGORY of deviations from desert—what we call *practical constraints*—consists of rules that depart from the abstract demands of justice but do so in order ultimately to advance the interests of justice. In the real world, we simply cannot achieve justice always and everywhere: limitations of time, knowledge, and money prevent us from identifying and punishing every offender. Accordingly, we must make some compromises to try to achieve as much justice as we can with the time, knowledge, and money we have. Sometimes these require us to create rules that cut some corners in terms of desert—rules that we know will lead to distortions from the ideal of justice in some, or even many, individual cases but that we think will track the just result in the vast majority of cases and will do so more efficiently than an ideal rule that did not cut corners. In the end, it is thought, these compromises will lead us to more, rather than less, real-world justice being done.

Frequently, the accuracy of these rules, in terms of whether they really do lead to just results more often than to unjust ones, will be debatable, but the important thing is that the terms of the debate are clear. The debate involves a disagreement over practice rather than principle. The advocates as well as the opponents of these rules are trying to support the principle of desert-based punishment; they simply differ in their opinions of how to achieve that result given concerns about the relevant practical constraints.

There are three distinct practical-constraint rationales driving rules that deviate from desert; chapters 2, 3, and 4 discuss these rationales in turn. Chapter 2 deals with the concern that, in some situations, a pure desert-based rule would allow the manipulation of juries into voting for improper acquittals. The rationale is used to justify the limitation or rejection of various exculpatory defenses or mitigation rules. Chapter 3 addresses several rules, such as statutes of limitation and the use of strict liability, that respond to concerns about the reliability of evidence and the unavoidable difficulty of using fallible or incomplete evidence to prove a person's guilt or innocence with any certainty. Chapter 4 turns to practices, such as plea bargaining and witness immunity, which are predicated on the claim that, given constraints on available time, resources, and fact-seeking capacities, the system can maximize justice overall by making compromises in individual cases.

The concerns driving all of these deviating rules are ultimately empirical rather than philosophical in nature, as they rest on the premise that each such rule or practice advances justice more than would a rule that, in the abstract, might seem more just. That premise is an assertion about objective fact, capable of proof or disproof. For this reason, the appropriateness of any such deviations can, at least potentially, be determined through objective analysis. Accordingly, the debates about the validity of these deviating doctrines admit of definitive resolution. It is merely necessary to shift the focus of the debates away from the abstract arguments of which legal academics are so frequently enamored and toward empirical research.

CHAPTER 2

Fear of Manipulation and Abuse

E ven under the best of circumstances, the criminal-justice system is unpredictable and imperfect. Our limited knowledge of people and events being what it is, complete accuracy is an unattainable goal. This inherent imperfection is only magnified when participants in the system do not seek accurate results, but seek deliberately to exploit loopholes for the sake of victory. The wish to avoid such potential abuses is one reason commonly given for deviating from a purely desert-based system of criminal liability.

According to this argument, certain rules that might seem desert-oriented in the abstract would be subject to *gamesmanship*—deliberate efforts by defendants and their lawyers to "game the system" and achieve an improper acquittal—and therefore would, if recognized, more frequently generate an unjust result than a just one. However theoretically desirable such rules may seem, the risk of abuse is seen as likely to make them counterproductive in practice, so the pure desert-based rule is rejected.

This approach is not a response to specific kinds of manipulation that targets a subset of cases where abuse occurs, but a preemptive strike seeking to prevent certain feared abuses from ever being possible. Hence our discussion in this chapter does not deal with rules so much as the lack of rules, or potential desert-enhancing rules that the law could recognize but does not.

This chapter discusses several such rules. Frequently the issue presents itself in the form of a defense that a defendant seeks to offer, but that the court rejects. For example, some defendants (such as Julio Marrero, in the case discussed immediately below) assert that they should not be held accountable for their offenses because they were operating under a mistaken, but reasonable, understanding of the law, which led them to believe they were committing no crime. The defense is often disallowed, as are other defenses such as an immaturity excuse or a "lesser evils" justification,[1] on the ground that case-by-case determination of such claims will (at best) waste time and (more likely) also lead to inaccurate results.

Sometimes the issue relates to the proper scope of a recognized defense, as where defendants (such as Andrew Goldstein, whose case is discussed later in the chapter) seek to introduce certain kinds of evidence of insanity or some other excusing condition that renders them morally blameless for their acts. Here, instead of categorically rejecting the defense, the response may be to narrow its definition or change the procedural context in which the defense operates (for example, in the case of insanity, by introducing a competing "guilty but mentally ill" verdict for the jury to apply in cases involving mental illness).

Finally, the issue may arise not only in the context of defining a defense, but also in defining an offense. The fear of abuse may lead the law to favor objectively defined culpability terms, which set out the states of mind that the law considers sufficiently blameworthy to merit punishment. For example, standards of negligence or recklessness, or the provocation requirement for manslaughter (the subject of the Gounagias case, discussed toward the end of the chapter), may refer to the perceptions and reactions of the "reasonable person." A strictly objective definition of *reasonableness* prevents a defendant from introducing dubious and confusing claims about how, under the circumstances, something *seemed* "reasonable" from her personal point of view. Yet many individuals may have a legitimate claim to a condition or circumstance that makes it more difficult, or perhaps impossible, for them to behave "reasonably" under the law, at least in some situations.

For all of these rules, the key question is whether the fear of abuse is legitimate and, moreover, so strong as to warrant a preemptive-strike approach that rejects potential genuine claims of blamelessness along with the feared bogus ones. The potential for abuse that may arise from recognizing a rule must be weighed against the potential for injustice that arises from rejecting it.

IS A FEDERAL PRISON GUARD A "PEACE OFFICER"?

Julio Marrero of the Bronx, New York, is a disabled Vietnam veteran who previously worked as an undercover agent in a Puerto Rican drug enforcement operation for the Department of Hacienda (Treasury). Now, in 1977, he works as a prison guard at the federal prison in Danbury, Connecticut, and is the father of six children ranging in age from three to eleven years old. (Two more children will arrive in the next two years.)

During his time as a guard at Danbury, Marrero has received death threats (as do many prison guards), including one from a recently released inmate. When off duty, he regularly carries a pistol for protection, having received weapons training when he was in the military police. At the military police armory in Manhattan, Marrero keeps space for several weapons he uses at the MP firing range.

Marrero purchased his pistol from a New York City gun dealer, Eugene DiMayo, who sold him the gun knowing that Marrero did not have a special New York gun permit, but believing—and advising Marrero—that, as a federal prison guard, he did not need one. DiMayo knew several other federal prison guards who similarly had bought weapons without a special New York gun permit, and he explained to Marrero that "federal corrections officers" are considered "peace officers" under the New York firearms statute, and "licenses are not required if proper identification is presented."[2]

On December 19, 1977, while off duty, Marrero visits a social club at 207 Madison Street in New York City. As he enters the club, he is searched by Officer Gary Dugan of the Seventh Police Precinct, who finds a loaded .38-caliber pistol on Marrero's person. Marrero explains that, though he does not have a permit, he does not need one because he is a federal corrections officer. He shows his identification badge. The police call the Danbury prison and confirm he is a guard there. Nonetheless, Marrero is arrested and charges are filed. Ten days later, Marrero is indicted for criminal possession of a weapon.

FIGURE 2.1.
Formerly a social club, now a Mexican restaurant, 207 Madison Street was where Julio Marrero was arrested on December 19, 1977. Photo by Paul H. Robinson.

At trial, Marrero pleads not guilty. The prosecution claims that Marrero violated section 265.02(4) of the Penal Law, a class D felony. They concede he would be exempt from such an offense under section 265.20(A) if he were a peace officer, as defined by section 1.20 of the Criminal Procedure Law. Under section 1.20, a "peace officer" includes, among other persons, any "guard of any state prison or of any penal correctional institution." But prosecutors read the word "state" as applying not only to the immediately following word "prison" but also to the later phrase, "any penal correctional institution." Thus Marrero, as a guard at a *federal* institution, is not a peace officer and therefore is not exempt from the offense.

The trial court, however, disagrees with that reading of the statute and agrees with Marrero's interpretation that the word "state" modifies only the word "prison" and not the phrase "any penal correctional institution." The judge dismisses the charge on May 3, 1978.

The prosecution appeals. Two years later, on December 11, 1979, in a 3–2 vote, the Appellate Division reverses the trial court's dismissal. A majority of the court concludes that, when read in its entirety and when harmonized with other sections of the law, the statute does not exempt off-duty federal prison officers. The case is sent back to the lower court for trial.

When the case comes back to trial court on remand, Marrero argues that he should be acquitted because his reading of the somewhat misleading statute, even if wrong, was a reasonable mistake. Other fellow officers, and teachers at the prison, had read the statute as he did. So did the gun seller. Indeed, so did the trial judge and two of the five appellate judges—meaning that of the six judges who have heard the case so far, half have agreed with Marrero's interpretation of the law. Given the statute's complexity, Marrero asserts, does not this level of disagreement among judges itself suggest that his mistake was entirely reasonable?

FIGURE 2.2.
Julio Marrero, circa
1984. Family photo.

But the trial court (a different judge this time) follows the old maxim that "ignorance or mistake of law is no excuse." Marrero is forbidden to offer his mistake theory to the jury as a defense. At trial, Marrero is convicted and, on July 9, 1982, he is sentenced to a three-year suspended sentence and a $500 fine, a conviction that will bar him from work in law enforcement or corrections. He appeals. The Appellate Division again rules against Marrero and upholds his conviction, this time without issuing a written opinion.

The state's highest court, the New York Court of Appeals, issues its judgment on April 2, 1987, almost ten years after the offense. The court concludes that public policy encouraging knowledge of and adherence to the law weighs against providing a defense for a reasonable mistake of law. Marrero's conviction is affirmed on a 4–3 vote. Because of his conviction, Marrero is fired from his job and is barred from other such work.

Even though the legislature rewrites the misleading statute to make other changes, it does not fix the misleading language. Even today, the persons exempt from gun-possession offenses are defined as "correction officers of any state correctional facility *or of any penal correctional institution.*" Is a guard at a nonstate "penal correctional institution" exempt from the offense? A person reading the new statute could easily come to the wrong conclusion.[3]

REJECTING A DEFENSE FOR REASONABLE MISTAKE OF LAW (OR FOR NECESSITY OR IMMATURITY)

Like New York in the *Marrero* case, nearly all American jurisdictions refuse to allow a defense for a person who acts under a mistaken, although reasonable, belief in what the law allows. Among American jurisdictions, New Jersey stands alone in providing a true defense of this sort, where a defendant will be excused for acting on a reasonable but incorrect interpretation of the law's requirements following a good-faith effort to ascertain those requirements.[4]

The reason for the nearly universal rejection of the defense is a fear that it would be easy to claim and hard to disprove. Recognition of such a defense, according to opponents, would reduce the overall number of criminal cases achieving a just result because the few meritorious assertions of the defense would be dwarfed by the number of spurious yet successful ones. These opponents recognize that rejecting the defense will sometimes lead to unjust results, but they claim that allowing the defense would lead to even more unjust results, as truly blameworthy persons would abuse the defense by obtaining improper acquittals.[5]

On the other hand, the *Marrero* case illustrates the inherent drawbacks of denying the defense. The case's outcome hardly seems just. Marrero had little reason to think he was committing a crime and had received seemingly reliable advice that he was not. Even half of the judges who interpreted the statute agreed with Marrero that it did not apply to him. Marrero's mistake seems entirely reasonable, and general consensus holds it unjust to impose criminal liability on one who could not reasonably have been expected to act otherwise than he did.[6]

Moreover, it seems increasingly likely, given the current trend in criminal legislation, that such reasonable mistakes will occur more frequently. As we discuss in chapter 8, recent years have seen a dramatic increase in the number of criminal offenses that punish minor or obscure regulatory infractions or other behavior lacking the seriously harmful or wrongful quality traditionally associated with criminal conduct.[7] And these offenses are not merely minor violations punishable by a fine, like a traffic violation; many of them carry the potential for serious punishment. This trend toward criminalizing morally or ethically trivial behavior is disturbing enough in its own right. But when coupled with a refusal to acknowledge that these numerous and complex rules are not intuitive or well known and that otherwise law-abiding people might violate them without realizing it, a great risk arises that unjust liability will be imposed frequently.

Does the risk of abuse outweigh this risk of injustice? We are aware of no empirical work that has considered, much less resolved, whether a reasonable-mistake-of-law defense, if allowed, is subject to frivolous claims, or whether such claims are successful with any frequency. As noted above, New Jersey stands alone in recognizing the defense, and while we have found no data proving that the defense presents no difficulty, neither are we aware of any reports that New Jersey criminals are commonly obtaining improper acquittals by asserting the defense. We are aware of only one published New Jersey state court opinion referring to the statutory provision providing the defense—and that opinion denies the defense.[8]

The same concerns that led New York to deny a defense to Marrero for a reasonable mistake of law have led many jurisdictions to deny defenses for a variety of other legitimate excusing and mitigating conditions. All of these refusals contravene the abstract demands of desert, which would dictate that such people do not merit punishment. Two other examples of such defenses are the lesser-evils justification and the immaturity defense.

The *lesser-evils* defense—sometimes called *choice of evils* or *necessity* or simply the *general justification* defense—illustrates the structure and operation of justification defenses generally by relying explicitly upon the rationale inherent in all justifications: while the actor may have caused the harm or evil of an offense, the justifying circumstances suggest that his conduct avoided a greater harm or evil than it caused. In the abstract, the lesser-evils justification is almost impossible to oppose. By definition, it applies only to conduct that is justified, and even desirable, under the circumstances. Breaking into a remote forest cabin to avoid a family's starving or freezing to death, or torching some crops in order to create a firewall that saves the city from an encroaching fire, is not conduct meriting condemnation. Punishing a person who performs such an act seems clearly to violate principles of desert.[9]

In practice, however, the merits of the lesser-evils defense are apparently less compelling, for many American jurisdictions deny it, and only a minority codify it.[10] As with the mistake-of-law defense, the reason for this decision lies in concerns about manipulation of the system. Legislatures don't like to let out of their hands this sort of broad power to define what will be punished, for fear that fancy-talking lawyers will take advantage of it and use it to persuade naive juries to do crazy things (or perhaps crazy juries will abuse it on their own).[11]

But here again, the debate regarding this deviation rests on contrary positive assumptions, not contrary normative positions.[12] Here, though, the correct answer to the underlying empirical question seems clear and favors the proponents of the lesser-evils defense. This justification relates only to conduct and not state of mind; its presence or absence in a given case is susceptible of proof by presentation of evidence in the courtroom (at least, to the extent that anything is). For the same reason, even if the defense is available, actors have no ex ante incentive or potential to game the system by attempting to cast their behavior in a certain light, for objective circumstances beyond the actor's control will ultimately govern the justifiability of her behavior. The standard American formulation of the defense makes clear that it is the community's, not the defendant's, balance of conflicting interests that controls and that any other specific justification defense or any other legislative predetermination of the balance of interests will preclude jury balancing to the contrary.[13]

Further, the justification rests on shared community norms regarding difficult moral choices. If the jury, selected as representative of those norms, thinks the justification should apply, then it should, almost by definition. Finally, although a number of states have had the lesser-evils defense on the books for a number of years, and it has been used,[14] there is little if any indication that it has been abused.

Another seeming deviation rooted in the same gamesmanship concern is the bright-line nature of the immaturity (or infancy) "defense," which is actually a rule governing the courts' jurisdiction over a defendant. All actors below a specified cutoff age are conclusively presumed to be immature and are tried in juvenile court, and all those above the age cutoff are presumed to be mature and are tried in adult court.[15]

Such an age cutoff formulation makes it easy to apply the defense, but it creates serious errors, for it results in a failure to excuse or even offer a mitigation of punishment for an older actor who is as immature as a typical underage actor and for whom we have reduced normative expectations.[16] The problem is only exacerbated by the increasing trend toward lowering the age at which juveniles can be tried and punished as adults.[17] It is not the transfer of a juvenile to adult court that creates the injustice. The injustice derives from the fact that, once transferred and tried in an adult court, immature offenders have no immaturity defense available by which their immaturity can be used to excuse them from blame.[18] Thus, the immature offender will not be excused even if his immaturity causes excusing conditions identical to those providing a defense to a disabled offender who is, for example, insane, involuntarily intoxicated, or coerced.[19]

The argument in support of bright-line maturity rules, even though application of those rules is likely to cause deviations from desert, is that case-by-case determinations of maturity are simply too complex and might enable too many psychologically mature defendants past the age of majority to sneak their way into juvenile court.[20] But we disagree. It is true that objective, easily applied criteria are always a virtue. In the realm of excuses, however, where the goal is to capture accurately a complex judgment of blameworthiness, subjective and judgmental criteria frequently are needed. Simply put, the empirical problem at issue here—assessing mental capacity and functioning—arises all the time in criminal law and is not normally abandoned simply because it is difficult.

Here, as elsewhere, flexible standards rather than bright-line rules should be used to address the problem. An approach more consistent with the goal of the immaturity defense would be a defense that looked to the actor's actual degree of immaturity. If a concession to easier application is needed, it can be achieved through rebuttable presumptions rather than through the irrebuttable presumptions contained in most current formulations.[21]

. . .

The mistake-of-law defense that Marrero asserted is often rejected in part because of a desire to incentivize sensible, careful, and clearly law-abiding behavior. We do not want clever would-be offenders to seek out and exploit loopholes or ambiguities in the criminal law, then claim later that they made a "mistake" for which the poorly written law, rather than the manipulative offender, should be blamed.[22] In other situations, the manipulation concern addresses a somewhat different issue: instead of the law's possible influence on offenders' decisions to engage in or avoid criminal behavior in the first place, the concern is that offenders will use legal rules to influence the outcome of their criminal cases after the fact.

An example is the insanity defense, illustrated in the Goldstein case below. Nobody would deliberately become insane, in the way that a person might deliberately make a "mistake" by ascertaining and maneuvering within the law's gray areas. Yet there is a fear that someone might commit an offense, then *pretend* to be insane for the sake of obtaining an acquittal in the subsequent legal proceeding. This fear drives efforts to narrow the insanity defense—but there is always the competing concern that narrowing the defense too much will lead to unjust convictions for some people who truly deserve an excuse.

"WHOOSH, WHOOSH, PUSH"

On January 2, 1999, Andrew Goldstein begins the new year with a visit to the emergency room. He is a shy twenty-nine-year-old who, unable to sleep, often walks the streets until dawn. Despite having been diagnosed with schizophrenia ten years ago, Goldstein lives on his own in an apartment in Howard Beach, Queens. He is in the ER to have his ankle examined. The doctors tell him he is fine, and he heads back home.

Born and raised in Queens and Little Neck, one of three brothers, Goldstein was a grade-school honors student who seemed on his way to a promising future, attending the elite Bronx High School of Science and then obtaining admission to the State University of New York at Stony Brook. However, when Goldstein was sixteen, in the middle of all this success, he was riding the bus and something clicked—he could no longer understand anything in the book he was reading; the words no longer made sense. His family was concerned and sought medical and psychiatric care. Goldstein was eventually diagnosed as a paranoid schizophrenic, prone to violence. He stayed in school, trying to overcome his disease, but his symptoms only intensified in college.

Goldstein was eventually hospitalized after pushing his mother and accusing her of poisoning his food. (His parents are now divorced, and he is largely estranged from both of them.) After release from Creedmoor Psychiatric Center, he tried to return to college several times, but found it too difficult to concentrate and to comprehend what he read. He was committed again in 1992 for assaulting a nurse, and he remained hospitalized for eight months. After release, Goldstein lived in a community residence for more than a year until being discharged in November 1994. He then moved into the Leben Home for Adults in Elmhurst, which gave him a place to live but did not provide supervision or counseling.

Goldstein's disease grew progressively worse. His hallucinations increased in frequency and duration, leading him to believe that aliens were sucking oxygen from the earth and that there was someone inside him controlling his behavior and movements. While medication helped to control some of his symptoms, it had side effects he did not like: drowsiness, dissociation, and stiffness. He knew there were newer medications that did not have these side effects, but they were expensive—too expensive for someone like Goldstein, living on $500 per month in welfare and $50 every once in a while from his father.

Goldstein's disease is aggravated by his denial of its effects, which include serious hallucinations and delusions. Goldstein also has hit at least a dozen people without provocation in restaurants, stores, hospitals, and subways. When the police arrive, he always admits what he has done and asks to be taken to a hospital. When reflecting on these incidents, Goldstein says that, each time it happens, he feels as if a spirit or ghost has entered him and taken over.

Goldstein continues to scrape by and is now living in a decrepit basement in Queens, in a one-bedroom apartment he shares with two roommates. He increasingly finds it difficult to cope and in late 1998, he is again hospitalized, from November 24 until December 15. Upon his release, doctors give him a week's worth of medication and tell him to get counseling. Goldstein has previously requested on several occasions that he be placed in long-term care at a state hospital or given a bed at a group home, but unfortunately, there are no vacancies at either type of facility, in part because of Governor George E. Pataki's recent state budget cuts.

Without supervision, Goldstein commonly misses taking his medication and then misses counseling appointments. Because of the poorly funded state mental health system, the only repercussion of failing to show up at an appointment is a letter requesting that he reschedule. Ignoring the latest letter when he returns from his January 2 ER visit, Goldstein shuffles off to his basement room to pace the rest of the day away.

FIGURE 2.3.
Andrew Goldstein.
Photo by Vern Lovic.

The next morning, January 3, 1999, Goldstein gets up and, forgoing his medication yet again, goes into Manhattan and stops in a Virgin Records store, where he listens to songs by Natalie Imbruglia and Madonna. Goldstein likes listening to music because he draws pictures in his mind to go with what he hears. After some time in the video section watching scenes from *The Good, the Bad, and the Ugly*, Goldstein heads to Dunkin' Donuts for an iced donut and a cup of water, then to McDonald's for a McRib sandwich and a Coke. Full, he heads to his brother's optical shop to visit, but his brother is not there. Goldstein visits another Virgin Records store and listens to Madonna again. It is now getting late and, hungry again, he heads to Wendy's for a steak burger and another Coke.

After his meal he walks uptown nine blocks to 23rd Street, where he walks down into the subway. Dawn Lorenzino is walking behind him and notices that he is acting strangely, "taking baby steps on his tiptoes" and then stumbling. She also notices that he is mumbling to himself. Once they reach the platform, Goldstein starts staring intensely at Lorenzino until she finally asks him what he is looking at. Goldstein backs away, troubled. He begins pacing so furiously that one man waiting on the platform says, "Yo, buddy, can you stop pacing, you're making us nervous." Goldstein stops and then goes up to another blonde woman on the platform, Kendra Webdale.

Kendra is from Fredonia, a small town in western New York. After graduating from SUNY Buffalo with a degree in communications, she worked for a couple of small weekly alternative papers in Buffalo, but then decided she needed more action in her life and moved to New York City. She worked first at a Queens newspaper and now is a receptionist in the recording industry, still hoping to make it big. She is heading out for the evening, wearing her favorite black boots.

Goldstein asks Kendra for the time. She replies and returns her attention to her magazine. Goldstein moves back to lean on the wall just behind Kendra. Soon they all hear the train rumbling toward the station. As it arrives, Goldstein darts from the wall and, as a witness later describes, "lurk[s] right behind [Kendra] Webdale with his fingers extend[ing] towards her shoulders." He then pushes her under the shoulder blades, hard enough for people on the platform to hear the sound of his arms hitting her back over the roar of the train. Kendra struggles to regain her balance but cannot. She is thrown directly into the train's path. The motorman pulls the emergency brake and closes his eyes, hoping to somehow avoid her. Kendra is decapitated, and her body is run over by the first three cars of the train.

The motorman, Jacques Lewis, jumps out of the train and asks Goldstein if he killed Kendra. Goldstein replies that he did and quickly says that he wants a doctor because he is a mental patient. Goldstein then begins to walk toward the north turnstile. Antonetta Alston, a commuter, sees him walking away and screams "murderer," ordering him to stop. She later notes that he looked scared and "recoiled like a child, pulling his arms up to his chest with his fingers pointed downward and trembling." She wonders what is wrong with him. Goldstein stands where he is and does not try to leave, though there is an exit nearby. Some passengers then stand guard around him, as another passenger fetches the police.

When the police arrive, one officer yells that he sees a leg on the tracks below. Goldstein looks at the other officers, glances toward the train, and says,

"I don't know the woman. I pushed her." Detective William Hamilton is the first to question Goldstein and notes that he seems to be alert, answering the detective's questions promptly.

Twelve hours later, Goldstein is again questioned. The session is video-taped. Goldstein says he knew that Kendra might get killed if he pushed her off the platform. When asked if pushing Kendra was wrong, Goldstein says yes, then adds, "Yeah, definitely. I would never do something like that." When pressed with the fact that he actually did do that, he says, "I know, but the thing is I would never do it on purpose." He explains, "I wasn't thinking about anything when I pushed her." Throughout the interview, Goldstein speaks in a "polite, chatty tone" and answers all questions posed. But he becomes con-fused when he talks about pushing Kendra onto the tracks. Attempting to ex-plain his actions and the spirits that overcome him, Goldstein says, "When it happens, I don't think, it just goes whoosh, whoosh, push, you know. It's like a random variable."

Psychiatric examinations show that at the time of the offense Goldstein continues to suffer from schizophrenia of the paranoid type, a disorder with these symptoms:

> The essential feature of the Paranoid Type of Schizophrenia is the presence of prominent delusions or auditory hallucinations in the con-text of a relative preservation of cognitive functioning and affect. . . . Delusions are typically persecutory or grandiose, or both, but delusions with other themes (e.g., jealousy, religiosity, or somatization) may also occur. The delusions may be multiple, but are usually organized around a coherent theme. Hallucinations are also typically related to the content of the delusional theme. Associated features include anx-iety, anger, aloofness, and argumentativeness. The individual may have a superior and patronizing manner and either a stilted, formal quality or extreme intensity in interpersonal interactions. The perse-cutory themes may predispose the individual to suicidal behavior, and the combination of persecutory and grandiose delusions with anger may predispose the individual to violence. Onset tends to be later in life than the other types of Schizophrenia, and the distin-guishing characteristics may be more stable over time. These indi-viduals usually show little or no impairment on neuropsychological or other cognitive testing. Some evidence suggests that the progno-sis for the Paranoid Type may be considerably better than for the other types of Schizophrenia, particularly with regard to occupa-tional functioning and capacity for independent living.[23]

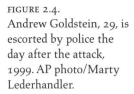

FIGURE 2.4.
Andrew Goldstein, 29, is
escorted by police the
day after the attack,
1999. AP photo/Marty
Lederhandler.

Goldstein is charged with second-degree murder and held without bail. He is placed under a suicide watch and ordered to undergo a psychiatric examination. Kendra's body is sent to Fredonia and she is laid to rest on January 6 in Dunkirk, New York, under a fresh layer of snow. Two months after Kendra's death, Goldstein is arraigned on second-degree murder charges. He is found fit to stand trial.

In New York, the insanity defense is available only for cognitive dysfunction—that is, failures in reasoning—not failures in control.[24] Thus, as long as Goldstein knew that what he was doing was wrong, he has no defense even if he had no ability to control his actions.

Goldstein's trial begins on October 7, 1999, nine months after Kendra's death. Faced with the legal irrelevance of Goldstein's lack of capacity to control his conduct, the defense must claim that he was not mentally aware and could not appreciate his actions—quite a challenge, given the nature of his mental dysfunction. During the trial, Goldstein rarely speaks, sometimes laying his head on his arms, other times staring straight ahead. He appears emotionless. None of his relatives attend any of the proceedings.

The prosecution argues that Goldstein is not insane, as the law defines it. Their line of argument is that Goldstein hates women. He was angry about still being a virgin, the prosecutors maintain, and it was no coincidence that the attack occurred on Goldstein's mother's birthday. The prosecution argues that after being rebuffed by one blonde woman (Lorenzino), Goldstein snapped and took out his anger on another blonde (Kendra).

After closing arguments, the jurors begin deliberations. During the second day of deliberations, Kendra's family publicly appeals for Goldstein to be convicted of murder. Eventually ten of the jurors decide to convict him, in large part because they are worried that if Goldstein is civilly committed, he will soon be released and back on the streets. But two jurors refuse to find Goldstein guilty, resulting in a mistrial. Goldstein shows little emotion and is transferred back to Bellevue, a noted psychiatric hospital in New York City. His family does not comment.

Goldstein remains in custody pending a retrial. His lawyers plan a new approach, to have him go off his medication so jurors can get a sense of the severe nature of his mental illness. Two weeks after going off Risperdol, Goldstein punches a social worker. Judge Carol Berkman forces a change of strategy when she orders Goldstein back on his drugs.

The second trial starts on March 22, 2000. The prosecution changes focus slightly, centering less on Goldstein's hatred of women and more on his actions just before pushing Kendra. At the start of jury deliberations, five jurors think he is guilty, three think he is not guilty by reason of insanity, and four are undecided. Once again, all are concerned that a verdict of acquittal, even if by reason of insanity, will lead to Goldstein's release from custody. One juror, a nurse, says that she is not sure that a conviction for murder would be right but that Goldstein's "planning, timing, and execution" convince her that he is dangerous. The jury finds that, although Goldstein was quite ill, he did know right from wrong and therefore did not satisfy New York's legal test for insanity. As the foreman reads the verdict, his face turns red, and he removes his glasses. Goldstein is convicted of second-degree murder. He shows no emotion.

At sentencing, Goldstein breaks his silence, saying that he is sorry. Judge Berkman gives Goldstein the maximum sentence: twenty-five years to life in prison. She calls Goldstein a "dangerous narcissist." He will not be eligible for parole for at least twenty-five years.

After learning the details of Kendra's death, Governor Pataki orders a review of state policies on releasing mentally ill individuals. Meanwhile, state lawmakers pass "Kendra's Law," a bill making it easier to involuntarily commit mentally ill people who fail to take their medication. They appropriate an extra $50 million for supervised housing. In the early part of the summer, Kendra's family sues seven private companies and clinics for letting Goldstein out. In the autumn, the family brings an additional suit against the city hospital system and the Metropolitan Transit Authority.

The week after the mistrial is declared in the first trial, New York authorities release a report concluding that Goldstein had received "uncoordinated treatment" and that the state had failed to recognize his dangerousness. Governor Pataki announces a $125 million program to improve care for the mentally ill. He has been criticized for cutting back the system's budget, but he insists that the new funding is not in response to any existing shortcomings.

Goldstein is presently serving his sentence at the Sullivan Correctional Facility in Fallsburg, New York. There is no record of any disciplinary violations.[25]

IMPROPERLY NARROWING OR REJECTING LEGITIMATE EXCUSES

There seems to be no doubt that Andrew Goldstein was seriously mentally disturbed when he committed his crime. Yet a jury found him not to be criminally insane and convicted him of second-degree murder. Is Goldstein's blameworthiness and deserved punishment really identical to that of a person without Goldstein's degree of mental illness who intentionally kills another?

Fear of the insanity defense's potential exploitation by offenders (or lawyers) who fabricate mental-illness claims, or the defense's expansion to cover defendants who may be troubled or maladjusted but are not truly mentally ill to an extent meriting exoneration, has led a few jurisdictions to abolish the defense altogether[26] and many others to narrow it substantially. Almost half of the jurisdictions now apply the traditional McNaghten "does not know right from wrong" test,[27] which allows a defense only for a cognitive dysfunction and not for control dysfunction, no matter how little control the offender has over his conduct. Another 20% of the jurisdictions have, like New York, adopted the American Law Institute's somewhat broader "lacks substantial capacity to appreciate the wrongfulness" formulation,[28] but these statutes, too, recognize no defense for impaired control, no matter how severe the impairment. Yet empirical research suggests clear shared intuitions in support of an excuse covering persons whose mental illness impairs their ability to control their conduct; abolition of the "volitional" aspect of the insanity defense controverts these shared intuitions.[29]

Some states have taken the step of introducing the "guilty but mentally ill" (GBMI) verdict as an additional option, providing an alternative to the "not guilty by reason of insanity" (NGRI) verdict.[30] (New York, the state in which Andrew Goldstein was tried, does not have the GBMI verdict.) The verdict does not do away with the insanity defense so much as create an atmosphere in which juries will be less likely to give it.

Although this verdict may appear to grant a useful third option to the jury in cases involving mentally ill defendants, it does not, for the practical effect of the GBMI verdict is the same as that of a standard "guilty" verdict. Upon a verdict of guilty but mentally ill, the court typically may impose the same sentence that would have been imposed had the defendant been found guilty of the offense charged.[31] The GBMI convict must be examined by psy-chiatrists before beginning to serve the sentence and, if the defendant is found to be in need of treatment, she will then be imprisoned in a criminal facility that can provide mental-health care. In most jurisdictions, however, these same examination and treatment procedures are in place for *all* con-victed offenders,[32] not only those who are found guilty but mentally ill. (Simi-lar civil commitment required-examination procedures exist for defendants *acquitted* under an NGRI verdict.)[33] In fact, although the GBMI verdict may seem designed to help mentally ill convicts, one of the few practical distinc-tions between GBMI convicts and typical convicts is that the GBMI convicts tend to receive *longer* sentences.[34]

Although less direct than outright abolition of the insanity defense,[35] the GBMI verdict also raises significant concerns that, far from helping mentally ill defendants, it actually leads to improper treatment. First, one must ques-tion why the factfinder in a criminal trial is an appropriate body to determine whether an offender is in need of psychiatric examination and treatment. The expertise of the jury is in finding the facts of past events and in apply-ing the community's notion of blameworthiness. The issue of the need for psychiatric treatment is a clinical one, appropriate for prison psychiatrists or other professionals rather than a lay jury. Referrals for treatment can be done more effectively and efficiently by the court after receiving the pre-sentence report, or by trained correctional officials. The GBMI verdict inter-feres with this sensible scheme and, worse, invites jurors to consider matters unrelated to guilt at a time when guilt is the sole issue before them. More-over, the verdict plays on jurors' ignorance of the consequences of an NGRI verdict (or a standard guilty verdict), encouraging the misperception that a GBMI verdict is the only way to incapacitate dangerously mentally ill per-sons while also providing necessary psychological treatment. Adding to the potential confusion is the likelihood that the jury will inadvertently confuse the statutory definition of "mental illness," relevant to the GBMI verdict, and the definition of legal "insanity."

Apparently, the verdict's potential to confuse and mislead jurors is not an unfortunate side effect for its proponents but rather its primary attraction. The legislative history strongly suggests that legislatures enacting the GBMI verdict intended it as a device to reduce insanity acquittals after constitu-tional mandates limited the use of civil commitment to preventively detain disturbed offenders.[36] As with other recent reforms narrowing the insanity defense, it is likely that the GBMI verdict produces injustice in order to avoid an illusory abuse. In the case of GBMI, however, the rule generating the in-justice is even more disturbing in that it does not overtly and honestly recognize the tradeoffs it is making between desert and other goals but rather is rooted in the insincere suggestion of an effort to harmonize desert with concerns about abuse.

The injustices produced by these kinds of reforms—barring an insanity defense for lack of control, no matter how severe, and subverting the operation of the defense with a GBMI verdict—are borne for no corresponding benefit, rendering these reforms inappropriate even on their own terms. Even if the fears of gamesmanship and abuse that drive such insanity-defense limitations were valid, a better means of addressing those concerns would be to shift the evidentiary burden of persuasion to the defendant for the insanity defense and other such defenses.[37] In any case, the empirical evidence strongly suggests that such fears are ill founded. For example, people generally believe, inaccurately, that the insanity defense is a commonly offered defense in criminal trials: one study found that people estimate that 38% of all defendants charged with crimes plead not guilty by reason of insanity (NGRI).[38] In reality, an insanity plea is exceedingly rare, raised in only a fraction of a percent of even felony cases.[39] (Also contrary to popular belief, more than half of the few cases where an insanity plea is introduced involve nonviolent offenses.)[40] In addition, even in the rare cases in which the insanity defense is sought, it is usually not granted,[41] yet the public perception is that it is commonly granted.[42]

Claims that the defense is abused and employed to manipulate juries are also belied by the fact that most NGRI pleas are not contested,[43] and the vast majority of NGRI verdicts—93%, in one study—are reached through negotiated pleas or rendered by judges in bench trials, rather than by juries.[44] The evidence directly refutes fears of rampant abuse and courtroom manipulation by attorneys representing sane defendants; in fact, most NGRI acquittees have significant prior histories of treatment for mental illness.[45] For each case like that of John Hinckley, who shot President Ronald Reagan and obtained a questionable NGRI acquittal, there are probably several cases like Andrew Goldstein, where the jury may vote to convict a truly disturbed person based on a sense that doing so is the only way to curb his dangerousness and get him needed help.

The choice between a guilty verdict and an NGRI verdict is not a choice between incapacitation and outright release. The actual effect of an NGRI verdict typically is to remand the defendant to state authorities for evaluation, supervision, and treatment.[46] This, indeed, is what happened in the notorious Hinckley case: Hinckley was transferred into a mental-health facility, St. Elizabeths Hospital in Washington, D.C., where he has remained for more than twenty years.[47] Few laypeople realize, though, that this result is the real consequence of an NGRI verdict; many assume that such a verdict is equivalent to a standard acquittal, leaving the defendant free to leave the courtroom under his own recognizance.

To make matters worse, the current system actively deters people from learning the real implications of the NGRI verdict, as many jurisdictions have rules explicitly discouraging, or completely disallowing, jury instructions that would inform the jury of the consequences of issuing an NGRI verdict.[48] Accordingly, there is a significant likelihood that juries will erroneously conclude that a guilty (or GBMI) verdict is either necessary to ensure that the defendant is not unconditionally released or the only appropriate way to guarantee needed psychological treatment for the defendant, or both.

These massive misperceptions of the practical significance of the insanity defense no doubt fuel the public's and its legislators' sense that the system is subject to pervasive abuse and that something must be done to limit the abuse.[49] They also indicate that concomitant fears about the manipulation of excuse defenses to achieve undeserved acquittals are grossly misplaced. It seems likely that eliminating or narrowing such defenses will lead to undeserved convictions in order to avoid only an illusion of abuse.

· · ·

The insanity defense generally applies to behavior that has no rational explanation, and the defense does not claim to offer any. Yet at times, the law also provides defenses or mitigations precisely because a person's conduct, though wrong and typically criminal, was motivated by some basis that seems reasonable or at least understandable. One such rule is the manslaughter mitigation, which reduces a person's liability for a killing that would otherwise be murder, based on a sense that some serious provocation incited the offender's homicidal response.

As with the other rules we have discussed in this chapter, concerns of potential manipulation by offenders seeking to stretch the boundaries of what the law considers "reasonable" have led some jurisdictions to impose strict limitations on the manslaughter mitigation and similar rules. Sometimes, though, the limitations draw arbitrary lines that exclude meritorious claims.

SODOMIZED AND TAUNTED, THE POT BOILS OVER

Like many Greek immigrants who made their way to Camas, Washington, in the early twentieth century, John Gounagias and Dionisios Grounas work at the local papermill. They also room together and frequent a local coffeehouse, a popular gathering place for the Greek community. On April 18,

1914, the day before Greek Easter, Gounagias and two friends are paging through a Greek magazine and come across an ad for a box containing a .32-caliber revolver and other miscellaneous articles. Gounagias considers the price to be a bargain and orders the box.

The next day, on Greek Easter, Gounagias and Grounas are both at home. Gounagias is drinking beer and becomes extremely drunk, almost to the point of passing out. The two men get into an argument, and Grounas makes many insulting remarks about Gounagias and his wife, who still lives in Greece. While Gounagias is laying helplessly on the floor in a semiconscious state, Grounas forcibly sodomizes him with an object and leaves the house. Upon recovering his senses, Gounagias gathers his things and moves out, re-locating to a house six or seven blocks away.

The following day, he runs into Grounas on the street and confronts him with what happened the previous night. Gounagias asks him why he did it, and Grounas laughingly replies, "You're all right, it did not hurt you." Gounagias pleads with Grounas not to tell any of their countrymen, to avoid the humiliation he knows it would bring. But Grounas is unmoved. From that point on, wherever Gounagias goes in Camas, his countrymen indicate by lewd gestures and remarks that they know what happened. Gounagias is constantly and brutally ridiculed about his rape and develops severe, debilitating headaches as a result.

About two weeks later, Gounagias's box arrives, containing the revolver. He obtains ammunition for the gun and stores it in a slit in the underside of

FIGURE 2.5.
Postcard of the Camas Mill, circa 1918. Camas-Washougal Historical Society.

his mattress. He continues to be taunted about being sodomized. A week later, Gounagias wakes up with a headache so excruciating that he cannot go to work. He tries to distract himself by going to the billiard hall, visiting the coffeehouse, and playing cards with the local baker. As the afternoon wears on, he becomes so depressed that he goes to the river intending to commit suicide but does not go through with it. He visits some friends and talks with them for a while, then meets a man from the old country and invites him back to his house where they converse for quite some time.

Gounagias goes to the coffeehouse again around eleven o'clock that evening and his feet scarcely cross the threshold before a rowdy group of fellow Greeks publicly taunt him, making laughing remarks and vulgar gestures about his rape. In his state of physical pain and emotional humiliation, Gounagias finally snaps. He rushes out of the coffeehouse enraged. He runs to his house, retrieves his gun from underneath the mattress, loads it, and runs up the hill to Grounas's house. It is dark inside, so Gounagias lights a match to find his way and discovers Grounas asleep in bed. Gounagias immediately shoots him in the head, emptying the revolver, firing five shots in all. He returns home, removing the empty shells on the way, puts the gun back inside the mattress, and gets in bed. Arrested shortly afterward, he is charged with first-degree murder.

At trial, the court refuses to admit any of the evidence concerning the provoking events that might reduce liability to manslaughter. Gounagias is convicted of first-degree murder.

He appeals to the Washington Supreme Court, arguing that the provocation evidence should have been admitted under the recognized mitigation of heat of passion.[50] The court denies his appeal, reasoning that Gounagias's actions in waiting nearly three weeks after the sodomy to kill Grounas are "wholly incompatible with sudden anger and heat of blood, as understood in the law of mitigation."[51] Thus, Gounagias's mitigation is barred because the common-law rule does not allow the mitigation if the defendant has had the opportunity to cool off after the provoking incident.

RELYING UPON A PURELY OBJECTIVE STANDARD

Traditionally, the common law imposed strict objective standards in defining such mitigations as the "reasonable provocation" standard distinguishing manslaughter from murder,[52] or in defining the culpable mental state of negligence.[53] All offenders were judged by the uniform standard of what a reasonable person would have done. It was thought that retreating from pure

FIGURE 2.6.
Washington territorial
capital, circa 1890. The
Supreme Court occupied
a portion of the
building. Courtesy
Washington State
Historical Society,
Tacoma.

objectivity by adjusting the reasonable-person standard to consider special characteristics or incapacities of the offender would introduce too much relativity into the determination of blameworthiness. Too many offenders, it was feared, would evade liability because their offenses may have seemed reasonable from their own viewpoints, however unreasonable in actuality. Accordingly, in assessing negligence, for example, the law tended to ignore differences in education, intelligence, age, background, and the like that might reduce our expectations for a particular actor.[54]

In cases involving the mitigation of murder to manslaughter, special characteristics or conditions of the defendant normally were ignored in determining whether the provocation that drove the person to kill was "reasonable."[55] Indeed, in some jurisdictions, only specifically defined circumstances could give rise to a mitigation for provocation.[56] Similarly, common-law courts held that no mitigation was available if the defendant had a reasonable period to "cool off" between the provocation and the killing.[57] (At the same time, however, the defendant's personal characteristics could be used to *deny* the mitigation: if the defendant was not actually provoked into a "sudden heat of passion" by a situation where a reasonable person would have been,[58] or cooled off before a reasonable person would have,[59] his unusual self-restraint would be taken into account and the defendant would receive no mitigation.)

The *Gounagias* case provides an example of this traditional commitment to a purely objective standard. Despite the ongoing nature of the provocation in *Gounagias*—the repeated taunts and ridicule that followed the initial act of object sodomy—and its clearly powerful cumulative effect on the defendant, the court in *Gounagias* imposed a strict standard regarding what constituted provocation and how much time could elapse after that provocation. Regardless of the actual impact of the events on Gounagias's state of mind, the court held that a "reasonable" person would have calmed down after the forcible sodomy, and therefore Gounagias was entitled to no mitigation as a matter of law—the jury would not even be allowed to consider the issue.

Many have criticized this strictly objective standard as too harsh and therefore contrary to the desert principle.[60] To ignore the provocation that inspired Gounagias's act, for example, is to ignore an important fact in the case that might well influence a careful determination of the extent of his blameworthiness. Such a killing by someone who had not suffered the humiliation that Gounagias had would be a substantially different case, essentially one in which a plausible provocation claim could not exist. Empirical studies confirm that most people share the view of these commentators that, under the demands of desert, an individual should not be held to a higher standard than he might legitimately be expected to meet.[61]

The Model Penal Code, developed several decades after *Gounagias*, promoted a more nuanced view that modified and, to some extent, partially individualized the objective standard. Under the Code, in judging whether someone has acted as a "reasonable person," the adjudicator is not to base that determination on an abstract, monolithic notion of a reasonable person, but is directed to use the viewpoint of a reasonable person aware of the facts known to the particular actor in question and "in the actor's situation."[62] The Code's commentary explains that a judge may interpret this last requirement broadly to include both the objective circumstances of the actor's situation and the characteristics of the actor.[63]

The modern view reflected in the Model Penal Code, an improvement over the cruder common-law rule, more closely tracks the requirements of the desert principle. Apparently, the concern that a partially individualized objective standard is subject to abuse and manipulation has decreased or has been supplanted by a heightened, and appropriate, emphasis on punishing offenders to a degree proportionate to their degree of blameworthiness.

Unfortunately, the fear of abuse continues to drive a significant number of American jurisdictions to rely on purely objective standards. In the provocation context, for example, several states adopting codes based on the Model Penal Code have explicitly rejected the Code's formulation and continue to employ a purely objective reasonable-person statutory rule.[64] States that still have older codes, uninfluenced by the Model Penal Code reforms, drive the figure even higher. One survey identifies twenty-three states that retain a reasonable-person formulation for provocation.[65] Another survey, based primarily on case law that either interprets a provision or determines law in the absence of a clear provision, concludes that forty-one jurisdictions still use an objective formulation for provocation, and only seven can be said to have clearly adopted the Model Penal Code approach.[66] The same survey concludes that sixteen states still use a purely objective standard for self-defense.[67] For the duress defense, purely objective standards are the rule rather than the exception. Although some states have adopted the Model Penal Code's approach for self-defense, nearly all have retained an objective formulation of duress.[68]

We believe that a better approach—in the sense of being as or more effective while not frustrating justice—is to allow use of a partially individualized reasonable-person standard as the Model Penal Code does, an approach that has not given rise to the feared manipulation and abuse. If skeptics remain concerned, further assurance could be provided by shifting the burden of persuasion for the mitigation or excuse to the defendant. We examine the details of this alternative approach in chapter 9. However skeptical one may be, there remains little justification for continuing in the use of purely objective standards that hold actors to standards that they cannot fairly be expected to meet.

PREVENTING OVER-INDIVIDUALIZATION OF AN OBJECTIVE STANDARD

Although strict adherence to an objective standard can lead to unjust results, the fear of exploitation is not irrational. *Over*-individualization can present the danger that motivated the common law's purely objective standard. Consider the legal dispute about the self-defense standard to use in the well-known case of the "subway vigilante," Bernhard Goetz, for example. The trial court invalidated the grand jury indictment because the prosecution erred, it concluded, in instructing the grand jury that the test

> was whether defendant's conduct was that of a reasonable man in defendant's situation. Penal Law § 35.15 repeatedly uses the phrase "he reasonably believes" and reasonableness is to be determined from the subjective viewpoint of a person in defendant's situation; an objective or hybrid test is inapplicable and it is not the mind of a reasonable person which is at issue, but rather, the state of mind of the defendant at the relevant time.[69]

The Appellate Division affirmed the dismissal,[70] approvingly citing this pattern instruction:

> The test the law requires you to use in deciding what this defendant was reasonably justified in believing is what this defendant himself, subjectively, had reason to believe—not what some other person might reasonably believe. You should place yourselves figuratively in the shoes of this defendant and, based on all the circumstances surrounding the encounter, as these, then and there, appeared to this defendant, you should decide whether or not this defendant in fact reasonably believed that the victim was about to use offensive deadly physical force against him, and that defensive deadly physical force was necessary to defend himself.[71]

But such language might be taken to direct a *complete* individualization of the objective standard, which would produce a purely subjective standard that would support claimed defenses based solely on irrational personal idiosyncrasies and thus reach far beyond legitimate notions of blamelessness or mitigation. For example, defendants have claimed mitigations or defenses, sometimes successfully, based on meek-mate syndrome,[72] black rage defense,[73] premenstrual stress syndrome,[74] television intoxication,[75] *Gone with the Wind* syndrome,[76] urban survival syndrome,[77] and the notorious "Twinkie defense."[78] Under a completely individualized standard, such questionable claims might well be granted, but clearly principles of desert require defendants to make efforts to resist law breaking, even if those people have impulses toward criminality not experienced by the average person. It is not every aspect of a defendant's situation that should give rise to an excuse or mitigation—how many people suffer a football-widow syndrome or an urban-survival syndrome?—but only those aspects sufficiently dramatic in their effects that we cannot reasonably have expected the defendant to have remained law abiding.

To avoid such abusive claims of mitigation or excuse, a significant number of American codes limit the possibilities for individualizing an objective standard in one context or another. As noted earlier, many codes do so by retaining the purely objective rules of common law. While that approach goes too far, for the reasons we give above, the concern that motivates them is understandable. The flexibility offered by formulations such as the Model Penal Code's represents a useful advance, but it is important that such formulations not be interpreted or expanded to create completely individualized standards of culpability and responsibility.

   While criminal-law theorists have not yet been able to articulate a comprehensive principle that defines what should and should not be allowed to
individualize the reasonable-person standard—perhaps the greatest challenge to the present and coming generations of theorists—there are clear
cases on each side of the divide on which there is consensus and which ought
to be distinguished even in the absence of an articulated general principle.[79]

   .   .   .

Although the decision to reject potential defenses or mitigations based on
fear of systematic abuses is one that seeks to advance the goal of desert, it
runs a serious risk of doing precisely the opposite. More often than not, the
concern with abuse seems an overreaction or mere speculation without factual support. Unless demonstrably harmful, these defenses should be given
a chance and abandoned only if experience proves them to be unworkable.

CHAPTER 3

Advancing Reliability

ANOTHER PRACTICAL CONSTRAINT cited as a justification for rules generating deviations from desert is a concern with reliability: either the untrustworthiness of specific pieces of evidence or the overall undependability of litigation outcomes more broadly. Unlike the rules proceeding from the fear of manipulation discussed in chapter 2, these rules do not respond to the peculiarly human element of potential *deliberate* abuse, but to the general, and unavoidable, difficulty of recreating past events. In other words, even if everyone is honest and nobody is trying to distort the result, there is still no guarantee that the result will be accurate, and in fact, there are various evidentiary problems that will make an accurate result difficult to obtain.

For example, the difficulty of proving a defendant's culpable state of mind—a fact that is necessarily a matter of speculation by all persons other than the defendant—can impose a serious burden on a prosecution charged with proving culpability beyond a reasonable doubt. Some appropriate efforts to punish the guilty might falter for lack of clear proof of culpability. It is therefore tempting to ease the prosecutorial burden by reducing the culpability requirement or by allowing indirect proof by other facts to facilitate or substitute for a finding of culpability. For example, strict-liability doctrines release prosecutors from the need to affirmatively prove a defendant's recklessness or negligence.[1] Yet, by their very nature, such doctrines open the door to the possibility of unjustly punishing morally blameless people like Raymond Garnett, whose case we discuss later in this chapter.

Other rules arising from a reliability concern will impose the cost of uncertainty on the prosecution, creating the potential to do injustice by *preventing* proper punishment. For example, statutes of limitation bar the prosecution of offenses after passage of a defined period of time, on the assumption that the evidence that would support a prosecution grows unreliable with age. Such rules enable offenders like Herbert Howard (discussed in the narrative immediately below) to avoid punishment altogether if they can avoid detection for a long enough time.

TOO LATE FOR JUSTICE

On the evening of March 16, 1978, Lauren Kustudick makes plans to meet her friends for an early St. Patrick's Day party at a dance club known as Some Other Place Lounge. She also has a crush on a guy who works there, and she hopes to see him. She gets dressed up and convinces her mother to drive her to the club. Lauren, known to friends and family as Lori, lives in Glenview, Illinois, a suburb of Chicago, and the club is nearby. Although Lori is only sixteen years old, her mother knows she is responsible and allows her to go. Lori gains entrance to the club by using a fake ID, but when she arrives, her friends are not there. Lori waits and waits. She passes the time by having a few drinks and talking to a few familiar faces she has seen at the club before.

Around 2:30 A.M., a young man (later identified as Herbert Howard) approaches Lori's table. "We're going now, my buddy and I are leaving now, and if you need a ride, we'll be happy to give you a lift down the street," says Howard. Lori accepts the offer, and Howard, Lori, and another man leave the club together. Howard opens the passenger-side door of a blue, two-door car with white vinyl bucket seats. Lori climbs into the back seat, and Howard sits in the front passenger seat. The other young man, a small and unimposing figure, gets in behind the wheel.

Lori lives only a few minutes from the club. As they approach the turn for Lori's street, she tells the driver, "Turn left up here." Howard responds, "Oh no, not yet." He flies over the seat and cracks Lori in the face with his fist, then begins to severely beat her. Lori cries out for help, begging for her mother, but each time she cries out, Howard beats her more. She pleads with the driver to stop the car, but the driver is of no help. Howard is screaming obscenities at Lori, spitting on her. He rips off Lori's clothes and forcibly

FIGURE 3.1.
Lori Kustudick (*center*),
accompanied by family
members, including her
mother (*left*). Photo
courtesy Lori Kustudick.

rapes her. Then he asks the driver if he wants to rape Lori; the driver says
that he does not. Howard chokes and bites Lori and burns her with a cigarette. The beating is so severe that it fractures her skull in multiple places.

After what seems like many hours, the driver of the car pulls into a gas
station and gets out to use the men's room. Lori notices that the driver's-side
door does not close completely. Howard sits up and leans between the two
front seats, opens the glove compartment and reaches inside to grab something. With Howard's weight shifted off her and his attention distracted, Lori
manages to squeeze out of the back seat and out of the car. She runs from the
car, and as she does she can hear his voice screaming after her, commanding
her to get back in the car.

At 4:04 A.M. on March 17, Officer Jack Hartmann of the Cook County
Sheriff's Department spots Lori running diagonally across an intersection,
completely naked. He follows and yells to her. As she stops, Officer Hartmann notices that she is bleeding profusely from her face and crying. Lori is
in shock and tells the officer, "I want to go home, I just want to go home." He
wraps her in a blanket and rushes her to Lutheran General Hospital. On the
way to the hospital, Lori attempts to convey the details of her attack, but has
great difficulty speaking due to her mouth injuries.

In the days that follow, the police, led by Investigator William Behrens,
attempt to locate Lori's attacker. From Lori's description of her attacker, a police sketch artist completes a composite drawing, but Lori says the drawing
does not resemble her assailant and that she cannot complete a better sketch.
The police interview Robert Fenton, a doorman working at Some Other Place

Lounge on the night of the attack. Fenton says that he knows Lori and that he watched her leave the club with two men on the night of the attack. Fenton tells the police that he also knows the man who approached and offered a ride to Lori, but asks for a few days to remember the man's name. Shortly thereafter, Fenton picks two photos out of a mug-shot book and correctly identifies them as the same person. This, he says, is the man who left with Lori. Fenton initially informs the police that the man's name is Junior, but when the police tell Fenton that the pictured man is Herbert Howard, Fenton agrees and says he remembers checking Howard's ID on the night of the attack. Investigator Behrens looks into Howard's criminal record and discovers that he was charged with unlawful restraint regarding a sex offense in 1977.

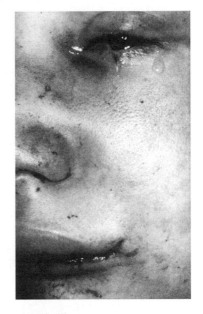

FIGURE 3.2.
Lori Kustudick in the hospital after her attack. Photo courtesy Lori Kustudick.

With this information in hand, the police interview Lori again. They present her with a book of mug shots, including Howard's photo. She scans the book, but does not select Howard's picture. The officer interviewing Lori points out Howard's photo to Lori, but she says that she does not recognize him. She finds herself unable to answer questions or offer a clear description of her assailant.

A few weeks after the rape, the police bring Howard to a local courthouse. They call Lori in to identify Howard as her attacker. Although she does not want to confront Howard, her mother convinces her to go. She is sick to her stomach at the courthouse, and she spends most of the time in the bathroom, shaking. "I walked in, did a fast look around, but like really not looking at anything and I said no and let's go and I just got up and I walked out and my parents had to follow me."[2] With no witness to testify against Howard, he is released.

The effects of the rape on Lori are far-reaching. She drops out of high school and drifts for a few years. She begins referring to the rape as "the accident." She trusts people less and yet takes needless risks, such as hitchhiking with total strangers. While maintaining an outer buoyancy, she dislikes physical contact or receiving affection or praise.

Around 1990, Lori decides to continue her education. She passes a GED test and begins taking courses at Oakton Community College. While in school,

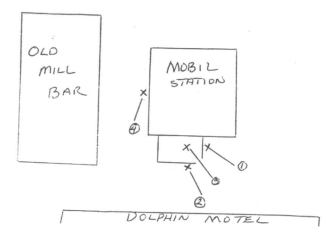

FIGURE 3.3.
Police sketch of location
of Kustudick's escape.
X's indicate locations
where things belonging
to her were found:
(1) purse and pantyhose;
(2) pants and blouse;
(3) bra and shoe;
(4) jacket and lighter.
Courtesy Cook County
Sheriff's Department.

Lori notices a strange change in her emotional state. She becomes extremely
flustered when she cannot understand a concept. She loses her bearings while
walking through the halls and finds herself crying in a bathroom stall. Lori
eventually sees a guidance counselor for help. After several conversations,
the counselor suggests that Lori seek help from a professional therapist.

In 1991, accompanied by her mother, Lori sees Lynn James, a rape therapist. As Lori conveys the details of the attack, her mother breaks down in
tears, but Lori shows no emotion. In spite of Lori's initial remoteness from
the experience, the therapy makes progress. She begins with one-on-one
counseling, then switches to group therapy. James's efforts break through to
her, getting her to realize that something horrible has happened and convincing her that the rape is something she must acknowledge and come to
terms with.

Lori agrees to learn about her rape and begins by searching for police reports. She contacts the Cook County police but initially fails to find any
records. She calls again and again, only to have the staff members tell her
that they are unsure whether the office would keep records from 1978. Finally, Sergeant Jerome Casserly agrees to look for the files, and a few days
later he locates her police report. He also gives her contact information for
Officer Kathy Lee, a female officer who had comforted her at the hospital
after the rape.

Lori continues her search. She obtains a file from Lutheran General Hospital, including X rays, additional photographs, and medical records from her
case. She returns to see her therapist, Lynn James, and they discuss her memories from the attack. James contacts Officer Lee, now working at Rolling
Meadows Police Department. James informs Lee, "I'm working with some-

one who very much would like to see you. . . . Her name's Lauren." Hearing only Lori's first name, Officer Lee immediately recalls her from more than fifteen years before. Lori meets with Officer Lee at the Rolling Meadows police station. They discuss Lori's case, and Lee explains that Officer Hartmann, the first officer on the scene the night of the attack, has passed away.

As Lori researches her case, she gradually remembers bits and pieces of the night of the attack, long since repressed. Lori wakes up in the middle of the night, thinking that her pillow feels like a vinyl seat. If a person suddenly appears near her, or an object falls on the ground making a loud noise, Lori feels her heart racing in her chest. She cannot watch television shows that portray graphic violence against women. Memories that were once a blank are now coming into focus.

Lori considers locating her assailant. She discusses the idea with Officer Lee, and they explore how they might go about it. Officer Lee obtains a book of mug shots, later described by Lori as "a big thick, thick book . . . like a couple of the yellow pages from Chicago together." Officer Lee secretly places two pictures of Howard taken at two different times in the book on separate pages. On October 6, 1993, Lori arrives at the police department but remains paralyzed by the thought of searching the book. Forcing herself to look, she is drawn to two photos, but cannot decide between them. She points out the two pictures to Lee, telling her that she can't be sure which of the two is her assailant. But the two photos are those of Herbert Howard that Lee had placed in the book. Lori tells Lee that she wants to prosecute Howard for his crimes.

The police think they have strong evidence against Howard. In addition to Lori's identification, the bouncer at the club had picked out Howard, and Howard's criminal record indicates that he is prone to this type of behavior. Assistant State's Attorney Jeanne Barrett believes that Lori has correctly identified her assailant. However, legal research determines that Howard cannot be tried. In the state of Illinois at the time of Lori's attack, all rape prosecutions carried a five-year statute of limitation. Because the time limit has passed, the state is powerless to pursue Howard for this rape.

Lori still sometimes reflects on this outcome to her case:

[A]s we're talking there's a little part that I will say to myself, and I probably will to the day I die, "Why the hell didn't I, couldn't I, pick him out that day when I was in that police station after I was beaten up?" . . . [A]fter all this time and all this, you know, . . . and all that help I had to get, we finally come back to the same person, and because I was unable to do anything [at] that time, you know, he got away with it. So that's something I have to live with.[3]

STATUTES OF LIMITATION

Statutes of limitation define a specified period after the commission of a crime within which the state must either bring a prosecution or forgo punishing the crime. Once the limitation period has run, prosecution is barred. The limitation period does not fully ensure rapid resolution of the case, however, as it relates only to the commencement and not the conclusion of criminal proceedings. Once the prosecution is under way, the statute of limitation is satisfied.[4] After that, the timeliness of the actual prosecution is controlled by the requirements of the defendant's right to a speedy trial,[5] which we discuss in chapter 7.[6]

The primary rationale for statutes of limitation is a deserved suspicion of the reliability of old evidence. With time, memories fade, witnesses die, and physical evidence disappears. In 1623, when a statute of limitation was first enacted in England,[7] these formidable problems for both prosecution and defense were avoided simply by barring prosecution after a fixed period. But time and circumstances have changed. Trial procedures now give defendants full opportunity to highlight the weakness of old evidence. It is the prosecution, which must prove the offense beyond a reasonable doubt, that suffers most from the deterioration of evidence over time. A prosecution case weakened by time can be easily exposed at today's trials in a way that it could not have been in 1623.

Long after the introduction of trial safeguards began to undercut the need for statutes of limitation, such statutes remained in force, perhaps because there was little motivation to repeal them. The weakness of old evidence gave prosecutors little interest in prosecuting older cases and provided a great, and useful, incentive to prosecute more recent ones expeditiously. Thus, statutes of limitation rarely had any practical effect (and gave prosecutors an easy answer to a victim or relative who unrealistically pressed for prosecution).

But that situation, too, has changed dramatically with a host of forensic scientific advances, of which DNA testing is only one. Early advances, such as fingerprinting, and more recent ones, such as videotape, also serve to undermine the stale-evidence argument on which statutes of limitation are based.[8] Prosecutors increasingly have reliable evidence in cases older than the limitation period, and future technological advances promise further increases.

Given these advances, the need for limitation periods has diminished, while the sense of outrage that attends their imposition has only increased. Even in Lori Kustudick's case, where nearly all of the evidence was based on the traditional (and sometimes unreliable) sources of personal memory and testimony, a compelling argument can be made that the prosecution should at least have the chance to present its evidence and to pursue a conviction against the alleged rapist. In cases involving physical evidence, whose reliability can be much higher and, perhaps more important, does not diminish over time, that argument becomes even more forceful, and the corresponding sense of injustice when the statute of limitation bars a prosecution becomes even greater.

Though the stale-evidence concern is the central and most enduring justification for statutes of limitation, it is not the only one. None of the other proffered reasons withstands scrutiny, however. For example, another rationale offered suggests that if the offender long refrains from further criminal activity, the likelihood increases that he has reformed, making criminal punishment unnecessary.[9] Even accepting this position's dubious theoretical underpinning—that criminal prosecution exists solely to induce behavior modification, rather than to punish past misdeeds or for some other purpose—such an argument simply calls for appropriate sentencing. A sentencing judge might conclude (or might not) that a rapist of seven years ago is less dangerous than one of two years ago. More important, it hardly follows that an offender who has delayed his capture for an earlier rape has not committed another one in the interim. But operation of the statute of limitation is not conditioned on his having remained crime-free. Even if he has raped several times in the interim, the statute of limitation will nonetheless bar prosecution for the first rape. (And, with conviction for the first rape barred, the offender will gain first-offender sentencing rather than repeat-offender sentencing for his second rape.)

Another rationale for statutes of limitation suggests that they "avoid prosecution when the community's retributive impulse has ceased."[10] But the best test of whether this is true in any given case may be whether a prosecutor with a docket of newer cases wishes to spend time and energy on an older case. In Kustudick's case, for example, the crime was serious enough that all of the law-enforcement authorities involved seemed eager to pursue prosecution despite the lapse of time. And, again, if the passage of time has indeed turned the desire for justice into compassionate forgiveness, then the shift in emotion can express itself in an appropriate sentence.

Another argument, phrased in economic terms, asserts that "[b]ecause potential criminals tend to discount the future at higher rates than society, punishing crimes long after they are committed will be inefficient. Punishments after a long lag have only a nominal deterrent effect, while they may cost society substantial sums."[11] This argument is similar to the time-to-reform argument noted above in that it assumes criminal law exists to serve a purely utilitarian objective—here, general deterrence—and that criminal-law doctrine should therefore be formulated based solely on its potential deterrent effect. Most people would disagree with such a role for criminal law and, as we discussed in chapter 1, even a good utilitarian should reject such a view.

More important, the argument itself, when examined carefully, suggests the futility of such a pure deterrence orientation. As we discuss in chapter 6, it is true that criminals tend to have extremely high discount rates. For that very reason, and a host of others, we question the validity of the overall project of achieving deterrence through manipulation of criminal-law doctrine. Such a deterrence-dominated view also ignores the potential expressive power of eliminating the statute of limitation, which would send a signal to criminals (and to law-abiding citizens as well) that law enforcement will not rest until a crime is solved, however long it may take and however much it may cost, because achieving justice is that important. Such a message emphasizes the moral component of the criminal law as an expression of shared values, rather than as a mechanism of social engineering and behavior control. In doing so, it may do a better job of promoting lawfulness than a calculated effort to maximize the system's deterrent efficiency.

While the original justifications for statutes of limitation are no longer valid—if, indeed, some of them ever were—the "justice cost" of retaining such nonexculpatory defenses can be high, as Kustudick's case illustrates. By overtly shielding guilty offenders from the punishment they deserve, statutes of limitation advertise the criminal-justice system as condoning a failure of justice, exacerbating the system's unfortunate reputation for treating criminal justice as a game. The system's much-needed moral credibility suffers when the system lets clearly guilty offenders go free, without even putting them to trial, because they weren't caught in time.

In short, statutes of limitation no longer serve a legitimate purpose, at least for serious offenses, but they continue to cause failures of justice and should therefore be abolished or greatly curtailed. Extension or elimination of limitation periods would not even necessarily foreclose pursuit of whatever delay-related interests they vindicate. Those interests could be pursued through claims that pre-indictment delay violated due process. Such claims are currently allowed even when an indictment is brought within the relevant statute of limitation.[12] Another method of addressing long-delayed prosecutions would be to alter the effect of the limitation rule so that it no longer presents a categorical bar to prosecution. A violation of the limitation period could give rise to a presumption of prejudice that the prosecution would have to rebut, or could create a defense contingent on the defendant's demonstration of prejudice.

Statutes of limitation vary widely across American jurisdictions. Five states impose no statute of limitation for any felony, allowing prosecution at any time: Kentucky, Maryland, North Carolina, South Carolina, and Wyoming.[13] Two others have hardly any limitation for felonies: Virginia provides a list of offenses for which a limitation period applies, which includes only a small handful of mostly regulatory felonies;[14] and West Virginia's only limitation for a felony is a three-year limitation on prosecutions for "committing or procuring another person to commit perjury."[15] All states exclude murder from any limitation period,[16] and at least eleven states extend that exclusion to other homicide offenses,[17] so that a delayed prosecution resulting in a manslaughter conviction will not lead to a failure to impose punishment, as might occur otherwise.[18] About a dozen states have also enacted special extensions of the limitation period for some or all crimes where the prosecution is based on DNA evidence.[19]

Other states, however, have relatively short limitation periods for felonies other than murder. Eleven jurisdictions impose limitation periods of seven years or less for all felonies, or nearly all felonies, other than murder: Arkansas, District of Columbia, Iowa, Maine, Nevada, New Hampshire, North Dakota, Oklahoma, Oregon, Utah, and Wisconsin.[20] Other states have staggered schemes with, it seems, varying underlying bases: sometimes extending the limitation across the board for more serious offenses;[21] sometimes imposing specific extensions apparently based on the difficulty of detection of the crime, such as for fraud, forgery, or embezzlement of public funds;[22] sometimes doing a little of both.[23]

Interestingly, despite these wide variations in limitation rules, we are aware of no demonstrated discrepancy in the experience of different states in terms of the central concern of limitation rules: improper outcomes based on stale, or vanished, evidence. Does the lack of limitation periods in Kentucky or Maryland translate into more improper convictions than occur in Arkansas or the District of Columbia? Though data are scarce, we suspect that the only long-past cases that are even pursued in states enabling such prosecution are those where the evidence is clear enough to overcome any concerns about delay and the crime is serious enough to warrant attention despite the passage of time.

The present special exception for murder only highlights the tension between the limitation period and the system's capacity, and desire, to do justice. Murder does not differ in an obvious way from other serious offenses in terms of the stated justifications for the limitation statute: the claims of "stale evidence" and that society's impulse for retribution and the offender's dangerousness diminish over time have equal application to all serious offenses— equally weak. It seems likely that the murder exception exists only because our desire to achieve justice is such that we could not stomach giving murderers a "free pass" if they went long enough without getting caught. Yet the need for justice applies to other serious offenses. At the very least, the

FIGURES 3.4, 3.5.
Lauren (Lori) Kustudick on August 11, 1999, at the signing of a bill to extend the statute of limitation for sexual assault. *Above*: Kustudick (*right*) with Governor George H. Ryan. *Below*: Kustudick (*center*) accompanied by state representative and members of the Illinois Coalition Against Sexual Assault (ICASA). Photos courtesy Lori Kustudick.

current exception for murder should be extended to include other serious felonies, such as sexual assault.

HOWARD AFTERMATH

In 1999, in part because of the efforts of Lauren Kustudick, the statute of limitation for sexual assault in Illinois was extended to ten years.[24]

In Herbert Howard's case, a rule rooted in the desire to promote accurate results prevented prosecution of a clearly blameworthy offender. The case of Raymond Garnett provides a stark contrast, as it offers an example of a rule whose underlying purpose is the same, but which can generate deviations from justice of the opposite kind, where undeserving defendants are improperly punished.

MISTAKES OF YOUTH

Raymond Lennard Garnett is a twenty-year-old man living in Silver Spring, Maryland, a town just outside Bethesda in the Washington, D.C., area. Of average height (5'8") and weight, he is mentally retarded, with an I.Q. of 52.[25] His guidance counselor at the public school reports his skills as seriously limited. He reads at about a third-grade level. His math skills put him on a fifth-grade level. He once attended special education classes but left school when the other students teased him mercilessly. He was then home-schooled for a time but later returned to school. He is often confused and sometimes gets lost. He was unable to pass any of the state's tests required for high-school graduation, so when he completed his studies he received only a certificate of attendance rather than a diploma. Although now twenty, he interacts with others and processes things much as would an eleven- or twelve-year-old.

In November 1990, a friend of Garnett's introduces him to Erica Frazier. Erica and the friend tell Garnett that Erica is sixteen years old, a fact later confirmed by her friends. In reality, she is only thirteen. Garnett is surprised that she is interested in talking to him. However, he likes her and enjoys talking with someone who does not make fun of him. Erica and Garnett talk on the phone off and on over the next several months.

On the evening of February 28, 1991, Garnett is stranded and wants to call someone to get a ride home. He notices that Erica's house is nearby on Liberty Heights Lane and approaches it about 9:00 P.M. Erica opens her bedroom window and, calling down to him, invites him to come up. She tells him

FIGURE 3.6.
Erica Frazier's house,
number 19306. Photo by
Catherine McAlpine.

to get a nearby ladder and to climb up to her window, which he does. The two sit and talk for a while. One thing leads to another and they eventually end up having consensual intercourse. Afterward, they talk and lay together for hours. Finally, at about 4:30 A.M., Garnett leaves.

Eight and a half months after their encounter, on November 19, 1991, Erica gives birth to a baby girl at the Shady Grove Adventist Hospital. Her mother, Brenda Freeman, had not been aware of the pregnancy before this.

The next day, Freeman contacts the Youth Division of the police to report the rape of her daughter. Erica explains that Garnett had visited and that it was her only sexual experience. It is confirmed that Garnett is the biological father, and he is arrested for statutory rape.

Garnett is indicted and arraigned on a charge of second-degree rape. The offense proscribes sexual intercourse with a person under fourteen by a person at least four years older than the victim. The offense is a felony and carries a sentence of up to twenty years in prison. At trial, Garnett's defense counsel tries to introduce evidence showing that Garnett acted with the belief that Erica was sixteen, because both she and her friends told him she was of that age. The defense also tries to show that Garnett is mentally twelve or thirteen (younger than Erica). But because second-degree rape is a strict liability offense, the court rules that evidence of his belief and his mental capacity are irrelevant. All that matters, the court rules, is that Erica was in fact under fourteen, that there was vaginal intercourse, and that Garnett is chronologically at least four years older than she.[26]

STRICT LIABILITY

In certain situations, the law imposes *strict liability* on criminal defendants, meaning that for one or more of the elements of an offense, no culpable mental state—such as intent or negligence—must be proved for the defendant to be convicted of the offense. Although imposing strict liability runs counter to the desert-based view that only blameworthy actors merit criminal punishment, the use of strict liability has been defended on several grounds.[27]

One rationale sees strict liability as serving an evidentiary, rather than a substantive, function. Under this view, the purpose of strict liability is to obviate a complex investigation of the defendant's mental state in a certain limited set of cases where that investigation seems unnecessary, typically because the person's very conduct is thought to reflect an indisputably culpable mental state. In other words, this *evidentiary* rationale sees strict liability as a mandatory, irrebuttable presumption that a person who commits a criminal act under certain circumstances must possess the culpable state of mind normally required for liability.

For example, in the statutory-rape context, the criminal provision defining the offense—such as that involved in the *Garnett* case—may impose liability for a sexual act with a minor without regard to the defendant's culpability, or lack thereof, as to the partner's age. Using the evidentiary rationale, proponents of such a strict-liability rule might argue that in most cases where a person has sexual intercourse with a minor, the offender's conduct reflects recklessness, or at least negligence, as to the other person being a minor. For example, the Model Penal Code provides strict liability as to the age of the victim when an offense punishes sexual conduct with a partner under ten years old.[28] It would seem to be the very unusual case in which an actor would not be at least negligent as to whether a sexual partner is under the age of ten—and even in the event of some mistake, the offender would surely know the other person to be a young minor who was *about* ten years old and would therefore be engaging in clearly wrongful conduct of some kind.

Other applications of strict liability are similarly defended using an evidentiary rationale. For example, the *felony-murder* doctrine—which imposes murder liability for a death caused in the course of a felony, whether caused intentionally or accidentally—has been defended on evidentiary grounds: people who commit dangerous felonies are usually aware, or should be aware, that a death may result during commission of the crime. The Model Penal Code explicitly employs an evidentiary rationale in its felony-murder substitute, which provides a rebuttable presumption of culpability supporting a murder conviction, rather than a categorical imposition of murder liability.[29]

Imposing strict liability, for any reason, suggests a willingness to sacrifice the dictates of desert, which would require a clear showing of culpability in each case. Clearly, imposition of liability where the minority of the victim was not known to the offender and could not reasonably have been known does not satisfy the desert principle, which proportions the extent of liability to the extent of blameworthiness and always requires *some* level of demonstrable culpability.[30]

For example, in the statutory-rape context, it is possible that, "under the circumstances known to [the actor]," a reasonable person "in the actor's situation"[31]—to use the negligence language of modern American criminal codes—might well make a mistake as to a sexual partner's age, particularly if the statutory cutoff age is at a level (such as fourteen years, the cutoff in the Maryland statute in Garnett's case) where significant numbers of persons on both sides of that age will have experienced puberty and be physically mature. Under such statutes, criminal law may impose serious liability based on insufficient blameworthiness.

The evidentiary rationale does not reject the importance of the principle of desert, however. The rationale is ultimately rooted in the position that, though facially inconsistent with the goal of desert, such presumptions of culpability actually promote desert, because they apply only in situations where it seems very likely that the actor truly had the level of culpability imputed to him, but where the practical difficulty (absent the presumption) of proving such culpability beyond a reasonable doubt creates the risk of improper acquittals. Accordingly, under this view, strict liability is not meant to express a substantive determination that culpability is irrelevant or unnecessary, but merely a practical determination that culpability is obvious and need not be put to proof. Doctrines relying on the evidentiary rationale for imputing culpability elements reflect a common legislative and judicial view that intrinsic constraints—limitations in juries' competence to draw proper inferences from evidence, in the capacity of the trial process to present all pertinent evidence, or in the ability of an investigation to find all relevant evidence—restrict the criminal-justice system's potential to achieve justice.[32]

Both of the factual underpinnings to the evidentiary rationale—first, that it is more difficult to convict criminals when full proof of culpability beyond a reasonable doubt is required; and second, that in the limited cases where criminal law imposes strict liability, the actor probably had some actual level of culpability anyway—have some merit. The systemic limitations on the discovery and presentation of evidentiary proof, especially proof of culpability, that drive the evidentiary rationale are very real. Society frequently must choose between hampered prosecution of blameworthy offenders and intrusive investigative methods or evidentiary advantages for prosecutors. And in many of the situations cited by strict-liability adherents, the actor will be at least negligent as to the harm he is risking. For example, many felons or accomplices should be aware that, by engaging in a felony where one of them plans to have a gun, a death might result.

Unfortunately, the doctrines and rules generated by the evidentiary rationale often have broader ramifications than intended or desired. A rule creating a presumption of a required element under circumstances suggesting that the element is present but cannot be proven can sometimes apply where the presumption is not warranted. There is always the risk that because no level of culpability is explicitly required, liability may be imposed even though an actor lacked any wrongful mental state, even negligence, as to the offense.[33] The *Garnett* case illustrates the point. Although most people might have been aware of a risk that Erica was underage, Garnett's mental deficiency suggests that he could not reasonably have been expected to have made such a judgment. Garnett probably was not even negligent, when judged by the negligence standard of most modern American criminal codes.

But just how often are strict-liability statutes applied, as in Garnett's case, to impose liability where no culpability exists? Of course, the very presence of strict liability statutes, even if they are not commonly used or needed, is troubling in that it undermines the moral authority of the criminal law.[34] Still, they are obviously more of a concern if it seems that many people are being convicted of serious crimes as to which they had no culpability. Many or most prosecutions for felony murder or statutory rape, though, may involve offenders who actually do possess some culpability—frequently at least recklessness, as the evidentiary rationale generally presumes—as to the relevant element, even though the statute requires none.

Because these offense provisions may be used to prosecute cases where culpability is present as well as those where it is absent, the frequency with which blameless actors are improperly punished is difficult to determine. For example, as to felony murder, F.B.I. statistics indicate that roughly one in six murders occurs in the context of some other felony, but the data indicate nothing about the typicality of the "classic" theoretical felony-murder situation, where murder liability is imputed despite the absence of culpability.[35] Many felony-context murders may be intentional killings that would properly count as murder even without a felony-murder rule.

Even so, the data may be instructive as to the appropriateness of the evidentiary rationale as a justification for an across-the-board felony-murder rule, as the statistics break down the "felony-type" murders by felony. Accordingly, they offer some indication of how often felony-context killings satisfy the premise of the evidentiary rationale: that such killings generally occur in high-risk situations where the danger to life is obvious, rendering direct proof of culpability unnecessary. In fact, many felony-context murders do arise with respect to felonies that might be thought to involve an inherent danger to human life, supporting the evidentiary rationale: for example, over the five years from 1998 to 2002, 47.7% of these murders occurred during a robbery, 3.7% during a burglary, and 3.1% during an arson.[36] Yet others seem more questionable: 26.5% of the felony-situation murders involved drug offenses, for which the *inherent* danger to life is not high, and another 13.9% of the total involved felonies that were not specified in the police reports.[37]

Because broad strict-liability rules may apply beyond the situations where the evidentiary rationale might justify them, it makes more sense to tailor the rules more narrowly to the rationale where possible. For example, as noted above, the Model Penal Code imposes strict liability as to age only where the victim is under ten years old. In most of those cases, the victim will not have reached puberty and the offender's negligence as to the minority of the victim will be obvious. Yet for sexual partners closer to the age of majority, who may be physiologically mature and thus overtly indistinguishable from a young adult, strict liability as to age may be too strict a rule.

In the case of felony murder, many jurisdictions adopt a narrow form of the felony-murder rule, which limits its application to those specific situations in which it is likely that the felon did have the extreme indifference to the value of human life normally required for reckless murder.[38] Yet even with a more narrow felony-murder rule, we should prefer rebuttable presumptions, such as the Model Penal Code's formulation, to conclusive presumptions. Specifically, felony murder and other strict-liability offenses should formally express the culpability being imputed as to the real harm or evil at issue, and defendants should have the opportunity to rebut the doctrines' presumption of such culpability. In chapter 9, we examine more closely the issues that arise upon such a shift of the burden of persuasion to the defendant.

Further, even if the existing strict-liability rules were put in place to reduce the number of improper acquittals, there remains the empirical question of whether any resulting erroneous convictions can be justified by the rule's benefits. Some see conviction of a few innocent persons as the necessary price for conviction of the numerous guilty persons who would avoid punishment without a somewhat overinclusive rule.[39] But in cases of clearly improper conviction, the evidentiary rationale loses much of its appeal and seems less attractive than a case-by-case adherence to the desert principle, which would require a showing of culpability. Certainly, the balancing of interests in the effort to achieve the agreed-upon goal of desert-based liability is complex. But for each doctrine of imputation supported by an evidentiary rationale, the empirical inquiry that should drive the balancing is clear: an investigation of the number of increased deserved convictions as against the relative increase in erroneous convictions.[40]

.   .   .

Both statutes of limitation and strict-liability rules run a serious risk of sweeping too broadly, either excluding or including some cases beyond those for which the underlying reliability concern genuinely applies. In some instances, however, reliability concerns offer persuasive reasons to adopt a rule that may occasionally frustrate desert, where the rule will, on balance, more often avoid injustice than create it. The constitutional rules governing confessions and lineups highlight the possibility of creating rules that are well tailored to address reliability issues while retaining enough flexibility to avoid injustices.

EXCLUDING COERCED CONFESSIONS
AND UNCOUNSELED LINEUPS

The Fifth Amendment codifies a long-standing common-law rule prohibiting the compulsion of self-incriminating out-of-court statements and their introduction at trial. The traditional basis for the prohibition was a concern that coerced confessions are inherently unreliable.[41] The concern seems well justified.

Moreover, and importantly, the rule does not reflect a deviation from the goal of doing justice. Rather, it is an evidentiary rule that makes a *case-by-case* judgment, considering the totality of the circumstances, regarding the factual reliability of a defendant's confession.[42] (Contrast this with, for example, the application of strict-liability rules, which categorically obviate any consideration of the factual particulars of the individual cases to which they apply.) Deeming a confession "involuntary"—in the sense that "the defendant's will was overborne at the time he confessed"[43] so that "the confession cannot be deemed 'the product of a rational intellect and a free will'"[44]—is tantamount to declaring that its tendency to create prejudice outstrips its probative value, and such evidence is typically excluded as a general matter.[45] Moreover, the exclusionary rule for involuntary confessions does not create a total bar to prosecution; it merely prohibits the use of a specific piece of apparently unreliable evidence. The prosecution may still pursue its case but cannot introduce the confession to support that case.

Even so, it has been argued that any legal rule requiring judges to exclude confessions they deem to be unreliable goes too far. Why not instead allow inclusion of the confession, along with inclusion of all evidence indicating its unreliability, and let the jury decide? Further, even if the confession is unreliable, other information or evidence that the police obtain based on it—the so-called *fruits* of the confession—might not be, and should therefore be admitted.[46] Yet some respond that excluding the fruits also promotes reliability, as it discourages the police from deliberately focusing all of their efforts on building a case against the person who confessed, which may both generate more unreliable evidence and distract the police from pursuing evidence that would point to the true offender and exculpate the defendant.[47] These arguments shade toward a debate about the proper role of legal rules in promoting or discouraging certain law-enforcement methods, an issue we address in chapter 7.

The rule barring the use of lineup identifications conducted without defendant's counsel present[48] also has a reliability rationale, to the extent that it aims to prevent the admission of inherently suspect identification evidence that may be highly prejudicial and lack significant probative value. Unlike the bar against the use of coerced confessions, however, the rule is not well tailored to its evidentiary purpose, as it creates a per se exclusion that operates even absent actual prejudice from counsel's absence. Therefore, some accurate and reliable lineup identifications may be excluded by the rule.[49] A formulation of the rule tailored more to a reliability rationale might create a presumption of unreliability that the prosecution could rebut with evidence that the lineup at issue was fair and nonsuggestive.[50] Enhanced attention to specific circumstances would retain the rule's power to exclude questionable evidence while allowing the flexibility to admit evidence having strong indications of reliability.

In short, although the rules barring admission of coerced confessions and lineups without counsel are constitutional in dimension, they generally serve a common evidentiary function. As such, they need be no more at odds with desert than other evidentiary rules, which are oriented toward a goal—ascertaining truth—that clearly accords with the desert principle. (By contrast, the rule demanding exclusion of confessions obtained in violation of the *Miranda* rules is grounded in a reason that genuinely admits the possibility of sacrificing desert. We discuss that rule in chapter 7.)

.   .   .

Reliability is obviously a legitimate goal and, indeed, is consistent with and generally seeks to advance the goal of doing justice. Even so, sometimes the pursuit of reliability has led to hard-and-fast rules that will generate results that run counter to the dictates of desert. For some rules, it seems likely that the cost of predictable deviations from desert will seem minor in comparison to the benefit of ensuring accurate results. In other cases, however, rules established to ensure just and accurate outcomes have underlying flaws suggesting that they instead subvert reliability, or advance it in many fewer cases than those in which it is subverted.

CHAPTER 4

Making the Most of Limited Resources

A THIRD PRACTICAL constraint used to justify doctrines of deviation from desert is the simple impossibility, given limited investigative and adjudicative resources, of finding, prosecuting, and suitably punishing every criminal offender. Police and prosecutors must be selective in their allocation of resources to focus on the most serious offenses and on offenses for which they can most certainly or easily bring a successful prosecution. From this tension between doing justice and limited resources springs the prosecutor's reliance on plea bargains: negotiated arrangements whereby an offender agrees to plead guilty, typically to a lesser offense than the one charged or in return for more lenient treatment at sentencing than he might expect if he had pleaded not guilty and been convicted. Prosecutors simply lack the resources to bring every case to trial, nor would they want to do so. Because police investigations do not always turn up overwhelming admissible evidence against the accused, it is not always clear ex ante whether a trial will result in a conviction. Accordingly, to clear their caseloads and make sure of getting at least half a loaf rather than none, prosecutors make deals.

The same basic justification supports the practice of granting witness immunity. It is an unfortunate reality that the most serious offenses often are the most difficult to prosecute. In particular, career criminals, wise to the ways of law enforcement, are careful to avoid leaving evidence that can be used against them, and they also tend to associate primarily with other career criminals. For this reason, every jurisdiction gives prosecutors discretion to grant some offenders immunity in order to establish a case against others.[1] Although witness immunity forecloses desert for some offenses or offenders by forgoing their prosecution, it arguably ultimately advances desert overall by enabling prosecutors to convict other, still more blameworthy offenders.[2]

One can look at the limited-resources issue in a rather different way: viewing these policies as true deviations from desert, resulting from our unwillingness to devote adequate resources to achieve true justice and to trade our privacy for more intrusive but more effective criminal investigation. From this perspective, plea bargaining is not rooted in an inevitable practical constraint but reflects a sacrifice of the desert goal in favor of competing social objectives (cost savings and personal privacy), and therefore properly belongs in our discussion in chapter 8, as an example of a distinct competing goal whose pursuit frustrates desert.

Although this alternative perspective may have some measure of legitimacy, for purposes of this project, we adopt the practical-constraint perspective, treating plea bargaining as consistent with the desert goal given unavoidable limitations preventing perfect law enforcement. We take this position for two reasons. First, some of the constraints, such as limitations on governmental intrusion, are so fundamental to how we define our society that to imagine a different world is to make the exercise purely fanciful. Second, not all of the relevant constraints on full and fair prosecution of all offenders relate to societal decisions about resource allocation or governmental intrusion; some are rooted simply in the fundamental impossibility of absolute empirical certainty or proof. Witness immunity and plea bargaining are necessitated in part by problems involving the availability of factual proof—if police always found a smoking gun, every offender could be convicted quickly and cheaply, regardless of the state's fiscal priorities or permitted governmental intrusion. On the other hand, society could spend a good deal more money on criminal investigation and allow more intrusion yet still not always find a smoking gun, a reliable witness, or the like.

A different argument in favor of plea bargaining sees the practice as a way of screening and quickly resolving, through a guilty plea, the many "easy" cases where evidence of guilt is clear.[3] This screening mechanism then enables attorneys to devote more time and effort to full, fair, and accurate adjudication, through a full-fledged jury trial, of cases that are closer on either the facts or the law. Seen this way, plea bargaining partially sacrifices desert in the easy cases by letting defendants bargain for reduced sentences—although the sacrifice is mitigated slightly by the certainty of conviction—while increasing the prospect of desert, for the guilty and innocent alike, in harder cases. Under this view, plea bargaining may have an ancillary benefit, which would be of particular significance for desert utilitarians: because the clear cases are resolved through bargains and only the gray cases are tried before juries, a jury verdict will rarely be seen as clearly wrong. As a result, the system's reputation for doing justice will be largely safe from the damage that patently inaccurate results would cause.[4]

A BARGAIN ON CONTRACT KILLINGS?

Salvatore "Sammy the Bull" Gravano is born on March 12, 1945, in Bensonhurst, a tough Italian neighborhood in southwest Brooklyn. The community feels like a small town, with the attendant insularity and suspicion of outsiders. Strangers are so closely monitored that the street crimes common elsewhere are rare, and the murder rate is one-third less than the New York City average. But Bensonhurst's relative safety comes with a large string attached: the Cosa Nostra. Many mob bosses live in Bensonhurst, and new members are regularly recruited from neighborhood street gangs.

Sammy catches the Cosa Nostra's eye at a young age, during an incident that earns him the nickname "The Bull." His brand-new bicycle, given by his parents for his tenth birthday, has been stolen, and Sammy gets word that it is parked next to a local fruit stand. He runs to investigate, discovering that two older and bigger boys have the bike. Undaunted, Sammy grabs the bike. A fight ensues, with Sammy taking on both boys, holding his own while getting plenty beat up in return. Some mob wiseguys are hanging out in front of the corner bar and come over to break up the fight. Sammy convinces them that the bike is his. One of the wiseguys tells the other boys to get lost and then boasts to the others, "Did you see this Sammy? He's like a little bull."

Due to an undiagnosed and humiliating case of severe dyslexia, Sammy dislikes school and fares poorly there. By age thirteen, his life revolves around the Rampers, the dominant youth street gang in Bensonhurst. The Rampers gain a reputation as one of the most dangerous gangs in the five boroughs, yet most people in the neighborhood think of them as "good neighborhood boys." They never burgle people's homes, only commercial businesses that have insurance to cover the losses. They also steal lots of cars, which are later sold for parts or shipped overseas and resold.

After dropping out of high school and being drafted into two years of army service during the Vietnam War, Sammy Gravano is approached by mobster Shorty Spero of the Colombo crime family. Spero convinces Sammy to join the family, where he starts off at the bottom, robbing and stealing, but quickly moves up in the ranks and into racketeering, as part owner of an after-hours club running a lucrative poker game in the back room.

One day, Carmine Persico, a captain in the Colombo family, summons Sammy and orders him to administer a severe beating to a Long Island washing-machine distributor who is having an affair with Persico's brother's wife. Persico explicitly instructs Sammy to bring back one of the man's ears. Sammy agrees, but has no intention of actually cutting off the man's ear. He ends up pleasing Persico, however, when he accidentally severs the man's little finger with a whack of his blackjack. The incident wins praise from Joe Colombo himself, and Sammy receives his first official hit assignment, Joe Colucci. Sammy kills Colucci, and when he thinks about the murder later, wonders:

> Am I supposed to feel remorse? Aren't I supposed to feel something? But I felt nothing, at least nothing like remorse. If anything, I felt good. Like high. Like powerful, maybe even superhuman. It's not that I was happy or proud of myself. Not that. I'm still not happy about that feeling. It's just that killing came so easy to me.

Sammy's run with the Colombos comes to an end when Shorty's brother, Ralph Spero, becomes jealous of Sammy's rising reputation, complaining that Sammy will be "made" before Ralph's own son (and Shorty's nephew), Tommy. Sammy is released from the Colombo family and joins the Gambino family as a hit man. In 1976, only eight years after joining the Cosa Nostra, he is "made," or promoted to the Gambino family's elite circle of members.

In late September 1985, Angelo Ruggiero, another member of the Gambino family, approaches Sammy with a proposal. Ruggiero tells Sammy that he wants to kill Paul Castellano, the boss of the Gambino organization, and promote John Gotti, then a *capo*, or captain, to boss. Sammy mulls this over in light of his dislike for Castellano and discusses the idea with Frank DiCicco, a trusted friend and high-ranking member of the family. DiCicco and Sammy decide they want to help with the murder. After meeting with other Cosa Nostra members to determine where their loyalties lie, the conspirators conclude that they must also kill Tommy Bilotti, Castellano's right-hand man.

Serendipitously, Castellano plans a meeting with various members of the Gambino crime family and, not suspecting any plot, asks DiCicco to attend. The meeting is to take place at Sparks Steakhouse in Manhattan on December 16. Because the area will be packed with holiday shoppers, it will be a perfect opportunity to kill Castellano and Bilotti, then escape into the bustling crowds.

On December 15, 1985, the four plotters—Gravano, Gotti, Ruggiero, and DiCicco—meet in the basement of Sammy's office along with a hit team of six additional men, including four shooters, to plan the murders. The next day, Gotti, Gravano, and nine others meet in a park a few blocks south of Sparks. The four shooters wear identical long white trench coats with black fur

FIGURE 4.1.
John Gotti, following his arrest at the Ravenite Social Club in 1990. AP photo/Andrew Savulich.

Russian hats. Walkie-talkies are distributed so the men can maintain communication during the hit.

Gotti and Sammy drive to a spot about a block away from the restaurant and wait. Growing impatient and restless, they circle the block and stop again at their assigned spot. Just then, they see Castellano and Bilotti drive past in a black limousine. Sammy signals the shooters over his walkie-talkie. At 5:26 P.M., Castellano and Bilotti park the limo in a no-standing zone about thirty feet from the entrance to Sparks. The street outside Sparks is bustling with shoppers and businesspeople.

The shooters approach the limo, and as Castellano and Bilotti get out of the limo, the gunmen open fire, sending pedestrians running and screaming. Castellano and Bilotti are killed, each taking six bullets to the upper body and head. Shell casings litter the ground by their bodies. Gotti and Sammy drive slowly up the block from their position and as they pass the scene, Sammy sees Bilotti in a pool of his own blood, turns to Gotti, and says, "He's gone." With Castellano dead, Gotti soon rises to power and becomes the boss of the Gambino family, with Sammy as one of his most important confidants and his top assassin.

Sammy unwaveringly fulfills his duties to the family, committing at least nineteen murders along with running gambling and loan-sharking operations. Even when assigned a hit he doesn't approve of, Sammy does it, later explaining, "What can I do? It's an order from the boss. This was the life I chose, and the boss was the boss."[5] In June 1986, Gotti orders Sammy to murder Robert DiBernardo, a captain in the Gambino family, for talking behind Gotti's back and "other reasons" he doesn't share with Sammy. Sammy shoots DiBernardo twice in the back of the head. In March 1988, Sammy becomes fed up with the "double dealing" of his close friend Liborio Milito, another made member of the family. He asks Gotti if he can get rid of Milito, and Gotti gives him the OK. Sammy calls Milito and invites him over to discuss the murder of another person. When Milito arrives, Sammy is sitting at a table, playing cards. Milito joins him at the table, and one of Sammy's henchmen comes up from behind Milito and shoots him once in the back of the head, then once under his chin.

In 1990, Gotti promotes Sammy to "underboss" of the Gambino family, second in command of the organization. In late 1990, Gotti and Louis DiBono, a member of the family who runs a drywall and construction business, have plans to meet to discuss the business, but DiBono does not show up for the meeting. Gotti is humiliated and orders Sammy to kill DiBono. Having hated DiBono for many years because he thinks him two-faced and double-dealing, Sammy gladly accepts the assignment. On October 4, 1990, a garage attendant in the World Trade Center finds DiBono dead in his Cadillac, shot three times in the head.

At 7:00 P.M. on December 12, 1990, fifteen agents from the F.B.I. and the New York Police Department raid Gotti's Ravenite Social Club at 247 Mulberry Street in Manhattan. At the time, twenty-seven people are in the club. The agents arrest Gotti, Sammy, and another senior family member, Frank Locascio. Sammy is charged with various gambling and loan-sharking offenses as well as, among other things, conspiracy to murder and the murder of Robert DiBernardo; conspiracy to murder and the murder of Liborio Milito; and solicitation of murder, conspiracy to murder, and the murder of Louis DiBono. Gravano faces life in prison for the charges.

Based on wiretap evidence providing more than 600 hours of taped conversations demonstrating Sammy's and Gotti's involvement in the Gambino crime network, federal agents feel confident in their case. The press and public don't necessarily agree, however. Gotti has been acquitted in three previous prosecutions over the last five years, earning him such nicknames as "The Untouchable Don" and "The Teflon Don."

During a bail hearing, prosecutors play tapes of secretly recorded conversations between Gotti and other members of the Gambino crime family. Sammy hears Gotti talking about him falsely behind his back and is outraged. On October 10, 1991, after eleven months in jail awaiting trial, he notifies two F.B.I. agents that he wants to meet with them. The agents suspect that Sammy's attorney may be involved in the family and fear that he will alert Gotti of Sammy's decision to testify, so they arrange for a phony voice-analysis test as a way to contact Sammy without his attorney present. After the fake voice-analysis test, Sammy leaves the testing area and his attorney returns to his place of business; but before Sammy leaves for his cell, federal agents call him back to the testing area. He says to the agents, "I want to switch governments."

Sammy informs the agents that he is willing to testify against Gotti but wants full immunity in return. The prosecutors refuse to grant total immunity, and Sammy agrees to admit to all of his previous crimes in return for a lenient sentence. He confesses to a total of nineteen murders, one conspiracy to murder, multiple acts of illegal gambling, loan-sharking conspiracy, and four acts of obstruction of justice. Sammy also agrees to be debriefed by the U.S. Attorney for the Eastern District of New York, the F.B.I., and any other law enforcement agencies that the U.S. Attorney requires. Furthermore, he agrees to testify in any proceeding as requested by the U.S. Attorney. In

FIGURE 4.2.
Sammy "The Bull"
Gravano testifying
about boxing and the
underworld, 1993. AP
photo/John Dunn.

exchange, the U.S. Attorney reduces Gravano's charge to a crime that carries a maximum of twenty years' imprisonment, as opposed to the life imprisonment that he was originally facing, and agrees not to charge him with any additional crimes based on evidence that he willingly supplies. If Sammy fully complies, the U.S. Attorney promises to recommend that the judge give Sammy a lenient sentence.

Beginning on March 3, 1992, Gravano takes the stand and testifies against his codefendants, including Gotti. "John was the boss," he testifies. "I was the underboss. I helped John run the family." For days, Gravano gives detailed testimony about the Gambino crime family and its crimes, including murders. Sammy is an extremely effective witness and with his testimony, the U.S. Attorney is able to convict John Gotti of all charges in the indictment. These include the murders of Castellano, Bilotti, DiBernardo, Milito, and DiBono and conspiracy to murder Gaetano Vastola. Sammy's testimony also helps to convict Locascio of all but one charge in the indictment. Both men are sentenced to life imprisonment without possibility of parole.

In accordance with his plea agreement, Sammy testifies in ten separate proceedings, and more than ninety officials from various state and federal agencies debrief him on organized crime. With his testimony, prosecutors convict or increase the sentences of roughly forty Mafia members, including the bosses of two other Cosa Nostra families. In April 1993, Sammy testifies before a Senate subcommittee on the involvement of organized crime in boxing.

At Sammy's sentencing on September 26, 1994, his contributions are noted on all sides. In a letter to the court, Senators Sam Nunn and William Roth ask for leniency, reporting that Gravano's Senate testimony provided "unique and valuable information that added measurably to the investigation." Judge I. Leo Glasser sentences Sammy to five years' imprisonment, followed by three years of supervised leave, and assesses a $50 court fine. Judge Glasser also gives him credit for the three years and nine months already served during the Gotti trial. At the end of the sentencing hearing, the judge comments on Sammy's "very significant change" since becoming an informant and states, "I hope I will never have occasion to be dismayed," to which Sammy replies, "I'm sure you won't, Your Honor."[6]

PLEA BARGAINING AND WITNESS IMMUNITY

Guilty pleas, rather than contested trials, account for the vast majority of criminal convictions: 90–95%, or even more, and the rate is rising.[7] Most of those pleas are the result of plea negotiations.[8] Plea bargaining comes in two forms: *charge* bargains, where the defendant pleads guilty to one or more charges in return for the prosecutor's agreement to dismiss any other charge(s); and *sentence* bargains, where the charges are not reduced but the prosecutor makes some commitment to pursue a favorable sentence for the defendant in return for his guilty plea. The federal sentencing guidelines make the "plea discount" explicit by reducing an offender's guideline sentence if he "clearly demonstrates acceptance of responsibility,"[9] which generally requires a plea of guilty.

The related practice of granting criminals immunity from prosecution, or reduced punishment, in return for their testimony is also very common. Even if one considers only the federal jurisdiction, prosecutors make hundreds of immunity requests each year (in the federal system, prosecutors must receive authorization from the Attorney General before granting immunity).[10] Moreover, prosecutors have other means, beyond formal grants of immunity, by which to bargain for witnesses' cooperation. Prosecutors increasingly obtain testimony through informal "cooperation agreements," which involve a prosecutor's informal promise not to prosecute a potential defendant, as opposed to a formal grant of immunity.[11] Further, under the federal sentencing guidelines that became effective in 1987, a prosecutor may request a reduced sentence—known as a "downward departure" from the otherwise authorized punishment range—for a defendant who has "provided substantial assistance in the investigation or prosecution of another person who has committed an offense."[12] This enables a prosecutor to use the prospect of a sentence reduction to induce a defendant to provide useful testimony, without fully sacrificing the ability to convict that defendant also. For the year ending September 30, 2001, some 9,390 sentences, or 17.1% of all federal cases, involved "substantial assistance" departures.[13] These figures relate only to the federal system; immunity grants in one form or another are also provided in each of the fifty states.

Are these practices—bargained-for charges or sentences, immunity, or downward guideline departures in return for a plea or testimony—justifiable? Should an offender escape deserved punishment because he agrees to plead guilty or helps prosecutors do justice in other cases? The problem and the tradeoffs it represents were put to prosecutors about as directly as possible when Sammy "The Bull" Gravano offered to testify against John Gotti and a host of other organized-crime figures in return for leniency.

The choice was a stark one. On the one hand, Gravano was a despicable character who had committed numerous murders and other serious offenses. On the other hand, his cooperation made history and enabled the prosecution of many other serious criminals. At Gravano's sentencing, Judge Glasser concluded, "There has never been so important a defendant in organized crime who has made the leap from one social planet to another. . . . His stature in organized crime is so unique. His unprecedented decision to cooperate encouraged others to cooperate."[14] The prosecution was equally complimentary, calling Gravano "the most significant witness in the history of organized crime in the United States."[15] They noted that Gravano had provided "extraordinary, perhaps even historic, assistance to our effort to dismantle the criminal empire he had helped maintain. . . . Simply put, Gravano's cooperation has been the signal event in the government's decades-long fight against the Mafia."[16] Yet Gravano had also killed in cold blood nineteen people, perhaps more.

The same problem, in less dramatic form, exists in the many cases where prosecutors allow reduced sentences in return for testimony or to forgo an expensive (and possibly risky) trial. The offender commonly receives less punishment than she would otherwise receive—that very inducement is what prompts the offender to testify or to plead guilty. The tension, and potential for results contrary to desert, seems highest in cases involving witness immunity, for as one commentator has observed and as the Gravano case exemplifies, "[T]hose defendants with the most information are usually those with the dirtiest hands—the more crimes you commit, the more criminals you know about. Trading plea concessions for information means giving the biggest breaks to the worst actors."[17]

Still, in principle, these prosecutorial practices do not necessarily reject, or run counter to, the goal of desert-based liability.[18] Instead, they are thought to be justified on the ground that, given the system's unavoidable resource limitations and the uncertainty of obtaining convictions at trial, more (and more blameworthy) offenders will be punished in a system with these practices than in one without them.[19] In fact, a system in which both parties can negotiate toward a reasonable punishment, instead of facing the uncertain, all-or-nothing outcome of a trial, may well tend to generate more accurate, consistent, and fair outcomes overall.[20] Even so, the practice of plea bargaining may be in tension with desert not because the bargained-for sentences are disproportionately or improperly low, but because the practice leads to disparate punishments for otherwise similarly serious offenders, with lower sentences for those who happen to plead guilty and higher sentences for those who happen to demand trial.[21]

Many of the attacks on the practice of plea bargaining—and there have been numerous attacks[22]—do not squarely address the issue of whether the practice advances or frustrates desert, but instead express different concerns.[23] Some critics of plea bargaining focus on the rights of criminal defendants, arguing that plea bargaining amounts to a forced, or at least unduly coerced, waiver of the trial right.[24] They also emphasize the inadequacy of the agency relationship between many defendants and their lawyers, who are often overworked, underpaid appointed counsel. Because the interests of the attorney may not be aligned with those of the defendant, attorneys may not satisfactorily pursue defendants' interests in plea negotiations.[25] (Another, somewhat more abstract, rights-based concern is that offering an inducement to plead guilty undermines the defendant's right, and perhaps moral duty, to use a guilty plea as a genuine expression of guilt.)[26] Defense attorneys may also simply lack the skill, time, or experience to adequately serve their clients.[27] Defendants' own emotions, or other impediments to acting in their own best interests, may also work to their detriment in striking a bargain. Excessive optimism, refusal to admit guilt, a tendency to discount the significance of long-distant punishment, and various psychological biases may all interfere with defendants' judgment.[28]

Such critiques are, at least by their explicit terms, centrally concerned with vindicating rights, rather than with advancing desert per se. Those rights, however, are themselves largely rooted in a desire to ensure accuracy in criminal punishment and ultimately to promote the aim of desert by ensuring that liability is not imposed on those who do not deserve it. Yet the rights-based critiques often do not address head-on the empirical question that fundamentally animates them: whether plea bargaining actually works any demonstrable unfairness to defendants in terms of the punishments they receive—a concern which, again, resonates with the desert goal rather than competing with it.

The right-to-trial and right-to-counsel (including counsel-as-imperfect-agent) arguments suggest that plea bargaining may depart from desert in the direction of imposing excessive, undeserved punishment. Some others share this view, asserting that bargaining creates a scheme that might encourage even innocent defendants to plead guilty for the sake of reducing their potential punishment.[29] Seen differently, the plea-bargaining system might generate excessive punishment for those who do *not* plead guilty, if the average negotiated plea or sentence leads to a fair punishment, whereas a sentence imposed after trial and conviction is higher than would be proportionate to the offense, effectively adding a "penalty" for asserting one's trial rights.[30] One commentator has argued, using the tools of game theory, that the institution of plea bargaining may actually increase sentences.[31]

Yet other critics claim that plea bargaining is troublesome in terms of desert for exactly the opposite reason: because the practice enables the pleading defendants to obtain *less* punishment than they deserve.[32] For example, just as defense counsel's incentives may not align perfectly with the defendant's, bargaining prosecutors do not have a direct incentive to maximize punishment in all cases, but may be motivated by other goals as well.[33] The same concern for insufficient, rather than excessive, punishment is also present with respect to the practice of witness immunity, as to which there would be no clear corresponding concern regarding defendants' rights. In the immunity or even the substantial-assistance sentencing departure situation, a defendant is clearly deriving a benefit that reduces his punishment below what would normally be considered appropriate.

Recently, some commentators have even questioned the basic assumptions of most analyses of plea bargaining. Specifically, they have questioned whether actual bargains bear any resemblance to what one might expect as a trial outcome,[34] or even whether they bear any significant relation to the relevant underlying legal prohibitions or sentencing rules.[35] If these claims are accurate—and there is much to suggest that they are for some, and perhaps for many, cases—they might seem to call into question the likelihood of plea bargains tracking desert.

But the consequences of these arguments for bargaining, as it relates to desert, are complex. The claim that bargains do not resemble the proper formal legal sanctions available is problematic from a desert perspective only if the law on the books tracks desert better than the bargains do. Yet in an era of ever-expanding criminal prohibitions and ever-escalating criminal penalties, there is reason to suspect this is not the case.[36] Indeed, there is good cause to suspect that legislators themselves are aware that the enhanced penalties they enact go well beyond deserved punishment and expect, if not hope, that bargaining prosecutors will routinely discount or ignore the harsh penalties for which the law provides.[37] Certainly, the reliance on prosecutorial discretion that the current dependency on bargaining reflects is troubling, as we have noted elsewhere.[38] Still, the relationship among desert, law, and bargaining is too complex to warrant a conclusion at this point that justice would be better served by following the letter of the law rather than allowing, or even encouraging, ad hoc negotiated settlements.

More generally, despite the numerous considerations advanced on both sides, the empirical soundness of the fundamental assertion that plea bargaining leads to systematic and improper deviations from desert, in either direction, remains uncertain.[39] Even the claim that bargaining creates new and improper discrepancies between the sentences of equally culpable offenders, some of whom plead while others do not, is debatable; absolute consistency might be a nearly impossible systemic goal even without bargains.[40] Available data suggest that guilty pleas and bench trials result in distinct but roughly similar sentences, yet the data also show serious sentence disparities between guilty pleas and sentences following jury trials. Figures for state-court felony dispositions in 1994 show that following a jury conviction, the average felony sentence was 143 months and the median sentence was 87 months, whereas following a guilty plea, the average felony sentence was 63 months and the median sentence was 48 months; the figures for bench trials are 84 months and 60 months.[41] These statistics might simply indicate that prosecutors refuse to plea bargain, or drive a harder bargain that encourages defendants to "take their chances" at trial, when the evidence is strong and the crime is serious—although that theory is in tension with the vision of plea bargaining as a screening mechanism to weed out cases where guilt is obvious.[42]

On the other hand, a similar debate exists as to the empirical support for the critical empirical assumption grounding the practices of plea bargaining and witness immunity: the belief that the system simply would not work without them, or at least, that the system is considerably cheaper and more efficient with them.[43] Some commentators have produced data indicating that, in the absence of plea bargaining, the system works much less smoothly.[44] But others maintain, based on other data, that the system could abandon plea bargaining and remain workable.[45] Some even maintain that plea bargaining has its own attendant inefficiencies which partially undermine its resource-saving goal.[46]

One recent contribution to the literature suggests an alternative to the traditional plea-bargaining system.[47] The proposal suggests using more rigorous early prosecutorial screening of cases to ensure that the initial charges against a defendant accurately reflect his crime, followed by strict curtailment of negotiations with defendants to reduce the charges later.[48] Its proponents maintain—with support from empirical data from New Orleans, which uses a similar system[49]—that enhanced screening and reduced bargaining would not drive up the administrative costs of the system, because many defendants would enter "open pleas" of guilty to the offenses charged (as opposed to bargained pleas to a lesser charge), rather than demanding a trial.

For those (like us) who take seriously the importance of maintaining the moral credibility and legitimacy of the criminal-justice system, such a scheme would have the potential advantage of reducing the appearance of the system as one where the lawyers, instead of the facts, determine the outcome.[50] Its proponents cite as one of its central strengths the increased transparency it would introduce to the currently opaque bargaining process, as offenses of conviction could be easily compared to offenses charged, and any reduction would be explicitly recognized as contrary to the system's goals.[51] Such increased transparency, in turn, could enhance the perceived legitimacy of the criminal-justice system. Of course, the proposed screening system is not perfect: it replicates the present system's qualities of denying most defendants a trial and making the prosecutor, rather than a judge or jury, the adjudicator who decides the central legal and factual issues.[52]

The central questions that should drive the debate over plea bargaining and witness immunity—which, as with other rules we have examined thus far, are empirical and not normative questions—address the fundamental issue of whether the criminal-justice system would come closer to maximizing deserved punishment with the practices or without them. Would many defendants who now negotiate a guilty plea to a lesser offense have pleaded guilty anyway? Does plea bargaining conserve resources, or does the time and effort spent on plea bargaining itself minimize such savings? Does plea bargaining even cause frequent deviations from deserved punishment, or do defendants actually tend to accept a roughly fair punishment for fear that an unduly harsh punishment might be imposed following trial and conviction? Does the number of convictions arising solely or mainly from the testimony of immunized witnesses—as opposed to convictions that would have occurred anyway, for which the grant of immunity would be counterproductive— suggest that the practice is desert-efficient? Would, or could, society spend more to reduce the deviation-causing constraints on the system if the plea-bargaining expedient were removed?

As yet, we have at best incomplete answers to these critical questions. At first blush, it seems entirely possible, perhaps likely, that the practices in question are sound from a desert perspective, for in using these practices, the prosecutor is (at least ostensibly) employing a desert-maximizing calculus *in each case* in deciding whether to agree to a grant of immunity or a plea bargain. Such an individualized approach would tend to avoid the problem, common with other rules we have discussed, of an insufficiently flexible general rule failing to adapt to recognize justified exceptions. But we adopt no categorical position here as to the propriety of these practices; our central point is to make clear the proper focus of analysis. Further attention to the questions we identify would direct analysis regarding the propriety of plea bargaining toward the crucial and hitherto largely unexplored areas of empirical analysis.

GRAVANO AFTERMATH

After Sammy Gravano serves his sentence, the government pays for plastic surgery; gives Gravano a new identity, "Jimmy Moran"; and moves him to Tempe, Arizona, in the Witness Protection Program. Gravano drops out of the program in 1998, unwilling to accept its limits on family contact, and is reunited with his wife, Debra, and their children. The F.B.I. continues to watch him and tries to keep his whereabouts secret.

Four years after his release, Gravano, his wife and two children, and forty other people are arrested on drug charges. Police and prosecutors identify Gravano as the boss and bankroller of an Ecstasy syndicate that imported the drug to Arizona from New York and California. No one in the F.B.I., Justice Department, Arizona Attorney General's Office, or Phoenix Police Department will comment on how Gravano is able to assemble a sizable drug operation while continuing to work with federal authorities in preparation for a trial against a notorious international fugitive.

On May 25, 2001, at the same federal courthouse in Brooklyn where he testified against John Gotti, Sammy "The Bull" Gravano and his son, Gerard Gravano, twenty-five, plead guilty to conspiring to distribute Ecstasy, having bought the pills from a New York City gang. In a Phoenix state courtroom, Sammy Gravano also pleads guilty to masterminding "the biggest Ecstasy ring ever to operate in Arizona," and Gerard pleads guilty to conducting a criminal enterprise and offering to sell and transport dangerous drugs. Sammy's wife, Debra, and daughter, Karen, are also involved. Debra pleads guilty to participating in a criminal enterprise, and Karen pleads to using telephone communications for drug-related transactions. "Sammy Gravano got the second chance of a lifetime, and he blew it big time," says Brooklyn assistant U.S. Attorney Linda Lacewell.

On September 6, 2002, a federal judge sentences Sammy Gravano to twenty years in prison, and on October 30, 2002, an Arizona state judge sentences him to nineteen years. Gravano will serve his state and federal sentences concurrently at a federal prison—four times the five years he served for confessing to nineteen murders in 1994. Gerard Gravano is sentenced to 9.25 years for his federal charges and 9.25 years for his state charges. Debra and Karen Gravano receive probation.

On August 18, 2003, the federal government charges Peter Gotti—brother of the late John

FIGURE 4.3.
Sammy Gravano is sentenced in 2002 after being found guilty of drug trafficking. AP photo/Michael Ging, POOL.

FIGURE 4.4.
Gerard Gravano shakes
hands with his lawyer
after being sentenced to
prison in 2002. AP
photo/Jack Kurtz,
POOL.

Gotti—and five other Gambino crime family members with conspiring to kill Gravano. In October 2003, Gravano testifies in the defense of the hitman they hired, indicating that he understood it to be only business and that there was little the hitman could do once given the order to kill.

On August 28, 2003, Gravano himself is charged with hiring a hitman to kill a New York City police detective, Peter Calabro, in 1980. Prosecutors in Bergen County, New Jersey, allege that Gravano hired Richard "The Iceman" Kuklinski and helped him to carry out the murder.[53]

II

SACRIFICING JUSTICE
TO PROMOTE OTHER INTERESTS

SECOND CATEGORY of rules that deviate from desert do so both in effect and in spirit. Whereas the rules we have previously discussed adhere to the desert principle in theory, but posit that practical constraints require certain adjustments when implementing that principle, this second category includes rules that effectively reject the desert principle in favor of some other competing interest. These rules truly create a gap between law and justice. They cannot be, and are not, justified in terms of the desire to achieve desert. Instead, they reflect a decision, whether conscious or inadvertent, to sacrifice the interests of justice to advance some other goal. Sometimes doing so is necessary or at least supportable. But some of these competing interests, we will argue, should instead be promoted through other mechanisms that do not distort the criminal-justice system's potential to do justice.

In the following chapters, we identify four competing interests that generate rules representing deviations from desert. Chapter 5 deals with the criminal law's wish to provide clear, fixed, ex ante rules defining the conduct it prohibits, commonly described as the criminal law's commitment to the "legality" principle. That principle forecloses liability for people whose acts, though blameworthy, do not fit within any clearly established prior criminal prohibition. At the same time, the interest in maintaining clear prohibitions also leads to doctrines that impose more liability than is deserved, as when a blameless offender is punished for fear that his acquittal would undercut the clarity of the prohibition he has violated.

Chapter 6 addresses the utilitarian goal of using criminal law to control or reduce crime. The goal has been used to justify various deviations from desert—typically, though not always, deviations in the direction of imposing more liability than is deserved—in the name of achieving increased deterrence, incapacitation of dangerous offenders, or rehabilitation.

A third goal, the subject of chapter 7, is embodied in those rules that seek to preserve a fundamental degree of procedural fairness, personal liberty, or systemic integrity by imposing restraints on police and prosecutors to curb governmental misconduct, even if doing so places some offenders beyond the reach of the law's substantive prohibitions. These rules generally deviate in the direction of preventing deserved punishment.

Finally, as we discuss in chapter 8, some rules promote interests completely external to the criminal-justice system, as with, for example, the granting of diplomatic immunity, which is thought necessary to facilitate international dialogue without fear of our diplomats abroad suffering criminal sanctions based on bigotry or reprisal.

CHAPTER 5

Living by Rules

O
NE DIFFICULTY WITH seeking to follow the demands of desert in every
case is that doing so might make the law too messy, complicated, or
unpredictable. If the law is to be obeyed and if the law is to be consistently applied—if it is truly to be *law*, rather than ad hoc decision making—
it must have clear and uniform prohibitions. Yet every broad prohibition, however much it seeks to pursue desert, may require an exception in unforeseen
situations. The potential tension between general rules and individualized
determinations of desert is obvious. A variety of legal justifications advocate
for resolving this tension in favor of creating and maintaining clear, bright-
line rules that admit no exceptions.

The virtues of clear prohibitions are many. First, imposing clear and uniform rules increases the likelihood of fair notice of the criminal law's commands. Beyond fairness issues, without such notice the law can hardly hope
to deter prohibited conduct. Second, developing clear rules, and then adhering to them, helps to minimize discretion in the application of criminal law.
Increased discretion on the part of police, prosecutors, judges, and juries increases the likelihood of unjustified disparity in application. Discretion also
reduces the predictability of law, undercutting its power to create order and
stability,[1] and greater discretion can introduce the potential for abuse of that
discretion.[2] Finally, requiring a clear ex ante declaration of the law, typically
through codification, allocates criminalization authority to the legislature,

the most democratic branch of government, rather than enabling ex post lawmaking by the courts.[3] For all of these reasons, most jurisdictions prohibit prosecution for offenses that are not statutorily defined in advance or whose definitions lack adequate clarity and precision to give a reasonable person notice of the conduct prohibited.[4]

Still, the demand for clarity comes at a cost in terms of the ability to obtain a just result in each case. It will sometimes lead to undeserved exoneration based on the lack of a clear written rule. Under what is known as the *legality* principle, people like Ray Brent Marsh (discussed immediately below), however deserving of vilification, may evade punishment because no explicitly stated legal rule was specified in advance to cover their conduct—sometimes precisely because the conduct is so bizarre and unique in its transgression that nobody thought to address it.

At other times, the desire for bright-line rules will lead to undeserved conviction based on Procrustean[5] adherence to the letter of a written rule. Where no written rule exists, the clarity concern forbids punishment, but where a written rule does exist, the same concern may demand punishment in all cases, even those that obviously fall outside of the law's spirit. Such was the case with Dudley and Stephens, discussed later in this chapter.

THREE HUNDRED BODIES IN THE BACKYARD

Noble, Georgia, is a small unincorporated cluster of houses and businesses off Highway 27 in Walker County, about twenty miles outside Chattanooga, Tennessee. Though people tend to live here for decades, they are not as close as they might be in a typical small town. "We come here and we stay here, but a lot of people don't know who their neighbors are," explains the video-store owner, who has been living here for forty-seven years. "It's a place where you don't need to worry about what's in your backyard."[6]

One prominent family in town is the Marsh family, descendants of Willie Marsh, who in the nineteenth century was the first African-American child in Walker County. In a county that is almost 94% white, the Marshes have become one of the more prominent families in town. Several generations of Marshes are buried in the family graveyard a few blocks from the Tri-State Crematory, a family business started by Tommy Ray Marsh in 1982.

Tommy Ray had been a postal worker but also worked digging septic tanks with a backhoe. In the mid-1970s, a family friend who ran a funeral home called Tommy Ray because he needed a grave digger. After a decade of digging graves, Tommy Ray bought a $20,000 cremation unit from Industrial Equipment & Engineering in Apopka, Florida, and opened Tri-State Crematory. Local newspapers reported that it was the first minority-owned crematory in the country.

Tommy Ray's family now owns and rents out a fair amount of land in Noble. He is a member of the Rotary Club. His wife, Clara Marsh, also is active in the community. After working as a schoolteacher for thirty years, she was Walker County Citizen of the Year and was both president of the Walker County Association of Educators and the first African American to serve as chair of the Walker County Democratic Committee.

In 1996, Tommy Ray has a stroke, which confines him to a wheelchair. His son Ray Brent Marsh now runs his father's cremation business. Like the rest of his family, Ray Marsh is well regarded in the community. He was a star sprinter at LaFayette High School, cocaptain of the football team, and a linebacker at the University of Tennessee at Chattanooga. Ray Marsh lives on the crematory grounds, with his parents.

When Tommy Ray started the business, cremations were rare in that part of Georgia, but they have become increasingly common, partly because they are less expensive than the alternatives. More than thirty funeral homes in the area now use Tri-State Crematory, which is the only independent crematory. The Marshes charge as little as $250, where other such companies tend to start at $600. (The cost cutting shows: one funeral director who did business with them noticed that there wasn't really any paperwork or tracking system, and the business, which is just in a shed, seemed a bit unprofessionally run.) Business has been good enough that the Marshes have never really needed to advertise.

For the most part, funeral directors are happy to let Ray Marsh continue his father's business. They know that there is sometimes abuse in the industry and that they should visit facilities or make unannounced inspections, but they never do because Tri-State has such prompt service and the family has a good reputation. Although in the past few years, Ray's parents and sister have broken regulations by signing papers as if they were licensed funeral directors, people have either not noticed or not cared. The local community likewise mainly tries to ignore the crematory tucked into the corner of their county. Neighbors don't go down to the nearby woods much.

After running the business for a year, Marsh has been having financial problems with the crematory. In August 1997, the cremation machine stops working. Marsh orders a $152 starter-motor part for the crematorium. For the past thirteen years, the family has declined service visits from the equipment company, so the service representatives are not surprised when Marsh says that no one needs to come to install the new part.

But after receiving the part, Marsh determines that he cannot fix the machine. Given the financial pressures on him, he decides nonetheless to keep accepting bodies for cremation, but he starts hiding bodies in the grove behind the crematory. He does not abuse them in any way, but simply dumps them on the property in whatever condition he gets them. The grove is already littered with dryers, broken chairs, and a house trailer. There are six rusty cars abandoned there, stuffed with rusted tools and other trash. Among the debris, hundreds of corpses start piling up. A baby is stuffed in a box in the back of a rusty hearse. Dozens of bodies are stacked like cordwood in sheds or half buried around the grove.

While Marsh lives among the bodies, he acts as if everything is normal. Unlike the smoke that can carry the smell of a crematory some distance, the localized smell of a body takes just two weeks to stop, so it isn't surprising that the neighbors haven't noticed what has been going on. For each new customer, Marsh continues to be prompt in arriving to pick up the body, the transit permit, the family's authorization, and the $200 check. He always insists on doing pick-ups and returning the "ashes" himself, often returning the next day. But in fact, Marsh often delivers a box of cement chips and limestone rather than cremated remains.

Marsh continues to be disorganized with his paperwork. He lets notices, bills, and papers, often unopened, pile up in the office and tucks them into corners around his home. Still, from the outside, things seem normal, though the locals later comment that they have not seen any smoke in a long time. In November 2001, the Atlanta office of the Environmental Protection Agency receives an anonymous call reporting that someone has seen "body parts" on Tri-State's property. The EPA turns the tip over to the sheriff's office, which briefly investigates, but as the investigators have no search warrant, they leave after a cursory look that fails to reveal anything.

By the beginning of 2002, Marsh has hidden bodies all over the property. His indifference may be rooted in depression or some other psychological disorder; a former F.B.I. profiler comments later that Marsh's behavior is like those who have a hoarding obsessive-compulsive disorder. He hoards all his papers, and stacks all the bodies, perhaps hoping to deal with them later. He doesn't make decisions about what to do about the problem, and as it gets harder to decide, everything just piles up in a disordered and haphazard fashion.

By now, the result looks like something out of a Stephen King novel. After five years, some of the bodies look like they have been there for decades and now seem almost skeletal. Others, once quasi-buried and embalmed, are now half disinterred, possibly to make them easier to stack later. Some are still dressed in formal wear; others are wrapped in hospital sheets and wearing a toe tag. More than twenty bodies are stuffed into a single cement vault that is designed to hold one coffin. Four other vaults are just as full. Some cremated remains are mixed among the rest. In all, there are about 340 bodies in the grove. The bodies now outnumber Noble's living population.

In February 2002, the Atlanta EPA gets another call. This time, representatives of the agency come to town to investigate. The next morning, February 15, a woman walking a dog finds a human skull, spurring a full investigation. As the first bodies are discovered, the county is horrified. Soon Dr. Kris Sperry, the state's chief medical examiner, is obliged to call in the Federal Disaster Mortuary Team, the group usually called when a cemetery is disrupted by a natural disaster. Dr. Sperry has performed more than 5,000 autopsies and viewed more than 30,000 bodies but is not prepared for what he sees around the crematory. During the first week of the recovery effort, he has nightmares.

By Saturday, February 16, the governor has declared "the Walker County incident" a state of emergency, making state funds available for the recovery efforts. He meets with a hundred families who dealt with Tri-State and agrees to pay the cost of identifying bodies to give the families closure. He vows to use the full powers of the state to investigate and prosecute. The sheriff says the Marshes are "good folks. I don't know what went wrong."[7]

The Marshes turn over their company records and generally cooperate with the authorities. A regulatory loophole that protected Tri-State (it was not "open to the public" and thus did not meet the legal definition of a "crematory") is quickly closed, and other states begin to review their licensing schemes.

On Sunday, a prayer service is held, while county employees comb the woods for bodies. Meanwhile, Marsh's sister puts up her house as a bond for $25,000 bail, and Marsh is released. His mother goes to church and reports that he is doing nicely. She refuses to talk about the case. "I don't have any-

FIGURE 5.1.
Police en route to the crematory. AP photo/Ric Feld.

FIGURE 5.2.
Workers removing
corpses from Ray Brent
Marsh's property in
February 2002. AP
photo/Mark Humphrey.

thing to say about the charges, if that's what they are. I'm just surrounding myself in the Lord and the people who support me."[8]

After the investigators clear away the bodies in plain view, they find the bodies stacked in the concrete burial vaults. Seeing the other vaults around the property, the crew stops trying to estimate numbers. Investigators set up a makeshift morgue on the site to process the bodies and help the families to identify them. People are asked to bring in photographs. Meanwhile, the Georgia Bureau of Investigation (G.B.I.) urges people to bring in the remains they were given so they can be checked. At the Walker State Community Center, people line up holding the "ashes" of loved ones received from Tri-State. Many of the containers turn out to be filled with dirt and cement chips.

On Thursday, February 21, underwater cameras spot a torso and skull in the lake behind the crematory. They begin to test the water for contamination, to see if it is safe for divers. Local residents are warned not to drink tap water.

By February 24, almost 300 bodies have been found. Investigators don't know when it will end. The families are devastated. When Pat Higdon's husband died of lung cancer, she couldn't afford a burial, so she chose to cremate him. "He looked like a corpse for two months before he died. He just laid

FIGURE 5.3.
Investigators collecting
bodies in the woods on
February 20, 2002. AP
photo/Mark Humphrey.

there with his mouth open and his eyes open," she says. "I can't bear to think he still looks like that, only he's lying in a shed or a creek somewhere."[9] Ellen West, on learning that the body of her mother, author Emmy Govan West, was among those discarded at the crematory, says, "When they called me and told me, it was worse news than her dying. I couldn't function."[10]

The funeral directors who trusted the Marshes are also reeling. One director sent more than 100 bodies there, including his brother Clyde. He says, "I don't sleep. It's a bad deal."[11] He has tried to comfort the families, who have told him they are praying for him and aren't blaming him. Other funeral homes have had civil suits brought against them.

The last body on the land is found on February 26. The next Monday, March 4, agents start draining the three-acre lake, which is eight feet deep at its deepest point. The potentially contaminated water is carted away in tankers, to keep it from affecting the local water supply. Eventually, using flat-bottomed boats, investigators probe the few feet of water that remain. No more bodies are found. Georgia has had to add $8.5 million to the state budget to cover the expenses of the excavation and search, which finishes on March 6, 2002. Investigators determine that over the course of more than five years, Marsh dumped 339 bodies on his property.

FIGURE 5.4.
Woman yelling at
Marsh outside the
courthouse. AP
photo/John Bazemore.

Georgia has laws against desecrating gravesites and coffins, but not against dumping corpses in the backyard. Funeral directors could lose their licenses for such abuse, but Tri-State continued to operate without a license because of the loophole in the Georgia regulation. Ray is arrested, but the prosecution struggles to find an appropriate charge. He is held for five counts of theft by deception for taking money for cremations he didn't perform.

LEGALITY

The criminal law's dedication to fair notice and clarity is instantiated in the *legality principle*. The principle does not define a single legal rule but rather is the overarching rationale that forms the basis for a collection of related rules: the constitutional prohibition against ex post facto laws,[12] the constitutional invalidation of vague offenses,[13] the rule of strict construction of penal statutes (also called the rule of lenity),[14] the statutory abolition of common-law offenses,[15] and the statutory bar to judicial creation of offenses.[16] The common objective of these rules is to bar criminal prosecution in the absence of a prior written definition of the prohibited conduct expressed with some minimum of clarity and conciseness.[17]

Several of the rules designed to promote legality—such as the ex post facto prohibition and the prohibition against vague offenses—are constitutional mandates and therefore apply always and everywhere in the United States.[18] Others are subject to modification. For example, the Model Penal Code replaced the strict rule of lenity with a more evenhanded rule of "fair import" for interpreting the meaning of penal statutes, and about half the states have followed suit.[19] Just how often the legality principle operates to prevent punishment of a blameworthy person is hard to track, especially because implementation of the principle will most often be reflected in an effectively invisible prosecutorial decision not to bring a case. Reversals of imposed convictions are considerably more rare, though they do occur.[20]

In today's criminal-law environment, legality has significant pro-desert aspects. As we discuss in chapter 8, modern criminal prohibitions have expanded to embrace literally thousands of regulatory offenses, many of which address conduct that is morally neutral. In this context, the legality principle serves an important function in limiting the reach of such offenses, so that they are not used to prosecute citizens who had little or no reason to suspect their behavior was not allowed.[21]

Yet at the same time, somewhat paradoxically, this proliferation calls into question the premises of the legality principle: the notion that criminalization decisions are better left to legislators than to the courts and should be specific. Recent trends suggest that what William Stuntz has called the "pathological politics of criminal law" often drives legislators toward criminalizing more and more conduct, less and less of which is worthy of moral condemnation, whereas courts are more likely to use restraint or carve out exceptions.[22] The demand for precision also encourages overcriminalization (and disserves the legality principle's objective of giving adequate notice of criminal prohibitions), as legislatures define numerous particular offenses rather than a handful of broader ones that would better reflect the relevant harms and underlying moral norms.[23] Stuntz concludes:

> In the guise of protecting the rule of law, we have generated its opposite. Criminal law is nominally legislative, prospective, and specific. In practice, it is none of those things. Oddly, part of the reason why is that courts have required those things, and in the process disabled themselves from participating in the definition of crimes.[24]

Accordingly, the legality principle can be said to both improperly expand and improperly curtail prosecutorial power. Enactment of numerous legislative prohibitions increases prosecutorial options in bringing a case, as well as both relying on and increasing prosecutorial discretion regarding the initial determination of whether to do so.[25] At the same time, legality rules prevent prosecution of clearly wrongful, but not specifically prohibited, conduct.

The desert-related costs of increased prosecutorial discretion are often intangible, but the costs of the legality principle's interference with the pursuit of deserved punishment are quite concrete and specific, as the case of Ray Brent Marsh illustrates. The inability to charge Marsh with any offense of desecration or abuse of corpses seems highly unsatisfactory when viewed from the perspective of desert. Marsh knew, or certainly should have known, that tossing the dead bodies into his backyard to decompose was condemnable conduct. He probably assumed it was a crime—and not just a theft offense for defrauding the bereaved families of their cremation payments. But the legality principle unequivocally bars Marsh from being charged with a body-mistreatment offense that did not exist at the time of his conduct and did not clearly prohibit it. That may allow a morally blameworthy person to escape punishment he deserves—certainly the families of the mistreated corpses feel that punishment is deserved—but without the limitations imposed by the legality principle, there would be no constraint on the power of the state to punish conduct after the fact, even though it had not made the illegality of that conduct clear in advance.

The unfortunate fact is that the legality principle *necessarily* will conflict with desert in some cases. There is simply no obvious way to enforce its strictures other than to forswear liability for anyone, even a clearly blameworthy actor, whose conduct is not clearly proscribed in advance. There is no apparent alternative means by which to promote legality, for legality interests cannot be divorced from the assignment of criminal liability; they can be given voice only in the process of imposing criminal liability and punishment. Although it is certainly possible, and perhaps legitimate, to consider desert interests more important than legality interests in those cases where they conflict, the critical fact for our analysis is that a choice between the two is necessary, for it is impossible to satisfy both.

The likelihood of such conflicts arising can certainly be reduced, however. To maximize criminal law's potential to achieve desert while also adhering to the legality principle, the first, best, and perhaps only resort is to encourage code drafters to be more thoughtful and more careful in the formulation and codification of offenses. Thorough and well-formulated criminal statutes enable legality and desert to work together, and even in synergy, rather than at cross-purposes. Further, dedication to process can be as important as attention to substance. Both legality and desert would benefit if legislatures were to put in place a mechanism for regularly reviewing and revising criminal codes as new forms of harmful conduct appear and existing codification flaws are exposed.[26]

Another way to address these conflicts would be to at least openly acknowledge them when they arise. A judge or jury prevented from imposing punishment on a deserving wrongdoer solely by virtue of a legality-based prohibition might at least be allowed to signal disapproval of the defendant's conduct via an alternative verdict, such as one declaring the defendant "not punishable" though blameworthy. We discuss further in chapter 9 the general possibility of using a more sophisticated verdict system to reduce deviations from desert.

Finally, it may be possible to tailor legality rules more narrowly to allow for some exceptions while still upholding the principles that underlie legality doctrines. One option is to give relevance to the defendant's culpability as to committing a crime. Even though the defendant's conduct is not criminal, so that her intentionality as to the conduct itself is not a crime, the defendant who believes her conduct to be criminal does have culpability as to its unlawfulness. A proposed (partial) resolution to this situation, then, would be to criminalize that culpability by creating an offense of "attempting to commit a crime."[27] In such a situation, there is a legislative enactment and notice concerns are not compelling, as the offense applies only when the defendant herself believes her conduct to be unlawful. Such an offense is a crude and imperfect resolution, however, as it would presumably have a specific punishment grade and would therefore be unable to tailor the severity of punishment to the moral gravity of a person's "crime."

MARSH AFTERMATH

By May 2002, 155 of the bodies have been identified. The charges against Ray Brent Marsh increase to 294 counts of theft by deception, in most cases two for each body identified: one for taking the money without performing the cremation and one for returning something other than the cremated remains. Brent's defense attorney, McCracken "Ken" Poston, Jr., who is representing the Marsh family in both criminal and civil cases, is trying to have the charges reduced to misdemeanors. Although the amount of money at issue in each case is not great, prosecutors successfully argue that Marsh had a fiduciary relationship with his customers and, therefore, the frauds are appropriately charged as felonies. Fifty-three civil lawsuits have been filed against the Marshes, including a potential class-action suit. In addition, Tommy Ray, Clara, and Marsh's sister LaShea, now a funeral director in Chattanooga, are each charged with one felony count for signing death certificates without being licensed funeral directors.

On September 23, 2003, Marsh appears in court to be formally informed of the charges against him. By now he is charged with 787 felony counts. He enters "no plea" to 439 counts of theft by taking and 122 counts of burial service fraud and pleads not guilty to 47 counts of making false statements. He also pleads not guilty to 179 counts of abuse of a dead body, the offense that prosecutors think comes the closest to covering Marsh's conduct. Unfortu-

FIGURE 5.5.
Marsh being led into
court on February 22,
2002. AP photo/John
Bazemore.

nately, the offense—which criminalizes only "defac[ing] a dead body"—is
not likely to be a successful ground for prosecution of his failure to bury or
cremate.

On that same day, Marsh's attorney files motions to change venue and to
declare Marsh indigent—which would oblige the state to pay for his legal defense. On December 2, 2003, Judge James Bodiford denies Marsh's request
for the state to pay for Marsh's expert witnesses, but partially grants Marsh's
request for a change of venue: the jury will come from a different county (on
June 3, 2004, the court decides that the jury will come from Lee County), but
the trial will take place in Walker County.

On November 19, 2004, prosecutors and Marsh's counsel present a negotiated guilty plea to the judge. On January 31, 2005, the judge accepts
Marsh's plea of guilty to four sets of charges: (1) 437 counts of "theft by taking" (and two counts of attempted theft by taking), (2) 179 counts of "abuse
of dead body," (3) 47 counts of "false statement," and (4) 122 counts of "burial service fraud." Marsh receives a twelve-year total sentence, to be followed
by probation.[28]

Ray Brent Marsh ultimately received a fairly substantial punishment,
but only by way of a plea agreement that centered on charges of theft and
fraud—as indicated by Marsh's earlier entry of "no plea," rather than a "not
guilty" plea, on those charges—and tacked on guilty pleas to numerous (and
legally questionable) "abuse of corpse" counts that added nothing to Marsh's
actual punishment. (For each of the four sets of counts, Marsh was sentenced
to twelve years, each sentence running concurrently with the others.) The
animating harm and evil of Marsh's conduct, his gross disrespect for the de-
ceased persons and for the feelings of their families, technically played no role
in his prosecution for theft. If Marsh had never cashed the payment checks,

FIGURE 5.6.
Ray Brent Marsh (*left*)
and his attorney, Ken
Poston. AP photo/Ric
Feld, POOL.

his "grove of horrors" would not have violated Georgia law and, under the legality principle, could not have been punished in any way.

. . .

The concern that criminal law must provide clear rules of conduct sometimes leads to the reverse sort of distinction from desert: punishing a blameless violator, for fear that a failure to do so will undercut the power and clarity of the prohibition. Such was the fate of Dudley and Stephens, whose crime (if any) occurred well over 100 years ago, but whose criminal case remains notorious to this day.

CANNIBALISM AT SEA

In early 1883, John Want, a prominent Australian lawyer and politician, arrives in England, looking for a fast, forty-ton yacht to buy and take back with him to Sydney. He eventually chooses the *Mignonette*, a fifty-five-foot yacht built in 1867. As the yacht is too large to ship as deck cargo, Want starts arranging to have the yacht sailed to Sydney. In November 1883, Thomas Dudley hears of Want's purchase of the *Mignonette* and applies to sail the boat for him. Dudley is employed, and plans are made to set sail in the spring of 1884.

Dudley, thirty-one, began his career as a seaman when he was just nine, following his mother's death. He worked hard and became a sailing master,

FIGURE 5.7.
Thomas Dudley.

winning yachting prizes and competitions. He takes on the task of sailing the *Mignonette* to Australia because he is thinking of emigrating there to find better opportunities. When Want hires him, Dudley becomes responsible for finding and organizing a crew. He selects Edwin Stephens as his mate, Edmund "Ned" Brooks as the able seaman, and Richard Parker as the ordinary seaman.

Stephens, thirty-seven, is an experienced seaman, married with five children, and a respected local figure active in the Young Men's Christian Association. Although Stephens holds a master's certificate and has considerable experience as a navigator, he has difficulty finding work because he was responsible for a shipping accident in 1877. It is clear to him that his career will never prosper if he remains in Southampton, so he decides to emigrate. With Want's consent, Dudley tempts Stephens into the journey on the *Mignonette* by offering him the captaincy of the ship once it gets to Sydney.

Ned Brooks, thirty-eight, is the son of a mariner and went to sea early. He was a reservist in the British Navy for a time and then became a yacht hand. He married, but later deserted his wife. He has known Dudley since 1879 and has been acquainted with the *Mignonette* yacht itself since it was built. Brooks apparently joins the *Mignonette* crew in the interest of emigrating to Australia as well. Dudley promises him work on the yacht in Sydney if Brooks decides to stay there.

Richard Parker, the ordinary seaman, is seventeen. Both of his parents had died by 1881; he started working at sea as a fourteen-year-old orphan. Parker wants to join the crew because he wishes to travel abroad, having never sailed on a long ocean voyage before. He also thinks he might emigrate to Australia. He hopes "to make a man of himself" on the trip, and Dudley talks to him about the trip as a rite of passage, promising to give Parker some schooling on the voyage. Dudley brings books on board the *Mignonette* for this very purpose. He also promises Parker work in Sydney on the *Mignonette* if Parker wishes to stay on there.

As captain, Dudley is paid a large flat fee to cover his expenses and is responsible for paying for repairs and provisions out of this sum. Dick Fox, who is hired to perform repairs on the *Mignonette* prior to its departure, says he notices that the ship's deadwood is "sick" (meaning that it has some rotten beams below the water line). Fox says the ship needs new timbers, an expensive repair job, but he is instructed to carry out repairs using the ship's own timbers, which is much less expensive. Dudley is an economical man and keeps the repair work to a minimum. Some officials think the *Mignonette* unlikely to survive the long voyage. The British Board of Trade's Marine Department considers the ship unfit for the trip, but because it is not technically unseaworthy, it cannot be prevented from leaving.

Earlier, when Dudley was looking for sailors to accompany him, there had been a general feeling in the community that the trip was a bad idea because of the yacht's small size. Three sailors who had initially signed on later thought better of the trip. Dudley eventually must pay Stephens, Brooks, and Parker substantially more than the going wage in order to secure their services. On the other hand, small yacht voyages across the ocean are not that uncommon, nor is the *Mignonette* a particularly small yacht, and Dudley and the crew believe they can make the voyage to Sydney.

Dudley and his crew sail from Southampton on May 19, 1884. The voyage as planned involves sailing 14,000 to 16,000 miles. Dudley and his navigator, Stephens, hope to reach Sydney within 110 to 120 days.

The boat leaves the last of the Cape Verde Islands on June 8 and sails into the South Atlantic, where it is winter. In order to secure good winds and avoid the chance of being run down by a larger ship, Dudley plots a course well to the west of normal shipping lanes. The crew expects, and receives, the strong and reliable southeast trade winds. On June 25, the winds become more variable, and on July 3, the winds cease and the *Mignonette* is becalmed in the South Atlantic until July 5, when it is caught in a storm 1,600 miles from the Cape of Good Hope. During the storm, an enormous wave sweeps over the ship, knocking a hole in the side. The ship's side collapses, partly because of the rotten beams below the water line.

Dudley realizes the ship is sinking, and he orders the dinghy lowered. He asks Parker to go below and pass up a barrel of water kept at the foot of the ladder leading into the hold. Parker does this and throws the cask of water into the sea as Dudley orders. Any attempt to lower the barrel directly into the dinghy would tear a hole in its bottom. Thus, the plan is to retrieve the cask, which will float, once the men are in the dinghy.

Stephens, Brooks, and Parker board the dinghy. Dudley retrieves six tins of provisions and the compass, then feels the ship start to founder and knows he must get to the dinghy. He tries to throw the provisions into the dinghy, but only one tin makes it. The men are able to recover one more of the tins along with some cotton waste. The water cask is lost, probably pushed out to sea by the strong wind.

Although maritime tradition holds that the crew need not follow the captain if their ship founders, Dudley remains in command of the dinghy. He successfully constructs a sea anchor and positions the dinghy so that its bow is to the wind, allowing them to survive the heavy seas. There is a hole in the

FIGURE 5.8.
As the *Mignonette* went down. Based on drawings by Edwin
Stephens/*Illustrated London News*.

dinghy, so the men must constantly bail, even though they plug the hole
with the cotton waste recovered from the ship. The nearest land is 2,000 nautical miles to the west. The normal steamship route lays to the east.

Dudley, Stephens, Brooks, and Parker survive the first night, but they
have no water and no food, except for the two one-pound tins of turnips they
salvaged from the ship. For three days, the four men eat nothing but turnips.
On the fourth day, July 9, 1884, Brooks spots a small turtle, and Dudley kills
it. They attempt to catch its blood, but seawater splashes over the side and
"contaminates" the blood. (It is believed by sailors of the time that seawater
is a kind of poison causing madness and death.) On that day, they consume
their second tin of turnips along with some of the turtle.

The main problem is not hunger but thirst. By July 13, all four are drinking their own urine. It does little to alleviate their thirst. Their lips and
tongues become parched and blackened, their feet and legs swell, and their
skins develop sores from constant exposure to sea and wind and from the
press of the crowded boat. They have no fresh water except the rain they
manage to catch in their oilskin caps from time to time.

They survive by eating the turtle slowly, consuming both the bones and
the skin until, on the twelfth day, July 17, the turtle has been entirely con-
sumed. At this time, Dudley first proposes that they draw lots to determine

FIGURE 5.9.
The dinghy, exhibited in September 1884 in the hall of the
Royal Cornwall Polytechnic Society in Falmouth.

which man should be killed to save the others' lives. Parker either does not
participate in the conversation or states that he will not draw lots. Stephens
and Brooks decide that discussion of the topic is premature. (At the time, cannibalism after a shipwreck is so common that suspicion of this practice among
surviving castaways is a routine reaction. The traditional course of action is
to draw lots, a practice viewed as legitimizing the killing and cannibalism.)

For the next eight days, the four eat nothing. On July 20, Richard Parker
drinks a considerable amount of seawater and becomes violently ill. He suffers from diarrhea, which further dehydrates him. He lays on the bottom of the
boat groaning and gasping for breath. He becomes delirious and then inter-
mittently comatose. Richard has been explicitly warned that drinking sea water
will kill him. Dudley again raises the issue of drawing lots, but the others ignore this suggestion. They say, "We had better die together." Dudley replies,
"So let it be, but it's hard for four to die, when perhaps one might save the rest."

The boat drifts on the ocean and remains more than 1,000 nautical miles
from land. Although they eventually fashion a rudimentary sail out of oars
and their clothing, they go no faster than about four knots. On the eigh-
teenth day, when they have been seven days without food and five days
without water, Dudley and Stephens speak to Brooks about what should be
done if no help arrives. Dudley and Stephens suggest to Brooks that one
should be sacrificed to save the rest, but Brooks disagrees. The sick and dying
boy, Richard Parker, to whom each understands they refer, is not consulted.

On July 24, Dudley again proposes to Stephens and Brooks that lots be
cast. Brooks still refuses to consent, and it is unclear whether Parker chooses

not to participate or votes against the idea. There is no drawing of lots. On this day, Dudley and Stephens speak of their families and suggest to one another that it would be better to kill the boy so that their own lives might be saved. Dudley proposes that, if no vessel appears by the following morning, the boy be killed. The next day, July 25, no vessel appears. Dudley tells Brooks that the boy should be killed. Stephens agrees to this again, but Brooks again opposes the plan. At this time, the boy lays at the bottom of the boat, helpless and extremely weakened by famine and drinking sea water, unable to fight but never agreeing to be killed.

Dudley offers a prayer, asking for forgiveness and mercy on them all if any of them should be tempted to commit a rash act. Then Dudley, after ordering Stephens to hold the boy's feet if necessary, goes to the boy and says, "Dick, your time has come, poor boy." Parker asks him, "What, me, sir?" and Dudley replies, "Yes, my boy." He stabs a two-inch blade into the boy's throat, killing him. Sharing the common sailors' belief that it is preferable to obtain blood from a living victim, Dudley and Stephens immediately drink as much blood as they can catch and cut out and eat the boy's heart and liver. All three men—Dudley, Stephens, and Brooks—use the oarlocks of the dinghy to cut the boy into pieces and feed upon his body and blood for four days.

At the time they feed on Parker's body, they are mere days from dying of starvation. The boy, being in a much weaker condition, would likely have died even sooner. At the time of the killing, there is no sail in sight, nor any reasonable prospect of relief. Stephens and Dudley see no chance of anyone surviving except by killing one of the others to eat.

Four days after the boy is killed, the dinghy is picked up by a passing vessel. Dudley, Stephens, and Brooks are all rescued. They are still alive, but all are near death. They eventually recover. It appears very likely that none would have lived to be rescued if they had not fed upon the boy.

After being rescued by the *Montezuma*, Dudley, Stephens, and Brooks are taken to Falmouth. All are weak and have difficulty walking. After resting for several hours, they go to the customs office. In accord with the Merchant Shipping Act of 1854, they are required to report any losses at sea. The men honestly and completely detail their time on the raft and Parker's death. Dudley's main objective is to make sure the truth comes to light. To this end, he answers all questions put to him, even reenacting his actions in killing Parker.

The superintendent reports them to the home office and to the Marine Department of the Board of Trade. They are arrested by the Falmouth harbor police and placed in jail. All three men are confident that they will be released once the full details of their ordeal are known. On their arrival in Falmouth, public opinion condemns the men for failing to cast lots. But by the time they are first called before the Falmouth magistrates, the full details of their ordeal at sea are publicly known. The magistrates release the men on bail, to cheers of approval from the crowd.

While preparing the case, the prosecution determines that a witness will be needed. Because Brooks did not consent to killing Parker, the prosecutor determines that his charges should be dropped. He then becomes the prosecution's star witness. Dudley and Stephens are headed for trial for murder in the assize court in Exeter.

The judge in Exeter, Baron Huddleston, is a strong, opinionated judge who often succeeds in convincing the jury to find in the manner he suggests. He feels that this case is an important one, necessary to declare that a civilized nation like Britain cannot endorse the barbaric custom of the sea. The decision of a single judge sitting in assize is not binding on others, so Huddleston wants to make sure that the case can be reviewed by a higher

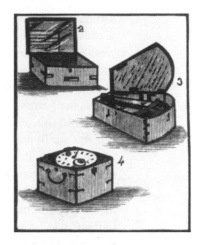

FIGURE 5.10.
Chronometer case used to catch Parker's blood for future consumption. *Illustrated London News.*

court. He convinces the grand jury to find a true bill of indictment giving a formal ruling of what he believes to be the law.

Nonetheless, Huddleston is fearful that the trial jury will release the men. He bars the defense attorney from presenting any argument regarding a potential defense of necessity, stating that no law exists to support such a defense. He presents a special verdict to the jurors, telling them that they can either find the men guilty of murder or agree to all statements in the special verdict. The jury agrees to the special verdict, which states that the men probably would have died if they did not have food in the four days prior to their rescue and that Parker would likely have died first. The verdict then states that the jury is leaving it to the court to apply the law to these factual findings.

To give the decision added weight, four additional judges are added to the decision-making court. After hearing arguments from both sides regarding the existence of a necessity defense, the court rejects the defense of necessity:

> Now it is admitted that the deliberate killing of this unoffending and unresisting boy was clearly murder, unless the killing can be justified by some well-recognized excuse admitted by the law. It is further admitted that there was in this case no such excuse, unless the killing

was justified by what has been called "necessity." But the temptation to the act which existed here was not what the law has ever called necessity. Nor is this to be regretted. Though law and morality are not the same, and many things may be immoral which are not necessarily illegal, yet the absolute divorce of law from morality would be of fatal consequence and such divorce would follow if the temptation to murder in this case were to be held by law an absolute defence of it. It is not so. To preserve one's life is generally speaking a duty, but it may be the plainest and the highest duty to sacrifice it . . . . The duty, in case of shipwreck, of a captain to his crew, of the crew to the passengers, of soldiers to women and children, . . . these duties impose on men the moral necessity, not of the preservation, but of the sacrifice of their lives for others, from which in no country, least of all, it is to be hoped, in England, will men ever shrink, as indeed, they have not shrunk . . . . It is not needful to point out the awful danger of admitting the principle which has been contended for. Who is to be the judge of this sort of necessity? By what measure is the comparative value of lives to be measured? Is it to be strength, or intellect, or what? . . .

It must not be supposed that in refusing to admit temptation to be an excuse for crime it is forgotten how terrible the temptation was; how awful the suffering; how hard in such trials to keep the judgment straight and the conduct pure. We are often compelled to set up standards we cannot reach ourselves, and to lay down rules which we could not ourselves satisfy. But a man has no right to declare temptation to be an excuse, though he might himself have yielded to it, nor allow compassion for the criminal to change or weaken in any manner the legal definition of the crime. It is therefore our duty to declare that the prisoners' act in this case was wilful murder, that the facts as stated in the verdict are no legal justification of the homicide; and to say that in our unanimous opinion the prisoners are upon this special verdict guilty of murder.[29]

The court's reasoning reflects two strands of thought, each of which upholds the virtue of maintaining absolute clarity in the criminal law. The first is simply that what is right is right. The court is willing to uphold—indeed, feels compelled to uphold—the highest and strictest moral standard, even if obeying that standard would mean the cost of additional human life, and even if it would be unreasonable to expect anyone (except, apparently, an Englishman) to uphold that standard. The second thought, which appears in the last few sentences of the first paragraph of the passage above, is that the only alternative to absolutism is relativism. If we cannot draw a bright line, how will we know whether someone has crossed the line? The final paragraph brings these two thoughts together into the general declaration that we must not allow anything, not even the pull of our own moral sensibilities in specific cases, "to change or weaken in any manner the legal definition of the crime."

Dudley and Stephens are convicted of willful murder and sentenced to death.[30]

DENYING LEGITIMATE EXCUSES (FOR THE SAKE OF CLARITY)

The opinion in *Dudley and Stephens* suggests a philosophy that the value of respecting innocent human life is an absolute that can never be outweighed, even in the interest of saving a greater number of lives.[31] Nonetheless, it seems equally clear that even if the sailors' conduct was not justified—as the court concludes it was not—the defendants should still be entitled to an excuse defense. Even the court concedes that the defendants' conduct was understandable given the circumstances. Most would agree that the heroic standard the court supports, requiring one to lay down one's life to avoid violating the law, is both unrealistic and unfair. Yet the court finds the defendants guilty of murder and sentences them to death, reasoning that to do otherwise would undercut the force of the law against killing and cannibalism, which in turn demonstrates the court's commitment to maintaining absoluteness and clarity in the criminal law's prohibitions.

Similar pressure for such clear line drawing exists in every case where an offender has violated the criminal law's rules of conduct but is blameless for doing so because he is entitled to an excuse defense.[32] The approach taken in *Dudley* will run contrary to desert whenever an unrealistic standard of conduct—such as imposition of an absolute conduct rule admitting no excuse—is followed in order to maintain the clarity of a rule. The conflict reflects an apparent tension between two functions of the criminal law: announcing ex ante the rules for people to follow and adjudicating ex post each case based upon the blameworthiness of the actor.[33]

Yet as we discuss more thoroughly in chapter 9, the apparent tension is an illusion. Both the ex ante rule-announcing function and the ex post adjudication function can be satisfied if we replace the crude current guilty/not-guilty verdict system with a more nuanced system that allows the jury's verdict to distinguish between the illegality of the conduct and the blameworthiness of the actor.

DUDLEY AFTERMATH

The public, the courts, and both defendants hope that the Queen will grant a pardon, once the official denunciation of conviction reaffirms the law's condemnation of the custom of cannibalism. The men wait in jail for seven days, expecting each day to receive a pardon. On December 11, the sentence is reduced to six months' imprisonment, to run from the date of judgment.

FIGURE 5.11.
Trial at Exeter of the *Mignonette* survivors. *Illustrated London News.*

The two men enjoy great notoriety for a short time (including wax sculptures in Madame Tussaud's), but soon fade into obscurity. They are forgiven by Parker's family.

Released from jail a year and a day after the *Mignonette* first set sail, Dudley and Stephens's sailing certificates are restored to them. But Dudley finds it difficult to get work in the yachting community and decides to make a new start, moving his family to Australia and becoming a tent and tarpaulin maker. Jack Want, the owner of the *Mignonette*, assists Dudley in his emigration. Dudley's business prospers, but in 1900, he dies of bubonic plague.

Stephens never quite recovers from the ordeal; he becomes depressed and ultimately turns to drink. He dies a poor man at the age of sixty-six.

Ned Brooks appears for a while in amusement shows but soon returns to the sea and dies poor and childless twenty-five years later.[34]

. . .

Like Marsh, Dudley and Stephens probably got about the punishment they deserved. But again, the criminal-law rules themselves get little credit for the result. On their own, they would have imposed the death penalty on persons who did little more than what others reasonably would have done in the same situation. Again, the system had to manipulate its way to an unobjectionable result. One can imagine a host of circumstances under which a royal pardon would not have been forthcoming. A system so dependent on discretion is ultimately too unreliable to be entrusted with the most severe sanctions that law can impose on an individual.

In some respects, the *Dudley*-type deviations and the *Marsh*-type deviations resemble one another. Both uphold, although in markedly different fashions, the principle that the criminal law's rules of conduct must be clearly expressed and carefully followed. However, there is little that can be done to avoid the legality costs reflected in *Marsh:* the legality conflicts with desert are nearly intractable. In contrast, the *Dudley* deviations are misguided and unnecessary; the announcement-adjudication conflict that produces the *Dudley*-type deviation does have a resolution: use of a verdict system that distinguishes between acquittals based on the absence of a rule violation and those based on a blameless rule violation. We discuss such a system in chapter 9.

SETTING BOUNDARIES: LEGALITY AND CHANGING NORMS

As we have discussed thus far, deviations from desert may arise because the criminal law wants to preserve the clarity of its prohibitions. A closely related but slightly different situation arises where the criminal law wants to *change* the existing social norm. In such cases, the law may enforce the pro-hibition overly broadly—perhaps by convicting some people who lack full culpability—in order to announce and reinforce the new conduct rule it seeks to establish. This is slightly different from the usual situation, exem-plified by the *Dudley* case, of "maintaining" an existing prohibition, for here the prohibition or norm is an evolving rather than an established one. Yet as with the *Dudley* rationale, which can be furthered by other means, we argue that the effort to promote adherence to new rules by enforcing them rigidly, where this is done at the cost of desert, is unnecessary and even counter-productive.

To take one case of the rationale in action, a significant and explicit goal of many of the substantial modern reforms in the law of sexual assault[35] is to change norms: specifically, to increase people's sensitivity to the impor-tance of obtaining clear consent to sexual intercourse.[36] In the context of "date rape," for example, there is much well-founded concern that the alarming in-cidence of often unreported cases of nonconsensual intercourse derives in large part from aggressive sexual conduct that current social norms condemn insufficiently, if at all.[37] Perhaps even more than the conviction of individual offenders, then, the greatest contribution that criminal law can make in the context of rape reform may be assisting in the norm-changing effort, so that society and each of its members are awake to the importance of clear consent. In pursuit of this goal, rape-law reformers have sought to expand the tradi-tional criminalization of rape, which required force and resistance or at least a threat of force,[38] to criminalize simply intercourse without consent.

Yet a broad prohibition against nonconsensual sex can seem weak, and unlikely to accomplish much, unless it is clear, unequivocal, and unwavering. If a man accused of the offense of "nonconsensual sexual intercourse" can obtain an acquittal by indicating that he mistakenly thought there was con-sent, the clarity of the prohibition against nonconsensual sex is partially undermined, diluting if not destroying its usefulness. After all, one central reason for the expansion of the sexual assault offense's reach is to instantiate, by means of a firm new conduct rule, a norm of obtaining clear, affirmative consent prior to sex. Failure to hold liable one who has disrespected the con-duct rule, even if accidentally, would undercut the new norm that the society seeks to strengthen: that sexual autonomy must be respected and consent carefully assured. Indeed, the expanded law seeks to cement the norm pre-cisely among the cohort of men who might otherwise tend to "accidentally" believe that consent exists.

Yet the only way to avoid such damaging acquittals is to make the of-fense one of strict liability. That is, the troublesome dilution of the norm would occur even if the mistake-as-to-consent rule is a narrow one, requiring only negligence as to lack of consent—i.e., providing a mistake defense if the circumstances were such that most other men would have reached the same conclusion, making the defendant's mistake nonnegligent. If such were the case, a defendant could win acquittal by successfully arguing that his honest belief in consent was one that most others in his situation would have shared, thus reinforcing the current social norms regarding what is an adequate inference of consent and thereby frustrating the push to change norms.

But use of strict liability here is problematic, both from the perspective of desert and in terms of the rule's ability to effectively change norms. With regard to desert, the use of strict liability to cement the norm is troubling, for culpability requirements are a defining feature of criminal law that distinguishes it from civil liability and civil commitment. Dispensing with culpability requirements debilitates criminal law's most unique and effective feature: its ability to bring moral condemnation to bear. A criminal law without blameworthiness requirements loses its critical power to condemn and stigmatize and therefore loses the very moral credibility that gives it the normative force to influence people's values and behavior that rape reformers seek to harness.[39]

Thus rape-law reformers and others seeking to shape social norms by adjusting criminal prohibitions seem to face a dilemma. Because they are in the norm-changing business, they, perhaps more than most, need a criminal law with strong moral credibility among the population they seek to influence. They need a criminal law whose liability judgments will be taken not just as the announcement of a new administrative rule that people are told to follow, like "put your trash out on Tuesdays," but rather will be taken as an authoritative statement of what is condemnable. Yet at the same time, they seek a clear and unwavering rule that shows that the criminal law truly means business when it comes to promoting and enforcing the norm in question.

The problem is that a strict rule, while it avoids acquittals that undercut the prohibition, may produce cases that serve as advertisements for the *injustice* of the criminal law generally and of the revised rape law (or other offense) in particular, creating sympathy for those who suffer liability and punishment without satisfying the usual test of blameworthiness. Rather than advancing the new conduct rule calling for careful attention and deference to a partner's consent, each such conviction may tend to generate suspicion of the conduct rule, perhaps putting the offender in the sympathetic role of oppressed victim of a criminal-justice system disinterested in a defendant's actual culpability.

Do reformers have no alternative but to pick between these two bad choices—no reform or potentially counterproductive reform? Are their only options to allow the acquittal of wrongdoers who have been insufficiently concerned about consent or to impose criminal liability in the absence of culpability and thereby suffer the "injustice" stories that can overwhelm and undercut the wrongful conduct message they seek to communicate?

We don't think so. Various mechanisms, both beyond the scope of a specific reform movement and within any such movement, are available to avoid or at least reduce the tension here. One broad-based change that would benefit these reformers would be the adoption of an "articulated verdict" system that would minimize the detrimental effect of no-culpability acquittals, as we note above and discuss in chapter 9. Such a system would allow the condemnation of the conduct (nonconsensual intercourse) and thus reinforce the new norm, yet would exculpate the blameless offender and thus preserve the criminal law's moral credibility. This enables the criminal law to effectively persuade the target audience that the conduct rule (such as "be careful as to lack of consent") ought to be taken as having real moral authority and thus will inspire people to support the rule and eventually to internalize it as part of their own moral system.

As to particular reforms geared toward norm shaping, we offer three suggestions for advancing a new rule's effectiveness.

First, liability rules must ensure blameworthiness as a prerequisite for criminal liability. This means requiring at least negligence or, even better, recklessness, as to lack of consent (or whatever other element the rule addresses). It also means using a partially individualized reasonable-person standard where appropriate, which will judge defendants by realistic standards that are within the range of what can be fairly expected of them, again ensuring that a conviction, where it occurs, will carry a credible signal of moral blameworthiness.[40]

Second, offense grading should reflect the relative seriousness of different violations. Thus, for example, intercourse by force with resulting injury should be distinguished from, and graded more severely than, intercourse by threat of force, which in turn should be graded more severely than intercourse without consent but also without force. In a related matter, one might want to reserve the condemnatory power of the "rape" label for the more egregious forms of sexual assault. The point here, again, is to build the criminal law's moral credibility with the community it seeks to influence by showing that it appreciates and tracks the differences in blameworthiness that the community members perceive.

Third, reformers should not expect the criminal law to do all the work. Rape law reform—and any attempts at using law to change norms—must be realistic about what is possible. Legal reform can be effective only as part of a larger agenda of education and societal awareness, including the public expression of disapproval by institutions other than the criminal-justice system. Criminal-law reform cannot be a substitute for public discussion, educational campaigns, and institutional programs, such as by universities and employers, about the need for greater attention to consent to intercourse. For we cannot expect criminal punishment to have a norm-changing condemnatory effect until the community knows and accepts that the new conduct rule does indeed describe a recognized wrong.

To see how these criteria can be significant, consider another example of recent norm-shifting efforts and their relation to clear prohibitions: drunk driving laws. Offense definitions for Driving Under the Influence, or DUI (also known as Driving While Intoxicated, or DWI) often depend on strict bright-line rules that set and maintain a firm and unwavering line for liability. For example, many states have adopted offenses prohibiting driving with a specific level of blood-alcohol content (BAC), such as 0.08 or 0.10%. Effectively, these rules look to BAC, rather than one's actual level of impairment or dangerousness, to decide when one should be held criminally liable.

In some respects, these bright-line rules might seem questionable or troubling. The BAC rules effectively impute an intoxicated state where none might be present—a person's blood-alcohol level might be elevated without any significant attendant impairment of physical skills or psychological awareness. Moreover, as a general matter, DUI offenses are essentially inchoate in nature: they are rooted in a concern that drunk drivers are dangerous and may cause harm to others or to property, yet they do not require the actual creation of any real danger, much less any resulting harm or injury. Indeed, in a sense, DUI offenses are an inchoate version of another form of offense— reckless endangerment—that itself is also inchoate, or at least does not require a resulting harm. DUI offenses are one step further removed, essentially punishing conduct tending toward endangerment, which tends toward injury. One might argue that many DUI offenders do actually create a danger, but if so, they could presumably be prosecuted for endangerment. The effect, and likely purpose, of DUI laws is to reach further, punishing some conduct that cannot be proved to create a danger, in order to establish and maintain clear rules about what behavior is punishable and inappropriate and, more broadly, to reinforce a strong norm against drinking and driving.

Yet interestingly, despite these potential concerns, DUI offenses are largely if not almost uniformly condoned, even applauded.[41] This is all the more interesting given how dramatic the legal shift has been since the 1980s. Clearly the relevant norm against operating a vehicle after consuming alcohol has taken firm root in American society. Why is this so? Why are DUI offenses such a success in terms of public opinion, given their complex (if not necessarily tenuous) relationship to standard criminalization decisions? Perhaps, to an extent, because DUI offenses and their history reflect some of the suggestions we have proposed above for norm-shifting offenses.

Although adherence to the first suggestion, a requirement of culpability, is not immediately apparent, the DUI situation commonly is seen as one where personal culpability exists, in the form of the driver's decision to voluntarily drink and drive. Just as the law and lay intuitions use the voluntary-intoxication decision as grounds for imputing recklessness in other contexts,[42] the DUI requirement of voluntarily drinking and driving ensures some degree of blameworthiness of the offender. As to the second proposed guideline, DUI is not graded the same as reckless endangerment or reckless homicide. It stands as a separate offense, and that offense typically fits within a hierarchy of offenses where escalating dangerousness, or resulting harm, leads to enhanced punishment.

Finally, norms regarding drunk driving have not only influenced (and been influenced by) criminal law but have also had a similar, mutually reinforcing dynamic with other legal reforms—such as changes in tort liability and increased minimum drinking ages—as well as being further strengthened by a great deal of extralegal norm-shaping work in the broader culture.[43] Such efforts, operating contemporaneously with the criminal-law developments, have helped to promote both respect for the norm and respect for the new laws designed to reinforce that norm. And as we discuss elsewhere, it is the internalization of the relevant norm, rather than the legal sanction itself, that may have the most significant impact on reducing the disapproved conduct.[44]

CHAPTER 6

Controlling Crime and Criminals

S EVERAL DIFFERENT REASONS for deviating from desert can be grouped together under the category of *utilitarian* or *crime-control* purposes. A utilitarian (or *consequentialist*) agenda is one that orients itself toward achieving some future goal, as opposed to redressing or correcting a past wrong, which is one common motivation—though, as we will discuss, not the only possible motivation—of a desert-based system of criminal law. For a utilitarian, justice has "utility" not as an end in itself, but as a means of increasing social welfare; specifically, criminal rules and their enforcement are expected to promote welfare by reducing the amount of crime in society.

In the area of criminal law, the broad utilitarian goal is advanced using three mechanisms, each of which has a targeted goal that is thought to promote the overall goal of crime reduction. *Deterrence* seeks to dissuade, in advance, those who may contemplate committing a crime in the future. An ideal, perfectly effective system of deterrent rules would need no enforcement, as the mere threat of sanctions would prevent potential crimes from ever occurring. *Rehabilitation* aims to transform those who were formerly motivated to commit crimes into law-abiding citizens. Unlike deterrence, rehabilitative efforts are typically applied after the fact to people who have already committed crimes (although in principle, there is no reason they need be so limited). Failing those two goals, a utilitarian system will also pursue *incapacitation*, to remove from society those who have shown themselves to be dangerous, undeterred by threat of punishment, and resistant to rehabilitation. Here again, the usual method is to incapacitate those who have already offended and are likely to do so again, but in the abstract, there is no reason that this method could not be used to incapacitate dangerous people before they commit any crime at all (indeed, such a tactic would be superior from a utilitarian perspective, as it would avoid the social cost of the first crime).

Numerous criminal-law rules seek to implement these three general utilitarian projects. Deterrence may be sought by using rules that impose serious punishment, perhaps even in the absence of culpability, for creating harms that society seeks to deter. One such rule is the felony-murder doctrine, which imposes liability for murder on any felon (such as DeSean McCarty, discussed in the narrative immediately below) whose felony causes the death of another person, even if accidentally. On the other hand, rehabilitation-oriented considerations may impose lighter punishment on a subset of offenders thought especially amenable to rehabilitation. For example, young offenders, even if fully responsible for their crimes, are often subject to rules reducing their exposure to punishment, the idea being that perhaps juveniles may yet be reformed. Then again, the incapacitation goal (like deterrence) tends toward increased punishment for those thought likely to commit future crimes, well beyond anything that might seem deserved or proportionate to their past deeds. Enhanced penalties for repeat offenders, such as "three strikes" laws, seek to incapacitate criminals whose recidivism is taken to suggest that they remain undeterred, incorrigible, and likely to continue their criminal ways unless incarcerated.

All three utilitarian goals and the general underlying goal of crime control are appropriate and desirable objectives. Even so, many of the specific rules that a strict utilitarian agenda generates are seriously problematic, including the rules we have just mentioned. We maintain that utilitarian considerations only rarely provide an *independent* justification for any rule. Many rules that satisfy other goals, such as the goal of desert, will also have utilitarian benefits. But where the two conflict, the utilitarian principle hardly ever (if ever) justifies the formulation of criminal-law rules that depart from the desert principle.

It makes sense to try to construct a criminal-law regime that will minimize the amount of crime in society. Of course, a system based purely on desert will also tend to achieve that crime-control objective, because the prospect of ex post deserved punishment for those who commit crimes provides a good ex ante incentive not to commit them. In short, desert deters. Indeed, one of us has argued elsewhere that a deliberate effort to pursue desert would better achieve the utilitarian crime-control aim than would a deliberate effort to construct a utilitarian system using the traditional mechanism of deterrence[1] or the mechanisms of rehabilitation and incapacitation.[2]

Yet even if this were incorrect, and desert had no inherent additional crime-control benefits relative to the utilitarian approach, it is not necessarily the case that desert has any inherent costs, either. For utilitarians to justify a liability scheme that departs from desert, they must show that the departure adds a *marginal* crime-control benefit beyond what a pure-desert model would already achieve.

As we shall discuss, however, in nearly all cases only scant, if any, evidence exists to suggest that utilitarian-based deviations from desert provide any such marginal benefit. In the case of deterrence, it is questionable whether criminal liability rules have much of an absolute deterrent effect, making it almost impossible to believe that tinkering around the edges by making particular liability adjustments will have any marginal deterrent effect. Similarly, the empirical evidence indicates that deliberate efforts at rehabilitation generally do not work (although certain narrow, targeted rehabilitation efforts may have some effect). As for incapacitation, it is certainly true that increasing jail terms will increase the amount of incapacitation, and more important, there is some evidence that doing so will have a concomitant impact on overall crime levels by taking would-be criminals off the streets. But the incapacitation goal need not be pursued through the criminal-justice system; civil commitment mechanisms could work as well and likely better. Therefore, manipulation of criminal-law rules to achieve incapacitation at the cost of desert is not justified.[3]

FLEEING AS MURDER

DeSean McCarty, seventeen years old, grew up with his mother and five siblings in the South Side of Chicago, an area known for its high crime rate. Growing up, DeSean had little contact with his father, who did not provide financial or emotional support to the family. Rather, DeSean's mother had a live-in boyfriend, an abusive drunk who often beat DeSean, his mother, and his siblings. DeSean would frequently run away from home. Now DeSean lives with his grandmother, near his girlfriend and their nine-month-old son. Although DeSean has not attended school regularly, he worked at Midway airport for a long time to provide financial support for his son and is planning to start classes toward his general equivalency degree.

DeSean has already had several encounters with the law. At age eleven, he began using drugs and was soon smoking four blunts (a combination of marijuana and PCP) and about $100 worth of marijuana a day. He later joined a local street gang. At the age of thirteen, DeSean was arrested for possession of cocaine and transferred to Juvenile Division custody, where the charges were ultimately dropped. Recently, DeSean was arrested twice for possession of controlled substances. These matters are still pending.

The Markham Police Department is familiar with DeSean, who also is known as DeSean Black, Ward DeSean, and Little D. A Markham officer recently tried to pull DeSean over on an outstanding warrant for carjacking. DeSean fled but was caught by the officers—but then he was released when the carjacking accusation turned out to be false. DeSean was arrested one other time on a claim of fleeing and eluding the police but was not convicted.

Andre Griffin is twenty-eight years old and lives in Chicago with his fiancée, Renell Brown, and their daughter. Late in the afternoon on Thursday, September 18, 1997, Renell asks Andre to take her 1982 Chevy Caprice to a mechanic for repairs. Andre takes the car, but instead of getting it fixed, he takes it to 154th Street in DeSean's neighborhood, thinking he can rent it out. At the intersection of 154th Street and Myrtle, Andre pulls over to talk to a woman who calls herself CoCo. The two have never met before. He asks her if she wants to rent a car, or knows someone else who might want to, in exchange for some cocaine. CoCo says that she might know of some people and tells Andre where to take her. When they get there, CoCo sees DeSean McCarty, whom she knows as "Little D." CoCo asks DeSean if he knows anyone who wants to rent a car for some cocaine. DeSean says that he would like to do so and tells them to meet him at 154th and Wood. At that location, DeSean gets in the car and gives Andre two dime bags of cocaine. They agree that DeSean will return the car at 9:00 that night.

Andre arrives at the specified location later that night, but DeSean never shows up. Andre does not report the car to the police as stolen. Andre sees DeSean two days later at an apartment building on 154th Street. He flags DeSean down and tells him to park the car in the back of the building. DeSean drives the car around back, but when Andre walks to the back of the building, DeSean drives away. Andre still does not report the car to the police as stolen.

At about 7:00 that evening, DeSean is parked on Marshfield Street. He looks in the rearview mirror and sees a Markham police car traveling

FIGURE 6.1.
DeSean McCarty.
Chicago Police
Department.

eastbound on 165th Street. A short time later, the police car passes again, this time going westbound. When he sees the police car, DeSean becomes nervous. He does not want to get caught in a stolen car, with two ounces of marijuana on him, and without a driver's license. DeSean starts the car and drives north on Marshfield to 163rd Street. While at a stop sign, he sees the same police car stopped at a corner on 163rd Street, headed eastbound. DeSean turns left on 163rd Street and heads westbound, past the police car. He looks in his rearview mirror and sees the police car make a U-turn in the middle of the street. The police car begins following DeSean, who continues and turns right on Wood Street.

Meanwhile, Officer Sean Laura, who is driving the police car, radios in that he is following a vehicle. Laura is twenty-five years old and has dreamed of being a police officer since he was three years old. In September 1995, Laura graduated from the Chicago Police Academy and was hired by the Markham Police Department. Laura hopes to become a state police officer and eventually an F.B.I. agent. He is taking classes at South Suburban College. On this evening, Laura is in the middle of his second shift of the day. He has worked his usual midnight shift, ending at 8:00 A.M., and is already back at work at 4:00 P.M. because he has agreed to fill in for another officer who requested the night off.

As Officer Laura approaches the Markham-Harvey border, the boundary of his jurisdiction as a Markham police officer, he notifies the dispatcher that he is going to make a traffic stop for "erratic driv-

ing." By the time DeSean reaches 159th and Wood Street, Officer Laura has turned on his emergency lights. DeSean does not pull over, but turns right onto 159th Street, driving forty-five to fifty miles per hour. The speed limit on 159th Street is forty. DeSean turns left on Ashland and heads northbound, with Officer Laura close behind. He is still driving at about the same speed, though the speed limit on Ashland is twenty-five. Deciding that he would be better off on foot, DeSean quickly turns into an alley and dumps the car in a weedy lot, leaving the ignition on as he starts running away.

DeSean runs north through a darkened backyard and gangway. Officer Laura, pulling up behind DeSean's abandoned car, turns off the ignition, grabs a flashlight, locks the car doors, and begins pursuing DeSean on foot. Using the radio on his shoulder, he notifies the dispatcher that he

FIGURE 6.2.
Officer Sean Laura.
Photo from *Daily
Southtown*, Tinley Park,
Illinois.

is engaged in a foot pursuit. The pursuit continues until DeSean runs between two parked cars and onto the street in front of 155th, followed by Officer Laura.

Officer Charles Brogdon of the Harvey Police Department is in the area of 154th and Vine streets, conducting a field interview, when he hears over the radio that an officer is pursuing a suspect coming into Harvey from Markham. Brogdon is twenty-eight years old and has been on the force for three years. (As it happens, he knows Sean Laura because they were classmates at both the Chicago Police Academy and South Suburban College.) When he receives the radio dispatch, Brogdon has been on duty for four hours.

Brogdon jumps in his car, turns on his emergency lights, and heads toward the reported pursuit. En route, Officer Brogdon hears from dispatch that the car chase has now become a foot pursuit in the vicinity of 155th Street. Brogdon enters the area, making a sharp left onto 155th, nearly hitting a tree on that corner. In this area, 155th Street is a two-lane, forty-foot-wide, asphalt-paved roadway, with residences and on-street parking on both sides of the street. The posted speed limit is twenty-five miles per hour in both directions. It is 7:15 P.M. and dark. The streetlights in the vicinity are obstructed by large trees lining the block. When Officer Brogdon turns onto 155th Street, he sees DeSean run across the street. Brogdon visually tracks DeSean and radios in, saying, "Harvey, he is running northbound going towards 154th." As Brogdon applies the brake, he feels a thump and the front wheel of his vehicle goes into the air.

Officer Laura, chasing after DeSean on foot, has run across 155th Street in front of the police car driven by Officer Brogdon and has slipped, causing his center of gravity to become lower than the impact point of the squad car. Rather than being thrown onto the hood of the squad car, Laura is pulled under the front tire. Officer Laura is dragged for approximately 100 feet before the police car comes to a complete stop. The lack of skid marks on the roadway indicates that the squad car did not brake strongly. Officer Brogdon was traveling approximately forty miles per hour when he hit Officer Laura. When the car finally comes to a full stop, Laura is pinned under the rear right tire.

Meanwhile, DeSean does not realize that Officer Laura has been hit. After reaching the other side of 155th Street, he continues to run, eventually hiding under a porch. After ten minutes, he figures the police officer is no longer following him, so he goes to a friend's house, where he changes clothes.

When Brogdon gets out of the car and realizes what has happened, he begins jumping up and down, crying and yelling, "That was Sean." By this time, other officers have arrived at the scene, and a crowd has formed. The neighbors offer to jack up the car, remove Laura, and perform CPR, but police tell them to wait until the ambulance arrives. Firefighters arrive at the scene, and it takes them twenty minutes to pry the vehicle off of Laura. He is rushed by helicopter to Ingalls Memorial Hospital, where the hospital's emergency staff works for more than an hour to save his life but is unsuccessful. He is pronounced dead at 8:58 P.M.

The police trace the license plates and registration of the vehicle to Renell Brown. They question Brown and Andre Griffin, who eventually admits that he lent the car to DeSean in exchange for drugs. Several witnesses at the scene of the accident also tell police that they saw a person they know as Little D running away on the night in question. The police catch up with McCarty, who admits to running away from Officer Laura on the night in question and states: "I truthfully didn't mean no harm [to Laura]. When you're scared, your first instinct is to run."

DeSean McCarty is arrested on Sunday, September 21, 1997, and charged with murder for causing the death of Officer Sean Laura.

.   .   .

After the accident, few statements are issued by the Markham Police Department. Markham police captain James Hunt, however, describes the events of September 20, 1997, as an "unfortunate, terrible accident that happened because of poor timing and poor lighting," and states, "There's nobody to blame." Officer Brogdon, though, is badly shaken by the accident and quits his job as a policeman one month later to take a job in construction.

DeSean McCarty is arraigned and pleads not guilty to charges of possession of a stolen motor vehicle, aggravated fleeing and eluding, and first-degree murder. Markham public defender Frank Rago is assigned to McCarty's case. Rago moves to dismiss the action, but Associate Judge Reginald Baker of Cook County denies the motion, stating that though it will be difficult for the prosecution to prove that McCarty was guilty of murder, it is premature to dismiss the case just yet. Based on this statement, the media attention the case has received, and the sympathy within the community for the death of Officer Laura, defense counsel Rago thinks it best to pursue a bench trial. McCarty waives the right to a jury.

The trial lasts for two days before Judge Baker, who then finds McCarty guilty on all counts. Frank Rago moves for a new trial, but his request is denied. At sentencing, McCarty takes the stand, asking for forgiveness for what he has done. Officer Laura's mother also takes the stand to give a victim impact statement. The judge sentences DeSean McCarty to forty years in prison.[4] After the sentencing, DeSean McCarty's grandmother states, "The judge said he made his decision to deter someone else from running from the police. Don't make an example of my grandchild."[5]

FIGURES 6.3, 6.4.
Markham police officer
Sean Laura's funeral.
Photos from *Daily
Southtown*, Tinley Park,
Illinois.

In April 2002, the appellate court affirms the trial court's judgment.[6] In April 2003, the Supreme Court of Illinois remands the case for reconsideration in light of another case they have just decided, reversing the rule that aggravated possession of a stolen motor vehicle is a "forcible felony" that can trigger felony murder.[7]

DETERRENCE

Modern criminal law often expresses a concern for deterrence that seems to equal, if not surmount, the desire to satisfy the goal of doing justice. It is hardly surprising, then, that the deterrence goal is sometimes successfully invoked to support rules that undermine the desert goal. Such rules include, for example, the imposition of strict criminal liability and broad formulations of the felony-murder rule,[8] as illustrated by the Illinois rule under which DeSean McCarty was convicted of murder.

Indeed, the deterrence rationale is ubiquitous. It arises in debates regarding all manner of rules, including rules we discuss elsewhere. In fact, the deterrence rationale sometimes arises on *both* sides of these debates, indicating that even advocates of deterrence are unclear about the empirical effects of doctrine on deterrence. For example, deterrence arguments are offered in support of corporate or enterprise liability, in opposition to corporate or enterprise liability, in support of limiting the liability of corporate officials to the board of directors or high management, in support of vicarious liability, in opposition to vicarious liability, in support of *Pinkerton* and "common design" rules in complicity, in opposition to strict liability offenses, in support of strict liability offenses, in opposition to liability based upon negligence, and in support of liability for negligent homicide and negligent assault with a deadly weapon. Deterrence is also the guiding rationale for some inchoate liability rules, including some rules that differ from each other: in support of a narrow "proximity" test for attempt, in support of a broad "substantial step" test for attempt, in support of limiting the renunciation defense to cases where the offender is successful in avoiding the offense, and in opposition to an impossibility defense for inchoate liability.[9]

Similarly, deterrence arguments are used to justify or oppose various rules relating to mitigations and excuse defenses, again including some rules we discuss elsewhere. To give just a few examples, deterrence arguments have been offered in support of an objective (unindividualized) standard of recklessness, in support of a purely objective (unindividualized) standard for the provocation mitigation to murder, in opposition to the individualized extreme-emotional-disturbance mitigation, in support of the partial-responsibility mitigation in murder, and in opposition to a general reasonable-mistake-of-law excuse and a duress defense. Deterrence arguments also have been used to support particular formulations of excuse defenses, including insanity-defense formulations featuring only a cognitive prong *and* formulations that also contain a control prong.[10]

Deterrence rationales also influence the grading of offenses. Promotion of deterrence through enhanced liability has been offered in support of aggravating offense grades according to type of victim (old, young, police officer, and others), location (such as selling drugs near schools), and class of offender (such as aggravation of terrorist threats by high schoolers). Similarly, deterrence arguments have been used in support of a separate offense of robbery (rather than relying upon offenses of theft and assault); in support of grading vehicular killing-while-intoxicated as manslaughter, without a show-

ing of negligence or even causation; in opposition to felony-murder liability
for killings by nonfelons during the felony; in support of the premeditation
aggravation for first-degree murder; in opposition to a mere grade reduction
for renunciation (preferring a complete defense); in support of grading inchoate liability the same as that for the substantive offense, but also in support of making an exception to this rule for first-degree felonies; in support
of grading thefts of livestock more than other thefts of equal or greater value,
because the former are particularly easy to commit and difficult to detect; in
support of a lower grade for intercourse upon invalid consent (that is, by mistake or trick) than by force; in support of grading theft by the amount stolen;
in support of reduced grading for "joyriding" (in comparison to theft); in
support of grading credit card fraud of even a trivial amount as at least a misdemeanor; in support of grading incest no higher than a midlevel felony,
even if the extreme moral indignation of the community would call for a
higher grade; in support of reduced grading for perjury; and in support of a
grading reduction for a kidnapper who "voluntarily releases the victim alive
and in a safe place prior to trial."[11]

Finally, the deterrence rationale is common in the formulation of a wide
range of sentencing rules and policies, including arguments in support of the
death penalty, in opposition to the death penalty, in support of automatic imposition of the death penalty on life-imprisonment prisoners who kill, in
support of jail time for drunk driving, in support of increasing fines to twice
the offender's pecuniary gain, in support of applying a mandatory penalty
enhancement for a subsequent offense to a second offense on a simultane-
ous conviction, in support of higher fines for corporate offenders, in support
of a judicially imposed minimum term of imprisonment, in support of fines
for offenses of pecuniary gain, and in guidelines for the exercise of judicial
discretion in setting the length of a prison sentence and the amount of a fine.[12]

Some of these numerous rules are consistent with, if not demanded by,
desert; others are clearly at odds with desert. All too often, the deterrence justification offered to support the rule is given credence regardless of whether
the rule promotes or impedes desert or whether the justification finds support in empirical data. Yet most doctrinal manipulations undertaken for the
sake of deterrence have not been shown to work, and there are good reasons
to believe that they are highly unlikely to be productive and even likely to be
counterproductive. Considerably more, and more robust, empirical analysis
is required to determine whether these manipulations offer any clear utilitarian benefit to offset their desert-related costs, including the utilitarian costs
of sacrificing desert, as well as the normative costs.

For example, rules allowing the imposition of strict liability, or punishment disproportionate to culpability, have been supported based on deter-

rence goals. Such rules transparently deviate from the desert principle, which would allow liability only where the offender has a culpable mental state and only to the extent of the blameworthiness that the existing mental state suggests. Indeed, the deterrence-based rationale for such rules essentially acknowledges that they will lead to deviations from desert, but holds that their added ability to achieve the competing goal of deterrence warrants the sacrifice of desert.[13] A closer look at the doctrines, however, reveals that in addition to their costs in terms of desert, they offer only questionable (if any) benefits in terms of the deterrence goal itself.

Felony murder is one such doctrine. The deterrence argument for felony murder holds that, although it may apply to some defendants who lack the culpability usually required for murder, there is significant deterrent value in threatening felons with severe sanctions whenever their felonies lead to someone's death. This will make them more careful when engaging in their criminal activity, a time when the danger of accidental injury is great and when comparably greater care is needed to avoid causing a death.[14] The rule also is thought to have the collateral effect of providing an additional deterrent to the commission of the underlying felony itself, especially where that felony is inherently dangerous.[15] An analogous deterrence argument frequently is made for strict liability in the context of prohibiting certain business activities involving a "danger of widespread harm occurring in case of mistake or accident,"[16] although the potential deterrent effects of strict liability are sometimes promoted in a more open-ended fashion.[17]

These deterrence arguments for felony murder, and other rules, suffer from two crippling flaws. First, it is not at all clear that deterrence-based rules actually work. That is, as an empirical matter, there are few data supporting the claim that they deter crime any more than a purely desert-based criminal system and good reason to suspect that they are actually counterproductive. Second, even if they did work, it appears that other rules could be substituted that would achieve just as much deterrence without as high a sacrifice of desert.

Social scientists have increasingly suspected that the criminal-justice system's threat of official punishment has only a limited effect in preventing crime.[18] The deterrence theory, particularly when used to justify the imposition of liability beyond the demands of desert, contends that increased marginal deterrence will arise from narrowly manipulating specific amounts of liability and punishment—that prospective felons will know, and think about, the difference between the negligent-homicide (or manslaughter) liability they might otherwise receive and the murder liability that the felony-murder rule provides and that this difference will alter their decision to commit the offense or their level of care in committing it. But in doing so, the argument assumes a widespread familiarity with the details of criminal-law rules that seems difficult to establish. It is almost inconceivable that De-Sean McCarty, in deciding to "rent" the car or in fleeing from the police, cal-culated his conduct in light of the state's broad felony-murder rule. Indeed, he probably would not know or surmise such a rule existed, even if he stopped to think about it.

The potential efficacy of deterrence policies is further hampered by the low risk of punishment an offender faces for the contemplated offense.[19] Li-ability and punishment rules will have no effect if the perceived risk of pun-ishment is too low for the potential offender to think it relevant. Moreover, the minimal deterrent power of this objectively low risk is compounded by subjective factors that cause potential offenders to further discount that risk.[20] Because of these difficulties, the only way to generate a sufficient de-terrent threat—if the system tries to do so only by tinkering with punish-ment levels—would be to increase punishments to draconian levels, but that solution would give rise to an entirely new set of problems. The greater the criminal-justice system's deviation from desert, the more it undermines its own moral credibility with the community it governs and the less influence it will have in shaping community norms and in gaining cooperation and ac-quiescence in its operation.

The very act of sacrificing desert to promote deterrence may actually cause a net *loss* of deterrence; a criminal-justice system that seeks to follow the dictates of desert may generate more effective deterrence than a deterrence-based, nondesert system would.[21] Social scientists increasingly believe that the criminal law's moral credibility is the true source of its power to gain compliance.[22] Each time the criminal law is used to punish blameless offend-ers, its moral foundation—the ultimate source of its ability to shape the com-munity and internalize individual norms and to stigmatize the conduct it prohibits—is incrementally weakened. Thus, any deterrence advantage gained by having the criminal law punish beyond the dictates of desert is purchased at a serious cost.

One recent and interesting study has directly inquired as to the crime-reducing effects of the felony-murder rule.[23] The study's results are quite surprising and illustrate the complexity of such deterrent effects. As the au-thor remarks:

[T]he results for robbery are inconsistent with either the predictions of proponents or opponents of the felony-murder rule. States that pun-ish robbery death more severely have higher share[s] of robberies that prove fatal. States that punish robbery death as either murder one or two even have higher numbers of robbery deaths due to guns. However one measures the felony-murder rule, states with stiffer penalties for this crime report greater numbers of victims of robbery-murder.[24]

A similar, though less statistically significant, result also obtains for rape: the rule may slightly reduce the overall number of rapes, but it also correlates with an *increase* in the number of rapes resulting in death.[25] One can only speculate about what causes these complex results (that is, the apparent tendency of those who engage in robbery or rape, when a felony-murder statute is in effect, to be slightly more likely to cause the deaths of their victims).

Ultimately, the study seems to suggest that the felony-murder rule does have an effect on conduct—yet at least some of its effect is to *increase* the social damage, rather than decrease it as the lawmakers intended. In any case, changes in conduct that amount to small fractions of a percent, as reported in the study, are hardly a ringing case for the overall efficacy of basing criminal-law formulation on an explicit deterrence justification, even at the sacrifice of desert. The study's results also illustrate other good reasons not to rely upon deterrence analysis in the formulation of criminal-law rules: the complexity of the dynamics of deterrence and our lack of information about those factors that are needed to accurately predict an effect. If anything, the study seems to argue against the usefulness of formulating the felony-murder rule in order to affect crime rates—even before one considers the additional costs of such a rule in terms of desert.

Even holding aside all of these questions about whether deterrence strategies work, however, the deterrence rationale is undermined by the availability of a variety of other, nondeviating, and potentially more effective methods to promote deterrence across the board. Instead of imposing high levels of punishment on those who do not deserve it, we might maintain serious (though still proportional and hence desert-based) punishment for legitimately blameworthy offenders or increase the resources used to combat and investigate crime.

Additionally, even where strict liability might make people behave more carefully, there is little reason to suspect it would be more effective in this regard than, say, a negligence rule. The negligence standard requires an actor to be as careful as she reasonably can be expected to be. What can strict liability add to that?[26] Strict liability might encourage people to be even *more* careful than the circumstances reasonably would require, but this seems a dubious goal and in any case an unlikely one to achieve. A broad felony-murder rule imposes murder liability even in cases, such as McCarty's, where the person's initial felony was not inherently dangerous and he would not have perceived any reason to behave more carefully than he did. Even while fleeing from the police, it is unlikely that McCarty would have appreciated the danger of accidental death while he was acting, much less that he would have thought to modify his behavior in an effort to reduce that risk.[27]

The deterrence-based agenda of modern criminal law has simply failed, on both moral and practical grounds. It fails to give defendants what they deserve—and admits this. But as is becoming increasingly clear, it fails also to achieve its own goal. It seems that pursuing desert is not only desirable for its own sake, but also because it holds out the potential to deter crime at least as well as, and perhaps better than, any other option.

REHABILITATION

Like the deterrence goal, the goal of rehabilitating offenders and thereby preventing future crimes has sometimes been used to justify practices that depart from desert (although in this case, in the opposite direction—imposing less punishment rather than more). As with deterrence, though, demonstrated results have not tended to vindicate the practices. The findings of numerous studies suggest that criminal-rehabilitation programs, as typically practiced, do not produce impressive or often even detectable reductions in recidivism for those who have participated in the programs.[28] Thus, where rehabilitation is used to justify a deviation from desert, the deviation is likely to be borne for little or no crime-control benefit. In most cases, there is little reason to think that effective rehabilitation even requires the sacrifice of desert, especially when a wide range of nonincarcerative sanctions are available to carry out deserved punishment. Imposing deserved punishment hardly impedes rehabilitation, and many would argue that it may help promote it. Further, it is entirely possible to support facilitative rehabilitation within the context of imposing deserved punishment without viewing rehabilitation as the underlying basis or justification for imposing punishment. For all of these reasons, rules that explicitly prioritize rehabilitation over desert are increasingly rare.

They are not extinct, however. An example of rehabilitative goals superseding desert interests is the system's treatment of mature, but young, offenders. Just as the presumption of maturity for actors above the current law's fixed cutoff age can lead to undeserved punishment, as discussed in chapter 2,[29] the chronological age cutoff also creates the converse problem of understating our normative expectations for the fully mature actor who is younger than the cutoff age. As long as an actor's chronological age is less than the statutory cutoff, the actor is entitled to the immaturity "defense," requiring transfer to juvenile court, with its more limited sentencing options. The escape from adult-level prosecution occurs even if the actor's level of maturity is such that he reasonably *could* have been expected to have avoided the violation.[30] Application of the defense is reduced to disputes over timing. In one case, for example, the defendant noted that he committed the offense at 9:45 A.M. on his birthday, but that he was not born until 12:50 P.M. of his birthday. Thus, he argued, he had not yet reached the cutoff age.[31]

Some of the failures of justice from this doctrinal shortcoming have been made moot by recent reforms reducing the age at which a defendant can be tried for a serious offense as an adult. A majority of American jurisdictions now allow eleven-year-olds to be tried as adults for some offenses.[32] But this reform only exaggerates the deviations from desert in the opposite direction. Once put to trial in adult court, a defendant has no mechanism by which he can raise his immaturity as an excuse. Thus, the new reforms increase the frequency with which offenders who are in fact blameless because of their immaturity will nonetheless be punished as if they were fully mature and therefore fully responsible for their offense conduct.

A better formulation of the immaturity "defense" would make it available in all prosecutions and would look not to an arbitrary cutoff age, but to an offender's actual level of maturity, perhaps using rebuttable presumptions to reduce the cost of the inquiry in typical cases.[33] Ultimately, the basis for the current law's treating mature minors as juveniles probably has less to do with blamelessness than with a belief in the possibility of rehabilitating those offenders.[34] Yet both interests would probably be better served by a more flexible rule enabling more individualized assessments of maturity.

.   .   .

In a practical admission that broad-based rehabilitation efforts are unlikely to produce results for many offenders, since the 1980s criminal policy has shifted away from rehabilitation and toward an increased emphasis on the third crime-control mechanism, incapacitation. The effort to remove from society those incorrigible offenders who have arguably shown themselves undeterrable and incapable of reform has led to rules such as those imposing greatly enhanced sentences for repeat offenders—people such as Charles Almond, discussed in the following narrative.

TV VIOLENCE

On March 4, 1963, a judge convicts Charles Almond of burglarizing an unoccupied building. Five years later, he pleads guilty to "throwing a missile"
(a rock) at an automobile occupied by his father-in-law and to breaking and
entering into the offices of the Peeler Oil Company. These three convictions
carry sentences of four, two, and eighteen years, respectively. No one is injured during any of his criminal acts. In 1988, Almond is given a suspended
sentence for bypassing the electric meter in his home.

On July 14, 1991, Almond, now fifty-nine years old, is at home with his
family in Augusta County, Virginia. Although possessing only a second-grade
education and unable to either read or write, he is self-employed as an automobile mechanic. Rather than enjoying his Sunday away from the automobile shop, Almond finds himself witnessing yet another installment of the
same endless dispute between his sons: what to watch on television. For unknown reasons, his adopted eight-year-old son, Anthony, and his twenty-
three-year-old son, Charles, Jr., are in a perpetual confrontation over which
program to watch. In the past, these disagreements have reached such a fer-
vor that Almond's only form of escape from the family turmoil was to go
fishing in the Chesapeake Bay.

On this day the arguments begin again, and as they continue become
louder and louder. Finally, Almond announces that he will put a stop to the
argument. He picks up a .22-caliber revolver that one of his sons has left on
a nearby table and shoots the television set. Shards of glass fly from the television when it explodes, nicking Almond's two-week-old granddaughter and
his stepdaughter. Although neither is seriously hurt, their parents nonetheless take them to King's Daughters Hospital as a precaution, at which point
the hospital's staff reports the incident to the sheriff's office. That office ob-

FIGURE 6.5.
Charles Almond fishing
on the Potomac River.
Family photo.

tains a search warrant for Almond's home, where officers find a number of other firearms, including two rifles, two shotguns, and two revolvers. The Augusta County district attorney, however, agrees to enter a *nolle prosequi* on the shooting charge, because Almond had not intended to injure anyone. He decides to charge Almond only with possession of firearms, which carries a two-year sentence under Virginia law.

FIGURE 6.6.
Almond and his
daughter in 2000.
Family photo.

For reasons that are not entirely clear, local authorities never prosecute Almond, but the case is referred to the U.S. Attorney's Office for the Western District of Virginia, which charges Almond under the career-offender sentencing provision with possession of a firearm as a felon.[35] A federal grand jury indicts Almond on March 4, 1992, and seven months later, a federal judge finds him guilty after a bench trial. In April 1993, Almond is sentenced to fifteen years in prison with no opportunity for parole for being an "armed career criminal." Almond will be in prison until he is seventy-five years old.[36]

INCAPACITATION

Like deterrence and rehabilitation, the third traditional crime-control mechanism, the incapacitation of dangerous offenders, similarly produces regular departures from desert. Sentencing guidelines that give great weight to prior criminal records[37] and "three-strikes" and related habitual-offender statutes[38] commonly double, triple, or quadruple the punishment imposed on repeat offenders, compared to first-time offenders convicted of similar crimes.[39] Such extended sentences are imposed because these offenders are seen as the most likely to commit future crimes, and added incarceration prevents them from doing so. As the *Guidelines Manual* of the U.S. Sentencing Commission explains, "[T]he specific factors included in [the calculation of the criminal history category] are consistent with the extant empirical research assessing correlates of recidivism and patterns of career criminal behavior."[40] Almond was sentenced under such a provision.

The expansion of rules designed specifically to achieve incapacitation is not limited to habitual-offender or recidivist-enhancement laws, but takes other forms as well. Gang membership and recruitment are now punished.[41] Jurisdictional reforms have decreased the age at which juveniles may be tried

FIGURE 6.7.
Almond during prison
visit by his family.
Family photo.

as adults.[42] These reforms boast as their common denominator greater official control over dangerous persons, a rationale readily apparent from each reform's legislative history.

Also departing from desert in favor of incapacitation are statutory offense-grading schemes that set the grade for an inchoate offense to equal the grade for the completed offense.[43] This grading judgment clearly conflicts with lay perceptions of justice—under which resulting harm aggravates an offender's blameworthiness and calls for greater punishment, and the absence of resulting harm has the reverse effect[44]—but makes good sense if the goal is to maximize control of dangerous people.[45] The offender who fails because police are lucky enough to interrupt his crime before its completion may be as dangerous as the offender who completes an offense, making both equally attractive candidates for incapacitation.

The criminal-justice system's focus on dangerousness and incapacitation also, though less frequently, causes distortions of the reverse sort: failures of justice, in which a person fails to receive the punishment deserved. This kind of error can occur both in the assignment of liability and in the assessment of the amount of punishment to be imposed. For example, the Model Penal Code makes available a mitigation, or complete defense, for inchoate liability when a person "presents no public danger" and the person's attempt was "inherently unlikely" to succeed.[46] Such a rule may make sense for a system designed to incapacitate the dangerous: incarcerating the nondangerous is a waste of preventive resources. But where the person fully believes that her conduct will cause a criminal harm, the person deserves punishment whether or not the chosen method actually is likely to succeed.[47]

Deviations from desert that underpunish are more common in sentencing, at least under the discretionary sentencing systems that were typical until the 1980s and that still exist in many jurisdictions. The judge who focuses on prevention instead of desert[48] will give a minor sentence for a serious offense if the offender is no longer dangerous. Thus, the recently discovered former Nazi concentration-camp official can escape the punishment he deserves because his advanced age (and the absence of the Nazi threat) make him no longer dangerous.

In design and in effect, all of these incapacitation-based statutes and rules violate the notion of basing punishment on desert. They tailor punishment based on the personal traits of, and its practical impact on, the criminal, rather than on the seriousness or blameworthiness of the offense, as a desert-based system would demand. In other words, they imprison categories of people defined as "criminals," rather than punishing individual people for their actual crimes. An initial portion of an imprisonment sentence may well be deserved, but it is followed by a purely preventive-detention portion that cannot be justified as deserved punishment.

One can construct a theory that makes a prior criminal record at least relevant to deserved punishment, as Andrew von Hirsch has done.[49] By committing another offense after having been previously convicted, such a theory argues, an offender might be seen as "thumbing his nose" at the system. Yet although such nose thumbing may justify some incremental punishment over what a first offense would deserve, it can hardly justify the vast increases in punishment for which habitual-offender statutes and sentencing guidelines provide—increases that lead the nose-thumbing portion of the punishment to dwarf the portion attributable to the crime itself.[50]

Consider the *Almond* case. Almond's crime of shooting his television, even considering the attendant endangerment aspect, hardly merits fifteen years' imprisonment. Indeed, the cumulative impact of his entire criminal career—whether or not he had been formally sanctioned and punished for his earlier crimes—probably would not warrant such severe liability, at least on desert grounds. Yet recidivism aggravations, such as three-strikes laws, are willing to tolerate this clear deviation from desert in the name of incapacitating dangerous offenders.

Yet, as with the deterrence-based rules we discussed above, these aggravations of punishment are not only undesirable in terms of desert but are also questionable even in terms of their own incapacitation rationale. In practice, three-strikes and related schemes turn good prevention on its head by detaining offenders only after their criminal career is sufficiently advanced to have the necessary three strikes, while failing to detain potentially dangerous criminals during their more crime-prone teens and twenties.[51] Many incapacitation-based rules thus do not even promote effective incapacitation and often amount to a simple waste of resources in incarcerating those who do not present a significant danger.

There is good reason to question the logic of incapacitation strategies as a general matter; the data available for specific efforts to reduce crime through incapacitation do not instill much additional confidence in the wisdom of those particular tactics. For example, the evidence regarding the crime-control benefits of three-strikes laws is, at best, mixed. Some studies conclude from available data that three-strikes laws do not achieve significant crime reduction.[52] Other studies, exploring criminal career patterns, suggest that such patterns make it unlikely that three-strikes laws will have much effect on crime rates at all—and even if they do, that such effect will be modest, given the costs of incarcerating so many offenders.[53] Still other studies assert that three-strikes laws do have some effect.[54]

But again, as with the deterrence-based rules we have discussed, even if such rules were clearly shown to further the utilitarian crime-control interest, they would not necessarily be justified, because that interest can also be advanced in other ways without suffering the costs inherent in the deviations from desert that the current rules generate. To the extent that a successful system for the incapacitation of dangerous offenders is possible, it should be implemented by creating a more expansive system of civil commitment that is open about its preventive nature. Such a solution would enable incapacitation, but would also allow the criminal law to maintain its moral force.

In chapter 10, we discuss in greater detail the option of openly admitting the use of preventive detention and employing such detention through an explicit civil commitment system, where its purpose can be achieved without distorting the criminal-justice system and where it can get the close scrutiny that it deserves. We also propose, in chapter 9, that the incapacitation goal often can be advanced in another way that would not distort justice: specifically, by taking such concerns into account when determining the punishment *method* but not when determining the punishment *amount*.

CHAPTER 7

_____

Controlling Police and Prosecutors

A SIXTH JUSTIFICATION OFFERED in support of deviations from desert is the need to curb misconduct by criminal-justice officials, whose zealous pursuit of criminals has the potential to overwhelm the desire for fair play and respect for individual rights. In turn, our desire to limit governmental intrusion and to promote procedural integrity sometimes appears to require a sacrifice of justice. What is at stake here is a tradeoff between the societal interest in effective law enforcement and the countervailing interest in preventing abusive or overly intrusive law enforcement.

Sometimes the tradeoff is clear or has effectively been made categorically, at least as a legal matter. Various rights and protections against improper prosecution are enshrined in the Constitution and therefore may not be sacrificed in favor of effective law enforcement. Such rights include the Fourth Amendment protection against unreasonable searches and seizures (the subject of the Eyler narrative, which begins this chapter), the Fifth Amendment rights and rules protecting against improperly obtained testimony, the right to a speedy trial, and the protection against double jeopardy (the subject of the Ignatow case, later in the chapter).[1] In many cases, recognizing and defending these rights has the effect—the intended effect—of limiting the state's power to pursue a prosecution, even where the subject of the potential prosecution is truly guilty if judged on the merits.

Some other rules are not of constitutional dimension, but are similarly designed to prevent improper prosecutions or other forms of governmental overreaching or intrusion. Rules barring trial of the incompetent, and the entrapment defense (discussed in the DeLorean narrative), are meant to prevent abusive or improper law enforcement or prosecution, even though they may also have the effect of preventing punishment of legitimately guilty parties. In all of these cases, whether the rule derives from the Constitution or not, the potential tradeoff between individual liberty and substantively accurate results presents a special situation that complicates, at least for some, the attractiveness of our unwavering commitment to these protections.

Some people may see little complexity here. One might adopt a categorical stance that the desert/control-of-government tradeoff should always be resolved in favor of effective law enforcement or, on the other hand, that it should always be resolved in favor of recognizing individual rights. Members of both of these groups, the diehard desert fundamentalists and the diehard anti–government-overreaching fundamentalists, would view the proper resolution of the conflict as obvious: each group would argue that its favored concern should simply trump the other all the time.

But others, probably most people, fall outside these groups and have strong principled commitments to *both* substantive desert and procedural restraints. Even for this camp, however, it may seem at first blush that the two principles are simply at loggerheads, and one must simply adopt a normative preference for one or the other. We seek to argue that, in at least some cases, there may be a method of accommodating both interests, and in other cases of balancing the two goals in a reasoned manner. That balancing turns on the relative value of the principles, not *as* principles, but as *practical* influences on the criminal-justice system's moral authority and therefore on its effectiveness.

As we discussed in chapter 6, one advantage of adhering to a desert distribution of liability and punishment is that doing so reinforces the criminal law's moral credibility, which in turn provides useful crime-control effects. But there is evidence to suggest that not only the justness of the system's results but also the integrity of the institutions and the fairness of the procedures that generate those results can affect the system's reputation. Moreover, the interests in integrity and fairness may exist independently of the interest in justice. Even if a system has sound liability rules, if it is considered biased or otherwise untrustworthy or if its procedural rules are perceived as unfair, its reputation may be tarnished, and it may suffer a reduction in its "legitimacy," as the literature in this area terms it.[2] Thus, maintaining the system's legitimacy by imposing basic requirements of fairness may promote compliance even though the same rules generate failures of desert that tend to undermine the public's sense of the system's moral credibility.

This argument differs from the standard argument advanced in favor of procedural fairness and judicial integrity, which accords these values some absolute stature that does not admit of interference or compromise. We argue that these principles should be weighed, as against the prima facie equally valid principle of desert, according to their *instrumental* merit: the extent to which they maintain the legitimacy of the legal system, thereby promoting respect for and compliance with the law.[3] This approach highlights the practical, as well as abstract, significance of these competing ideals while also providing a criterion for testing the propriety of any given rule offered to advance them. Looking to public perceptions of the mandates of procedural fairness gives us a mechanism to distinguish between those rules that truly are needed to preserve the system's legitimacy and those rules that do not advance a reputation of legitimacy. The critical question to ask is this: if a particular rule were not provided, would it undercut the public's perception of the legitimacy of the system and thereby incrementally undercut people's willingness to comply with the system's demands? Or would providing the rule—thus increasing the likelihood of failures of desert—have the opposite effect, making the system seem more like arbitrary game playing that takes no interest in the substantive merits or facts of the case?[4]

RELEASED TO KILL

Larry Eyler, thirty, is a man of contradictions. He has a big round baby face and a shy, quiet manner, but his 6'1" body is all muscle. His behavior is childlike and naive, yet he can be cunning when necessary. Eyler's greatest inner conflict, however, revolves around his sexuality. Though attracted to men ever since he can remember, he can barely even talk about the subject. Perhaps as a consequence of his strict religious upbringing, he is terribly ashamed of his sexual orientation, and with Eyler, this shame translates to violence. When he engages in sex, he is brimming with rage. He is into bondage and enjoys tying up his partners and cursing at them. More than anything else, Eyler likes to inflict pain on his partners—so much pain that sometimes they die.

By day, Eyler has a seemingly regular life in Terre Haute, Indiana, working in the Vigo County offices and sharing an apartment with David Little, a middle-aged library science professor. Eyler has had a steady romantic relationship for the past year with John Dobrovolskis, a married man who lives in Chicago (Dobrovolskis's wife, Sally, is well aware of his homosexuality, but she still prefers to live with him). The relationship, however, is not al-ways calm—there are frequent heated phone arguments, and added tension based on Little's undisguised hatred of Dobrovolskis, which causes Eyler stress. Sometimes Eyler ties Dobrovolskis up during intercourse, but he does not hurt him.

Eyler reserves his most violent tendencies for other people and other times. Late at night, he likes to cruise the roads to gay bars in uptown Chi-cago, carrying in his pick-up truck a "torture kit" which includes knives, a metal-tipped whip, a sword, handcuffs, and tear gas. On December 19, 1982, Eyler picks up a hitchhiking Steven Agan, who has met Eyler before because he works at a car wash that Eyler patronizes. But it is a different Eyler that Agan encounters in the pick-up truck—one with a butcher knife and a grim determination to live out his dark fantasies.

Eyler drives north on Route 63 to an abandoned farm near the tiny town of Newport. At knifepoint, he orders Agan to take off his shirt, then hand-cuffs him, gags his mouth, and drags him into a shed. With a rope, he ties the terrified Agan to a beam. He unbuckles Agan's belt and pulls his pants down. Eyler goes back to the pick-up for his equipment, then meticulously sets up a stage of ritual torture, setting flashlights that make dramatic light. Then he

FIGURE 7.1.
Larry Eyler at the Indiana State Police post in Lowell after Eyler was stopped for a traffic violation, September 30, 1983. Courtesy Indiana State Police.

slowly stabs Agan in the chest. Agan, unable to scream through his gagged mouth, tries to avoid the knife, but his actions only excite Eyler. In a frenzy of rage, Eyler makes deeper and deeper gashes on his victim's abdomen and throat. Agan bleeds to death, but Eyler does not stop; he continues to mutilate the dead body. After he calms down, he drags the body into a wooded area and drives away. Agan's mutilated body is found nine days later, on December 28, 1982, but the police have no clue as to the killer's identity.

By early 1983, more bodies of young men are found along the highway routes between Chicago's northern suburbs and Terre Haute. Most of these men are homosexual; some are hustlers. All are found mutilated in a similar fashion. Indiana police suspect a serial killer and set up a special multiagency task force to do the investigation, charging Sergeant Frank Love with its daily operation.

FIGURE 7.2.
Steve Agan, 23, from Terre Haute, Indiana. He was found stabbed to death near Newport, Indiana, on December 28, 1982.

An informant calls in and identifies Eyler as the murderer, telling Love that Eyler is into bondage, that he is violent during sex, and that he regularly cruises the routes where the bodies were found. The informant adds that Eyler was involved in a stabbing in Terre Haute in 1978. (Eyler had picked up Mark Henry and sexually abused him at knifepoint, then stabbed him when he tried to run away, abandoning him in a field, but Henry managed to stumble to help and was taken to a hospital. Eyler was apprehended—the police even searched his truck and found his torture kit—and charged with aggravated battery, but when it came time for the trial, his lawyer offered Henry $2,500, which Henry accepted, agreeing to drop the charges.) Trying to verify this lead, the task force puts Eyler under partial surveillance, though it does not search Eyler's car or apartment. Eyler is seen cruising the routes to Chicago late at night and entering gay bars. Sometimes he picks up hitchhikers.

Unaware of the investigation, Eyler continues to prey upon young men. At midnight on August 30, 1983, he picks up Ralph Calise by Chicago's lake front. Calise, young and poor, lives on welfare and sells small quantities of drugs. Eyler drives with Calise to an open field just south of Lake Forest, where he again handcuffs and gags his victim, unbuckles his belt, pulls down his pants, and begins the torture. Slowly, Eyler inflicts seventeen deep cuts to Calise's chest, abdomen, back, and neck, cutting deeper and deeper until he

FIGURE 7.3.
Larry Eyler outside Andy's Liquor Store, Greencastle, Indiana, July 1983. Photo by undercover officer of Indiana task force.

punctures Calise's lungs and cuts his liver; the blood splashes from Calise's dead body onto Eyler's pants and runs into his boots.

This time, though, Eyler does not make a clean getaway. The earth is damp, and his boots and the pick-up's tires leave marks on it. Investigators from the Lake County sheriff's office find the body the next day. They make cast prints of the boot and tire marks, but still have no clue about the murderer's identity. Investigators in Illinois connect with those in Indiana to share their information, but the investigation stalls.

In the wee hours of September 30, 1983, Eyler picks up Daryl Hayward, a young drifter from Arkansas who is hitchhiking on the Dan Ryan Expressway to get a ride to a funeral in Indianapolis. Eyler tells Hayward that he can take him there, and Hayward mutters, "Tonight's my lucky night."

After some time, Eyler whispers, "I have a fantasy."

"What is your fantasy?" Hayward asks.

"Tying people up," Eyler answers and adds, "I'll give you $100 if I could tie you up. I get off like that. It's just someone being helpless for a while, being tied up, that gets me off." Eyler promises that he will not hurt Hayward and will untie him after the act. Hayward refuses at first, but is swayed by the offer of $100. Eyler heads south on Interstate 65 and pulls over near a ditch. Eyler hands Hayward a plastic grocery bag with ropes and tape. In the ditch, Eyler asks Hayward to take off his shirt. The loud noise of the highway traffic makes Hayward uneasy, and he asks, "Why don't we go where nobody can see us?"[5] Eyler agrees and suggests that they go to a quiet barn he knows.

As the two men emerge from the ditch, around 7:00 A.M., Indiana state trooper Kenneth Buehrle passes by in the opposite direction. Parking along the interstate is prohibited, and Buehrle makes a U-turn to check the truck. He sees that one of the men is carrying a bag, which makes him suspicious. Eyler and Hayward get into the pick-up and start driving away, but Buehrle follows and pulls Eyler over. He checks Eyler's driver's license and writes him a warning ticket for illegal parking on the interstate. When he asks Eyler what they were doing in the ditch, Eyler says he needed to go to the bathroom; and when Buehrle asks to see the bag Hayward was carrying, Hayward tries to deceive him and hands him his personal bag instead of the grocery bag with the ropes and tape. Buehrle's

FIGURE 7.4.
Ralph Calise, 28, was found stabbed to death on August 31, 1983, in a farmer's field east of the Tri-State Tollway in Lake County, Illinois.

suspicions intensify, and he radios Max Hunter, the dispatcher at Lowell police post, to check the registration.

As Hunter hears the driver's profile, he realizes that it matches the wanted notice of "Larry Eyler—wanted for possible suspect in murder cases," which was posted on the clipboard of the day's assignments. Hunter excitedly informs Buehrle of the match, and Buehrle immediately calls the shift supervisor for instructions. The supervisor, John Pavlakovic, says to get Eyler and Hayward to the post for interrogation and to impound the vehicle, but says nothing about arresting the two men.

In the meantime, two officers join Buehrle on the scene, and Eyler and Hayward are patted down in search of weapons, handcuffed, and placed in different police vehicles. One of the officers searches the pick-up and finds the bag with the ropes and tape, which Buehrle identifies as the one he saw the men carrying. Hayward breaks down and tells them that Eyler offered him $100 for bondage sex. Eyler and Hayward are read the *Miranda* warnings but are not told whether they are under arrest or on what charges.

At the post, the local officers do not know what to do with Eyler and Hayward. The wanted notice about the "possible suspect" does not include any orders or directions about what to do with the suspect, so they put Eyler in a cell and urgently ask the task force to come and deal with the situation. Love and two other task force officers fly in by helicopter, and Love starts questioning Eyler, asking about his sexual preferences. Eyler refuses to talk about this subject but is otherwise very cooperative, answering any question and agreeing to virtually all of the officers' requests, including a search of his pick-up truck. Eyler denies any involvement in any murders.

An officer from the post comes in to give back the belongings taken from Eyler before he was put in the cell. One of the task force officers glances at Eyler's boots and suspects that they match the footprints taken at Calise's murder scene. Pavlakovic asks Eyler if the police may keep the boots, and Eyler agrees.

In the meantime, police technicians search the truck for fingerprints and take ink impressions from the tires. They find Eyler's knife with blood on it. When Eyler hears about it, he says, "If it's got human blood, it's mine. I cut myself and went to County Hospital."[6]

FIGURE 7.5.
Eyler's boots and knife, containing blood matching Ralph Calise's; Eyler's truck tire matching the cast from the crime scene. Police photos.

Love is concerned about Eyler being held for so long without being charged, because it could be viewed as an illegal arrest. "You've got to charge him," he tells Pavlakovic. "Soliciting for prostitution isn't much, but it's all we've got."

Pavlakovic refuses, saying, "Bond's one hundred dollars, and Eyler's got a one-hundred-dollar bill. What would be the point?"[7] Tension builds up between the local and task force officers, time drags on, and still no charges are brought. Eventually, at about 7 P.M., twelve hours after being stopped by Officer Buehrle, Eyler is told that he can take his pick-up truck and go. Shortly after Eyler leaves the Lowell post, officers from Lake County arrive and are angry to hear that Eyler was not charged and was released.

The next morning, October 1, Love and another officer come to David Little's apartment with a search warrant based on the previous day's incident and questioning. Eyler and Little, who are in the apartment, are cooperative and agree to the search. The officers take many of Eyler's personal items, as well as telephone bills and credit cards. At police headquarters, a study of the phone bills reveals that Eyler made calls to Little and Dobrovolskis from pay phones near the scenes of at least nine murders attributed to the "Highway

FIGURE 7.6.
Members of the Central Indiana Multi-Agency Investigation Team. *Left to right*: James Rhineberger, Sergeant Frank Love, and William "Billy Bob" Newman. Photo by Paul Klatt.

FIGURE 7.7.
David Schippers, a
Chicago criminal defense
lawyer, represented
Eyler in the Calise
murder proceedings and
during the suppression
hearings and trial for the
murder of Danny
Bridges. Courtesy David
Schippers.

Killer" and just a short time after the murders
were committed. Likewise, a study of the credit
card records reveals that Eyler bought gas near
some of the murder scenes. In the following weeks,
three additional searches of Little's apartment are
made; his pick-up truck is taken, so that new tire
impressions can be made; and the police take from
Eyler blood and hair samples.

Eyler's boots, knife, and pick-up tires are sent
to police and F.B.I. crime laboratories. The F.B.I.
lab technician finds human blood inside Eyler's
boots. The blood type is Calise's, which is different
from Eyler's. The Indiana State Police crime lab
gets the same results for the blood on the knife. In
addition, Eyler's boots and pick-up tires exactly
match prints taken where Calise's body was
found. Eyler is arrested and charged with Ralph
Calise's murder; he cannot pay the release bond,
which is set at $1 million.

Little and Eyler's family hire David Schippers,
a Chicago attorney, to represent Eyler. Schippers
studies the case and decides to file pretrial suppression motions based mainly on the contention
that Eyler was illegally arrested on September 30.
Among other things, the motions seek (1) to
suppress the evidence seized, and the statements made in the Lowell police
post, on September 30; (2) to quash the search warrant of October 1 and to
suppress the evidence seized based on that warrant; (3) to suppress evidence
seized on October 3, meaning Eyler's pick-up truck; and (4) to quash three
other search warrants executed in October and November, under which the
samples of Eyler's hair and blood, among other things, were taken.

The pretrial hearings on these motions revolve around whether the war-
rantless search and seizure conducted on September 30 were lawful under the
Supreme Court's 1968 decision in *Terry v. Ohio*. Under *Terry*, the police can
briefly detain and search someone—an activity that came to be known as a
"*Terry* stop"—based on a "reasonable suspicion" of criminal activity, which
is a lower standard than the "probable cause" usually required for a full-
fledged arrest.

At the hearing, the prosecutor contends that Buehrle justifiably pulled
Eyler over for a parking violation, then came to identify Eyler as a murder
suspect, which allowed for a *Terry* stop for further investigation. Even if the

stop was technically improper, the state claims, Buehrle acted in good faith and not with any intent to harass Eyler or violate his rights. The prosecutor also argues for application of the "inevitability exception," which allows the admission of evidence gathered from an illegal search if the evidence would have been discovered anyway.

Defense attorney Schippers argues that "if the State's attorney's theory is adopted, the police may grab anybody they will on any type of pretext whatsoever. And if they luck out and during the course of their investigation, no matter how long it takes, they come up with the same probable cause for some kind of arrest, then that will 'legitimize' the original detention."

The judge rules that although the original stop was valid under *Terry,* there was no legal justification for taking Eyler into custody after that stop. Therefore, "his seizure was, and seizure of his person, and his personal property and his truck was, at this point, illegal." Although an initial *Terry* stop was justified, the bounds of such a stop were exceeded, and though not formally charged, Eyler was effectively arrested without probable cause. The judge particularly criticizes the search made by officers at the scene when the bag with the ropes and tape was found:

> This was not a search incident to a valid arrest, it was not a search where, under the circumstances, it was valid for purposes of protection of the officers, it was not a search where the officers had any probable cause to believe contraband or evidence of a crime was present at that time in the vehicle. Therefore, the seizure of that particular bag from the truck was clearly illegal and violative of the Constitution.

The judge holds that everything done on September 30, 1983, including the seizure of Eyler's boots and knife, stemmed directly from the initial illegal arrest. He rejects the state's arguments that the officers' conduct was acceptable because they acted in good faith and that there was independent probable cause to arrest Eyler for patronizing a prostitute. Accordingly, the judge grants the motions to suppress the evidence gathered on September 30.

As for the October 1 search and the evidence it produced, after excluding the illegally obtained earlier evidence from the affidavit supporting the

FIGURE 7.8.
Ray McKoski, who headed the Lake County state's attorney team that handled the suppression hearing in the case against Eyler for his killing of Calise, 1984. Courtesy Judge Ray McKoski.

search warrant, the judge rules that there is no longer probable cause to support the warrant. Accordingly, he rules that anything seized in the October 1 search was also illegally obtained and must be suppressed. But as to the evidence seized and statements made on October 3, the judge applies the inevitable-discovery doctrine, concluding that the police would have seized the truck even without using the illegally obtained information.

The state's attorney is stunned. The court has suppressed all of the most important evidence—the knife and the boots with Calise's blood on them and the phone and credit card bills found on October 1—making it impossible to prosecute the case effectively. The tires, though matching the cast prints taken from the murder scene, are by themselves too circumstantial to uphold a murder conviction. The state plans to appeal the judge's rulings, but that process will take a long time.

Following the decision, Schippers requests release on bond, and Judge William Block sets it at $10,000. Eyler is free to go. Sheriff Robert Babcox watches Eyler get into a car, together with his mother and attorneys, and drive off toward Chicago. "He is freed to kill," says Babcox. "Hell, it's only a matter of time."

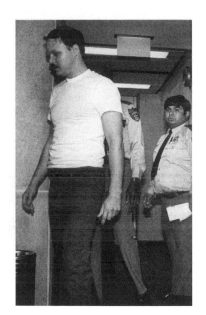

FIGURE 7.9.
Eyler leaves Judge William Block's courtroom in Waukegan, Illinois. He then asserts his innocence at a news conference, November 2, 1983. *Daily Herald* photo.

Under the bond terms, Eyler cannot leave Illinois. On February 29, Little comes from Terre Haute and signs a rent application for an apartment at 1628 West Sherwin Avenue. Schippers offers Eyler a job painting his offices. Eyler does a good job and receives more opportunities, but he also returns to his old friends and habits. The relationship with Dobrovolskis starts anew, but with the same friction: the telephone "screaming sessions," the jealousy, the animosity between Little and Dobrovolskis with the attendant anxiety for Eyler.

In early April 1984, a teenage drifter called Cowboy disappears from the streets of uptown Chicago. Some time after that, a homeless person finds a pale human hand while going through the trash in a dumpster behind Eyler's apartment. He runs to the nearest phone and dials 911. The police dispatcher thinks he is a lunatic or a joker and hangs up.

In July, Schippers succeeds in forcing the police to return the pick-up truck. Soon, Eyler re-

FIGURE 7.10.
Danny Bridges's
dismembered body is
found in garbage bags in
a dumpster behind
Eyler's Chicago
apartment building.
Photo by Robyn
Ross/WMAQ.

turns to his nightly rides, although he cannot cross the state line. On Friday, August 17, Little comes for a weekend visit, which sets off a series of fights between Eyler and Dobrovolskis. After Little leaves, a stressed and infuriated Eyler gets in his pick-up to cruise the night.

Searching the streets for prey, Eyler finds Danny Bridges, a fifteen-year-old prostitute working the street. Eyler picks him up and they go back to Eyler's apartment. Eyler promises Bridges extra money for bondage sex, and Bridges agrees. When Eyler ties Bridges with a rope and then forcefully gags his mouth, Bridges becomes scared and starts to resist, but Eyler hits him hard on his right eye and stuns him. Then Eyler finishes tying Bridges up and unveils his torture kit; he uses his butcher knife and a newly added awl to cut Bridges and puncture his chest, ultimately perforating the heart and left lung, killing him.[8]

EXCLUSIONARY RULES

The so-called Fourth Amendment exclusionary rule provides that when police obtain evidence from an improper search or seizure, that evidence is inadmissible in a subsequent prosecution of the person whose rights were violated.[9] Other, similar exclusionary rules prevent admission of criminal confessions obtained in violation of the Fifth Amendment or of the warning rules established in *Miranda v. Arizona*.[10]

These rules, and the rule requiring dismissal in cases involving violations of the Sixth Amendment speedy-trial right, enforce vital constitutional protections. Yet at the same time, the remedy they employ to do so has great potential to undermine the significant competing goal of punishing the guilty, as the *Eyler* case demonstrates. However clearly the evidence may have shown that Eyler had committed several heinous murders, the judge's ruling that it was obtained illegally foreclosed its use at trial, making a conviction essentially impossible. Thus, a deviation from desert is created for offenders like Eyler, whose guilt is unquestioned and who therefore clearly merit criminal liability, yet who go unpunished because an exclusionary rule prevents use of the evidence of their crimes. (It is also worth noting that, in addition to preventing punishment of the guilty in specific cases, the exclusionary rules may also cause deviations from desert in another, less direct fashion. By directing resources toward motions to suppress that are ultimately unrelated to factual guilt or innocence, these rules may divert resources from the pursuit of vigorous defenses in cases where defendants are factually innocent.)[11]

How often exclusionary rules operate, as in *Eyler*, to prevent conviction of defendants is hotly debated. As to the *Miranda* warnings, for example, estimates of their impact vary widely. One analysis looked at numerous prior studies and concluded that *Miranda* led to lost convictions in 3.8% of all criminal cases, meaning that "[r]oughly 28,000 arrests for serious crimes of violence and 79,000 arrests for property crimes slip through the criminal justice system due to *Miranda,* and almost the same number of cases are disposed of on terms more favorable for defendants," in any given year.[12] Another analysis, though, countered that proper examination of the same studies leads to a finding that "the properly adjusted attrition rate is not 3.8 percent but *at most* only 0.78 percent . . . for the immediate post-*Miranda* period, and most likely even less today."[13] As for the Fourth Amendment exclusionary rule, the Supreme Court has cited statistics claiming that the rule causes the release of between 0.6 and 2.35% of felony arrestees—a seemingly small percentage but one that translates into a large absolute number of cases.[14] Yet the dissent in the same Supreme Court case cited other studies (and also some of the same ones) to support a smaller effect.[15] In one recent study of about 400 judges, prosecutors, and defense counsel, the respondents estimated, based on their own practical experience, that Fourth Amendment claims were offered in about 7% of all criminal cases and Fifth Amendment claims in about 4% of all cases—but estimated success rates for those claims were quite low, ranging between about 10 and 12%.[16] In any event, however frequently these rules have an impact, it is clear that the impact they have is (among other things) to frustrate the goal of imposing deserved punishment on known offenders.

A bit of clarification is in order here, for some people might contend that the source of the deviation from desert lies in the Constitution itself, rather than in the exclusionary rules that enforce its mandates. If the investigating officers had not violated the Constitution, the argument runs, they would not have obtained the evidence in the first place, so the end result would be the same: a guilty person would avoid punishment. This argument is at least partly true; obviously, the constitutional prohibition of, say, unreasonable searches and seizures places some limits on law enforcement that would not otherwise be there. Even so, the argument neglects the possibility that the officers could have obtained the evidence in question *without* violating the Constitution—and might have, had a more effective system of incentives and sanctions encouraged them to comply with the law.

Further, even where the Constitution itself operates to prevent detection of criminals, such investigative failures are distinct from the perversions of justice that the exclusionary rules foster. First, constitutionally induced failures to find offenders or evidence take place outside the system of legal adjudication, so that they do not bring the adjudicative process into disrepute. Second, in the public mind, they do not occur with respect to a specific criminal. They exist only as an abstract weakness of law enforcement generally. For both of these reasons, such failures are diffuse and invisible and relate not to particular deviations from desert but to systemic limitations on the potential to find and convict offenders. They are therefore properly seen as inherent practical restrictions on what law enforcement can achieve, similar to the budgetary constraints and other evidence-gathering problems we discussed in chapter 4. Our attention, then, is properly directed toward the exclusionary remedy, not the substantive constitutional imperatives it enforces, as a source of deviations from desert.

Those deviations are considered necessary for purposes of achieving an important goal, namely, deterring the police and other state agents from conducting unconstitutional searches and seizures or engaging in improper interrogation techniques.[17] Indeed, the Supreme Court repeatedly has noted that the rules are not directly mandated by the Constitution, but are a remedy designed to achieve the goal of preventing misconduct by police and prosecutors.[18] The deterrence objective is not the only possible justification for an exclusionary rule[19]—we discuss others below—but because the Court has relied on that particular objective when making its decisions about the rule's scope, the rule has evolved such that its current formulation is incompatible with any other basis.[20]

The same rationale underlies other related rules, such as the "fruit of the poisonous tree" doctrine, which prevents introduction not only of the evidence obtained directly as a result of the illegal activity but of any other evidence it leads to.[21] In fact, the curbing-misconduct rationale underlies the fruit-of-the-poisonous-tree rule even where the justification for denying the initially obtained evidence is not curbing misconduct but rather a concern about reliability.[22] For example, if the police beat a confession out of a murderer, the confession might be unreliable, and it makes sense to exclude it on that ground alone. But if the murderer then tells them where the bodies are hidden, the later-found bodies are quite reliable evidence, and the reliability concern alone would not warrant their exclusion.[23] (Note that the later-found bodies do *not*, however, make the confession itself any more reliable. The confession, considered *in vacuo* as a piece of evidence, is unreliable; to the extent that extrinsic evidence makes it appear more trustworthy, it is that extrinsic evidence that truly indicates the defendant's guilt and on which the prosecutor should have to rely to demonstrate that guilt.)

The curbing-misconduct rationale, then, is critical to a number of key exclusionary rules and other related rules. Yet that rationale is based on an empirical assumption—that the rules actually deter misconduct—which should require some support before it is used to justify rules known to create departures from desert. The available evidence, however, hardly suggests that the benefits of these rules in terms of curbing improper conduct offset their desert-related costs. A deterrence strategy is only effective if it creates a significant likelihood of a meaningful penalty for engaging in the conduct it aims to deter,[24] yet it remains highly uncertain whether the existing rules manage to do this. There has never been a clear demonstration that the exclusionary rule and the *Miranda* warnings have actually reduced the number of unconstitutional searches and seizures or improper interrogations.[25] Even advocates of these rules admit that there is little hard evidence of their deterrent effect, arguing instead—with some justification, admittedly—that the question of their deterrent power *vel non* is difficult and perhaps incapable of empirical demonstration.[26]

Consider, for example, the potential penalty for a police officer's failure to follow the Fourth Amendment's requirements. The exclusion of evidence against an offender is, to be sure, a significant sanction, but its costs are borne largely by society as a whole and experienced only indirectly by the officer. The officer may suffer some reputation costs when his misconduct leads an offender to go free, but the extent of such costs is unclear, as is the issue of whether the benefits of obtaining convictions using similar improper practices that go undetected in other cases offset those costs in part or in full.

Moreover, the likelihood of experiencing the cost may not be significant enough to make up for its small magnitude. Even if an exclusionary rule operates to exclude evidence, the offender may be convicted anyway, in which case the officer will think, "No harm done." Additionally, the officer may figure that there is little risk involved in conducting a search and seizure, for without the evidence obtained thereby there may be *no* chance of obtaining a conviction. And in the situations where obtaining a conviction is not the sole, or even the central, motivation for conducting the search, the officer simply will not care about the prospect of exclusion leading to acquittal. There are a variety of such situations, including:

> arrest or confiscation as a punitive sanction (common in gambling and liquor law violations), arrest for the purpose of controlling prostitutes and transvestites, arrest of an intoxicated person for his own safety, search for the purpose of recovering stolen property, arrest and search and seizure for the purpose of "keeping the lid on" in a high crime area or of satisfying public outcry for visible enforcement, search for the purpose of removing weapons or contraband such as narcotics from circulation, and search for weapons that might be used against the searching officer.[27]

The Supreme Court itself has recognized that an exclusionary rule will be "powerless to deter invasions of constitutionally guaranteed rights where the police either have no interest in prosecuting or are willing to forgo successful prosecution in the interest of serving some other goal."[28] Thus, even if the resulting evidence is likely to be excluded—in some situations, even if it is *certain* to be excluded—a police officer will often have little incentive to avoid conducting an improper search.

Yet, to make matters worse, it is *not* always certain, or perhaps even likely, that evidence will be excluded, notwithstanding an officer's constitutional violation. This might happen for any of several reasons. The police may have managed to cover up the violation or the defendant might not be aware of it or might plead guilty. Or the evidence may be admitted for some "collateral use" rather than directly to prove guilt. Illegally obtained evidence, though not admissible as part of the prosecution's case-in-chief, may nonetheless be used in some circumstances to impeach a defendant's testimony.[29] It may also be used in a sentencing hearing, grand jury proceeding, federal civil tax proceeding, or civil deportation proceeding.[30] Another possibility is that a results-oriented judge, disgusted that another clearly guilty defendant may be exonerated, will simply find that no violation occurred because there was no true "search" or "seizure" or will fit the violation into one of the ever-expanding "exceptions" to the Fourth Amendment and *Miranda* rules.[31] In a great variety of situations involving conduct in violation of a defendant's constitutional rights, then, law-enforcement officials sometimes suffer no penalty under the current remedial scheme. In sum, it is entirely possible that the exclusionary rules impose the costs of deviation from desert in return for little corresponding deterrent benefit.

But as mentioned, deterrence is not the only possible justification for the exclusionary rules and perhaps not even the best one. It may also be argued that exclusionary rules are important mechanisms for promoting the legitimacy of the criminal-justice system, insofar as they are seen as necessary means of maintaining the integrity of the judicial branch as an institution charged with upholding the Constitution. This view was emphasized in some of the Supreme Court's early exclusionary-rule cases.[32] In more recent years, however, the Court has subordinated judicial integrity concerns to, or merged them with, the goal of deterring law-enforcement abuses.[33] Accordingly, the Supreme Court has created exceptions for the rule for various situations where its deterrence value seems minimal, showing little regard for a concomitant sacrifice of judicial integrity.

Accordingly, the impact of the exclusionary rules (as they are currently formulated) on the perceived integrity of the judicial branch is likely quite attenuated; the very inconsistency of the rules themselves suggests that they do only a poor job of maintaining judicial integrity. For example, if the courts' integrity demands that they refuse to countenance, or to become complicit in, any violation of the Constitution, one would expect that the courts would exclude all such evidence, whether obtained by an official within or outside their jurisdiction and regardless of the type of proceeding in which it was to be introduced. Yet such is not the case.[34] Additionally, we would expect the existing good-faith exception to the exclusionary rule[35] to undermine judicial integrity; if the courts are supposed to forswear complicity with any violation of the Fourth Amendment, they should not care about the mental state of the officials who committed the violation.

At least as currently conceived, then, the exclusionary rules hardly seem to promote recognition of the judicial branch's integrity, and so any legitimacy cost from abandoning them altogether would likely be limited. On the other hand, great potential benefits might support expansion of the rules to properly promote the goal of integrity, if doing so would enhance the system's legitimacy. But at present, the rules seem constructed to maximize their own cost and minimize their own benefit: they clearly sacrifice desert and are so defined as to render any possible enhancement of the system's integrity negligible, in the name of serving a deterrence goal whose basis is empirical, yet unproved, both in terms of absolute effect and of relative advantage over other methods.

The exclusionary remedy, then, is troublesome in terms of desert and questionable in its deterrent effect. Moreover, it may be counterproductive in terms of protection of the underlying right, to the extent that the unappealing prospect of imposing the remedy discourages courts from finding any violation of the right.[36] Indeed, one key question regarding the exclusionary rules and the speedy-trial rules we discuss below is whom these powerful remedies deter more effectively: the police and prosecutors, from engaging in wrongful conduct, or the courts, from finding that such conduct amounts to a constitutional violation mandating the remedy. The first effect is the rules' aim; yet the second effect, which is the last thing the rules' advocates (or anyone else) would want, may also be as powerful, or more so.

We discuss other possible ways of implementing the exclusionary remedy at the end of this chapter, and we discuss civil alternatives to that remedy in chapter 10. As to the specific question of illegally obtained confessions (such as those resulting from *Miranda* violations), an additional potential solution also may exist: mandatory videotaping of police interrogations of suspects. Videotaped or recorded interrogation has long been advocated[37] and has been implemented for some time. Britain imposed a recording requirement in 1988,[38] and by 1990, about one in six police departments in the United States—one in three, for departments serving populations of more than 50,000—had instituted videotaping for at least some interrogations.[39] Minnesota and Alaska mandate recording of interrogations, and Texas effectively imposes a similar rule by barring admission of an oral confession unless it has been recorded.[40] Illinois recently created a statewide pilot program to videotape interrogations in all first-degree murder cases.[41] The ABA's House of Delegates recently approved a report urging law-enforcement officials to adopt videotaping.[42]

SPEEDY TRIAL

Another constitutional right rooted in notions of fair play and curbing governmental abuse and whose remedy leads to potential deviations from desert is the speedy-trial right.[43] Although mandated by the Constitution, today the right is effectively guaranteed by, and enforced under, statutes dictating the period within which a defendant must be tried.[44] The federal Speedy Trial Act, for example, requires commencement of trial within seventy days after a defendant's indictment or appearance before the court, subject to numerous exceptions that extend the period, including a catchall allowing the judge to grant a continuance that would serve the "ends of justice."[45]

Mandating the timeliness of trials is clearly a good and necessary rule—without it, the state might be able to detain prisoners indefinitely without trial. The right has two related, and important, underlying purposes: it protects against the possibility of prosecutorial gamesmanship through delay (in this respect, it operates as a sort of post-indictment "statute of limitation" requiring expeditious case management); and it protects the disruption of an individual's life occasioned by pending criminal charges, either due to direct state restrictions on liberty (such as pretrial incarceration or bail restrictions) or due to the lingering cloud of public odium hovering over the individual while charges are unresolved.[46]

Even so, as with the exclusionary rules, the remedy that typically attends a denial of the speedy-trial right or a violation of a speedy-trial statute—dismissal of the indictment with prejudice[47]—creates an unnecessary deviation from the goal of desert. (At the same time, the definition of the remedy has helped to shape the substantive contours of the right itself, perhaps harmfully, because the severity of the remedy may encourage courts to read the underlying right more narrowly.)[48] Indeed, the speedy-trial remedy is more powerful than the exclusionary remedy, as it leads to a complete dismissal of charges, rather than merely to the exclusion of evidence in a criminal proceeding.

Additionally, as with the Fourth Amendment exclusionary rule, the speedy-trial remedy is vastly more likely to benefit the guilty than the innocent, at least in its direct ramifications. The guilty suspect released because of a speedy-trial right violation has obviously escaped the likelihood of conviction and punishment. But what of the innocent person who would have been acquitted in any event? Had that person been tried in a timely fashion, he would have obtained the same result as attended the speedy-trial claim—release from custody—but he would have obtained it earlier. What does that person receive for having his release delayed? At present, nothing.

There is no particular reason to think that dismissal with prejudice is "the only possible remedy"[49] for a violation of the speedy-trial right.[50] Maintaining the right, but substituting alternate remedies for a violation, would preserve basic fairness and generate disincentives for prosecutors to game the system without creating such an extreme distortion from the goal of desert.[51] To prevent prosecutorial gamesmanship,[52] as well as to minimize or redress infringement on liberty, the system could provide for release from pretrial confinement,[53] money damages,[54] a reduction in sentence,[55] dismissal without prejudice (an option allowed as a remedy for federal Speedy Trial Act violations, though not constitutional violations),[56] or some combination of these, as the circumstances warrant and allow. Because the right itself serves multiple goals—so that violations of the right can vary in both type and extent[57]—courts should be free to craft a specific remedy to a specific violation. And, as important, allowing more flexible remedies would make courts more likely to recognize the presence of a speedy-trial violation in the first place.[58]

Unlike the double-jeopardy and incompetency rules, for which there are no obvious alternative remedies but to forgo or delay prosecution, respectively, the exclusionary rules and the speedy-trial remedy are not the exclusive methods available to safeguard the interests they protect. We have already discussed various alternative remedies for the speedy-trial right; some of these remedies could also be used to replace the exclusionary rules and are discussed more thoroughly in chapter 10. Because such viable alternatives exist—and also, in the case of the exclusionary rules, because there is no clear indication that the rules effectively safeguard the relevant interests to begin with—the existing remedies are more likely to undermine than to enhance the system's moral credibility and its legitimacy.

EYLER AFTERMATH

Eyler uses a hacksaw to cut up Bridges's already mutilated body, which he then puts in large gray garbage bags. This takes him until the afternoon, when he takes the bags out to the dumpster of the next building. Because the bags are heavy, it takes him a few trips. Both the janitor for Eyler's building, Al Burdicki, and the janitor at another neighboring building see Eyler taking garbage bags past the dumpsters for his own building to throw them into the dumpster next door. Back in the apartment, Eyler repaints the walls to cover up the blood.

Early Tuesday morning, the janitor at the neighboring building sees the heavy gray bags in his dumpster and, knowing they do not belong to his tenants, rips one open. Inside he sees the upper part of a human leg. He calls the police, and the responding officer talks with him and several other janitors, who identify Eyler as the one who dumped the bags. More officers arrive, and one of them remembers that Eyler is a suspected serial killer. The officers find and arrest Eyler, then seal the area.

Later, the officers come back with a search warrant. The apartment looks clean and tidy, but a methodical search produces abundant evidence: the body is identified, the hacksaw and awl are found, and traces of Bridges's blood are found all over the apartment. Two of Eyler's fingerprints are found on one of the bags, one of them on its inside. On Schippers's orders, Eyler makes no statement and offers no explanation for the evidence.

The multiple counts against Eyler, including murder and aggravated kidnapping, mean that he faces the death penalty. The case receives wide media coverage. Bridges's funeral, his horrible death, and the way Eyler previously evaded prosecution draw a lot of public attention. The details of the overwhelming evidence connecting Eyler to Bridges's murder become widely known.

FIGURE 7.11.
Police and sanitation workers search for evidence after a young man's body parts are found behind Eyler's residence in Chicago, August 21, 1984. Photo by Howard Greenblatt.

Against this background, an Illinois appellate court hears the state's appeal from the earlier decision to suppress evidence in the Calise murder case. On April 26, 1985, the court, by a vote of 2–1, denies the appeal and affirms the lower court's ruling.

At the trial for the Bridges murder, Little testifies for the state. Eyler does not testify. The jury convicts on all counts, and Eyler receives a death sentence.

Eyler changes representation, and his new lawyer, Kathleen Zellner, cuts a deal with the State's Attorney's Office in Indiana. In exchange for the state's promise not to pursue the death penalty, Eyler gives a full confession to Steven Agan's murder, including detailed testimony asserting that Little also participated. Eyler pleads guilty, and on December 28, 1990, exactly eight years after Agan's body was found, he is sentenced to sixty years in prison. Little is also indicted and tried, but despite Eyler's testimony as the main prosecution witness, the jury is unconvinced and acquits Little.

Zellner also tries to make a deal with the Illinois State's Attorney's Office. In exchange for commuting the death sentence to life imprisonment, Eyler offers to confess to twenty unsolved murders and to name his accomplices in some of the murders. The Cook County state's attorney rejects the offer, calling it "extortion of the most venal and gruesome nature" and adding that he will not let Eyler benefit from being a mass murderer.

In addition, Zellner appeals the conviction in the Bridges murder case. The appeal is pending before the Illinois Supreme Court when, on Sunday, March 6, 1994, Eyler dies in the infirmary at Pontiac Correctional Center from AIDS he contracted in 1984.[59]

. . .

The Fourth and Fifth Amendment exclusionary rules seek to deter improper behavior by police and other law-enforcement officials when they investigate crimes. The prohibition against double jeopardy at issue in the Ignatow case below, on the other hand, prevents improper prosecutions and therefore applies to a different set of officials at a

FIGURE 7.12.
Eyler arrested, 1984.
Courtesy Court TV.

different point in the criminal-justice process. Even so, the underlying situation is the same: a rule designed to curb governmental overreaching that will potentially prevent deserved punishment.

PICTURES IN THE HEATING DUCT

Since divorcing his wife of thirteen years (and gaining custody of their three children) in 1973, Melvin Ignatow has become more cocky and flashy. He wears expensive jewelry, drives a Corvette, has his hair dyed and permed, belongs to singles clubs, and dates younger women. A college dropout, he works for an import-export firm in Louisville, Kentucky, which is where he met Mary Ann Shore. The two have dated for ten years, during which time Mary Ann has cared for Ignatow's children when he traveled on business. But now, in September 1986, a friend of the forty-eight-year-old Ignatow has set him up on a blind date with thirty-four-year-old Brenda Schaefer, an X-ray technician in the office of Dr. William Spalding. Ignatow's friend is dating Schaefer's best friend, Joyce Smallwood. The couples double-date for a river cruise on Ignatow's thirty-two-foot boat.

Schaefer is also divorced. She married Charles Van Pelt in December 1971, but the marriage began to crumble after a few years, in part because of problems with physical intimacy. Although Brenda liked to kiss and hug her husband, she was very inhibited with respect to the physical act of making love. They divorced after four years, after which, like Ignatow, Schaefer changed her appearance and lifestyle. She had plastic surgery on her nose and breasts, had her teeth straightened, and began to frequent singles bars and date men with money who would buy her jewelry and take her on trips.

Ignatow and Schaefer's relationship becomes serious, and on Valentine's Day 1987, Ignatow proposes. Ignatow gives Schaefer a custom-designed 2.3-carat engagement ring, but they do not set a wedding date. Ignatow is thrilled about his involvement with this younger, beautiful woman, describing their relationship as an "ego trip,"[60] yet he continues to have sexual encounters with Mary Ann Shore, who is bitter about being dumped for Schaefer. Schaefer's work schedule usually permits her to see Ignatow only on weekends, and several of Schaefer's coworkers and friends believe her relationship with Ignatow has more to do with her material needs than any emotional attachment to him.

Schaefer becomes increasingly depressed. Coworkers at Dr. Spalding's office notice that her work is suffering and that she seems very nervous. Schaefer tells many friends and family that she has come to dislike and to fear Ignatow and that she intends to break off her engagement. She tells Linda Love that one time she woke up with Ignatow leaning over her with a rag doused in chloroform. When asked what he was doing, he said that he was trying to help her sleep. Schaefer confides to some that Ignatow has oc-

FIGURE 7.13.
Mel Ignatow and Brenda Schaefer as a couple. Courtesy Schaefer family.

casionally forced her to take "sex drugs"[61] and that after taking the pills, she awakes without clothing or any idea of what has happened.

Meanwhile, Ignatow complains to Shore that Schaefer is "frigid" and that he wants to hold a "sex-therapy" session at Shore's home "to bring [Schaefer] out of that."[62] The session is scheduled for Saturday, September 24, 1988. Ignatow also asks Shore to help him dig a hole behind her house. She objects, telling him that she does not want to be part of whatever it is he plans to do. Ignatow assures Shore that he only intends to scare Schaefer, and Shore acquiesces. The pair test Shore's house to see if screams inside the house can be heard outside.

The Wednesday before Ignatow's planned "therapy" session, Schaefer tells the women at the office that she has left Ignatow. He calls her at work that Friday and becomes belligerent when told she is busy, so Schaefer reluctantly accepts the call and says to him, "I told you never to call me again."[63] Schaefer later tells a coworker that she intends to meet Ignatow the next day to give him back his jewelry and fur coat, adding that she is frightened of Ignatow. That night, Schaefer speaks with her sister-in-law and tells her that she suspects Ignatow has been following her home from work. She also says she has plans to see Dr. Jim Rush, her former serious romantic interest,

FIGURE 7.14.
Mary Ann Shore
testifying in court. Photo
by Michael Hayman,
© *Courier-Journal.*

that Sunday. (Meanwhile, that afternoon, Ignatow brings a shovel, a wooden paddle, a camera, film, plastic garbage bags, tape, a pair of gloves, rope, and a bottle of chloroform, as well as some sex toys, to Shore's house.)

By 4:00 P.M. on Saturday, Schaefer picks up Ignatow for their last meeting. They go to Gold Star Chili at Hike's Point, where Ignatow suggests that they visit a friend of his who has expressed interest in buying Schaefer's jewelry. Around 5:30 or 6:00 P.M., Ignatow and Schaefer arrive at Shore's home. Ignatow sits Schaefer down on the couch and tells her about his "sex-therapy" idea. She gets up to leave, but he forces her back down on the couch, telling her that "she [needs] to have this because she [is] just very cold-natured."[64]

He has a checklist on a yellow piece of paper, listing all of the steps of his "sex therapy." First, he forces Schaefer to stand against a wall and disrobe while he takes pictures. Next, Ignatow strips off his clothing, leaving on only his dark socks, ties Schaefer to a coffee table, and forces her to have anal sex for two hours. Ignatow orders Shore to photograph him and Schaefer, but tells Shore to leave his head out of the pictures. Ignatow then moves Schaefer to the bedroom, where he forces more sex acts on her, while Shore takes more pictures and participates in Schaefer's abuse. Schaefer cries during the assault and at one point, starts screaming as Ignatow strikes her with the wooden paddle. Shore, eventually too scared and disgusted by Ignatow's further indecencies to continue, flees to the kitchen, leaving Schaefer in the bedroom with Ignatow.

Ignatow pours chloroform onto a handkerchief and covers Schaefer's mouth and nose with it. Unsure of whether Schaefer is dead, Ignatow ties a rope tightly around her neck to choke her, then emerges from the bedroom and announces to Shore that Schaefer is dead. Shore enters the bedroom and sees Schaefer on the bed with her hands tied and a rope tight around her neck. Ignatow folds Schaefer's body into the fetal position and ties it tightly with ropes. Ignatow and Shore then wrap Schaefer's body in garbage bags and bury her in the backyard.

Ignatow changes his clothes, throwing away the dirty ones. He puts the incriminating materials in the trunk of Shore's car. He then punctures the rear tire of Schaefer's car and pushes a nail into the hole. Wearing gloves, he gets into Schaefer's car and drives to Interstate 64. Shore follows him in her car. Ignatow leaves the car on the side of the highway and tells Shore to drive him home. Alone at his house, Ignatow puts Schaefer's jewelry and the photographic film of the torture in a plastic bag and tapes it to the inside of a floor heating duct.

The next morning, at 6:08 A.M., a police officer spots Schaefer's car on the shoulder near the Breckinridge Lane overpass. The car has a flat right rear tire, a broken rear window, a missing radio, and an unlocked passenger side door.

There is damage to the left rear corner of the trunk lid, and the trunk lock has been pried. The back seat and the outside of the car are splattered with what looks like blood.

At noon, having discussed Brenda's apparent disappearance with her mother, Essie, earlier that morning, Ignatow visits the Schaefers and spends the afternoon with them. He seems nervous and jittery, and occasionally he whimpers like a child, but he does not shed tears. Schaefer's brother Tom and his girlfriend, Linda Love, go to the police station and meet with detective Jim Wesley. Love tells Wesley everything Schaefer has said about Ignatow and his creepy behavior, so Wesley decides to interview Ignatow. Wesley and two other officers question Ignatow at his home, where he carefully recounts the events of the previous day—speaking, oddly, from prepared notes. He tells the officers that Schaefer picked him up at 3:00 Saturday afternoon and they went for a drive. He fills them in on the details of the drive, mentioning every stop. The officers leave, feeling very unsatisfied and agreeing that Ignatow seems cold and methodical.

The investigation continues with little progress. Ignatow is asked to take a lie-detector test, but he refuses, claiming that such a test would put too much stress on his weak heart. Other people come forth with stories of Schaefer's whereabouts on the day of her disappearance that conflict with Ignatow's

FIGURE 7.15.
"Missing Person" poster.
Courtesy Schaefer
family.

$25,000 REWARD

BRENDA SUE SCHAEFER

Missing since Saturday Evening,
September 24, 1988
Age 36 years   Height 5'4''   Weight 110 Lbs.
Eyes Brown   Hair Brown
Last seen wearing a Light colored short sleeve
sweater, blue jeans and red shoes.

claims. Members of the Kentucky Rescue Association spend eighty hours searching for Schaefer's body in the Ohio River, but come up empty-handed. Dr. Spalding starts a reward fund for information on Schaefer's disappearance that grows to $16,000 in just two weeks. Ignatow does not contribute to the fund.

Investigators receive useful information from one of Schaefer's coworkers, who happens to know a hair stylist who knows Shore and to whom Shore had confided about Ignatow's control over her and her inability to get over her relationship with him. Suspicion of Shore's involvement in Schaefer's disappearance is heightened by information from Robert Spoelker, who pays Shore $125 a week to baby-sit his children. Spoelker's records show that Shore did not work on Saturday, September 24. A background check also reveals five arrest warrants for bad checks. Wesley and the F.B.I. decide that the bad-check charges may be used as leverage if Shore refuses to cooperate.

Shore comes to the police station for questioning and takes a polygraph test, which she fails. When Wesley confronts Shore about her test results, she becomes agitated and refuses to say anything else. Wesley allows her to leave but has a police officer follow her. That night, Shore is seen walking in the rain with Ignatow. Wesley is notified at home of the situation. Unmarked police cars pull up next to the couple. Ignatow remains calm and tells Shore to cooperate. At the station, Wesley grills Shore, demanding to know what she knows. He tells her that he knows Ignatow killed Schaefer and that Ignatow does not care about her, but Shore does not budge. Wesley can sense that she has something she wants to say so he pulls out all the stops, threatening her with the bad-check charges. Still, she does not cooperate. At 12:45 A.M. on February 14, 1989, Shore is fingerprinted and put in jail on five warrants for bad checks under $100.

Some months later, Shore is called to testify before a federal grand jury. U.S. Attorney Scott Cox asks Shore how many times she had seen Schaefer before the disappearance. Shore replies that she had seen Schaefer only once. When Cox later asks what Schaefer looked like the last time she saw her, Shore responds, "You mean the last time?"[65] Cox then points out the discrepancy in Shore's statements as Shore turns pale and leaves the jury room. On January 9, 1990, Shore confesses to the F.B.I. and the police that she was present when Ignatow killed Schaefer at Shore's rented house. She leads the police to the woods behind her house, where she and Ignatow buried Schaefer, and also agrees to wear a concealed microphone for a conversation with Ignatow. In return, the authorities agree to charge Shore only with tampering with physical evidence.

Shore tapes a conversation with Ignatow in which he orders her to resist investigators' requests for a lie-detector test and refers to Schaefer's burial site, by way of assuring Shore that the body will not be found. The next day, Ignatow is arrested and charged with murder, kidnapping, sodomy, sexual abuse, robbery, and tampering with physical evidence.

On January 10, after hours of digging in Shore's backyard, the police bring in Bingo, a German shepherd. Within fifteen minutes, Bingo picks up a scent, and after the officers dig for a few minutes, their shovels hit a black plastic bag. A smaller plastic bag is found a couple of hours later. The bags are brought to the autopsy room of Humana Hospital University, where the medical examiner removes Schaefer's clothes from the smaller bag, then turns to the larger bag. The body is wrapped in four overlapping plastic bags sealed by tan plastic tape. Her skin is badly decomposed and her facial features have disappeared. A forensic odontologist helps to identify Schaefer by her teeth.

On December 2, 1991, the day before jury selection begins for Ignatow's murder trial, Mary Ann Shore pleads guilty to tampering with physical evidence. Ignatow's trial proceeds until December 21, when the jurors begin deliberating. Most believe that Ignatow is involved somehow, but there are problems they can't get over. First, Shore does not seem to be a reliable witness. Ignatow's lawyer has done a good job portraying her as a jealous, vindictive ex-girlfriend. Second, the thirteen-minute taped conversation between Shore and Ignatow has turned out to be a disappointment for prosecutors. The defense argues that Ignatow is simply talking about a safe that he had loaned to Shore. Ultimately, the jury acquits Ignatow of kidnapping and murdering Schaefer.

On February 3, 1992, Mary Ann Shore is sentenced to the maximum five years in prison for tampering with physical evidence.

On October 1, 1992, Ronald and Judith Watkins, the current owners of Ignatow's former home, are changing the carpet. In a plastic bag taped to the

FIGURE 7.16.
Diagram of the hallway of Mel Ignatow's home where photos of Brenda Schaefer's sexual torture are discovered in a heating duct hidden beneath a carpet. Court discovery document.

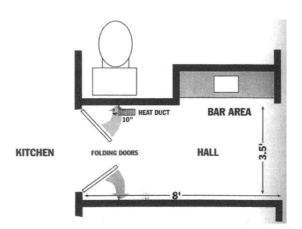

inside of a floor duct, they discover undeveloped film and jewelry and notify the F.B.I. The film is developed, revealing about 100 pictures of "sexual acts, sadomasochistic bondage, disrobing, and torture of Brenda Sue Schaefer."[66] But Ignatow has already been acquitted for Schaefer's murder, and the double-jeopardy bar prohibits prosecutors from trying Ignatow again.[67]

DOUBLE JEOPARDY

Sometimes a just outcome must be sacrificed to prevent what seems like manifest procedural unfairness, even if the unfairness works no actual prejudice to the defendant's case. An example is the constitutional rule proscribing double jeopardy, which is applied even if the case against the defendant is now clear. Another rule, which prevents trial when a defendant is not competent to participate in the proceedings, is more directly related to unfairness that leads to prejudice. Both of these rules—double jeopardy and incompetency to stand trial—impose valuable and necessary limitations on the exercise of the government's prosecutorial power. Still, the rules' potential to lead to serious failures of justice, as highlighted by the *Ignatow* case, suggests the exploration of limitations on each of them that might enable the system to avoid some of the most serious failures of justice while also satisfying the underlying fairness concerns they protect.

The ban on double jeopardy, which prevents a person from being tried twice for the same offense,[68] serves two purposes: (1) ensuring against prosecutorial harassment, thus guaranteeing finality and repose for the defendant following a single criminal proceeding; and (2) promoting accuracy—by preventing the state's representatives from simply retrying a defendant until they get a conviction.[69] Only the first of these two goals may conflict with desert; to the extent that the rule promotes reliability, it advances desert. Yet the two goals are intertwined. In many cases, we cannot know whether the initial acquittal or the later conviction truly captures the truth of the situation. Allowing multiple "dress rehearsals" until the prosecution "gets it right" might actually enable prosecutors to induce a jury to get it wrong.

The extent to which the double-jeopardy bar prevents desirable prosecutions is unclear. As with statutes of limitation, statistics regarding the actual frequency of the bar's operation are extremely difficult to obtain. In one six-state survey of about 400 judges, prosecutors, and defense attorneys, the respondents estimated that the double-jeopardy bar plays a role in about two to three of every thousand criminal cases, either by providing an asserted defense or by causing prosecutors to forgo prosecution.[70] Firmer statistics are difficult to come by, as the rule's main impact is to prevent the initiation of the second prosecution (rather than to cause acquittal or dismissal of a pending prosecution), and there is no reason for prosecutors to maintain records indicating the cases resulting in acquittal for which they would have brought renewed prosecutions if they could. Moreover, it is not clear that lifting the bar would have uniformly good consequences in terms of achieving desert. Perhaps the existence of the prohibition encourages prosecutors to bring their best possible case the first time around, and it may also decrease the risk of prosecutorial gamesmanship, thereby advancing desert.

At the same time, cases such as Ignatow's offer obvious reasons to wish that double-jeopardy protections could be more narrowly drawn. It is almost certain that a second prosecution against Ignatow, in which the pictures of him torturing Brenda were admitted, would lead to a conviction. It is also clear that in Ignatow's case, if a second prosecution were allowed, it would not occur because overzealous prosecutors were hell-bent on tormenting Ignatow or because they had used the first trial as a dress rehearsal for a later chance to prosecute again. Rather, the reason for the second prosecution would be simply that new evidence has suddenly emerged—evidence that the authorities did not know about and could not have found through ordinary diligence the first time around.

But while the failure of justice in Ignatow's case is hard to accept, there are only limited ways to gain the benefits of the double-jeopardy rule except to honor the bar even where it frustrates justice, as in *Ignatow*. It seems nearly certain that a world without a double-jeopardy rule would have a countervailing set of injustices that, on balance, would be unacceptable. Importantly, where double jeopardy leads to deviations from desert, there commonly is no alternate remedy; modifying the remedy to allow a second prosecution would destroy the substance of the right.

Even so, the substance of the right itself admits of a variety of readings under Supreme Court precedent, some of which are more consistent with the goal of desert than others. Given these numerous and equally plausible alternative readings, as one commentator has noted, "we can isolate the type of government harassment we wish the Clause to guard against, and this, in turn, can inform our definition of [a] 'double jeopardy offense' in a modern world."[71] An interpretation seeking both to promote desert and to prevent prosecutorial abuse would strive to minimize the prosecution's capacity to harass or engage in dress rehearsals while maintaining some flexibility to allow for the prosecution and punishment of blameworthy offenders.[72] More specifically, a reading of the Double Jeopardy Clause seeking to maximize the promotion of desert would likely tend to define strictly the boundaries of jeopardy—that is, to impose specific requirements governing when jeopardy "attaches"[73] or, probably more important, when it ends. A desert-based reading might impose a categorical bar on reprosecution only where the first trial resulted in a verdict. Where proceedings are terminated prior to a verdict but after jeopardy has attached (as with a dismissal or mistrial), there might be a more flexible rule for determining whether the bar should apply—for example, creating a presumption of finality that the prosecution may overcome by demonstrating that the premature termination caused no prejudice.[74] A desert-based reading might also be sympathetic to notions of "continuing jeopardy" that might, for example, consider allowing prosecutorial appeals before a verdict of acquittal is held to be final.[75]

Additionally, a desert-sensitive reading of the double-jeopardy bar might refuse to consider a defendant who obtained acquittal by means of fraud.[76] Such a rule might apply to a defendant like Ignatow, whose improper efforts to frustrate law-enforcement efforts—in ways that themselves would amount to criminal offenses, such as obstruction of justice, tampering with evidence, and perjury, of which he was eventually convicted—were central in preventing an effective prosecution in his first trial.

Of course, it would remain necessary to keep in mind and guard against the possibility of prosecutorial manipulation, which may tend to tilt the playing field and distort outcomes so that desert is *not* realized. These concerns, however, do not necessarily justify an expansive reading of the Double Jeopardy Clause, as they might also be addressed through case-by-case review under the Due Process Clause.[77]

Interestingly, the British government has recently narrowed the scope of the double-jeopardy ban—which, of course, is not a constitutional rule there, as Britain has no constitution.[78] The new UK rule applies to specified "qualifying offences"[79]—such as murder, manslaughter, kidnapping, sexual offenses, arson, and certain drug offenses[80]—and allows retrial after acquittal if the director of public prosecutions consents to having a prosecutor apply for a retrial order and if the Court of Appeal grants the application.[81] The director is to give consent to an application only if there appears to be "new and compelling evidence" against the defendant, if the retrial would be "in the public interest," and if the retrial would not violate any of the United Kingdom's treaty obligations.[82] The Court of Appeal must grant the application if satisfied that "new and compelling evidence" does exist and "if in all the circumstances it is in the interests of justice . . . to make the order."[83] Relevant considerations as to the latter requirement include the likelihood of a fair trial; the passage of time since the first trial; the likelihood that the new evidence could have been presented in the first trial, but for prosecutorial error; and the existence of any other prosecutorial failure "to act with due diligence or expedition."[84] Unusually under British law, the reform applies retrospectively, allowing a second prosecution for those who were acquitted prior to the change.[85]

Other nations are also considering such reforms. For example, in New Zealand, the Law Commission has proposed an exception to the ban for offenses whose maximum punishment exceeds fourteen years.[86] Retrial would require that an acquittee secured the acquittal through an "administration of justice" offense—such as perjury, fabricating evidence, or corrupting witnesses—and that the acquittee was then convicted of that administration offense.[87] With additional proposed qualifications similar to those in the United Kingdom—such as consideration of the passage of time and "the interests of justice"—the New Zealand High Court would be entitled, in such cases, to order a second trial.[88] A Criminal Proceedings Bill including the proposed change, along with a proposal to modify the jury unanimity requirement to allow conviction based on an 11–1 vote, was introduced to Parliament on June 22, 2004, and is currently pending.[89]

We discuss these alternative interpretations of the U.S. rule and proposed changes to the British and New Zealand rule for two reasons. First, they demonstrate that popular concern with the fairness and justice of results in the criminal-justice system is real and significant. But second, and equally important, they demonstrate the important point that popular and political reactions to the system's failure to achieve justice in specific cases often run the risk of being overreactions, replacing crude rules that erred in one direction with equally crude rules likely to err in the other direction. The cases we discuss in this book are precisely the kind that can lead to popular outrage and political action—and should. Yet it is crucial to recognize that the solutions to the problems these cases raise are rarely obvious or simple. To assume otherwise is to neglect the difficulty of pursuing justice itself, much less the other systemic goals we discuss in this book and, in doing so, to place justice in continued jeopardy.

IGNATOW AFTERMATH

Although his face is not shown in the newly discovered photographs, markings on his body and his watch identify the man in the pictures as Mel Ignatow "beyond any doubt." Ignatow is arrested and ordered by the court to undress and have his picture taken.

A federal grand jury indicts Ignatow for committing perjury, inducing Mary Ann Shore to commit perjury, and lying to F.B.I. agents investigating Schaefer's disappearance. The indictment charges Ignatow with lying to the

FIGURE 7.17.
Ignatow, with his
attorney, Jay Lambert,
when Ignatow is
sentenced for perjury.
Photo by Durell Hall, Jr.,
© *Courier-Journal*.

federal grand jury when he said that he did not know what happened to Schaefer's engagement ring, that the last time he saw Schaefer was September 24, 1988, after she dropped him off at his home, and that he had nothing to do with Schaefer's death.

Knowing that he is protected by the double-jeopardy provision of the Constitution's Bill of Rights, Ignatow confesses to the murder of Brenda Schaefer and pleads guilty to the perjury charges. On November 13, 1992, Ignatow is sentenced to eight years and one month in federal prison, without eligibility for parole. However, he earns a year off the sentence for good behavior, and he receives two years' credit for the time he spent in jail while awaiting the trial. He is released from prison five years later, on Halloween 1997.

In 2001, Ignatow is charged again with committing perjury, this time for his testimony during another trial—that of Dr. Spalding, who after Schaefer's disappearance threatened Ignatow and was convicted of making "terroristic threats." Ignatow is convicted and sentenced to nine years in prison. He is currently scheduled to be released in August 2007.[90]

INCOMPETENCY

Another rule that promotes fairness, but may do so at some cost to desert, is the incompetency defense. Where a defendant cannot understand the nature of the proceedings against her or adequately assist counsel in preparing a defense, such incapacity bars trial.[91] Even after trial, incompetency may bar conviction, sentencing, or execution of the sentence.[92] Although the reasons for these other incompetency bars differ from those that bar trial (they do not, for example, implicate the defendant's participation in his own defense), several jurisdictions provide a single incompetency defense that may be raised at any time during the process to bar further proceedings.[93] The defense does not present a total bar to the imposition of sanctions against criminals. One who is found incompetent to stand trial may be committed to a mental institution until such time as the defendant has gained sufficient competency to proceed, subject to certain limitations.[94]

The competency requirement has several bases. First, it derives in part from a due-process notion that it is unfair to prosecute a defendant who is unaware of the nature of the proceedings or unable meaningfully to participate.[95] The right to a fair trial, the right of the defendant to testify in his own behalf, and the right to confront witnesses all support a competency requirement.[96] The Sixth Amendment guarantee of the assistance of counsel also supports the requirement; the counsel right has little meaning if the defendant is unable to communicate with, understand, and inform counsel of matters necessary to an adequate defense.

A related justification is the need to maintain the dignity of criminal proceedings.[97] Because the rationales underlying the competency requirement include concerns other than the defendant's personal rights, the defendant may not waive the right to be competent to stand trial. Further, if the defendant is incompetent to stand trial, it is unlikely that the defendant has sufficient capacity competently to waive the right to competency.[98]

The competency requirement also stems in part from the desire to ensure accuracy and reliability in criminal proceedings. Where the defendant cannot participate in the preparation of the defense, there is increased risk of an inaccurate result.[99] The potential unreliability problem—which, after all, is rooted in a desire to achieve desert—urges the exercise of caution before making a decision to limit the scope of the defense. This concern is clearly not the only one, however, for even if there were irrefutable physical evidence of guilt, the incompetency defense would prevent punishment. Indeed, because many states (following the old common-law rule) bar the sentencing of an incompetent defendant, the incompetency defense would exist even if the defendant mounted a full defense and became incompetent only after judgment was rendered.[100]

While, to some extent, the competency requirement is meant to advance desert,[101] complete prohibition of criminal proceedings against all incompetent defendants (and their probable resulting civil commitment) can generate deviations from desert in both directions. Without trial, blameless offenders can be improperly detained and blameworthy offenders can escape the punishment they deserve.

A number of methods have been suggested for avoiding deviations from desert from a finding of incompetency. These include requiring reasonable efforts to treat the defendant and prepare him for trial,[102] and, as the Model Penal Code proposes, allowing the defendant to go forward with "any legal objection to the prosecution which is susceptible of fair determination prior to trial and without the personal participation of the defendant."[103] These procedures are sensible because, to the extent feasible, they seek to define boundaries for the incompetency defense that maximize its ability to harmonize the goal of fairness with the sometimes conflicting goal of desert.

.   .   .

A final rule, the entrapment defense, recalls the constitutional exclusionary rules in that it relates to deterrence of misconduct by the police rather than prosecutors. Here, an offender receives a defense because the police played too active a role in bringing about the offense—perhaps through a "sting" or similar operation. This defense is not mandated by the Constitution, but its underlying purpose and effect are the same as for the Fourth and Fifth Amendment rules.

A WINGED CAR POWERED BY COCAINE

Early in his career in the automotive industry, John Zachary DeLorean is recognized as a brilliant engineer. While some consider him brusque and erratic, he seems to know what people want and moves swiftly up the ranks of the Detroit elite. But by the 1970s, although successful at General Motors as one of the youngest division managers and then as the head of Pontiac, DeLorean clashes with the administration over attitude, company structure, even style of dress (he tends toward sideburns and bell-bottoms rather than blue suits). People say he has "gone Hollywood," as traveling for business brings him in contact with new social circles and the allure of sunny California.

By 1973, DeLorean, now thirty-eight years old, is divorced from his first wife, remarried, divorced from his second wife (a twenty-year-old), and married to his third wife, LA fashion model Christina Ferrare. A few months before this third marriage, he is asked to resign from GM. Though he loses his $650,000 salary, DeLorean is excited, as he plans to start his own company. He tells the press that he will make a luxury car that will be more fuel efficient and will have more safety features than any other in the market, as well as "gull-wing" doors that open from the top.

DeLorean has numerous critics, though, many of whom object to more than his lifestyle. While he advocates for various charities and is a vocal pro-

FIGURE 7.18.
John DeLorean in his high-rise Manhattan office. Photo by Woodfin Camp/
Anthony Howarth.

ponent of civil rights, he also has alienated many of the people with whom
he has worked in the past, typically over money issues. An inventor named
Peter Avrea claims that DeLorean cheated him out of hundreds of thousands
of dollars by not protecting the patents that DeLorean was hired to maintain.
A car dealer in Wichita claims that DeLorean ruined his car dealership—and
stole his gull-winged Mercedes 300SL to use as a "model."

None of this bothers DeLorean. After many years, his dream is being
achieved. In 1977, he establishes the DeLorean Motor Company and eventually decides to build its production plant in Dunmurry, Northern Ireland,
which desperately needs jobs and which lures him there with an investment
package of $134.1 million in loans from the British government. With Amer-
ican investors like Sammy Davis, Jr., seeing DeLorean's newest endeavor as
a good tax shelter, DeLorean is able to get the company started without much
of his own money.

After some early design problems, the first model, DMC-12, is finally
shipped from the company's new plant. But the technical conflicts between
the engineers whom DeLorean wooed away from GM and the new partners
he has acquired from Lotus create time and cost constraints that make it hard
to implement many of the originally planned innovations. The conflicts are
just one cause for the chronic cash shortage the factory faces. DeLorean's
tendency to mix company spending with private purchases, like a small
Nevada-based snowmobile company and art for his New York office, don't
help the beleaguered car company, either.

FIGURE 7.19.
DeLorean seated inside the DMC-12 at Earl's Court Motor Fair in London, 1981.
Photo © Hulton-Deutsch Collection/CORBIS.

Though the stainless-steel cars sell well when they first come out, the luxury-car market slows down, and some at the company grow concerned that there is a limited market for a monochrome, nonconvertible two-seater priced at $25,000, which is higher than the comparable cars by Porsche and Mercedes. The cars also have a few mechanical problems. Johnny Carson, the official spokesman for DeLorean cars, has his car break down after driving it just a few miles. When a new part is rushed over, the replacement also breaks. A man who climbs into a display vehicle at the Cleveland Museum finds that the doors won't open. He is trapped for hours.

Finally, in 1980, after providing another loan of $33 million beyond the original investment of more than $130 million, the British government makes clear that enough is enough—it will put no more money into the company. More than that, in October 1981, Prime Minister Margaret Thatcher orders a police investigation of the company's finances after an upset former employee brings copies of company memos and files to show, among other things, how casually money has been spent and that DeLorean's personal investment in the company is much less than required. The company is cleared by the British reviewers, but then the cars themselves begin to have more technical problems. In late November, the more than 2,000 DeLoreans on the road have to be recalled to correct a problem.

By January 1982, the company's finances are in dire straits. DeLorean authorizes the firing of almost half of the company's 2,600-person workforce after the British government refuses an additional loan. The government begins a new review process to determine if the company can survive at all. By February, the company is in receivership, which puts total control of the company and its finances under an appointed financier, a situation tantamount to a declaration of bankruptcy. Trying to put the best spin on it during an interview, DeLorean says he is "delighted at the outcome," explaining that the government now has to deal with the debt problem.

FIGURE 7.20. DeLorean is bombarded by the press about the health of his car company. Photo *Automotive News,* photographer Joe Wilssens.

Finally, after months of trying to find a way to keep the car company open, the British government announces in May that the factory will be closed by the end of the month. Hours later, however, DeLorean announces that he has new backers who will provide the $37 million needed to keep the plant open. He doesn't reveal the sources but says they are "an individual and a bank." Those around him have heard this kind of vague promise of funding from an unknown source before and are extremely skeptical.

By June, DeLorean seems to have run out of ideas but then thinks of the conversations he has had with his former neighbor James Timothy Hoffman. Hoffman and DeLorean are acquaintances through their sons and have discussed their respective business troubles in very general terms. While DeLorean spent years making a name for himself in the business world, Hoffman also found success—in the drug trade, dealing cocaine. Hoffman had called DeLorean earlier to interest him in investing in a drug deal. (Unknown to DeLorean, however, Hoffman was actually calling because he was caught by the F.B.I. in 1981 and has agreed to help them to find others involved in drugs in return for a reduced sentence. Realizing the importance of remaining valuable to the agency, Hoffman is always looking for someone he can turn over to the government.)

When DeLorean returns Hoffman's call in June, the conversation gets more specific. In the course of their phone call, Hoffman mentions that he has made money smuggling drugs from Colombia and Thailand. The men agree to meet on July 11 at the Marriott in Newport Beach, California, to discuss matters further. At the meeting, DeLorean brings up the idea of their transacting a drug deal. The next day, Hoffman calls his F.B.I. supervisors and tells them that John DeLorean has approached him about selling drugs.

On July 13, in the first of many taped calls, DeLorean explains to Hoffman that his company has $40 million in cars but no cash, so he would like to proceed with the proposition they discussed. During the meeting, an F.B.I. camera hidden under the table records DeLorean's muffled voice explaining that his tax man can reconstruct past records, making anything look legitimate. As the deal is explained to him, the profits from the cocaine can be channeled through Eureka Federal Savings in San Carlos, California, so it will seem legal. DeLorean, a little relieved, explains that he doesn't really care where the money comes from—it could come from drugs, organized crime, anything, as long as it eventually comes through a recognized financial institution.

On September 4, DeLorean meets with Hoffman in Washington, D.C.; unknown to DeLorean, the meeting is videotaped. DeLorean agrees to provide $1.8 million to fund a drug deal to raise the $40 million he needs to save his company. He is reassured by Hoffman's claims that he won't be easily connected to the transactions.

Hoffman warns DeLorean that he had better not agree now and try to back out later without a good reason. He follows this up with a reminder that he doesn't want DeLorean to take part in something with which he isn't comfortable, that the car maker can pull out at any time. "I won't be mad, I won't be hurt, I won't be anything," Hoffman says. "If you can get the money somewhere else and it's better circumstances, I'd say do it." But DeLorean has made up his mind. He explains that he appreciates the option to leave, but, "Well, I want to proceed."[104]

On September 8, DeLorean travels to San Carlos, California, to meet the drug dealer's crooked banker, "James Benedict"—actually, F.B.I. agent Benedict Tisa. The banker lays out a plan to include a person "very successful in bringing in cocaine."[105] This refers to William Hetrick, a fifty-year-old pilot who reportedly runs drugs and has a lifestyle clearly beyond the means of a flight-service operator with no clients. The F.B.I. considers him to be one of the major cocaine traffickers in southern California but has not been able to catch him smuggling.

DeLorean and Hoffman meet at the Bel Air Sands Hotel to discuss the details, and DeLorean talks with Hetrick; on September 28, they meet again at the Bonaventure Hotel in Washington, D.C. DeLorean is introduced to the bearded Mafia kingpin "Mr. Vicenza," actually DEA agent John Valestra.

FIGURE 7.21.
William Hetrick. *Los Angeles Times* photo by Larry Sharkey.

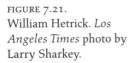

While they eat lunch, the undercover agent discusses rates of payback with DeLorean, estimating that "from that particular cocaine purchase"[106] he could have $10 million within forty-eight hours.

Trying to work out a deal, DeLorean suggests that he give Vicenza 50% ownership of DeLorean Motor Car, Inc. as collateral and then let the Mafia man buy the cocaine with his own money. In a letter dated September 29, he signs over 500 shares of DeLorean Motor Company stock to Vicenza and 5,000 to Benedict. (According to later estimates, this is his entire voting stock in the company.) From the table, DeLorean calls pilot Hetrick and says awkwardly, "They'd like to go ahead with those monkeys you had up in San Francisco."[107] "Monkey" had been used before as code for a kilo of cocaine. The plan to meet is finalized.

On Monday, October 18, Hetrick and his assistant, Steven Arrington, arrive at the Los Angeles airport with more than sixty pounds of cocaine, worth about $24 million. They are arrested immediately. Meanwhile, Hoffman calls DeLorean about the arrival of the cocaine, and DeLorean makes arrangements to fly to Los Angeles the next morning.

On the morning of October 19, the British government announces that it will close the DeLorean plant in Northern Ireland permanently. That same morning, DeLorean flies to Los Angeles to complete his part of the drug transaction. (Neither he nor the British government knows that meanwhile a legitimate banker has been desperately calling DeLorean's office. She just needs his signature to finalize a loan that could salvage the company. She is told that he is on his way to Los Angeles.)

In Los Angeles, DeLorean goes to the airport's Bel Air Sands Hotel. His room is wired and video cameras are running. Still oblivious to the set-up, when DeLorean enters the room, he is confronted with an open suitcase of cocaine and leans forward to examine it. There is about fifty-five pounds in all. In 1982, a kilo (2.2 pounds) sold for $50–60,000 to distributors and for up to $400,000 a pound at the retail level. DeLorean picks up one of the kilo bags, saying that it is better than gold. "Just in the nick of time," he beams. Glasses of champagne are passed around, and DeLorean toasts "a lot of success for everyone."

A knock at the door interrupts the celebration. Agent Jerry West enters. "I'm with the F.B.I. You are under arrest for narcotics law violations."

While the British government reels from the news of the arrest—and the fact that the DeLorean Motor Company owes more than $70 million to creditors—DeLorean is held in jail overnight. News of the arrest rocks the nation; it is even announced during the World Series game. His investors are stunned, and many realize they are ruined. On Wednesday morning, the F.B.I. files an affidavit that adds to the DeLorean charges his plans to import heroin from Thailand. He pleads not guilty to all nine counts of narcotics violations. Bail is initially set at $5 million but is raised to $10 million after prosecutors reevaluate his flight potential.

DeLorean can't raise the $500,000 cash needed for release on the $5 million bail and spends ten days in Terminal Island Federal Prison. He hires Warren Commission attorney Joseph Ball, who has a reputation for being skilled at behind-the-scenes negotiations, and Howard Weitzman, who has successfully represented Mafia figures and one of Charles Manson's family members. Weitzman eventually leads the defense team. DeLorean signs over one of his estates to pay the legal fees.

The DeLorean Motor Company files for bankruptcy and is later sold to Consolidated International Inc., which assumes about $8.7 million in debt. The Internal Revenue Service broadens its investigation of DeLorean to look into possible tax fraud. By August, 132 Oppenheimer investors have also filed suit against DeLorean and Oppenheimer for misappropriating $18.7 million collected for research and development.

After nine months in jail, on June 13, 1983, William Hetrick changes his plea to guilty and agrees to testify against DeLorean. Two weeks later, the third defendant, Arrington, also pleads guilty, though he does not agree to testify. DeLorean is left to stand trial alone.

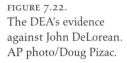

FIGURE 7.22.
The DEA's evidence
against John DeLorean.
AP photo/Doug Pizac.

The trial is postponed three months from the January 7 start date, then again in April, and again in June. Even before the trial begins, two books are published about DeLorean's life. In October, the case's publicity reaches a new level when CBS News obtains a copy of the tape of DeLorean's drug bust and shows it on the Sunday night news broadcast. The nation sees De-Lorean gleefully examining the cocaine and then being handcuffed by police.

On March 5, jury selection finally begins. Potential jurors fill out forty-page questionnaires and are interviewed individually. The trial is followed closely by many. Each morning, DeLorean arrives in court in his chief attorney's Mercedes with his wife, Christina. Legal experts speculate on what statement his fashion-model wife will make each day with her outfit, and re-porters get daily updates of her wardrobe. As he leaves the court each day, DeLorean is often greeted by well-wishers. Groups of teenagers try to get autographs.

Within the trial itself, DeLorean's defense focuses on a claim of entrapment, asserting that his criminal efforts were induced by Hoffman and other agents of the government. At the close of evidence, the judge dismisses one of the nine counts and drops two of the twenty acts, leaving the essential charges the same but sending an encouraging message to the defense.

On August 16, 1984, after twenty-nine hours of deliberations, with a break for an unrelated bomb threat, the jury acquits DeLorean of all charges, based on his entrapment claim. Greeting the press after an unusual two-hour meeting with the judge and jury, DeLorean announces that "as a Christian, I hold no animosity, no grudges."[108]

The following year—though still fighting charges of embezzlement and defending against numerous civil claims brought by various DMC creditors and others, including his own lawyers, whom DeLorean has not paid—DeLorean goes on a book tour to promote his autobiography and also announces his plans to build a new, fast luxury car.[109]

ENTRAPMENT

The defense of *entrapment* allows a person to claim that, although he did commit an offense, he did so because he was encouraged to do so by the police (or by an agent of the police). John DeLorean, for example, was able successfully to claim that he had been "set up" to do a drug deal that he would never have committed if law-enforcement authorities had not lured him into doing so. The United States is one of the few countries in the world where the entrapment defense is recognized. The federal government and all fifty states allow the defense of entrapment.[110] Estimates vary as to the success rate of the defense. One recent six-state survey of 400 judges, prosecutors, and defense counsel found it successful about a third of the time.[111] In another survey of judges, prosecutors, and defense attorneys in Tennessee, the defense prevailed at trial in fewer than one in a thousand cases, though defense attorneys claimed that it also affected the final outcome of a case (as by influencing a plea-bargained sentence) in as many as 1.4% of cases.[112]

Within the United States, jurisdictions disagree over how the defense should be formulated.[113] The apparent terms of the disagreement concern how much the defense should focus on the police conduct and how much it should focus on the *effect* of the police conduct on the defendant. The *objective* formulation explicitly defines the defense as addressing, and seeking to prevent, improper police behavior. Under the Utah statute, for example, unlawful entrapment occurs whenever police conduct "creat[es] a substantial risk that the offense would be committed by one not otherwise ready to

commit it."[114] The defense does not require that the *defendant* be "not otherwise ready to commit it." It is available, without regard to the defendant's
predisposition, if the police conduct is such that it might cause an offense by
"one not otherwise ready to commit it."[115] Under such a definition, the key
question in the DeLorean case would be: was the operation of the police's
"sting" of DeLorean objectively inappropriate? This conception of the defense has nothing to do with desert, because it focuses on the appropriateness of the *police's* conduct, which is beyond the defendant's control, rather
than on the blameworthiness of the defendant in committing the offense.
Even a fully blameworthy offender who would have committed the offense
were there no police involvement is eligible for the defense under this objective formulation.

The *subjective* formulation, on the other hand, seems to cast the defense
as more related to desert, concentrating on the actual effect of the entrapping
conduct on the individual actor's free choice. The Delaware statute, for example, permits an entrapment defense only if the defendant is "induced" to
commit an offense that he (the defendant) "is not otherwise disposed" to commit. Under this formulation, the defense is given "because the wrongdoing
of the officer originates the idea of the crime and then induces the other person to [commit the offense] when the other person is not otherwise disposed
to do so."[116] Under a subjective formulation, the defendant's predisposition
to commit the offense is central (and evidence of predisposition is not necessarily limited to the defendant's conduct prior to the entrapping conduct).[117]
Such a subjective formulation would ask: did the police's conduct induce De-
Lorean to commit the crime, when he would not otherwise have done so?

The U.S. Supreme Court cases that define the federal entrapment defense
(there is no federal entrapment statute) show competition between the objective and subjective formulations. In *Sorrells v. United States*,[118] the Court
adopted the subjective formulation: that the entrapment defense is intended
to prevent conviction of "otherwise innocent" individuals who have been
lured into the commission of a crime they had no predisposition to commit.
A long line of cases has upheld this characterization of the defense.[119]

But an equally long line of concurrences and dissents, beginning with the
concurrence of Justice Roberts in *Sorrells*, has viewed the entrapment defense as rooted in the notion that the integrity of the judicial process must
not be sullied by the use of improper police conduct to procure convictions.
Under this rationale, the defendant's predisposition is immaterial; the only
relevant question is the degree to which the police have overstepped the
bounds of appropriate behavior.[120]

Authority also exists for a due-process defense independent of the entrapment defense.[121] This defense, rooted in the Constitution, is essentially a

more demanding version of the objective formulation; it operates only where police conduct offends "the canons of fundamental fairness, shocking to the universal sense of justice."[122] Several states have adopted a due-process defense broader than the federal defense, based upon the due-process provisions of the relevant state constitutions.[123]

The difference between the objective and subjective formulations is significant, but closer examination reveals that it is not a distinction that is relevant to desert, for although the subjective formulation might appear to be a desert-related excuse, similar to duress, which exculpates the defendant because she is coerced to commit an offense,[124] such a characterization is unfounded.[125] A duress defenses applies when the pressure on a defendant to commit an offense is so strong that he cannot justly be held accountable for his resulting offense conduct. The "induced" requirement in entrapment is somewhat analogous, for example, to the coercion requirement in duress. But a duress defense is not given simply because an actor was subject to coercion, just as an insanity defense is not given simply because the actor has some mental illness. A proper excuse requires that the offender's disability be sufficiently strong in its effects that one could not reasonably have expected the actor to have avoided the violation.[126]

Yet nothing in the entrapment defense, even in the subjective formulation, ensures that the defense will be given only if an overwhelming degree of coercion is present. Under the entrapment defense, the requisite degree of inducement of the offender is dramatically lower than the level of coercion that would be necessary for an exonerating excuse. The subjective formulation typically requires no more than a showing that the actor would not have committed the offense but for the officer's inducement. For example, DeLorean may receive the defense merely by showing that he would not have done so in a less-tempting situation; he need not show that he was *compelled* in any way to take the money, just that he was *tempted* or encouraged to do so.

Further, if the subjective formulation represented a true excuse, there would be no reason to limit the defense to cases of inducement by government agents and to exclude from the defense similar inducements by private citizens, as the entrapment defense does.[127] Clearly, if a private citizen had, using the same degree of temptation, induced DeLorean into a scheme to buy drugs—that is, if Hoffman had just been Hoffman and not a government agent—DeLorean would have had no defense. Thus, even the subjective formulation must ultimately derive its intellectual legitimacy (or lack thereof) from a concern with wrongdoing or overreaching by state actors. Under either formulation, the true primary reasons for the entrapment defense are the nonexculpatory interests of deterrence and estoppel: deterrence of improper police inducement and avoiding the apparent unfairness of allowing the government to induce an offense and then prosecute it.

The purpose of the entrapment defense is thus similar to that underlying the exclusionary rules,[128] which we discussed earlier in this chapter—preventing police misconduct—although the effect of the rule is even more severe in this context. Instead of merely limiting the evidence that may be presented against an accused offender, the entrapment defense provides an absolute bar to criminal liability. Yet, while several attempts have been made to determine whether the exclusionary rules actually deter law-enforcement abuses, that critical empirical issue remains largely unexplored with respect to the entrapment defense. We are aware of no empirical research to indicate whether the existence of the entrapment defense, or the use of one formulation of the defense rather than another, actually reduces the frequency or severity of coercive police tactics. (As with the exclusionary rules, though the defense obviously deprives at least some misconduct of its effect ex post, this does not necessarily suggest that it alters police behavior ex ante.) In short, there has been no demonstration that the cost of the rule in sacrificing desert is offset, in whole or in part, by any corresponding benefit.

We argue in chapter 10 that a better approach—more effective and not justice frustrating—is to use administrative procedures to sanction law-enforcement officers and officials who violate rules limiting police and prosecutorial conduct.

MORAL CREDIBILITY "VERSUS" LEGITIMACY: EVALUATING THE TRADEOFFS

Returning to the general theme with which we began this chapter—the conflict between substantive justice and procedural fairness and its possible resolution—can we say anything generally about the relative significance of these two principles in influencing the system's reputation as an authority whose rules and results merit deference? The relationship between the law's ability to induce compliance based on its substantive articulation of moral rules with which the public agrees (its *moral credibility*) and its ability to do so based on the public's general view of the law's procedural fairness (and, hence, its *legitimacy*) is complex. Normally, "morality and legitimacy reinforce each other."[129] Indeed, although procedural rules play a substantial and possibly critical role in determining legitimacy,[130] to some extent legitimacy is also rooted in the public's substantive agreement with the law's moral content.[131] The legitimacy-morality relation may work in the opposite direction as well: legitimate institutions may promote norms that the governed individuals will then internalize and adopt as their own.[132]

Still, there are times when the two conflict.[133] Some initial efforts have been made to explore the relative strength of moral credibility and legitimacy in inducing compliance with the law.[134] For example, one study finds that when making decisions about imposing punishment, subjects tend to prioritize substantive desert; for example, where guilt is clear, people tend to seek the just outcome even at the cost of procedural fairness.[135] Other work further supports the significance of moral credibility,[136] though there is also some work suggesting a substantial role for legitimacy.[137] In any case, at present we have only highly incomplete information on the issue. Given the increasing awareness of the significance of the system's credibility and legitimacy in sustaining and strengthening social institutions and in promoting compliance with law, this area presents a fertile and crucial set of issues for further research.

Some procedural rules we discuss may have such an effect in promoting public faith in the criminal-justice system as to make up for the demoralization costs of their deviation from desert.[138] But on the other hand, if the rules are not "cost effective" in promoting the system's legitimacy to an extent that outweighs their damaging effects in violating desert, then they must find their justification elsewhere, or they should more appropriately have their interests advanced through alternative, nonviolating mechanisms.

Perhaps one option for issues that are found to involve significant reputational tradeoffs between substantive moral credibility and procedural legitimacy would be to replace the existing hard-and-fast mandatory rules with a more flexible approach that weighs the relative costs for each case.[139] Canada, for example, currently employs such an approach with respect to exclusionary-rule issues:

> Where . . . a court concludes that evidence was obtained in a manner that infringed or denied any rights or freedoms guaranteed by this Charter, the evidence shall be excluded *if it is established that, having regard to all the circumstances, the admission of it in the proceedings would bring the administration of justice into disrepute.*[140]

The ALI's Model Code of Pre-Arraignment Procedure proposes a similar method.[141]

Another option may be to allow substantive sensibilities to inform the content of procedural rules, as Christopher Slobogin and William Stuntz have, in different ways, suggested doing with the Fourth Amendment. Slobogin argues that the rules governing search and seizure should track public views of the relative "intrusiveness" of different types of government interference, so that officials' behavior would comport with people's feelings about what types of intrusion are acceptable.[142] Stuntz argues that the scope of the Fourth Amendment's protections should vary based on the seriousness of the substantive crime being investigated, so that greater intrusions would be allowed for more-serious offenses—thus reducing, though not eliminating, the deviation from desert.[143]

In conclusion, we wish to make clear what our point is *not*. We have no wish to suggest that procedural rights are unimportant, nor even that they are less important than desert. We seek only to explore the ways in which the tensions between the two might be reduced, hopefully at the expense of neither. Indeed, as we have seen for specific rules, such as the exclusionary rules and the speedy-trial right, the tension between procedural fairness and desert is currently often resolved against procedure and in favor of substance, as courts narrow the scope of procedural rules for the sake of avoiding their application to prevent punishment of the guilty. A closer examination of the relationship between substance and procedure and a serious effort to explore new solutions for the enforcement of these rights might well promote a more robust understanding of the rights themselves, as well as a reduction of—or at least, a well-reasoned and empirically sound justification for—their tendency to interfere with implementation of the desert principle.

CHAPTER 8

Promoting Interests Unrelated to Criminal Justice

A SEVENTH AND FINAL justification offered for departures from desert is that such departures are sometimes necessary to promote an interest external to the criminal law. Sometimes these departures involve rules that impose punishment where none is deserved. For example, criminal liability is sometimes imposed on corporations even though a corporation is a fictitious entity that cannot be blameworthy or be "punished" in any meaningful sense. Other offenses criminalize trivial, morally neutral behavior that happens to run afoul of some governmental regulation—such as the Lindseys' camping at a time outside the specifications on their permit, discussed immediately below. In both sets of cases, criminal punishment is imposed in the absence of genuine moral blame. Yet corporate liability and the criminalization of regulatory violations are thought to serve important noncriminal purposes, as powerful levers allowing civil regulatory agencies to enforce their authority and fulfill their missions.

In other cases, a policy interest outside the criminal law will be used to prevent the imposition of deserved punishment. Permitting diplomatic immunity from criminal prosecution in this country prevents acts of retaliation against our diplomats abroad; official immunities for domestic political officials ensure freedom of action to perform their official duties. These immunities apply even in cases, such as that of Manuel Ayree (discussed below), involving a known repeat offender whose criminal responsibility is clear.

In all of these instances, the criminal law is employed to advance a governmental purpose unrelated to the objectives of criminal justice itself.

CRIMINAL CAMPING

A portion of the Snake River in Idaho is surrounded by Nez Perce National Forest to the east and Wallowa-Whitman National Forest to the west. This area comprises a part of the Hells Canyon National Recreational Area and has been designated a part of the Wild and Scenic River System created by federal law. Hells Canyon and Snake River provide a highly valued opportunity for wilderness adventure.

However, local adventurers may not simply do whatever they please; the area is heavily regulated for environmental and safety reasons. People may ride on the river only at certain times, because the rapids are often fast and dangerous. Camping is limited to designated sites. Camping in other areas is restricted, both to protect people from changes in the water levels, which can rise and drop quickly, and to prevent overcrowding. The National Forest Service maintains a permit system that allocates campsites and time slots for river riding. Launch times are spaced so that people on the river will not bump into one another. The process allows permit holders to enjoy the wilderness experience while assuring their safety. The Forest Service also regulates the building of fires along the river, prohibiting fires during the summer, when the area presents a fire hazard; a fire built on the beach during that period may spread to the forest. Finally, there are regulations to preserve the appearance of the surrounding environment: people must clean up after themselves and carry their waste in appropriate containers. The geographic reach of the federal regulations is limited, however, as the 1976 Hells Canyon Recreation Act gives jurisdiction over the areas below the high-water mark to the states of Idaho and Oregon. Those camping below this mark do not need federal permits.

In July 1977, Benjamin "Scott" Lindsey is twenty years old, and his brother, Tom Lindsey, is twenty-six. Tom works as a truck tender for a drill on the Brownlee Dam, while Scott is recovering from a motorcycle accident. Tom has floated the Snake River a few times and wants his brother to experience the thrill. Tom Lindsey has a reputation for having an antigovernment, antiregulation attitude. As a result, confrontations between Tom and Forest Service agents are common.

Despite this sour relationship, Tom decides to follow the federal regulations and obtains ten permits from the Forest Service in Halfway, Oregon. The permits allow for rafts to be launched only after 9:00 A.M., though, and Tom finds this restriction inconvenient, as he wants to get an early start on the day. Also, Tom is primarily interested in fishing, which is better done earlier in the morning than later. Thus Tom, Scott, and six of their friends launch their rubber raft a couple of hours early, at 7:00 A.M., with Tom leaving a note for the Forest Service agents, explaining to them his situation and detailing his camping plans.

That evening, the group makes camp above the main rapid, known as High Mountain Sheep. The next night, they set up camp below Granite Creek on a gravel bar. (This area is below the high-water mark and therefore under the jurisdiction of the state of Idaho.) An outfitter notices that the Lindseys are using a gas stove; he reports that the brothers have built a "fire" in violation of the federal regulation. Other campers complain to the Forest Service that the Lindseys are mocking the permit system by floating before permitted hours.

After receiving these complaints, three Forest Service law-enforcement agents, Mike Merkley, Ace Barton, and Dick Ziegler, determine to arrest the Lindseys. They fly to the area by helicopter and land at the Lindsey camp, destroying it and blowing the campers' belongings into the river. The agents try to arrest the Lindseys, but leave after the Lindseys threaten to drown Mike Merkley. Soon thereafter, Merkley files a complaint against the Lindseys, omitting the other six members of the group. Tom Lindsey later receives a letter revoking his permits.

Tom Lindsey goes to the Halfway Recreation Center and shows the agents the stipulation in the Hells Canyon Recreation Act that states that no permit is needed to camp below the high-water mark. He does not hear from the Forest Service for some time, but eventually he receives a letter informing him that he has been indicted for the felony crimes of camping without a permit and building a campfire without a permit.

The brothers refuse to appear in court, and a warrant is issued for their arrest. Three months after the indictment, Tom Lindsey is dragged off the toilet in his trailer-park home and arrested in front of his frightened four-year-old daughter. His foreman and supervisor, who also live in the trailer park, witness the arrest, and Lindsey later loses his job. Meanwhile, Scott Lindsey is taking a whirlpool bath at the high school for his motorcycle injury when police pull him out of the water and arrest him.[1]

FIGURES 8.1, 8.2.
Snake River, Hells
Canyon. Courtesy
USDA Forest Service.

FIGURE 8.3.
Tom Lindsey (*center*),
accompanied by friends
Mike Foster (*left*) and
Tom Tumbleson, aboard
a boat on the river.
Courtesy Tom Lindsey.

CRIMINALIZATION OF REGULATORY VIOLATIONS

Governmental regulation has shown an increasing, and disturbing, tendency
to criminalize actions other than those the community would conceive of as
morally condemnable conduct. The trend toward criminalization has led to
an astounding 300,000 or so federal "crimes,"[2] extending criminalization beyond even the domain of traditional *malum prohibitum* offenses to criminalize conduct that is "harmful" only in the sense that it causes inconvenience
for bureaucrats. The practice is not unlike the deterrence-based rules we examined in chapter 6, which commonly call for punishments well beyond an
offender's moral desert for the sake of discouraging what is seen as improper
or undesirable conduct. Regulatory crimes differ, however, in that not only the
amount of punishment but the very *imposition* of criminal punishment—
as opposed to some available civil sanction, such as a fine—seems questionable and out of step with a desert-based scheme for criminal liability.

   As the *Lindsey* case illustrates, many federal regulations are now routinely converted to federal crimes, and often serious crimes, for the sole purpose of giving regulators greater leverage in enforcement. But this criminalization of regulatory violations deviates from the goal of desert, for it punishes
behavior that is morally neutral and frequently objectively trivial. Tom Lindsey was subject to criminal liability for each of the offenses of launching his
raft two hours early and using his gas stove.[3]

   The enactment and enforcement of such trivial offenses are themselves
far from trivial, however. Such provisions undercut the moral force of the
criminal law and may have potential spillover effects on law enforcement or

prosecution. Some people might cite prosecutorial discretion as a panacea for any legislative overreaching, but such discretion is as likely to exacerbate as to counteract the dangers of overcriminalization. The *Lindsey* case suggests that regulatory offenses can lend themselves to selective enforcement. The authorities seem to have identified Tom Lindsey as a troublemaker, and it is possible that they targeted Lindsey in advance. In any case, it appears that they seized the opportunity to arrest and prosecute Lindsey with a zeal that would be lacking in the usual case. But regardless of the circumstances of Lindsey's case, it is generally true that regulatory offenses depend upon officials' sensible use of discretion, and such reliance on discretion at any level only opens the door to the type of selective, disparate treatment that the criminal law should combat, rather than promote.

In addition to expanding criminal liability to include minor conduct, the proliferation of regulatory crimes is counterproductive on its own terms. First, by imposing criminal liability in cases lacking in moral blameworthiness, the practice undermines the very characteristic of criminal law that regulatory-offense advocates seek to press into service.[4] *Criminal* penalties are thought desirable because they bring to bear the moral condemnation that civil liability does not, but using criminal sanctions in morally neutral cases only dilutes criminal liability's condemnatory effect over time.

The current trend toward blurring the criminal-civil distinction is particularly disconcerting because it offers no direct advantages, even with respect to the very cases brought within the expansion. By criminalizing these offenses, we do not effectively access more severe sanctions. Regulatory offenses are exactly the cases for which the likelihood of a prison sentence is most remote. The majority of regulatory offenses are misdemeanors, for which a serious prison term is not authorized. Even for the most egregious forms of these offenses, where danger to life or property is created, the likelihood of a significant incarcerative sentence is not high. For example, in fiscal year 2001—the most recent year for which data are available—of the 1,410 federal defendants convicted of a felony considered a "regulatory offense," less than half were sentenced to any period of incarceration, and the median sentence for those was only fifteen months. A total of seventy-eight people who violated agriculture, antitrust, food and drug, or transportation laws received a sentence of incarceration, and the median sentence was no more than 13.5 months for any of those categories. More regulatory offenders receive either probation or a suspended sentence (or no sentence) than receive any imprisonment. Many of those who receive any genuine punishment are required to pay a fine or restitution—penalties also available as civil, rather than criminal, sanctions.[5]

LINDSEY AFTERMATH

Chief Judge Ray McNichols of the District of Idaho dismisses the case against the Lindseys, concluding that the federal government does not have jurisdiction over acts occurring on state property.[6]

The government appeals, seeking to enforce its regulations in the area below the high-water mark. The Ninth Circuit Court of Appeals rules that the federal government has the power to regulate conduct on nonfederal land when doing so is reasonably necessary to protect adjacent federal property or navigable waters. The Forest Service agents are satisfied with the Ninth Circuit decision, which allows the agency to enforce its regulations on the Snake River. The case is remanded to the district court, but the prosecuting attorney does not pursue the case further.

Tom Lindsey continues to be harassed by Forest Service agents for years. He is currently an independent miner and driller, using family-held mineral claims near Interstate 95. Scott Lindsey works as a carpenter.

CORPORATE CRIMINALITY

As with regulatory crimes, imposition of criminal liability on corporations is often justified on the ground that it gives civil sanctions more teeth.[7] Criminal prosecution of corporations, the argument goes, provides a deterrent that civil actions cannot: the stigmatization of criminal conviction.[8] Proponents note that while some civil wrongs might be condemnable, many are not; thus, civil liability sends at best an ambiguous message.[9] Only criminal liability, it is argued, can bring moral stigmatization to bear.

But such corporate criminal liability seems inconsistent with desert, although here for a different reason than the deviations we have seen elsewhere: it does not make intuitive sense in terms of desert to assign "blame" to a fictitious, conceptual entity. Because condemnation of a nonhuman entity has no clear moral meaning, each such conviction creates ambiguity about the criminal law's distinguishing feature and primary concern: its focus on moral blameworthiness. To try to use that special characteristic where personal blameworthiness cannot exist is to erode and undermine the criminal law's most important asset.

A case in support of corporate criminality might be argued on desert grounds, but that case remains, at best, unsettled. Some recent psychology scholarship on what is called "group entitivity"[10] and philosophy scholarship on "plural subject theory"[11] do suggest that it is possible—indeed, some argue that it is natural and perhaps routine—to assign "intent" or other such notions of unitary agency to groups as well as to individuals. Accordingly, it may not be absolutely certain that shared societal intuitions of morality would regard the assignment of blame to an organization such as a corporation to be inherently incoherent or improper. We find this work interesting and promising, and if further work offers convincing evidence that imposition of blame on collective entities is in keeping with widely shared notions of desert, our objections to corporate criminality on desert-based grounds might well be more muted. At present, however, a clear affirmative case that our shared norms do support extension of blame to abstract entities, rather than only to individuals, has yet to be made.[12] Absent any such explicit and well-supported justification or basis, attribution of *moral* sanctions to legal fictions is counterintuitive and questionable.

The complexity of assigning blame to a corporation is highlighted by the difficulty of determining how to impose punishment, as opposed to some merely deterrent or restitutionary sanction, on such an entity. Quite obviously, the corporation cannot be made to feel, or experience in any way, whatever penalty the state imposes. Only individuals can truly be punished—and we would emphasize that typically they can and should be punished in these situations. Even if corporate behavior is in some sense group behavior, tools already exist for prosecuting group criminality—through conspiracy or complicity liability—and can be employed to bring serious criminal punishment to bear on those who truly deserve it. If anything, efforts to prosecute the corporation itself increase the likelihood of confusing the issues or distracting from the goal of punishing the blameworthy individuals rather than the nonsentient corporation.[13] Though some have maintained to the contrary that "corporate liability may make it easier to convict the individual defendants,"[14] this assertion—as with most empirical assertions in the area of corporate criminality—lacks confirmation from supporting data.[15] Prosecutorial efforts to pursue the larger entity may waste resources more properly devoted to punishing the people—usually, it seems, a fairly small inner circle of wrongdoers—who can be held to moral account and who can feel the sting of that punishment.

The potential cost that corporate criminality presents to the criminal law's credibility would be all the more difficult to justify if the civil prosecution of organizations would be, or could be made, as effective as criminal prosecution.[16] Some writers have argued that, on balance, civil liability is actually *more* effective than criminal liability in gaining organizational compliance.[17] The difficulty of determining how specifically to punish a corporation is reflected in the current mechanisms for trying to do so, which merely replicate other, noncriminal penalties. The most serious criminal sanctions—deprivation of life or liberty—are not available against an organization. The available sanctions are essentially the same as those available under civil law: fines, orders for restitution, and orders requiring or limiting future organizational action. Some features of criminal procedure, such as a speedy trial, may be considered more attractive in gaining compliance than the comparable civil procedures, but the legislature could alter the civil procedures for organizations in these regards if doing so were thought necessary to exact greater compliance.

In fact, *criminal* rules can limit the effective prosecution of organizations in ways that legislatures cannot get around. Constitutional guarantees, such as those requiring proof beyond a reasonable doubt and barring double jeopardy, are available to an organization in defending a criminal action, but not in defending a civil action.[18] Further, criminal law's general disapproval of strict liability and negligence liability[19] may limit the prosecution of organizations when it ought not; many of the objections to such liability have little force in the context of corporate liability. Civil actions can therefore provide a greater possibility of liability for a greater number of offenses with less demanding elements of proof. The empirical evidence—what little there is—bears out this conclusion, as there is next to no evidence that criminal liability deters corporate misconduct[20] and some reasons to believe that it does not.[21]

Both regulatory "crimes" and corporate "crimes," then, could be dealt with as effectively, and probably more effectively, through the civil rather than the criminal system. Further, civil mechanisms could tailor liability and enforcement to focus on issues other than the blameworthiness of past behavior. For example, the imposition of civil fines and other remedies could incorporate consideration of post-offense internal reforms that will prevent future regulatory or other violations.[22]

As we discuss in more detail in chapter 10, we believe that the best approach for such quasi-crimes is to use administrative sanctions imposed by regulatory agencies as is done in other countries and, to a lesser extent, in the United States. This change would be largely symbolic, but nonetheless significant, for it would reinforce the useful distinction between civil and criminal law and promote the criminal law's moral authority, and it would do so without diminishing the range of penalties typically available against the relevant offenders.

.   .   .

Some protected categories of official or public servant—such as members of a diplomatic mission, judges, prosecutors, and others—may receive immunity from criminal prosecution by virtue of their positions. Immunity is thought to be necessary to enable these officials to perform their jobs properly and to prevent malicious or retaliatory prosecutions against them. At the same time, immunity comes at a serious cost, as it prevents liability for known offenders, some of whom commit serious crimes.

THE DIPLOMATIC RAPIST

On January 8, 1981, "Jane" (not her real name) boards the crowded bus home from work and thinks about her boyfriend, who is out of town. When the bus reaches her stop in the Upper East Side of Manhattan, she squeezes her way out of the bus and heads for the grocery store on the corner. Grocery bag in hand, she makes her way across the street to her apartment building. She stops in the entryway of her building, as always, to check her mailbox before unlocking the inside door. Before the door locks behind her, a young black man, who will be identified later as Manuel Ayree, catches it and enters the building. Short but powerfully built, he is dressed nicely, in a tie and well-pressed slacks, and is carrying keys in his hand. Jane assumes he lives in the building. He leisurely climbs the stairs behind her, lighting a cigarette on his way up. He follows her up to her high-rise apartment and approaches the door across the hallway from hers.

As soon as she unlocks her door, she feels him press against her back. In a thick accent, he says, "Do everything I say or I'll kill you. I have a gun." Jane tells him that she will do anything he wants and pleads with him not to kill her. Although her heart is pounding and her mind is racing, she manages to appear calm so as not to agitate the man. As they enter the kitchen, he grabs a steak knife. Once again, he threatens her, prodding her stomach with it. She offers him money to leave her alone. He ignores the offer and asks if she lives alone. She lies and says that she does not. "If you don't tell me the truth, I am going to kill you. Do you live alone?" he demands. She admits to living alone as she hands him the few dollars from her wallet. She hopes that he will leave now. She thinks about telling him that she has a venereal disease to deter any sexual assault, but the words do not surface. He orders her into the studio. The convertible sofa is still open from the previous night. He tells her to take off her pants and lay face down on the mattress. He pulls down his own pants and enters her anus. She screams from the pain and starts crying. After intercourse, he withdraws and wipes himself with her blanket.

He orders her under her bed and tells her to go to sleep and never wake up. At this point, she is sure that he means to kill her, but then she hears him walk out the door and down the stairs. She picks herself up and eventually telephones the police. She is taken to the emergency rape unit, where she is questioned by police and examined by nurses. After a sleepless night at a

FIGURE 8.4.
High-rise on the west
side of York Avenue
between 88th and 89th
Streets, New York City.
Photo by Geoff Gentile.

friend's apartment, she receives a telephone call from Detective Pete Christiansen asking her to meet him at her apartment. There, she recounts the horrors of the previous night.

Later that winter, Ayree victimizes Carol Holmes, a freelance proofreader in New York, using a similar modus operandi. He enters her building with her before the outside door closes behind her, then approaches her and presses something against her back, warning her that he has a gun and forcing her up the stairs to her apartment. There he grabs a knife off the table and places it under her chin, threatening again to kill her if she disobeys. He orders her to take off her clothes and lay down on the mattress in her living room, where he has forcible anal and vaginal sex with her. He then pulls up his pants and heads for the bathroom. She follows him, completely naked, hoping to make him feel uncomfortable enough to leave. He lights a cigarette and burns her with it. Suddenly, they hear a door slam and loud footsteps. Carol recognizes the sounds as a neighbor descending the stairs. Ayree panics and flees. Still naked, Carol runs after him, screaming, "Stop him, stop him! He raped me." There is no response, and Ayree escapes. An ambulance takes her to the rape unit of Lenox Hill Hospital, where she is questioned, examined, and given medication. At the police station, she is questioned by Detective Christiansen.

Following the attack, Carol begins to have nightmares of men breaking into her apartment and attacking her. She hears reports that her rapist has been seen by others in the neighborhood, which heightens her fears of another encounter with him. She becomes obsessed with finding her attacker. Every afternoon, Carol scours the neighborhood with her boyfriend, Bruce.

Meanwhile, Detective Christiansen's frustration builds as the rapes continue. Nearly all of the rapes occur on the Upper West Side, and each time, the rapist's methods are the same: he follows a woman into her apartment building, pretending to be a fellow resident, then forces her into her apartment, and rapes her. At least ten such rapes, in addition to Jane's and Carol's, have now been reported. By February 1981, with help from Carol, Jane, and other victims, Christiansen is able to come up with a composite sketch of the rapist. He hands copies of the sketch to undercover agents and tells them to concentrate on the Yorkville neighborhood.

That Friday, Carol and Bruce set out on their daily search for the rapist. They pass a grocery store on the corner of 89th Street and continue past the Carnegie Animal Hospital and the Stuyvesant Square Thrift Shop around the same time that Manuel Ayree leaves his apartment building and walks across 89th Street toward Second Avenue. He is spotted by two undercover policemen in a yellow taxi, who recognize his face from the composite sketch Detective Christiansen gave them. At the same time, Detective Christiansen heads south on Second Avenue in his unmarked police car. Parking his car on the curb at 89th Street, he gets out and walks over to the corner pay phone. Ayree passes the Carnegie Animal Hospital and the Stuyvesant Square Thrift Shop while the taxi creeps along behind him.

Carol and Bruce, meanwhile, decide to turn around just as they approach 88th Street. As soon as they turn around, Carol sees Ayree walking toward them. She stares at Ayree as he walks by them and tells Bruce that Ayree is the rapist. Immediately, Bruce grabs Ayree, and a fight ensues. Carol rushes to the pay phone on the corner of 88th Street and tells the operator to call 911. The police in the taxi, as well as Detective Christiansen and two more undercover agents posing as joggers, arrive on the scene. Ayree is shoved into the back seat of the taxi and taken to the police station.

At the police station, Ayree demands to be released, announcing that he has diplomatic immunity. Detective Christiansen moves quickly, calling the other victims to come and identify Ayree as their attacker. He has little luck contacting most of the victims, but finally reaches Jane at work. Upon hear-

FIGURE 8.5.
Near the intersection of 2nd Avenue and 88th Street, New York City, where Carol
Holmes's boyfriend confronts Ayree. Photo by Geoff Gentile.

ing that Ayree has been caught, Jane runs out of her office and heads toward
the station. However, members of the Ghanaian mission arrive sooner and
identify the rapist as nineteen-year-old Manuel Ayree, son of the third at-
taché to the mission. Carol confronts the group, recounting her horrible experience. Jane arrives at the police station, where she is introduced to the
Ghanaians as another of Ayree's victims. In a viewing room, Jane hears
Ayree's voice and knows for sure that Ayree is the rapist.

About forty-five minutes after arriving at the police station, Manuel Ayree
walks out, a free man. "I told you I had diplomatic immunity," he snickers.
He laughs tauntingly as he walks by Carol and leaves.

Carol immediately consults lawyers from the firm of Beldock, Levine,
and Hoffman. Hoping that the U.S. State Department will force Ghana to
waive Ayree's immunity, the lawyers work all weekend to prepare a complaint.
All the while, Seth Ayree, Manuel's father, denies his son's guilt and makes
accusations of racism. On Monday, February 9, the law firm files a civil complaint against Manuel Ayree. At the same time, State Department officials
meet with Ghanaian officials and warn them that if Ayree does not "voluntarily" leave, he and his family will be deported.

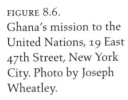

FIGURE 8.6.
Ghana's mission to the
United Nations, 19 East
47th Street, New York
City. Photo by Joseph
Wheatley.

On Tuesday morning, a press conference is held, in which Ghanaian officials announce that Manuel Ayree will be leaving the United States and will not return. They also announce that the case will be fully investigated in Ghana. Manuel Ayree leaves the United States that night. He is never investigated nor brought to trial in Ghana.[23]

DIPLOMATIC AND OFFICIAL IMMUNITY

The diplomatic agents of foreign states and many of the members of their missions are granted immunity from criminal prosecution by the Diplomatic Relations Act of 1978,[24] which adopted the Vienna Convention of Diplomatic Relations: "a diplomatic agent shall enjoy immunity from the criminal jurisdiction of the receiving state."[25] The Act grants full immunity to the "diplomatic agent" (that is, the ambassador) and the agent's family and administrative and technical staff, but grants only limited immunity to other members of the mission. The diplomatic agent's service staff, for example, is granted immunity only for acts committed in the performance of official duties. The personal staff of the ambassador receives no immunity nor do members of the mission who happen to be citizens of the United States.[26] Some 200,000 residents of the United States—mostly in Washington, D.C., and New York—are entitled to diplomatic immunity, and roughly 40–50 of those people commit a crime in the United States each year.[27]

Underlying the immunity rule is the fear that subjection of foreign diplomats to criminal prosecution in this country might lead to reprisals abroad.[28] But the potential of such a defense to produce serious deviations from desert is illustrated by the Ayree case. At some level, such immunity is a necessary evil, for there is no other practical way to accomplish the goal of reciprocal protection and prevention of reprisals. But two useful limitations can minimize the deviations and their effects.

First, a reformed verdict system and special procedures may allow the criminal-justice system to note its condemnation of the offense, though it is unable to punish it. We discuss the details of this possibility in chapter 9.

Second, immunity can be extended only to the degree that it is necessary to achieve its purpose—and in fact, this is often done. The modern scope of diplomatic immunity has been narrowed in many instances to limit its breadth to that which is functionally necessary for the performance of the diplomat's duties.[29] Further, a diplomatic agent's grant of immunity is not a grant of total impunity. The host state may declare a diplomat to be persona non grata and request the sending state to recall the diplomat or terminate the diplomat's service.[30] If its request is denied, the receiving state may refuse to recognize the person as a member of the mission.[31] While the diplomat who has lost protected status in this fashion may not be punished for previous offenses,[32] most legal authorities suggest that the injured state may restrain the offending diplomat until expulsion is possible.[33] Further, the agent enjoys the immunity as a representative of, and by the grace of, the sending country. A diplomat may be liable for trial and punishment under the laws of the sending country.[34] Or that country may waive its diplomat's immunity and thereby subject the diplomat to criminal prosecution in the host state.[35] These alternatives offer at least some prospect of bringing an immune criminal to justice. But, as the Ayree case illustrates, even these mechanisms often do not prevent serious failures of justice.

Judicial, legislative, and executive immunities, or what as a group might be called *governmental* or *official* immunities, are similar to diplomatic immunity in that they generally protect government agents and officials from criminal prosecution and conviction for conduct within the scope of their official duties.[36] A distinct governmental immunity exempts officials from arrest, as opposed to prosecution; such immunity generally is only temporary and is designed to permit the performance of official business without interference.[37] (Official immunities usually do not merely bar conviction, but bar prosecution, and are normally decided by the court, resulting in dismissal of charges rather than a not-guilty verdict. For example, legislative immunity protects legislators "not only from the consequences of litigation's results but also from the burden of defending themselves.")[38]

Some of the immunities may seem similar to justification defenses, such as self-defense, where otherwise prohibited conduct is allowed because of some countervailing interest. The interest advanced by immunities is clearly distinct, however. Justifications provide a defense because the actor's conduct in committing the offense avoids a greater harm or furthers a greater good. Immunities, like other nonexculpatory defenses, rely instead on public policy interests that are advanced not by the defendant's offense conduct, as with justification defenses, but rather by forgoing the defendant's conviction. The offender is not punished, not because his conduct is justified, but rather *despite* the fact that he may deserve punishment. Even if an official's conduct is by all measures criminal and blameworthy, public policy interests may urge that we forgo conviction to avoid the potential chilling effect on official actions.

It may be that little can or should be done to restrict the scope of present governmental immunities. But, as with diplomatic immunity, at the very least a refinement of the verdict system can provide a disposition of "unpunishable violation" that would enable the system to make clear that, although criminal liability and punishment must be withheld, the official's conduct is nonetheless morally blameworthy. Such a change would avoid the misleading signals sent by the dismissal of charges in such cases, which might be taken as moral exoneration of the offender. That is, the criminal-justice system can protect its moral credibility by making clear that it is not simply indifferent to the violations. The challenge here, as with diplomatic immunity, arises from the fact that there commonly is no official adjudication; the defense bars even the prosecution. We discuss the possibility and operation of an alternative verdict system in chapter 9.

III

REGAINING MORAL CREDIBILITY

A S THE PRIOR discussions make clear, many doctrines that deviate from desert do promote important interests, but that does not mean the doctrines are necessary or justified. Often these rules could be replaced by rules that would promote the same underlying interests as, or more, effectively yet would not produce deviations from desert—or, at least, not as many deviations. Many of these alternative mechanisms are complex enough or raise such serious issues of their own that they merit examination in some detail.

We argue for two general types of reform. The first group of reforms, the subject of chapter 9, would occur within the criminal-justice system. Specifically, we argue that shifting the burden of persuasion is a more rational response to potential abuses than the deviation doctrines rooted in fears of manipulation. Also, a more detailed verdict system would avoid the need for some deviation doctrines and might mitigate the distortion caused by others. Finally, a system incorporating alternative punishments to incarceration, but also measuring each punishment method according to a common metric of units of punishment, might better achieve the various crime-control goals discussed in chapter 6 without compromising the goal of desert.

The second set of reforms, examined in chapter 10, deals with changes that can be made outside the criminal-justice system to deal with problems that currently arise within, or are treated within, the system. In some cases, civil law offers a better mechanism for advancing the interests now advanced by a criminal-law doctrine that deviates from desert. We suggest, for example, that civil damages or administrative sanctions may be a better (i.e., potentially more effective, as well as more just) means of dealing with official violations of rights than the current method of excluding reliable evidence in criminal proceedings. We also discuss the possibility of developing a distinct administrative system, as exists in other countries, to impose liability for minor administrative violations and corporate wrongdoing, which are commonly (and inappropriately) dealt with in the United States through the criminal-justice system. Finally, an open system of post–criminal-term civil commitment could provide a more honest and effective means of providing protection from dangerous offenders than the current system, which uses criminal liability as a method of achieving cloaked preventive detention.

CHAPTER 9

Criminal Justice Reforms

S EVERAL OF THE possible reforms we have noted concern changes to the
criminal-justice system. Specifically, we said in chapter 2 that shifting
the burden of persuasion is a more rational way to prevent potential
abuse than the existing deviating doctrines that are justified by the abuse
concern—yet the Supreme Court's constitutional case law appears to limit
the ability of a jurisdiction to pursue this option. Similarly, in chapter 6, we
pointed out that a more detailed verdict system would avoid the need for some
deviating doctrines and might mitigate the moral credibility damage caused
by others—yet Anglo-American criminal law has traditionally forbidden almost anything but a general verdict. We also argued, in chapter 7, that the
current system of incarceration could be replaced with a more nuanced system that would allow, and even facilitate, use of various nonincarcerative
methods of punishment. In this chapter, we offer a more thorough discussion
of these proposals.

SHIFTING EVIDENTIARY BURDENS

As we discussed in chapter 2, efforts to curb courtroom gamesmanship ultimately seek to advance the goal of desert. Even so, they often are suspect.
The problem of gamesmanship often is more apparent than real, and the fear

of abuse is an overreaction without factual support. There is no indication, for example, that recognition of the mistake-of-law defense that was denied to Julio Marrero—the federal prison guard arrested for possession of a firearm—would open the floodgates to a host of bogus "mistake" claims by blameworthy defendants.

The uncritical tolerance of such abuse-based deviations may have been more understandable when the real costs of deviation from desert, which we discussed in chapter 1, were obscure. But those costs, once recognized, should not be tolerated unless there is evidence of the asserted abuse, not just a groundless hypothetical worry about it. The proponents of these deviating rules should have the burden of proving that their exploitation concerns are valid and that their proposed departure from justice-in-theory leads to greater justice-in-fact. In addition, they should have to refute the viability of any proffered approach that might protect against abuse without sacrificing desert.

One such approach, rather than denying altogether a potentially abused defense, would simply shift the burden of persuasion for the defense to the defendant. (For the nonlawyer reader, the phrase *burden of persuasion* is roughly equivalent to the common understanding of the expression *burden of proof*. It governs who must ultimately persuade the jury, or other fact-finder, and how convincingly they must do so—that is, whether they must prove a fact or element "beyond a reasonable doubt," or by "clear and convincing evidence," or some other standard.)[1] Such a shift in the burden of persuasion would make it difficult for defendants to successfully raise frivolous defenses but would enable defendants to present and to litigate an issue and obtain an acquittal where the facts truly do support a defense.

Excuse defenses, in particular, typically involve state-of-mind or mental-capacity questions as to which the defendant has unique access to the most relevant information. Thus, there is already a fair reason to have the burden of persuasion allocated to the defendant. Also, such defenses enable the defendant to avoid liability even though all of the usual elements of the prosecution's claim of an offense have been demonstrated—a standard criterion for shifting the burden of persuasion to the defendant in a civil setting.[2] Because the question of a possible excusing condition typically arises only in cases where it is undisputed that the defendant did violate the criminal law's prohibitions, it seems appropriate to shift the burden to the defendant to demonstrate such a condition.

For example, the current bright-line, all-or-nothing approach to the immaturity defense, which is based solely on the defendant's age (and which we discussed in chapter 2), could be replaced with a more flexible system using shifting presumptions or burdens of persuasion. An actor below a given age might be presumed immature unless the prosecution proves otherwise. An actor above a given age might be presumed mature unless the defense proves otherwise. (In the latter situation, if the defendant were too old for the juvenile court to have jurisdiction, the defendant might be given a full-excuse defense or some form of mitigation, as is currently done for defendants with other incapacities.) There is precedent for such a rebuttable presumption approach both in state codes and at common law.[3] To rebut the presumption, the party should have to prove not only the disability of being abnormally immature, but also that the effect of such immaturity was to cause an excusing condition sufficient to render the actor blameless for the offense charged. This solution would accomplish two goals: it would maximize the number of defendants assigned to the proper judicial forum, whether juvenile or adult court (thus also addressing the parallel difficulty of underage, but "mature," offenders);[4] and it would enable the maturity issue to play a role in the determination of liability, rather than only in the application of jurisdiction.

With respect to the insanity excuse, instead of eliminating the defense (or part of it) altogether or otherwise limiting its substantive scope, a better solution would be to keep the parameters of the defense the same, but to shift the burden of persuasion for the defense to the defendant. It is instructive that in the infamous *Hinckley* case—where John Hinckley, who attempted to assassinate President Reagan, was found not guilty by reason of insanity—then-existing District of Columbia law placed on the prosecution the burden of disproving the insanity defense beyond a reasonable doubt.[5] Had relevant law provided otherwise, as is the case in the majority of American jurisdictions,[6] the reform-provoking *Hinckley* acquittal might never have occurred.

With respect to several of the problematic doctrines we have discussed—specifically, the reasonable-mistake-of-law, immaturity, and insanity defenses—legislatures are free to craft such a solution. The Supreme Court has upheld as constitutional provisions that shift the burden of persuasion to the defendant as to a general excuse such as insanity.[7] Using a similar reform to avoid the use of strict-liability rules, however, would pose a problem under current law.

As noted in chapter 3, some advocates of strict liability defend it as an effective negligence per se (or recklessness per se) rule. They claim that although a person who commits, say, felony murder or statutory rape may lack culpability in some exceptional cases—such as that of Raymond Garnett, the mentally retarded twenty-year-old who did not know his sexual partner was underage—such culpability will be present in the large majority of cases. Supporters of this basis for strict liability point to the significant burden placed on prosecutors when they must prove culpability beyond a reasonable doubt and also cite the dangers to society that may arise if such prosecutions are less successful. Moreover, they cite the higher prosecution costs that would arise if strict liability were not permitted.

Where a genuine case can be made for the special difficulties of prosecution together with the special need for effective prosecution, a better approach than strict liability would be to retain a culpability requirement for criminal liability but to shift the burden of persuasion to the defendant.[8] Several other countries already do this. In Canada, for example, "strict liability" allows the defendant to rebut the presumption of culpability (while "absolute liability," which applies to minor offenses not involving mandatory incarceration, does not).[9] Britain has used a similar approach, though less consistently; its form of strict liability has been called a "halfway house" between negligence liability and absolute liability.[10] The courts of Australia and New Zealand go further, adopting a general rule that demonstrated lack of culpability will exonerate a defendant, and other Commonwealth nations in Asia and Africa adopt explicit statutory rules allowing a good-faith defense to strict liability.[11]

These countries all effectively exchange the *irrebuttable* presumption of culpability embodied in American strict-liability rules for a *rebuttable* presumption. The defendant would have the opportunity, under this approach, to prove that he lacked any culpability as to some significant aspect of the offense and thus that his conduct was not blameworthy under the circumstances.

Unfortunately, the Supreme Court's decisions under the Constitution as to the permissible boundaries of burden shifting have discouraged states from pursuing this avenue of reform. A line of cases from the 1970s indicates that the government must bear the burden of persuasion for any issue defined as an offense element—though, importantly, the cases do not impose such a requirement for issues characterized as "defenses" or "mitigations." The first of these cases, *In re Winship*, held that the prosecution must prove beyond a reasonable doubt "every fact necessary to constitute the crime with which [the defendant] is charged."[12] In *Mullaney v. Wilbur*, this was held to include *disproving* the defendant's claim of provocation; provocation under the Maine murder statute was seen as inconsistent with the required element of malice aforethought.[13] In *Patterson v. New York*, however, the Court held that the state need not carry the burden of disproving the defendant's claim of "extreme emotional disturbance" (a modern, expanded form of the provocation mitigation), which was interpreted not as something negating a required offense element but rather as providing an independent doctrine of mitigation.[14]

This constitutionalization of a ban on burden shifting for most culpability issues effectively encourages the imposition of strict liability by means of irrebuttable presumptions of culpability, as with the felony-murder rule. Consequently, the ban ultimately works to the detriment, not the benefit, of people accused of criminal wrongdoing—people like Raymond Garnett—for it obviates the need for *any* proof, much less proof beyond a reasonable doubt, as to the culpability issue.

To eliminate the problem, the courts should narrow the limitation on burden shifting to include only the objective elements of the charged offense—conduct, attendant circumstances, and result—that define the harm or evil of the offense or the culpability requirements that establish a higher-grade offense (as in the grading of homicide). We thus propose a rule that gives states a relatively modest ability to shift the burden of persuasion: forbidding burden shifting for proof of all objective offense elements and disproof of all objective elements of a justification defense, but allowing burden shifting for some minimum culpability requirements and all excuse issues (specifically, allowing burden shifting for all excuse defenses, as is allowed under current law, and for minimum culpability requirements *if* the element as to which defendant will bear the burden reflects an *increase* in the minimum required culpability level relative to preexisting law). The dissenters in *Patterson* supported a substantially similar approach, although they cast it in terms of defining defenses vis-à-vis offenses rather than the culpability elements of an offense.[15] In fact, a footnote from the majority opinion in *Patterson* also strongly suggests that such an approach is acceptable. The footnote clarifies that *Mullaney* did not foreclose the possibility of shifting evidentiary burdens for culpability issues, offering the explicit example of a possible "defense" to the felony-murder rule under which a defendant could prove by a preponderance that he lacked culpability.[16]

Such an approach would have three virtues relative to current Supreme Court law. First, it is conceptually coherent, unlike current law, which generally forbids burden shifting,[17] but sporadically allows it,[18] based largely on whether or not the formal structure of the provision casts the issue as an "offense element." Such an approach elevates form over substance for no good reason. As the Supreme Court itself has recognized,[19] legislatures have almost total discretion to define an issue as an "element" or a "defense," as they see fit. Second, the proposed approach would maintain strict proof requirements on the prosecution where they are most appropriate—with respect to factual issues involving whether the defendant unjustifiably caused the harm or evil of the offense. Finally, this approach would encourage the development of nuanced and sophisticated liability rules that benefit both individual defendants and the cause of justice, rather than blunt imputation rules that impose strict liability, abandoning the blameworthiness inquiry entirely.

REVAMPING THE VERDICT SYSTEM

Some of the deviations we have discussed could be mitigated by simply modifying the current verdict and disposition system. These deviations include
rules based on a desire to maintain clear conduct prohibitions, even at the
cost of desert (discussed in chapter 5), and certain nonexculpatory defenses
designed to achieve goals unrelated to criminal justice (discussed in chapter
8). The current general verdict of "not guilty" obscures distinctions between
bases for acquittal and thereby makes the meaning of every acquittal dangerously ambiguous. Replacing the monolithic not-guilty option with a variety of possible verdicts that make clear the basis for acquittal—whether
there has been no violation, a justified violation, a blameless violation, or an
unpunishable violation—enables the operational structure of criminal law to
maintain the clarity of the law's conduct prohibitions and to make the scope
of those prohibitions transparent.[20]

Thus, a "blameless-violation" verdict for Dudley[21] would make clear that,
although punishment would be improper because of an excusing condition,
he did violate society's rules of conduct when he killed and drank the blood
of his ship's cabin boy. Only a "no-violation" or "justified-violation" finding
would signal that the defendant had complied with the rules of conduct;
other verdicts would reflect a determination that the conduct is condemned
and should be avoided by others in the future. Such a system would maintain, and indeed clarify, the law's commands while also better serving the
goal of maintaining the criminal law's moral credibility with the community.
Dudley would not be punished, but neither would his acquittal send a message that such killing and cannibalism is somehow acceptable conduct.

This system also would provide benefits in nonexculpatory-defense cases
where competing social or political goals require retention of a deviation-
producing defense, such as diplomatic immunity or official immunity.[22] Where
a nonexculpatory defense precludes imposition of deserved punishment, a
"not-punishable" verdict would at least make clear that the offender's conduct is not necessarily condoned and the offender is not necessarily blameless. Manuel Ayree would at least be subject to a not-punishable verdict—
making clear that he had committed numerous rapes but was subject to a
freestanding immunity defense—rather than the ambiguous nonverdict of
the current system. The not-punishable verdict would prevent the false
claim, all too easy under the current system, by which the recipient of a
nonexculpatory defense equates the absence of liability with a conclusion
that he did nothing wrong.[23]

It might even be desirable to retain some of the nonpunitive or indirect
consequences of conviction for offenders receiving a not-punishable verdict,

as is often currently done with pardoned offenders.[24] Such collateral consequences of conviction can include loss of some basic rights and privileges,[25] such as citizenship; employment opportunities;[26] the capacities to litigate, to testify, or to serve as a juror or court-appointed fiduciary; voting, parental, and marital rights; and the rights to carry a firearm, to inherit, and to receive insurance, pension, and workers' compensation benefits. Other collateral consequences of conviction can include increased likelihood of civil forfeiture, civil restraint or injunction, civil liability, and civil commitment.[27] Finally, collateral consequences of conviction can extend to impeachment of an offender in a subsequent trial where the offender is a witness or a defendant/witness,[28] and aggravation of the sentence for a subsequent offense.[29] Thus, the child molester whose conviction is barred by the exclusionary rule or the entrapment defense might nonetheless be denied a license to drive school buses.

A not-punishable verdict could be used to authorize sanctions short of conviction and formal punishment. A nonexculpatory defense ought to authorize prosecutors to seek such sanctions (upon a showing that the defendant acquitted with a not-punishable verdict did in fact commit the offense) where needed. By branding the defendant as a blameworthy violator, the not-punishable verdict would also enable imposition of the informal or extralegal sanctions that currently flow from the stigma of criminal conviction—sanctions that should certainly apply to offenders like Ayree, a serial rapist who was beyond the direct reach of criminal justice.

Because nonexculpatory defenses exist to support social policy concerns and do not reflect the blamelessness of the individual offender, there is no reason that society should not modify such defenses, or their consequences, to achieve competing policy objectives. The scope and effect of such defenses should derive from a balancing of social interests rather than a categorical decision to advance one interest while completely losing another (doing justice).

The greatest practical hurdle to maintaining these consequences—and, indeed, to implementing the not-punishable disposition itself—is that many nonexculpatory defenses bar criminal prosecution, not just criminal liability. For example, diplomatic immunity bars trial of the defendant, as do incompetency and double jeopardy, which might also allow for not-punishable verdicts. Similarly, official immunities often are litigated as legal issues prior to trial. Thus, a not-punishable verdict in such cases would not conclusively establish that the defendant is actually blameworthy. The diplomat asserting immunity might also be innocent.

But these difficulties are not insurmountable; they can be resolved through procedural rules. A judge who finds that a defendant is not amenable to prosecution for nonexculpatory reasons may, when dismissing the charges, impose a not-punishable disposition on the defendant. If a defendant receiving such a disposition wishes to dispute the matter, the issue of blameworthiness could be litigated at a separate hearing. Where collateral consequences of conviction are sought to be imposed, the burden should be on those who seek to impose the collateral consequences to meet the normal burdens of proof of trial. Obviously, the cost of establishing the offender's guilt commonly will not be worth the benefit of the collateral consequence. But in some cases—the child sexual abuser acquitted because of entrapment or a statute of limitation who now seeks a school bus driver's license, or the immune perjurer who is now the witness in a death-penalty case—the cost may well be worth the effort. The expenditure of resources to obtain these consequences might be warranted in only a limited number of cases, but surely it makes more sense to enable imposition of such a disposition for those cases than merely to grant a blanket "not guilty" to all such offenders.

USING ALTERNATIVE PUNISHMENT METHODS

In chapter 6, we discussed how the goal of desert frequently conflicts with, and is currently often compromised in favor of, traditional utilitarian crime-control interests. The deterrence and incapacitation goals seem to demand ever-higher criminal sentences to keep offenders off the streets and to discourage others from committing crimes. The goal of rehabilitation sometimes suggests reductions in punishment that may fail to give a blameworthy offender what he deserves. This clash with desert may seem inevitable given the contrasting concerns of desert, which is backward-looking and seeks to punish past offenses, as compared to crime control, which is forward-looking and seeks to prevent future offenses. A crime-control orientation may deem to be relevant a host of factors about the offender and the community at large that do not relate to blameworthiness.[30]

Yet it is possible to accommodate both concerns—at least, to a much greater degree than is currently done. This potential exists because notions of desert concern primarily the *amount* of punishment and not the *method* of punishment. At present, the system focuses almost exclusively on two types of criminal punishment: incarceration and probation. Yet various other sanctions are currently available, including house arrest, weekend jail, electronic or other monitoring, fines, victim restitution, community service, personal or family counseling, drug treatment, regular drug testing, and mandatory job training. These other options are typically described as "intermediate sanctions" because they seem more restrictive and punitive than probation but less so than imprisonment.

Thus, if the dominant behavioral influence of the offense is drug addiction, a treatment program and counseling might better reduce future violations than will imprisonment. If poverty and hopelessness are contributors, then job training may be useful. If inattention to the harm caused victims is part of the explanation for the offense, the victim restitution and various "restorative" processes, such as mediation and sentencing circles, may reduce future violations.[31]

All of these modes of punishment are viable options for desert-based liability; all of them impose some degree of intrusion, aggravation, or suffering for the offender. Thus, so long as the total "bite" of the punishment imposed is that which the offender deserves, they can be as effective as imprisonment in imposing the punishment deserved. For more serious offenses, requiring a high level of punishment, these nonincarcerative options may become more useful by increasing their punitive bite. That is, some more onerous aspects might be added or introduced. For example, fine limits or amounts might be pegged to an offender's assets or income. This practice is followed elsewhere, as in Finland, where a well-to-do senior Nokia executive was handed a fine of $103,000 for speeding.[32] Another option is the use of "shaming" mechanisms, such as the publication of the names of offenders and the nature of their crimes.[33] Some nonincarcerative or quasi-incarcerative sanctions may be made more restrictive or severe, as by requiring an offender to serve a work furlough from a spartan halfway house (for whose costs the offender might have to pay) rather than from home or mandating community service assignments of more unpleasant tasks.

The key to ensuring that the total bite remains constant regardless of the method(s) of punishment is a conversion system showing the amounts of different punishments required to obtain an equivalent punishment effect. In other words, there must be a single "currency," a unit of punishment, that may be converted into various types of actual punishments without any change in its value in terms of punitive impact. With such a conversion system in place, sentences could consist of an assigned number of units of punishment that, although fixed in amount, would be flexible in mode of implementation— each unit could be used to "purchase" the relevant amount of *any* available punishment method deemed to be appropriate to maximize future crime prevention, given the particular characteristic of the offender at hand.

One could fashion a superior sentencing system, then, by providing fixed, uniform, desert-based rules for assessing the number of units of punishment to impose, yet granting judges (or corrections officials, as deemed appropriate) discretion in translating those units into the punishment method(s) that would be most effective in preventing future crime given the particular traits of the offense or the offender.[34] (One potential advantage of a fungible units system is that, so long as the total punishment level remains constant, it can be constructed to enable transition from one mode of punishment to another at the "back end"—by correctional officers who may wish to modify the mode of liability while the convict is serving a sentence—as well as at the "front end," when the judge originally imposes sentence.) A concomitant practical benefit of the system is that it would likely ameliorate the high financial and social costs of prison overcrowding—and would do so without letting offenders off with less punishment than they deserve.

The greatest practical difficulty in implementing such a system may be the problem of establishing the equivalency of a punishment unit among the alternative punishment methods. Translating all of the sanctions listed above into a single metric, so that one punishment unit equals X days in prison, which equals Y hours of community service, and so on, may seem a daunting project. As it happens, however, empirical studies have already done such evaluations, indicating perceptions of the relative bite of various modes of criminal liability with respect to one another.[35] These studies strongly suggest the plausibility of establishing the punishment ratios needed for an effective units-of-punishment system. Implementation of such a system could drastically reduce the extent to which the imposition of criminal liability is thought to force tradeoffs between desert-based punishment and crime control.

Some states have already made steps toward incorporating a units-of-punishment approach. Washington has a system in which, for sentences of one year or less, eight hours of community service, or one day's "partial confinement," may substitute for one day of confinement.[36] Oregon's sentencing guidelines grid provides for a maximum number of "sanction units" for forty-six combinations of offense and offender criminal history where presumptive incarceration periods do not apply. One sanction unit may be satisfied by sixteen hours of community service or by one day in jail, residential custodial treatment, house arrest, or work release.[37] These schemes are by no means comprehensive—they could include more sentencing ranges and more varieties of sanctions, such as fines—but they certainly offer some indication of the feasibility of the idea for at least some offenders.

The available intermediate sanctions may seem relatively tame compared to incarceration, which may lead some readers to worry that the actual practice of employing punishment units will inevitably fall short of the goal of doing justice, or else that the units system will prove workable only for the most minor offenses.[38] This is a legitimate concern, and the units approach surely has some limits, but we urge three counterpoints. First, in the current system, the relatively even less severe method of probation is used with high frequency, even for felonies. For example, in the year 2000, nearly a third of all state-court sentences for convicted felons—and more than one in five for violent felons—imposed only probation, with no jail or prison time.[39]

Second, the cost of imprisonment and the paucity of prison space often translate into defendants receiving—or at least, serving—sentences that are transparently shorter than they deserve, based on any assessment of the absolute gravity of the offense or the proper proportional punishment relative to other offenses. Numerous accounts describe a current system in which, to ameliorate prison overcrowding or to make way for new convicts (who are often, it is asserted, drug offenders whose offenses are subject to mandatory minimum sentences), many criminals—including violent felons—must be released before serving their full sentences.[40] The problem has been discussed on the floor of Congress, where Senator Spencer Abraham of Michigan described the rise in crime in Philadelphia after a federal judge required the release of prisoners to ease overcrowding.[41] Increased use of alternative punishments—either in lieu of or along with some incarceration—might relieve this pressure, reserving long prison terms for those who truly deserve them and ensuring that such terms are actually served by those criminals who do deserve them.

Finally, and perhaps most important, the punitive impact of incarceration—the extent to which it is felt as punishment by the person experiencing it—may be greatly exaggerated. Of course, any systematic imposition of punishment can produce some degree of deterrent bite. But a deterrence-based system faces the challenge of modulating the threatened punishment bite to achieve optimum deterrence. Lawmakers typically assume they can do this by simply altering the length of prison terms. But in reality, the studies suggest that this aspect of the deterrence calculus is neither simple nor predictable. The forces at work in determining perceived amount of punishment are complex.

For example, the "hedonic adaptation" and "subjective well-being" studies suggest that the standard for judging perceived punitive effect changes over time and conditions. In a famous paper, Brickman and Campbell introduced the idea of the "hedonic treadmill."[42] The essence of the notion is that over time, people who move from a neutral psychological state to a set of circumstances that initially produces a better, more-positive state come to adapt to that new set of circumstances, eventually lapsing back to neutrality. A person who wins the lottery, or moves to southern California from a place with poor weather, is initially euphoric, but over time she reverts to her previous neutral level. This adaptive effect has been found to work in both directions; both those suffering accidents making them paraplegics and those winning the lottery tend to adjust similarly to their new circumstances, treating them as their new neutral state.[43] Applying these concepts to the specific context of prison incarceration, a recent study concluded that "although incarceration is designed to be unpleasant, most of the research on adjustment to prison life points to considerable adaptation" over time.[44] Thus, as a prison term continues, it can become increasingly less painful in effect, although its monetary cost per unit time remains constant, making each unit increasingly less cost effective.

Further, the "duration neglect" studies suggest that the *intensity* of the punishment experience, rather than its *duration*, has the greatest influence on its perceived severity.[45] In these experiments, the amount contributed by duration to the remembered experience of pain was small.[46] Accordingly, it seems inappropriate to structure the criminal-punishment system as if prolonging the duration of a prison term will lead to constant, uniform increases in its punitive bite. Indeed, because the studies show that remembered intensity is highly influenced by the *end-point* intensity—which, as the adaptation-to-circumstances effect indicates, *decreases* with increased duration—it is possible that the overall remembered bite of a prison term decreases as it gets longer.

This psychological evidence is relevant in three ways. First, it suggests that, in terms of defining equivalent amounts of punishment that will equal one unit, it may take a lower amount of an alternative punishment to equal a corresponding prison term than might at first be supposed. This is increasingly true as the potential prison sentence gets longer, as days of imprisonment are not fungible in terms of their punitive bite: because of the rapidly diminishing marginal punitive impact noted above, the first 30 days of incarceration are more "painful" than days 100 to 130 and *much* more painful than days 1,000 to 1,030. Accordingly, a finely tuned units-of-punishment system might not treat all incarceration days as equal, but give additional weight to the earlier ones, making it easier to trade later ones in favor of alternative sanctions.

Second, this evidence suggests that the project of achieving specific deterrence—discouraging offenders from offending again—by imposing ever-longer prison sentences is thoroughly misguided. The longer the term, the less bad it may seem in the offender's memory. As one grows accustomed to imprisonment, and each day seems less onerous than the previous one, both the average perceived punishment of a day in prison and the seeming severity of the days at the very end—that is, the days that the offender is likely to remember best—decrease rapidly. As prison seems more manageable, or at least less harsh, the prospect of returning becomes less daunting.[47]

Third, the psychological data suggest the utility of alternative punishments, especially to the extent that those punishments may be combined with incarceration so that the sting of each day in prison may be more keenly felt. For example, an offender who is let out of prison each weekend will be given enough of a recurrent taste of freedom that the renewed experience of entering prison again may have a greater overall punitive effect than if he had been in prison the whole time.

CHAPTER 10

Employing Civil Rather Than Criminal Processes

S EVERAL OF THE reform proposals we have mentioned share the position that the civil law offers a better mechanism for advancing the interests now advanced by a criminal-law doctrine that deviates from desert. In chapter 8, we urged a system of administrative violations to replace criminal liability for regulatory violations or criminal liability for nonhuman entities. In chapter 7, we suggested that civil damages or administrative sanctions may be a better means of dealing with many official violations of rights than the exclusion of reliable evidence or the outright dismissal of charges. In chapter 6, we proposed an explicit system of post- criminal term civil commitment, which we argued would provide a more honest and effective means of protecting the society from dangerous offenders than would using criminal justice as a system of cloaked preventive detention. We discuss each of these proposals in more detail below.

USING ADMINISTRATIVE, INSTEAD OF CRIMINAL, SANCTIONS FOR REGULATORY VIOLATIONS

The United States commonly provides administrative procedures for enforcing governmental regulations. The unfortunate trend toward criminalizing regulatory violations derives in part from lawmakers' desire to invoke the greater sanctions and the stigma available from criminal liability. The desire for a bigger stick is understandable, but as we demonstrate in chapter 8, it is not clear that the use of criminal law is a necessary or desirable means of getting one. Several European nations—including Germany, Italy, and Spain—have devised an alternative system that defines noncriminal "violations" or "infractions" and enforces them through administrative agencies.[1] As one commentator describes:

> Pursuant to [Germany's Law on Infractions], a legal entity could be fined up to one million German marks [approximately $650,000]. These fines also include forfeiture of any windfalls occasioned by the illegal activity and thus, in certain areas such as antitrust, could exceed the limit in a penalty of several millions of marks. Non-criminal monetary sanctions have also been introduced in Scandinavia for violations of state regulations, such as emissions standards. In 1987, Austria established the general power to confiscate any profits gained as a result of a violation. This sanction was understood as a remedy *sui generis* and not as a criminal fine.[2]

Other nations, such as France and Belgium, have included administrative sanctions on an ad hoc basis whenever, in the course of drafting a statute, it seems suitable to do so.[3] For example, Belgium's 1993 money-laundering statute, designed to prevent the use of banks for money-laundering purposes, empowers the Belgian banking authority to impose fines of up to 50 million Belgian francs (approximately $1.58 million) on violating banks.[4] These enforcement mechanisms "have neither the status of criminal sanctions nor that of purely administrative measures."[5] Thus, they reflect societal disapprobation without confusing or muddying the more severe moral assessment of blameworthiness reflected in a finding of criminality.[6]

Such administrative mechanisms also provide additional benefits beyond their preservation of the criminal law's unique focus on desert. Because they are not criminal in nature, the adjudication procedures need not provide all of the procedural rights that exist in the criminal-justice system, although of course lawmakers are free to maintain such procedural rights as seem useful and appropriate. For example, in the German system, "although the *Geldbussen* [fines] are imposed by administrative bodies, an appeal lies to a criminal court," so that "the rights of the defence are guaranteed."[7] Allocating jurisdiction to the administrative system also helps to remove from the criminal-justice system "the kinds of public order or 'victimless' crimes . . . that clog American criminal courts and aggravate problems of police and prosecutorial discretion."[8] Further, providing enforcement through an agency rather than the criminal court may be desirable where the offenses involve technical matters better handled by an administrative body with expertise in the relevant regulatory field.[9]

In the context of corporate criminal liability, mechanisms for administrative sanctioning need not maintain the fiction of a corporate *mens rea*— which raises thorny issues of when the corporation "deserves" vicarious criminal liability for conduct necessarily performed by its agents, rather than by the corporation itself. An administrative sanctioning system can retain more flexibility in deciding whose acts may lead to corporate liability and when those acts will do so, or may obviate altogether the requirement of showing that any particular person acted with culpability. (This last benefit would likely be increasingly slight vis-à-vis current American law, as courts have stretched the doctrine of *respondeat superior* to allow broad imputation of criminal conduct and culpability to corporations. For example, under modern American rules for corporate criminality, it is not necessary for the same individual actor to provide both the conduct and the state of mind required by the offense, and the knowledge of different persons may be aggregated even when no single person possesses an offense's requisite state of mind.[10] Further, a corporation often may be liable for its representatives' acts undertaken with only apparent rather than actual authority[11] or even acts that violate company policy.[12] But all of this, needless to say, merely highlights the complexity, and perhaps vacuity, of attempting to impute criminal culpability to a nonhuman entity and how out of step the rules enabling corporate criminal liability are with the everyday rules governing criminal liability.)

There is no reason to believe that such an administrative sanctioning approach could not work in this country. Indeed, to an extent, such a system already exists.[13] Various federal agencies are vested with the power to bring civil proceedings against regulatory violators, which allow the same penalties—including monetary fines, forfeiture, loss of government benefits and privileges, injunctive relief, expatriation and deportment, and restitution[14]— that are typically imposed by criminal courts for regulatory and corporate offenses. Indeed, civil administrative remedies are often considered *more* effective sanctions than corresponding criminal sanctions, and not just because the procedural rules and burden of proof are more favorable to the enforcing authority. As one group of commentators has observed:

> Persons faced with the possibility of losing their money, property, business, or livelihood, may be more likely to adhere to the governmental statutes and regulations than if they face a lower probability of a short prison sentence. Because the burden of proof in criminal proceedings is so high, the probability of conviction is relatively low. . . .

Even in cases where the procedural requirements have been met, juries are often reluctant to convict corporate officials, even though a criminal conviction may result in lesser penalties than those provided for under civil provisions.[15]

As a result of the reduced likelihood of conviction, the good chance of avoiding any prison time after conviction, and the brevity of the prison time even if it is ultimately imposed, perhaps it should not be surprising that the availability of criminal sanctions seems to have done little to prevent major American corporate scandals and wrongdoing.

Current criminal proceedings and remedies involve additional bureaucracy and waste. Although federal agencies usually conduct the initial investigation into a violator's misconduct, they generally are not empowered to bring criminal actions themselves but must refer such cases to the Department of Justice (DOJ) for prosecution.[16] Administrative civil enforcement is more efficient than criminal enforcement for other reasons as well. As mentioned, there are lower procedural thresholds and evidentiary burdens in the civil context. Partly for this reason, administrative proceedings tend to enable greater speed and efficiency of resolution. Further, the government can avoid the costs of litigation by allowing private enforcement via *qui tam* and other suits that enable aggrieved citizens to sue in place of the government or on its behalf. Finally, there is often the potential for higher monetary recovery against violators in civil suits.[17]

Thus, eliminating existing criminal authority and using the civil administrative system to prosecute quasi-criminal "infractions," as some jurisdictions term them, perhaps with stiffer penalties than currently exist for civil violations, would accomplish three goals. First, it would eliminate the existence of morally trivial criminal offenses that blur the criminal-civil distinction and undercut the moral authority of the criminal law. Second, it would abolish the current redundant system whereby agencies can bring civil actions and the DOJ can also bring criminal actions.[18] Third, a modified civil system could enable increased flexibility as to procedural and evidentiary issues.[19] At the same time, because most of the administrative agencies that would implement this mechanism already exist and have well-developed executive and judicial divisions, carrying out this proposal would not require severe disruption nor would it create vast new bureaucracies.

The experiences and examples of other countries instruct us that administrative remedies can be sufficient to sanction and deter regulatory violations. There is little reason, then, to dilute the force of the criminal law by using it to enforce rules that have little relation to findings of moral blameworthiness.

CONTROLLING POLICE AND PROSECUTOR MISCONDUCT WITHOUT LETTING THE CRIMINAL GO FREE

In chapter 7, we discussed various desert-violating rules and remedies, such as Fourth and Fifth Amendment exclusionary rules and the speedy-trial right, whose aim is to curb prosecutorial and police misconduct—and we questioned whether these rules actually advance that goal in practice. Yet even if those rules do deter misconduct, that fact is not enough to justify them; the rules should be retained only if they are better than any other available practical means of achieving their goal. The fact is that alternative, nondeviating mechanisms are available that would promote the control-of-officials goal while also advancing the desert goal.

One frequently advocated alternative means of curbing police misconduct is to require that the violating officials literally pay for their misdeeds, either in the form of compensation to those whose rights they have violated or by payment of a fine to some administrative body. Numerous commentators have proposed various formulations of this alternative, specifically as a replacement for the Fourth Amendment exclusionary rule.[20] A bill that would replace the Fourth Amendment exclusionary rule with a civil-damages remedy against police was introduced in Congress, but not enacted.[21] Another proposal would enable criminal defendants to obtain a reduction in sentence, rather than exclusion of the evidence, on showing a violation, in order to maintain their incentive to litigate the issue even without the exclusionary remedy in place.[22] (We consider this a less-attractive alternative, because it still produces a deviation from desert, albeit a lesser deviation. We mention it only because it may be a more attractive alternative for those who insist that the violation of rights should affect the criminal disposition.) Similar proposals relating to interrogation procedures, rather than to searches and seizures, are less common, but also appear. For example, a Minnesota statute provides for law-enforcement officials to pay a $100 penalty to any suspect to whom they deny the right to consult with counsel during a pre-arrest interrogation.[23]

The literature in this area is exhaustive. Rather than seeking to recapitulate these sources in brief summaries that may distort the subtleties of some proposals, we refer the interested reader to them.[24] While we will not discuss the merits of each proposal, we offer here some general observations about how the proposals relate to the goal of minimizing deviations from desert.

First, although the alternative remedies are nearly always proposed in connection with the Fourth Amendment exclusionary rule, there is no reason to think they could not be equally useful as replacements for, say, the entrapment defense or the speedy-trial remedy. All of these rules share the same goal—to curb official misconduct or overreaching—and it seems entirely possible that a solution that achieves this goal in the place of one rule may, with a few modifications, work as well in the place of others. Both the exclusionary rule that prevented the use of key evidence of Eyler's killings[25] and the entrapment defense that enabled DeLorean's acquittal for his drug deal[26] effectively sought to punish the police who used improper or unfair practices to catch them, rather than to exonerate the defendants based on any lack of blameworthiness. A monetary or administrative sanction could directly penalize the police tactics employed against these offenders while still allowing effective prosecution.

Second, such an alternative system for sanctioning official misconduct could operate not only in cases involving violations of the rights of the guilty but also in cases involving violations of the rights of the innocent—unlike the present exclusionary rules, the speedy-trial remedy, or the entrapment defense, which benefit only those (such as Eyler and DeLorean) who have committed an offense and need a defense or evidentiary exclusion. Some have denounced this only-helps-the-guilty criticism of the rules as misleading, claiming that because the focus of the rules is ex ante deterrence of future misconduct and not ex post compensation for those whose rights have already been violated, they actually benefit us all by giving voice to the protections of the Fourth Amendment and preventing future infringements of our rights.[27] But of course, this is a defense of the Constitution itself—or of the general goal of preventing governmental overreaching—and not of the exclusionary rules. *Any* remedy that provides effective ex ante deterrence of police misconduct and that effectively enforces the Constitution's mandates would provide this benefit. Moreover, whatever the stated goal, there is no doubt that one effect (whether sought or ancillary) of the present rules is to provide an ex post remedy and to provide it only to guilty offenders.

Third, these alternative remedies would actually work as remedies and not just as behavior-modification devices. Typically, legal remedies are meant to serve, and do serve, both as ex ante deterrents to future undesirable conduct and as ex post compensation or restitution for past misconduct. Yet the exclusionary rules do not fit this mold, as they are meant to operate only as ex ante deterrents. They are not intended as restitutionary measures for victims of constitutional violations; if they were, it would make little sense to have, for example, an exception leaving victims of "good-faith" violations with no remedy.[28]

It is somewhat reassuring to know that the rules are not meant to be compensation measures, for they do a poor job as such. As noted, they aid only the guilty and not the innocent—implying that the Bill of Rights exists solely to protect against improper criminal convictions, when its true purpose is to prevent improper intrusions on liberty, which may be suffered by law-abiding citizens as well as criminals. The law-abiding citizen who is pulled over, detained, and subjected to the indignity of a baseless search surely merits some form of compensation as much or more than does Larry Eyler, who suffered only the indignity of having his heinous crimes discovered. Accordingly, it makes sense to look for a remedy that operates the way most remedies do: both as a backward-looking restitutionary measure and as a forward-looking behavior-modification device. A direct monetary sanction, paid by offending officials to all injured citizens, would avoid the unfortunate disconnect between the current exclusionary rules' general aim and their particular effects.

Finally, the most important issue is not whether alternative remedies are applicable to rules beyond the Fourth Amendment or whether they work better as remedies to injured parties, but whether they would achieve the central goal of curbing misconduct more thoroughly and directly than do current rules. On this score, it must first be pointed out that the performance of the current remedies—exclusion of evidence, acquittal through an affirmative defense, or dismissal of charges—is dubious.[29]

There is every reason to think that potential personal liability for offending officials would indeed get their full attention and deter misconduct. Indeed, one might speculate that such alternative control mechanisms have failed to be implemented in part for fear they may be *too* effective—that they would paralyze police, and the resulting inaction would increase crime.[30] But one can well imagine that a compromise can be struck where police or prosecutors are treated fairly when their violations are judged, and some but not too much deterrence is provided. (Note that this is one instance where the conditions for effective deterrence actually do exist: informed officials facing enforceable standards of conduct.)

Perhaps most important, a legal sanction that punished offending individual officials, either directly or by promoting institutional reforms that would hold violators accountable,[31] would create a powerful incentive for those officials actually to learn and follow the law governing search and seizure. Indeed, it would ensure the development of familiarity with at least some aspects of the relevant law, as each allegedly offending officer would be a party to the proceeding that determines the propriety of his questionable search. At the moment, it is at best unclear whether police officers generally understand the numerous and complex constitutional rules regulating their conduct.[32]

If we value the importance of doing justice, it is at least worth exploring such alternative methods of controlling police conduct without perverting justice.

DISTINGUISHING DANGEROUSNESS FROM BLAMEWORTHINESS

As we discussed in chapter 6, the current criminal-justice system, in its efforts to achieve the utilitarian goal of incapacitation, sometimes confuses detention of the dangerous for preventive purposes with detention of the guilty for punitive purposes. Yet punishment and prevention are different functions that logically use different criteria and that call for different procedures. Trying to use a single system to perform both functions ensures that neither will be performed effectively. Today's mixed system, in which preventive detention is cloaked as criminal justice through the use of such mechanisms as three-strikes laws, suffers problems both in doing justice and in protecting society.[33]

Moreover, there is no need to compromise one to advance the other, for the conflict between justice and prevention can be avoided by simply segregating the two functions: by having a criminal-justice system that focuses exclusively on imposing the punishment deserved for the *past* offense and having a post–criminal-incarceration civil-commitment system that looks only to protecting society from *future* offenses by a dangerous offender. The sticking point in this proposal is *not* in having a criminal-justice system that is guided only by justice. That is what most laypersons assume the criminal-justice system has always sought to do and what they generally want it to do. The difficulty comes, instead, with the open recognition of a system of preventive detention.

There is precedent for preventive detention. Many states presently have some form of civil commitment operating to protect society. Most jurisdictions allow civil commitment to detain dangerous persons who have mental illnesses, drug dependencies, or contagious diseases.[34] Further, providing a more direct precedent, many states presently have post–criminal-incarceration civil commitment of "sexual predators."[35] Under these civil-commitment programs, the government can attempt to detain an offender at the conclusion of his criminal term if it can show continuing dangerousness. (Unlike our proposal, however, there is no indication that the current sexual-predator legislation excludes reliance upon dangerousness in setting the initial criminal commitment. It is less a segregated punishment-prevention system than a cloaked preventive-detention system followed by an additional, explicit preventive-detention system.)

Despite the precedent, there will be concern about creating a broader system of explicit preventive detention. One obvious concern is that the post–criminal-incarceration preventive-detention proposal might be held to be unconstitutional. While the permissible scope of civil commitment has recently been expanded slightly, it still appears to require not only a finding of dangerousness but also some additional factor, such as mental abnormality.[36] But this would be an odd result: barring civil commitment with its periodic review of dangerousness for a dangerous murderer, but permitting on preventive grounds, as the Court explicitly does, life imprisonment without parole for a petty-fraud offender.[37]

Beyond the issue of constitutionality, some will take the view that a detention system is simply undesirable or dangerous, and those concerns are understandable; the *Gulag Archipelago* potential for governmental abuse is admittedly real. It is important to keep in mind, however, the extent to which such problems and abuses already exist under the current criminal system. For example, part of preventive detention's bad reputation stems from an objection to its quality of having the punishment precede the offense. Yet that same objection can be made of the present system of de facto preventive detention through expanded offense definitions or in sentencing, where, for purely incapacitative purposes, an offender is given an incarcerative punishment far beyond what any desert-based scheme would impose. Obscuring the preventive character of such extended detention by imposing it under the criminal-justice system may reduce open controversy and public outrage, but it does not alter the underlying fact that the incarceration is justified by fear of an offense that has not yet been committed.

Finally, some might question—not without reason—the capacity of a civil-confinement system to accurately predict which offenders remain dangerous and pose an ongoing threat. We agree that, at present, experts have only limited ability to empirically predict which particular offenders are likely to re-offend—although the quality of their predictive power seems to be increasing over time.[38] But consider how much poorer a job the current system of cloaked detention through criminal incarceration is doing, with its crude and across-the-board sentence enhancements that subject *all* offenders in a given category to greatly enhanced punishment, with no consideration whatever of their individual dangerousness. A civil-commitment system whose goals are explicit and whose methods seek directly to maximize those goals would stand a much better chance of minimizing the unnecessary detention of "false positives" than the current system does. And if the predictive accuracy of dangerousness assessments were too low, that failing would have to be explicitly addressed and overcome. In the current system, there is no accountability if three-strikes or other laws prove to preventively incarcerate vast numbers of offenders for no good reason.

In any case, given that the alternative to an explicit system of preventive detention is the present system of cloaked preventive detention, the risks of reform are worth taking. An explicit system of post–criminal-incarceration preventive detention would be better for both the community and potential detainees.[39]

The community would be better off because such an explicit preventive-detention system offers both more justice and better protection from dangerous offenders. Giving the criminal-justice system a better chance of doing justice is valuable for its own sake and also means greater moral credibility for the system, thus greater long-term crime-control power. Better protection is offered because an explicit preventive-detention system, which can look directly at a person's present dangerousness, stands the best chance of accurately assessing who is and who is not dangerous. Accuracy is enhanced further by periodic reevaluations, rather than the present system's need to make a single prediction of dangerousness years in advance. Greater accuracy means a higher rate of detention of the dangerous, resulting in better protection, and a lower rate of detention of the nondangerous, reducing waste and unnecessary infringements on liberty.

A segregated, explicit preventive-detention system also benefits the potential detainees, for many of the same reasons. Better accuracy in prediction means less detention of nondangerous offenders. Periodic reevaluation means detention more frequently limited to periods of actual dangerousness; if the dangerousness disappears, so does the detention. But if the detention is characterized as deserved punishment for a past offense, as under three-strikes provisions and the like, there is little reason to revisit the justification for the detention, and indeed no such reevaluation currently takes place. Instead, the present system avoids periodic review by hiding behind the veil of deserved punishment for which fixed terms are appropriate.

In addition, acknowledgment of the preventive nature of the detention also logically suggests a right to treatment, nonpunitive conditions, and the principle of minimum restraint, meaning greater freedom for those who are detained. When a person is detained for society's benefit rather than because of deserved punishment, logically the conditions of detention ought to be nonpunitive. Where confinement is imposed as deserved punishment, on the other hand, the offender has little justification to complain about punitive conditions; the point of the imprisonment is to bring about suffering, within the bounds of human dignity. By cloaking preventive detention as punishment, then, the current system need not justify its failure to provide nonpunitive conditions of detention. Further, the extent of restraint justified by prevention logically should be limited to the minimum required for the community's safety. If house arrest, an ankle bracelet, drug therapy, or other non-incarcerative conditions provide adequate protection, then greater restraint cannot be justified. But because no such minimum-restraint principle applies in the application of deserved punishment, the current system spares authorities from having to show that the detention imposed is the least-restrictive adequate method for protection.

Beyond all of these reasons, an open, explicit system of preventive detention ought to be preferred precisely because it is open rather than cloaked. No one can guarantee that a legislature or court will not attempt to abuse its power. But an open system makes it harder, not easier, to abuse the system. The openly preventive nature of the system subjects it to closer scrutiny, as it should, while the present cloaked system escapes such scrutiny. Instead of the current debates—which typically reduce to disagreements about, for example, whether three-strikes sentences are "too long"—the debate would shift to the many aspects of preventive detention that cry out for debate: what is the reliability of the predictions of dangerousness? Is the threatened danger sufficient to justify the extent of intrusion on personal liberty? Are there less-expensive or less-intrusive measures that would as effectively protect the community? Under the current cloaked system, these issues escape examination and debate.

Imagine, for example, a legislature trying to pass an explicit preventive-detention statute that would provide for life detention following a third conviction for a minor fraud offense, the disposition provided by the statute in *Rummel*.[40] Such legislation would be difficult to defend and unlikely to find support in any political quarter. Indeed, imagine the Supreme Court's review of *Rummel* if Rummel were being preventively detained. Life terms without possibility of parole may be common in a criminal-justice system, where horrible crimes can deserve severe punishment, and thus are more likely to seem acceptable when imposed in the criminal context. But life commitment, with no further dangerousness review, in a civil preventive-detention system would be preposterous on its face.

In short, if there is a danger of governmental abuse of preventive detention, it is at its greatest when that preventive detention is cloaked as criminal justice.

Doing Justice in a Complex World

THIS BOOK HAS made several basic claims. First, doing justice is important—not only for its own sake, but because failing to do justice has
practical costs in addition to whatever intangible moral costs we may
associate with it. Second, despite the importance of doing justice, criminal
law often sees fit to do something else—sometimes with good reason and
sometimes (it seems to us) not.

More specifically, we have identified eight general objectives that drive
criminal law and have explored the tensions between one of those objectives—justice, or desert—and the other seven. In conducting this survey of
the reasons and rules that may conflict with desert, we have done three
things: we have surveyed and listed the purposes that underlie criminal-law
doctrine; we have surveyed and categorized the specific doctrines that potentially lead to violations of the desert principle; and we have suggested what,
if anything, can be done to eliminate or reduce the dissonance between those
doctrines and the desert goal.

The consequences of that dissonance, where it exists, are real. To offer a
final illustration of those consequences, we offer an example we have discussed little so far: drug laws and drug policy. In the area of drug policy, both
substantive criminal prohibitions and the methods of enforcing those prohibitions involve numerous and frequent deviations from justice, falling into

nearly all of the categories we have identified. As a result, drug laws (and, to some extent, the criminal-justice system as a whole) have lost significant credibility, which predictably makes efforts to uphold those laws even more difficult.

First, criminal drug offenses often lack elements seen as central to desert or contain elements that may poorly track desert. For example, they often punish mere possession, rather than affirmative conduct, and also may require little or no culpability as to key elements of the crime, such as the quantity of drugs possessed or sold. These rules may reflect a concern with potential abuses of the kind we discussed in chapter 2 or an effort to foster reliable results by easing the state's difficult burdens of proof, as we discussed in chapter 3.

Second, the enforcement of those crimes involves practices in tension with desert. Owing to resource constraints of the kind we discussed in chapter 4, law-enforcement officials cannot pursue every drug offender. Unlike other crimes, because drug transactions are consensual, police enforcing drug laws are not responding to a report of a past crime but must go out looking for present crime.[1] They tend to look where offenders will be easiest to find. Often, this means disproportionately concentrating on low-income, high-minority neighborhoods, where drug sales are more likely to occur in street transactions or at specific places.[2] In addition, probably more than any other area of criminal law, the jurisprudence of the exclusionary rules we discuss in chapter 7 has been influenced by, and has in turn influenced, the war on drugs. Accordingly, drug enforcement, from the perspective of those against whom the laws are enforced, must highlight both the arbitrariness of the exclusionary remedy's application and its failure to deter police misconduct—especially since the remedy offers nothing to innocent victims of improper searches or unjustified stops.[3] Further, because drug crimes involve consensual conduct and typically involve large-scale conspiracies with many members, practices such as witness immunity, which we discussed in chapter 4, are also crucial in prosecuting drug offenders. Accordingly, some offenders are punished severely, based on the testimony of their luckier or more clever colleagues, while other, perhaps equally culpable, offenders receive little or no punishment.

Finally, once offenders are caught, the penalties for drug violations are frequently draconian. Even acknowledging that drug crimes can be seen as seriously blameworthy conduct meriting considerable punishment, it is hard to disagree with the assessment that "drug penalties dispensed by American criminal justice systems frequently have strained or broken basic notions of proportionality (when compared to sentences for other more serious crimes)."[4] Indeed, many aspects of sentencing do not even seem to claim any basis in desert, but rather heighten penalties on claims of the kind we discussed in chapter 6, involving the need to deter drug activity or to incapacitate the dangerous offenders who deal drugs by getting them off the streets.[5]

What is the result of all of this? Drug laws are widely violated, and in areas where drug laws are enforced most regularly, the criminal-justice system generally is seen as suspect if not clearly illegitimate. People subjected to the enforcement of drug laws — or their family members, friends, or neighbors — are thereby introduced to a world whose rules often seem to bear little or no relation to the goal of giving people what they deserve. Should we be surprised that these people view the system as unfair?[6] As we have discussed throughout this book, this loss of systemic credibility or legitimacy in the eyes of the public, or a subset of it, weakens the law's authority and its power to induce compliance.[7]

In fighting the war on drugs, because we are so willing to forgo desert in favor of other goals, we may be losing one of our greatest weapons: the ability of a just legal system to command respect and therefore to promote obedience.[8] Perhaps worst of all, when crime rates do not go down, the standard response is merely to increase enforcement efforts and punishment levels in an effort to achieve greater deterrence, which only further undermines the law's moral credibility, ensuring that compliance will not increase and may even decrease.

The point of this discussion is not to say that no rule that deviates from justice is ever acceptable or supportable. Many are, at least some of the time. Our effort here has been to make clear the costs of sacrificing justice and to at least examine the rules that lead us to incur that cost. Some such rules may be inevitable; some seem dubious even on their own terms; some could be replaced by other, more desert-friendly rules; and for many, the answer is simply that we do not know how great a cost they impose or how much of a benefit they provide. One of our goals has been to point out just how much we don't know and how much more empirical study is needed to address our lack of knowledge.

We do not expect that this book will categorically resolve all, or perhaps even any, of the debates surrounding the doctrines we have discussed. We also acknowledge that no solution or combination of solutions will ever entirely eliminate systematic, much less occasional or haphazard, deviations from the dictates of desert. Yet we believe that by clarifying the terms of these debates, we may generate reform proposals that would strike a better balance between the numerous goals at play in our criminal-justice system. It is our hope that the careful enumeration and categorization of the various purposes and problems of criminal law might enable a clearer understanding of how to realize its purposes and minimize its problems.

NOTES

INTRODUCTION

1. See Lockyer v. Andrade, 538 U.S. 63 (2003).

2. See Justice Anthony M. Kennedy, Speech at the American Bar Association Annual Meeting, at 4 (Aug. 9, 2003), available at http://www.supremecourtus.gov/publicinfo/speeches/sp_08–09–03.html.

3. See Deborah W. Denno, *The Perils of Public Opinion*, 28 Hofstra L. Rev. 741, 754 (2000) ("Opinion polls in the United States and other countries show that the public has little knowledge of the nature and extent of crime. Moreover, what little knowledge the public has is substantially distorted. . . . [F]or example, a common public misperception is that crime rates are increasing, particularly rates of violent crime, when in fact they are declining or stabilizing. Likewise, the great majority of offenders and parolees do not become repeat offenders, in contrast to widespread public beliefs that they do. In general, then, the growth in public concern over crime appears unrelated to any escalation in crime rates or the proportion of crimes involving violence."); cf. Julian V. Roberts, *Public Opinion and Youth Justice*, 31 Crime & Just. 495, 499–500 (2004) ("Polls in several Western countries reveal that the public hold[s] a distorted view of the magnitude (and nature) of the juvenile crime problem. Thus [members of] the public believe that juvenile crime rates are constantly rising, and they overestimate the recidivism rates associated with juvenile offenders. . . . As with perceptions of crime by adults, public views of juvenile crime and justice are systematically distorted in the direction of seeing the problem as being worse than it is."). For more on the public's views about crime rates and other aspects of the criminal justice system, see generally Julian V. Roberts & Loretta J. Stalans, *Public Opinion, Crime, and Criminal Justice* (Westview 1997).

4. See Francis T. Cullen et al., *Public Opinion about Punishment and Corrections,* 27 Crime & Just. 1, 38 (2000) (noting that Washington's three-strikes law passed by a three-to-one margin in a 1993 referendum, and that California's three-strikes law passed by 72% to 28% in a 1994 referendum; also citing national polls conducted in 1994 by Time/CNN (showing 81% support for three-strikes laws) and by The Wall Street Journal/NBC (showing 76% support)).

5. See Michael Vitiello, *Reforming Three Strikes' Excesses,* 82 Wash. U. L. Q. 1, 24 n.192 (2004) (citing polls indicating over 60% of Californians would amend the state's three-strikes law to limit it to violent felons); see also Cullen et al., supra note 4, at 39 (discussing a 1995 opinion poll of Cincinnati residents, showing strong support for the general idea of a three-strikes law, but also showing support for various limitations and exceptions when respondents are asked about possible specific cases).

6. Modern academics have become comfortable with a criminal-justice system that does not do justice (more on this in later chapters), but laypersons generally have not. They still assume that criminal liability and punishment ought to depend upon a person's moral blameworthiness. See, e.g., John M. Darley et al., *Incapacitation and Just Deserts as Motives for Punishment,* 24 Law & Hum. Behav. 659 (2000) (empirical study suggesting that laypersons do not take account of correlates of future criminality in setting punishment, especially when other protective mechanisms than the criminal-justice system are available, but look instead to blameworthiness); Cass R. Sunstein et al., *Do People Want Optimal Deterrence?,* 29 J. Legal Stud. 237 (2000) (discussing two reported experiments suggesting that people do not spontaneously think in terms of optimal deterrence and that people would have objections to policies based on the goal of optimal deterrence); Kevin M. Carlsmith et al., *Why Do We Punish? Deterrence and Just Deserts as Motives for Punishment,* 83 J. Personality & Soc. Psych. 284 (2002) (empirical study suggesting that laypersons do not consider difficulty of detection or publicity—classic deterrence factors—in setting punishment).

7. William J. Stuntz, *The Pathological Politics of Criminal Law,* 100 Mich. L. Rev. 505 (2001).

0. See Paul H. Robinson & Michael T. Cahill, *The Accelerating Degradation of American Criminal Codes,* 56 Hastings L.J. 633 (2005), Paul H. Robinson & Michael T. Cahill, *Can a Model Penal Code Second Save the States from Themselves?,* 1 Ohio St. J. Crim. L. 169 (2003).

CHAPTER 1

1. See infra "A Further Word on What We Mean by 'Doing Justice.'"

2. It is true, though, that "public opinion" can be unreliable in assessing what justice requires in a given case. We refer here not to the popular pronouncements of what justice demands in sensational cases covered by the media, for example, but rather to the shared *deliberative* sensibilities of the public. Even the lynch mob knows the difference between a lynching and justice. The justice we discuss here is not what public or private persons may scream for in a well-publicized case—where,

among other things, facts are typically omitted, embellished, or distorted by media coverage—but what shared principles of justice, developed in a neutral context marked by sober reflection, would suggest if applied.

3. See Paul H. Robinson & John M. Darley, *Justice, Liability, and Blame: Community Views and the Criminal Law* (Westview 1995) (hereinafter Robinson & Darley, *Justice, Liability, and Blame*).

4. Paul H. Robinson & John M. Darley, *The Role of Deterrence in the Formulation of Criminal Law Rules: At Its Worst When Doing Its Best*, 91 Geo. L.J. 949, 971–74 (2003) (hereinafter Robinson & Darley, *Role of Deterrence*).

5. See Paul H. Robinson & John M. Darley, *Does Criminal Law Deter? A Social Science Investigation*, 24 Oxford J. Legal Stud. 173 (2004), appendix available at http://www.law.upenn.edu/fac/phrobins/OxfordDeterrenceAppendix.pdf; Robinson & Darley, *Role of Deterrence*, supra n. 4; Paul H. Robinson, *Punishing Dangerousness: Cloaking Preventive Detention as Criminal Justice*, 114 Harv. L. Rev. 1429 (2001).

6. See generally Paul H. Robinson & John M. Darley, *The Utility of Desert*, 91 Nw. U. L. Rev. 453 (1997) (hereinafter Robinson & Darley, *Utility of Desert*).

7. See generally idem; Robinson & Darley, *Justice, Liability, and Blame*, supra n. 3.

8. See idem at 14–27.

9. While "harm-based" retributivism contends that an actor deserves less punishment when the resulting harm does not occur, "intent-based" retributivism looks to the actor's state of mind and holds that the fortuity of the result should not matter. Compare Andrew Ashworth, *Criminal Attempts and the Role of Resulting Harm under the Code, and in the Common Law*, 19 Rutgers L.J. 725, 738–44, 770 (1988) (discussing these two positions and adopting the intent-based view, concluding that "[a] rational system for judging human behavior should pay attention to choice, not chance"); Sanford Kadish, *The Criminal Law and the Luck of the Draw*, 84 J. Crim. L. & Criminology 679 (1994), with George Fletcher, *Rethinking Criminal Law* § 6.6.5, at 482–83 (Little, Brown 1978) (arguing for differential punishment of attempts and completed crimes); Leo Katz, *Why the Successful Assassin Is More Wicked Than the Unsuccessful One*, 88 Cal. L. Rev. 791 (2000); Michael S. Moore, *The Independent Moral Significance of Wrongdoing*, 5 J. Contemp. Legal Issues 237 (1994).

10. See Robinson & Darley, *Justice, Liability, and Blame*, supra n. 3.

11. See Norval Morris, *The Future of Imprisonment* 73–76 (U. Chicago 1974); Norval Morris & Marc Miller, *Predictions of Dangerousness*, 6 Crime & Just. 1, 35 (1985).

12. See Andrew von Hirsch, *Past or Future Crimes: Deservedness and Dangerousness in the Sentencing of Criminals* 40 (Rutgers 1985).

13. Recent empirical research demonstrating much sophistication in shared lay intuitions of justice seems consistent with this view of desert. See, e.g., Robinson & Darley, *Justice, Liability, and Blame*, supra n. 3. Presented with a dozen or more scenarios describing similar but different cases, subjects in the studies generally agree on the rank and even the relative gap separating the cases as to the amount of punishment deserved. Some of the subjects impose generally longer sentences, some generally shorter sentences, but both harsh and lenient sentencers typically agree on

the *pattern* of relative blameworthiness among the cases, even when the factual differences among the cases are slight. Further, the agreement among subjects cuts across class, gender, education, race, income, religion, and most other significant demographic variables. See idem at 226.

14. See Paul H. Robinson, *Desert, Crime Control, Disparity, and Units of Punishment*, in *Penal Theory and Practice: Tradition and Innovation in Criminal Justice* 93–107 (Antony Duff et al., eds., 1994). This is the insight that makes possible our "units of punishment" proposal in chapter 9.

15. The remainder of this subsection summarizes the arguments made in Robinson & Darley, *Utility of Desert*, supra n. 6. For more recent work supporting that article's thesis, see Janice Nadler, *Flouting the Law*, 83 Tex. L. Rev. 1399 (2005) (empirical study finding that perception of one rule as unjust makes people more likely to disregard other, unrelated laws).

16. See Robinson & Darley, *Utility of Desert*, supra n. 6, at 495–96.

17. See Robinson & Darley, *Utility of Desert*, supra n. 6, at 484.

CHAPTER 2

1. The lesser-evils defense is a "justification" because it relates to the actor's conduct, claiming that the behavior in question was acceptable and perhaps even commendable. Immaturity and mistake of law, on the other hand, are "excuse" defenses because they do not involve any claim that the conduct was justified or appropriate, but rather maintain that the actor in question had some personal condition or mental state that takes away his responsibility or fault for the admittedly improper conduct.

2. Affirmation of Facts, Brief for the Defendant, Para 6 (Para 2, Page 2), Joel Stewart, Esq., attorney for Marrero.

3. The facts of the *Marrero* case are derived from the following sources: State v. Marrero, 507 N.E.2d 1068 (N.Y. 1987); State v. Marrero, 71 A.D.2d 346 (N.Y. App. Div. 1979); State v. Marrero, 404 N.Y.S.2d 832 (1978); Indictment of Julio Marrero, Supreme Court of the State of New York, *State v. Julio Marrero*, Dec. 29, 1977; Notice of Motion for the Defendant, Supreme Court of the State of New York, *State v. Julio Marrero*, Mar. 1, 1978; Answering Affidavit for the District Attorney of New York, Supreme Court of the State of New York, *State v. Julio Marrero*, Mar. 20, 1978; Notice of Motion for an Order Pursuant to CPL Section 160.50(1)d, Supreme Court of the State of New York, *State v. Julio Marrero*, Sept. 22, 1978; Notice of Motion, Supreme Court of the State of New York, *State v. Julio Marrero*, Nov. 6, 1981; Brief for the Prosecution, Supreme Court of the State of New York, *State v. Julio Marrero*, Dec. 15, 1981; Indictment of Julio Marrero, number 5423/77 in the Supreme Court of the State of New York, *State v. Julio Marrero*, Dec. 21, 1981; Request to Charge for the Defendant, Supreme Court of the State of New York, *State v. Julio Marrero*, Jan. 20, 1982; Affirmation of Facts, Attorney for Mr. Marrero, Supreme Court of the State of New York, Jan. 1982; Brief for the Defendant-Appellant, Court of Appeals of the State of New York, *State v. Julio Marrero*, July 1986.

4. See N.J. Stat. Ann. § 2C:2–4(c)(3); Paul H. Robinson et al., *The Five Worst (and Five Best) American Criminal Codes*, 95 Nw. U. L. Rev. 1, 50 (2000). It is not uncommon, however, for jurisdictions to give a defense for a reasonable mistake of law based upon an official misstatement of law—a defense based largely on an estoppel argument. See Paul H. Robinson, *Criminal Law* 547–49 (Aspen L. & Bus. 1997) (hereinafter Robinson, *Criminal Law*).

5. See, e.g., John Austin, 1 *Lectures on Jurisprudence* 483 (Robert Campbell, ed., 5th ed., Murray 1885, reprint 1972) ("The only sufficient reason for the rule in question, seems to be this: that if ignorance of law were admitted as a ground of exemption, the Courts would be involved in questions which it were scarcely possible to solve, and which would render the administration of justice next to impracticable. If ignorance of law were admitted as a ground of exemption ignorance of law would always be alleged by the party, and the Court, in every case, would be bound to decide the point."); People v. Snyder, 652 P.2d 42, 44 (Cal. 1982) ("The rule rests on public necessity; the welfare of society and the safety of the state depend upon its enforcement. If a person accused of a crime could shield himself behind the defense that he was ignorant of the law which he violated, immunity from punishment would in most cases result.") (quoting People v. O'Brien, 31 P. 45, 47 (Cal. 1892)); cf. Dan M. Kahan, *Ignorance of the Law Is an Excuse—But Only for the Virtuous*, 96 Mich. L. Rev. 127, 129 (1997) ("Punishing those who mistakenly believe their conduct to be legal promotes good (that is, moral) behavior less through encouraging citizens to learn the law—an objective that could in fact be more completely realized by excusing at least some mistakes—than by creating hazards for those who choose to rely on what they think they know about the law.").

6. See generally Paul H. Robinson & John M. Darley, *Justice, Liability, and Blame: Community Views and the Criminal Law* (Westview 1995).

7. In legal terms, such conduct is referred to as *malum prohibitum*—"bad because prohibited," meaning that the offense's legitimacy derives from the legislative declaration itself and not from any sense that the banned conduct is morally wrong in principle—as opposed to *malum in se*, or "inherently and obviously bad."

8. See State v. Guice, 621 A.2d 553, 558 (N.J. Super. 1993).

9. Of course, one might want to punish the *unknowingly* justified actor. While his conduct may be objectively justified, he has shown his willingness to act unjustifiably. Whether he deserves full liability or only attempt liability is a matter of dispute. See Paul H. Robinson, *Competing Theories of Justification: Deeds vs. Reasons*, in *Harm and Culpability* 45–70 (A. P. Simester & A. T. H. Smith, eds., Clarendon 1996).

10. See Paul H. Robinson, 2 *Criminal Law Defenses* § 124(a) n. 1 (West 1984 & 2004 supp.) (listing jurisdictions that allow and deny the defense).

11. See *Final Report of the National Commission on Reform of Federal Criminal Laws: Proposed New Federal Criminal Code* § 601 Comment (1971) (suggesting that a choice-of-evils provision would be "a potential source of unwarranted difficulty in ordinary cases" and that case-by-case exercise of prosecutorial discretion would be preferable); Law Commission for England and Wales, *Criminal Law Report on Defences of General Application* 19–32 (Law Com. No. 83, 1977), reprinted in 9 Law

Comm'n Reports 25–38 (1980) (opposing codification of defense and supporting abolition of common-law defense). But cf. 2 *A Criminal Code for England and Wales* 230–31, Comment on cl. 43 (Law Com. No. 177, 1989) (criticizing previous Law Commission report and proposing a "duress of circumstances" defense).

12. And here again, the participants in the debate often provide no empirical support for their positions. See, e.g., sources cited supra n. 11.

13. Model Penal Code § 3.02(1) & 3.09(1).

14. See 2 Robinson, supra n. 10, § 124(a) n. 1 (listing authorities).

15. See 2 Robinson, supra n. 10, § 175 n. 1 (listing authorities).

16. In *State v. Jamison*, for example, the defendant was denied an immaturity defense, despite his "mental age" of 11.7 years, because his chronological age of 17 put him over the statutory age cutoff for the immaturity defense. 597 P.2d 424, 428 (Wash. App. 1979), aff'd, 613 P.2d 776 (Wash. 1980). In some jurisdictions, the insanity defense is formulated broadly enough to provide a defense in such a case. The Model Penal Code, for example, uses the phrase "mental disease *or defect.*" Model Penal Code § 4.01. While a mentally retarded actor may be excused under this formulation, a defense still may not be available to the actor who is immature for other reasons, such as having had a childhood of isolation. Developmental retardation, as opposed to physiological incapacity, might be thought to fall outside the scope of "mental disease or defect."

17. As one recent article notes:

> According to the National Center for Juvenile Justice in Pittsburgh, in the past four years, 30 states and the District of Columbia have jumped on the bandwagon of harsher treatment of juveniles—sometimes by expanding the list of crimes excluded from juvenile court jurisdiction, sometimes by sending ever-younger offenders to adult court.
>
> States are also allowing prosecutors to file certain charges directly in criminal court, empowering juvenile court judges to impose adult-style sentences and mandating the transfer of certain cases out of the special courts that handle young offenders. According to the Justice Department, judicially approved transfers to criminal court jumped 68 percent between 1988 and 1992.

Lisa Stansky, *Age of Innocence—More and More States Are Telling Teens: If You Do an Adult Crime, You Serve the Adult Time,* 82 A.B.A. J. 60, 61 (Nov. 1996); see also Stephen J. Schulhofer, *Youth Crime—and What Not to Do about It,* 31 Val. U. L. Rev. 435, 438 (1997); cf. generally Lisa S. Beresford, Comment, *Is Lowering the Age at Which Juveniles Can Be Transferred to Adult Criminal Court the Answer to Juvenile Crime? A State-by-State Assessment,* 37 San Diego L. Rev. 783 (2000) (discussing trend toward increased adult-court prosecution, but also claiming that resulting liability in adult court is frequently no more severe than in juvenile court).

18. What states have instead is a provision transferring jurisdiction to juvenile court for all defendants below a given age. See generally 2 Robinson, supra n. 10,

§ 175. In some jurisdictions, a blameworthiness assessment of sorts is made in juvenile court. For example, in *In re Gladys R.*, 464 P.2d 127, 132–33 (Cal. 1970), the defendant successfully argued in juvenile court for the use of the immaturity defense provided in section 26 of the California Penal Code. Thus, to be found a ward of the court, the court must decide that the juvenile knows the wrongfulness of the conduct constituting the offense. This approach is useful in correcting one of the errors of current formulations: it excludes blameless underage violators from punishment, through criminal or juvenile jurisdiction. But it fails to correct the other kind of error; it continues to conclusively presume the maturity of all offenders over the cutoff age.

19. Insanity, involuntary intoxication, and duress all excuse a violator who has caused the harm or evil prohibited by an offense but who, because of some disability, lacks the capacity to appreciate the wrongfulness of her offense conduct or lacks the capacity to conform her conduct to the requirements of law. See, e.g., Model Penal Code §§ 2.08(4), 2.09(1), 4.01(1). Because a person's lack of maturity can cause these same excusing conditions, an immaturity defense logically should be part of the criminal law's system of excuses. For a general discussion of the conceptual analogy among excuses, see Robinson, *Criminal Law*, supra n. 4, § 9.1.

20. Cf. Stephen J. Morse, *Immaturity and Irresponsibility*, 88 J. Crim. L. & Criminology 15, 31 (1997) ("[H]uman beings are epistemologically incapable of evaluating the criteria for responsibility with such subtle precision. Thus, the law does adopt a bright line test."); see also Ill. Ann. Stat. ch. 38, ¶ 6–1 [now 720 ILCS 5/6–1], Comment 322–23 (Smith-Hurd 1972) ("[T]he Committee sought to accomplish . . . the elimination of the [rebuttable] presumption of incapacity thereby withholding from the jury an unsatisfactory and uncongenial task. The solution arrived at is the simple proposition providing that criminal capacity shall not be deemed to exist below the age of thirteen.").

21. We discuss potential reforms based on the use of presumptions and modifications of the burden of persuasion in chapter 9.

22. For an extended presentation of this argument, see Kahan, supra n. 5.

23. American Psychiatric Association, *Diagnostic and Statistical Manual of Mental Disorders* 313–14 (4th ed., 2000).

24. N.Y. Penal Law § 40.15 (Mental disease or defect) reads:

> In any prosecution for an offense, it is an affirmative defense that when the defendant engaged in the proscribed conduct, he lacked criminal responsibility by reason of mental disease or defect. Such lack of criminal responsibility means that at the time of such conduct, as a result of mental disease or defect, he lacked substantial capacity to know or appreciate either:
> 1. The nature and consequences of such conduct; or
> 2. That such conduct was wrong.

25. The facts of the *Goldstein* case are derived from the following sources: Salvatore Arena & Barbara Ross, *Mistrial in Subway Push; Jurors Deadlock, 2 Back In-*

sanity, N.Y. Daily News, Nov. 3, 1999; Salvatore Arena et al., *Train-Push Jury Probe*, N.Y. Daily News, Nov. 5, 1999; Author Unknown, *A Bizarre Case Filled with Twists and Turns*, N.Y. Post, Mar. 23, 2000; K. C. Baker, *Pushed to Her Death—Straphanger Shoved to Tracks*, N.Y. Daily News, Jan. 4, 1999; Julian E. Barnes, *Insanity Defense Fails for Man Who Threw Woman onto Track*, N.Y. Times, Mar. 23, 2000; Julian E. Barnes, *Second Murder Trial Opens in Subway Shoving Case*, N.Y. Times, Mar. 4, 2000; Nina Bernstein, *Hospitals Face Lawsuit by Kin of Victim in Subway Push*, N.Y. Times, May 25, 1999; Michael Cooper, *Man Accused in Subway Death Says He Tried a Similar Attack Before, the Police Say*, N.Y. Times, Jan. 6, 1999; Michael Daly, *Shover Chose Perfect Spot*, N.Y. Daily News, Nov. 3, 1999; Donna De La Cruz, *Pushing Death Rattles Subway Riders*, Bergen (N.J.) Record, Jan. 5, 1999; Donna De La Cruz, *Subway-Pushing Suspect Claims He Tried It Before*, AP, Jan. 6, 1999; Fredric U. Dicker, *Pataki in $125M Push to Aid Mentally Ill*, N.Y. Post, Nov. 10, 1999; Jim Dwyer, *'85 Case Shows How Official Tried to Play Blame Game*, N.Y. Daily News, Jan. 5, 1999; Joseph Fried, *Subway Killer's Push Is Still Felt Today*, N.Y. Times, Mar. 3, 2002; Patricia Hurtado, *Anger or Illness? Prosecution Cites Rage in Fatal Subway Push*, Newsday (N.Y.), Oct. 8, 1999; Patricia Hurtado, *Jury Deadlocked: Mistrial Declared in Fatal Subway Pushing Case*, Newsday (N.Y.), Nov. 3, 1999; Patricia Hurtado, *Witness Calls Subway Killing Unreal*, Newsday (N.Y.), Oct. 13, 1999; Laura Italiano, *Kendra's Killer Gets the Max*, N.Y. Post, May 5, 2000; Laura Italiano, *My Kendra Deserved Fair Jury, Mom Says*, N.Y. Post, Nov. 5, 1999; Laura Italiano, *Schizophrenia Splits Subway Push Jury*, N.Y. Post, Nov. 1, 1999; Laura Italiano, *Subway Killer May Have Stalked Victim*, N.Y. Post, Oct. 16, 1999; Laura Italiano, *Subway-Push Juror Was Convicted of Hitting Cop*, N.Y. Post, Nov. 4, 1999; Laura Italiano, *Victim's Mother Feels for Killer's Mother*, N.Y. Post, Nov. 3, 1999; N. R. Kleinfield & Kit R. Roane, *Subway Killing Casts Light on Suspect's Mental Torment*, N.Y. Times, Jan. 11, 1999; Samuel Maull, *Mentally Ill Man Convicted of Subway Shove Murder*, AP, Mar. 23, 2000; Samuel Maull, *Mistrial Declared in Fatal Subway Push*, AP, Nov. 3, 1999; Samuel Maull, *Murder Trial of Subway Push Suspect Opens*, AP, Oct. 7, 1999; Samuel Maull, *Psychiatrist Says Subway Push Killer Did Not Know He Was Doing Wrong*, AP, Oct. 19, 1999; Samuel Maull, *Second Suit Filed in Subway Pushing*, AP, Oct. 15, 1999; Bill Porter, *Mourners Told to Remember Kendra Webdale's Life, Not Death*, AP, Jan. 7, 1999; Graham Rayman, *Subway Attacks Thwarted*, Newsday (N.Y.), May 23, 2000; David Rohde, *Defense Witness Barred in Subway Trial*, N.Y. Times, Oct. 27, 1999; David Rohde, *Expert Disputes Schizophrenia Defense*, N.Y. Times, Oct. 23, 1999; David Rohde, *In Court, Psychiatrist Rebuts Defense Claim in Train Killing*, N.Y. Times, Oct. 26, 1999; David Rohde, *Juror Who Rejected Guilty Vote in Subway Killing Had Just Been Convicted*, N.Y. Times, Nov. 4, 1999; David Rohde, *Jury Hears Confession in Killing*, N.Y. Times, Oct. 16, 1999; David Rohde, *Prosecutors Press Theory that Killer Hates Women*, N.Y. Times, Oct. 20, 1999; David Rohde, *Witness Tearfully Describes Fatal Subway Shoving*, N.Y. Times, Oct. 9, 1999; Barbara Ross & Salvatore Arena, *Kin Seeks $40M in Push Slay*, N.Y. Daily News, Oct. 15, 1999; Barbara Ross & Dave Goldiner, *Push-Slay Jurors Get Charge Option*, N.Y. Daily News, Mar. 22, 2000; Laura Siegle, *Train-Push Jury Still Out*, N.Y. Daily

News, Nov. 1, 1999; Gene Warner & Kevin Collison, *WNY Woman's Dream Is Ended under Wheels of Subway Train*, Buffalo News, Jan. 5, 1999; Michael Winerip, *Oddity and Normality Vie in Subway Killer's Confession*, N.Y. Times, Oct. 18, 1999; Michael Winerip, *The Way We Live Now: 11–21–99: The Juror's Dilemma*, N.Y. Times, Nov. 21, 1999.

26. Idaho Code § 18–207; Kan. Stat. Ann. § 22–3220; Mont. Code Ann. § 45–2–101; Utah Code Ann. § 76-2-305.

27. Ariz. Rev. Stat. Ann. § 13–502; Cal. Penal Code § 25; Colo. Rev. Stat. Ann. § 16–8–101; Fla. Stat. Ann. § 775.027; Ga. Code Ann. § 16–3–2; Iowa Code Ann. § 701.4; La. Rev. Stat. Ann. § 14; Minn. Stat. Ann. § 611.026; Roundtree v. State, 568 So.2d 1173 (Miss. 1990); Mo. Ann. Stat. § 552.030 (modifying the standard language slightly to "incapable of knowing *and appreciating*"); State v. Harms, 650 N.W.2d 481 (Neb. 2002); N.J. Stat. Ann. § 2C:4 1; Finger v. State, 27 P.3d 66 (Nev. 2001) (finding unconstitutional the legislature's attempt to abolish the insanity defense and applying the McNaghten test instead); State v. Vickers, 291 S.E.2d 599 (N.C. 1982); Ohio Rev. Code Ann. § 2901.01; Okla. Stat. Ann. Tit. 21 § 152; 18 Pa. Cons. Stat. Ann. § 314; S.C. Code Ann. § 17–24–10; S.D. Codified Laws § 22–1–2; Tex. Penal Code Ann. § 8.01; Price v. Commonwealth, 323 S.E.2d 106 (Va. 1984); Wash. Rev. Code Ann. § 9A.12.010.

28. Ala. Code § 13A–3–1; Alaska Stat. § 12.47.010; Del. Code Ann. Tit. 11, § 401; 720 Ill. Comp. Stat. Ann. 5/6–2; Ind. Code Ann. § 35–41–3–6; Me. Rev. Stat. Ann. tit. 14, § 14; N.Y. Penal Law § 40.15; N.D. Cent. Code § 12.1–04.1–01 (requiring also that "an essential element of the crime charged [is] that the individual act willfully"); Tenn. Code Ann. § 39–11–501.

29. See, e.g., Robinson & Darley, supra n. 6, at 128–39; Daniel S. Bailis et al., *Community Standards of Criminal Liability and the Insanity Defense*, 19 Law & Hum. Behav. 425 (1995).

30. See Barbara E. Bergman & Nancy Hollander, 1 *Wharton's Criminal Evidence* § 2:13 at 85–86 & n. 24 (15th ed., 1997 & 2005 supp.) (describing the GBMI verdict and listing the jurisdictions that have adopted it).

31. See 2 Robinson, supra n. 10, § 173(h); Anne S. Emanuel, *Guilty but Mentally Ill Verdicts and the Death Penalty: An Eighth Amendment Analysis*, 68 N.C. L. Rev. 37, 47 (1989) ("The Michigan statute provides, as do all guilty but mentally ill statutes, that the court may impose any sentence that could be imposed upon a defendant found simply guilty.").

32. See, e.g., Cal. Penal Code § 2684 (prescribing terms for transfer to state hospital of mentally ill prisoners); D.C. Code Ann. § 24–302; Mich. Comp. Laws Ann. §§ 330.2001–.2006; 50 Pa. Cons. Stat. Ann. § 4408; see also National Advisory Commission on Criminal Justice Standards and Goals, *Corrections* 184 (1973).

33. See infra nn. 46–47 and accompanying text.

34. See Henry J. Steadman et al., *Before and after Hinckley: Evaluating Insanity Defense Reform* 8 (Guilford 1993). This is likely due to a suspicion that mentally ill individuals are unusually dangerous and need to be incapacitated to prevent them from committing more crimes. That suspicion, and the resulting sentence aggrava-

tions, are driven by a utilitarian crime-control rationale for criminal liability. We examine such rationales in chapter 6. As our discussion there and in chapter 10 (discussing the potential role of civil commitment) will make clear, we take the view that the longer sentences strongly hint that GBMI is being used to usurp the role of civil commitment (protecting society from persons who present a danger for the future) rather than to fulfill the proper role of criminal liability (sanctioning offenders for their blameworthy conduct in the past).

35. Implementation of GBMI to induce "compromise verdicts" or otherwise discourage NGRI verdicts may do as much to undermine the insanity defense as would total abolition. In simulated trial studies, introduction of a GBMI option decreases the number of NGRI verdicts. See, e.g., Ronald L. Poulson, *Mock Juror Attribution of Criminal Responsibility: Effects of Race and the Guilty but Mentally Ill (GBMI) Verdict Option*, 20 J. Applied Soc. Psych. 1596, 1600, 1604–05 (1990); Caton F. Roberts & Stephen L. Golding, *The Social Construction of Criminal Responsibility and Insanity*, 15 Law & Hum. Behav. 349, 359–60 (1991); Jeffrey C. Savitsky & William D. Lindblom, *The Impact of the Guilty but Mentally Ill Verdict on Juror Decisions: An Empirical Analysis*, 16 J. Applied Soc. Psych. 686, 694 (1986).

Yet the actual experience of states that have enacted GBMI is unclear. Data for some states suggest that the GBMI verdict has had its intended effect of reducing NGRI acquittals. See, e.g., Steadman et al., supra n. 34, at 111 ("Prior to the reform [of enacting GBMI in Georgia], someone pleading insanity for a violent crime had better than a 1 in 4 chance of being acquitted; after the reform his or her chances dropped to 1 in 7."); Lisa A. Callahan et al., *Measuring the Effects of the Guilty but Mentally Ill (GBMI) Verdict: Georgia's 1982 GBMI Reform*, 16 Law & Hum. Behav. 447, 451–52 (1992) (after enactment of GBMI in Georgia, the rate of NGRI pleas remained about the same, but the rate of acquittals decreased from about 22% to about 12%); cf. R. D. MacKay & Juliann Kopelman, *The Operation of the "Guilty but Mentally Ill" Verdict in Pennsylvania*, 16 J. Psychiatry & L. 247, 254–55, 262, 268 (1988) (decrease in NGRI in Pennsylvania following enactment of a GBMI statute, but cause unclear, as criteria for NGRI were made more restrictive at same time); Ingo Keilitz et al., *The Guilty but Mentally Ill Verdict: An Empirical Study* (Inst. on Mental Disability and the Law, Nat'l Ctr. for State Courts 1985) (decrease in NGRI in Alaska following enactment of a GBMI statute, but cause unclear, as criteria for NGRI were made more restrictive at same time).

Still other data indicate that the GBMI verdict has not reduced, and may even have increased, the number of NGRI pleas and acquittals. See, e.g., Carleton A. Palmer & Mark Hazelrigg, *The Guilty but Mentally Ill Verdict: A Review and Conceptual Analysis of Intent and Impact*, 28 J. Am. Acad. Psychiatry & L. 47, 51–53 (2000) (citing research and concluding that "there is no evidence to suggest that the GBMI verdict is reducing NGRI verdicts"); George L. Blau & Richard A. Pasewark, *Statutory Changes and the Insanity Defense: Seeking the Perfect Insane Person*, 18 L. & Psych. Rev. 69 (1994) ("In Michigan, investigations have consistently belied the hypotheses [regarding reduced NGRI acquittals] underlying the GBMI verdict's promulgation. . . . The experience of Illinois with the GBMI verdict parallels that of Michigan. In fact, in Illinois, the introduction of the GBMI verdict brought an increase in NGRI acquittals."); Ingo Keilitz et al., *The Insanity Defense and Its Alternatives: A Guide for Policymakers* 43 (Inst. on Mental Disability and the Law, Nat'l Ctr. for State Courts 1984) ("[T]o the extent the GBMI verdict [in Michigan] was intended to decrease NGRI acquittals, it has failed.").

If effective abolition is the objective, abolishing the insanity test openly would better further the interests of informed debate and reform. In any case, all such restrictions on the defense risk deviations from desert to avoid only an illusion of abuse.

36. See, e.g., Donald H. J. Hermann & Yvonne S. Sor, *Convicting or Confining? Alternative Directions in Insanity Law Reform: Guilty but Mentally Ill versus New Rules for Release of Insanity Acquittees*, 1983 B.Y.U. L. Rev. 499, 582 ("The rationale for the GBMI verdict stems from a legislative concern that the insanity defense is too easily proved, while the abolition of automatic commitment of insanity acquittees in some states has made civil commitment of persons found NGRI more difficult."); see also People v. Ramsey, 375 N.W.2d 297 (Mich. 1985) (major purpose of GBMI statute is to lessen the number of persons relieved of all criminal responsibility by way of NGRI verdict); State v. Neely, 819 P.2d 249, 252 (N.M. 1991) (suggesting that legislature's purpose in enacting GBMI statute was "to reduce the number of improper or inaccurate insanity acquittals and to give jurors an alternative to acquittal when mental illness is believed to play a part in an offense"); State v. Hornsby, 484 S.E.2d 869, 872 (S.C. 1997) (purposes of GBMI statute were to reduce the number of insanity acquittals and provide mental health care for GBMI inmates); Robinson v. Solem, 432 N.W.2d 246, 248 (S.D. 1988) ("[O]ur legislature intended to provide an alternative verdict available to a jury to reduce the number of offenders who were erroneously found not guilty by reason of insanity."); People v. Smith, 465 N.E.2d 101, 106 (Ill. App. 1984) ("In the instant case, the legislature intended to provide a statute that reduced the number of persons who were erroneously found not guilty by reason of insanity and to characterize such defendants as in need of treatment."). Limitations on civil commitment were thought to risk imprudently the release of dangerous insanity acquittees back into the community.

37. We discuss this reform, which has already been adopted by numerous states, in more detail in chapter 9.

38. See Valerie P. Hans, *An Analysis of Public Attitudes toward the Insanity Defense*, 24 Criminology 393, 406 (1986); see also Eric Silver et al., *Demythologizing Inaccurate Perceptions of the Insanity Defense*, 18 Law & Hum. Behav. 63, 67–68 (1994).

39. See Lisa A. Callahan et al., *The Volume and Characteristics of Insanity Defense Pleas: An Eight-State Study*, 19 Bull. Am. Acad. Psychiatry & L. 331, 334 (1991). Note that this is less than 1% of all *felony* cases, while the lay participants estimated insanity pleas for 38% of all persons charged with *any* crime. See also Richard A. Pasewark & Hugh McGinley, *Insanity Plea: National Survey of Frequency and Success*, 13 J. Psychiatry & L. 101 (1985) (reporting median rate of one plea per 873 re-

ported crimes); Stephen G. Valdes, Comment, *Frequency and Success: An Empirical Study of Criminal Law Defenses, Federal Constitutional Evidentiary Claims, and Plea Negotiations*, 153 U. Pa. L. Rev. 1709, 1723 (2005) (survey of 400 judges, prosecutors, and defense counsel reports insanity claims offered in less than 1% of cases).

40. See Steadman et al., supra n. 34, at 111; see also Callahan et al., supra n. 39, at 336.

41. One study reports that the average acquittal rate for insanity pleas is 26%. See Callahan et al., supra n. 39, at 334. Pasewark and McGinley report a success rate of 15% of pleas. See Pasewark & McGinley, supra n. 39, at 106; see also Valdes, supra n. 39, at 1723 (reporting success rate of under 24%).

42. See, e.g., Hans, supra n. 38, at 406 (reporting study indicating that public believes that over 36% of all NGRI claims, constituting perceived 14% of all criminal cases, result in NGRI verdict); Mary Frain, *Professor Says Insanity Defense Seldom Works*, Telegram & Gazette (Worcester, Mass.), Jan. 19, 1996, at B1 (quoting chair of psychiatry at the University of Massachusetts Medical Center as saying that general public believes the insanity defense is used in 20–50% of all criminal cases).

43. See Michael J. Perlin, *A Law of Healing*, 68 U. Cin. L. Rev. 407, 425 (2000) ("Nearly 90% of all insanity defense cases are 'walkthroughs'—stipulated on the papers.").

44. See Callahan et al., supra n. 39, at 334.

45. See, e.g., Michael R. Hawkins & Richard A. Pasewark, *Characteristics of Persons Utilizing the Insanity Plea*, 53 Psychol. Rep. 191, 194 (1983); Steadman et al., supra n. 34, at 56.

46. See, e.g., 730 Ill. Comp. Stat. 5/5–2–4.

47. See, e.g., Judith Havemann, *City Unveils Design for Scaled-Down St. Elizabeths*, Wash. Post, Oct. 10, 2002, at T3 ("The most famous current court-ordered patient [of St. Elizabeths] is John W. Hinckley Jr., found not guilty by reason of insanity of attempting to assassinate President Reagan in 1981. He has been in St. Elizabeths since 1982, allowed out only on visits supervised by hospital staff.").

48. See, e.g., People v. Stack, 613 N.E.2d 1175, 1183–84 (Ill. App. 1993); see generally Thomas M. Fleming, *Instructions in State Criminal Case in Which Defendant Pleads Insanity as to Hospital Confinement in Event of Acquittal*, 81 A.L.R.4th 659 (1990 & 2004 supp.).

49. See Michael L. Perlin, *"The Borderline Which Separated You from Me": The Insanity Defense, the Authoritarian Spirit, the Fear of Faking, and the Culture of Punishment*, 82 Iowa L. Rev. 1375, 1375 & nn. 5–6 (1997) (citing polls suggesting that "ninety percent [of Americans] believe that the insanity plea is overused").

50. The doctrine provides:

> That if the act of killing, though intentional, be committed under the influence of sudden intense anger or heat of blood obscuring the reason, produced by an adequate or reasonable provocation, and before sufficient time has elapsed for the blood to cool and reason to reassert itself, so that the killing is the result of temporary excitement rather

than of wickedness of the heart or innate recklessness of disposition, then the law, recognizing the standard of human conduct as that of the ordinary or average man, regards the offense so committed as of less heinous character than premeditated or deliberate murder.

State v. Gounagias, 88 Wash. 304, 311–12 (1915).

51. The facts of this case are derived from *State v. Gounagias*, supra n. 50.

52. See Wayne R. LaFave, *Criminal Law* § 15.2(b), at 777–78, 784–85 (4th ed., West 2003); Andrew Ashworth, *The Doctrine of Provocation*, 35 Cambridge L.J. 292, 298–300 (1976); Richard G. Singer, *The Resurgence of Mens Rea: I: Provocation, Emotional Disturbance, and the Model Penal Code*, 27 B.C. L. Rev. 243, 251 (1986).

53. See LaFave, supra n. 52, at § 5.4(b)(2); 2 Robinson, supra n. 10, § 61(a) at 209–15.

54. See, e.g., State v. Williams, 484 P.2d 1167 (Wash. App. 1971) (holding that loving parents with little education were negligent in failing to get needed medical care for their seventeen-month-old child, who died from complications from what began as a toothache).

55. In England's famous *Bedder* case, for example, the court upheld the conviction of an eighteen-year-old who, told by a doctor that he was impotent, nonetheless hired a prostitute and attempted to have intercourse with her. See Bedder v. Director of Public Prosecutions, 1 W.L.R. 1119 (1954). When he was unable to perform, the prostitute taunted and mocked Bedder, who flew into a rage and killed her. The court held that the jury was properly instructed to ignore any possible influence of Bedder's impotence. See idem at 1123 ("If the reasonable man is . . . deprived in whole or in part of his reason or the normal man endowed with abnormal characteristics, the test ceases to have any value."); see also Glanville Williams, *Provocation and the Reasonable Man*, 1954 Crim. L. Rev. 740, 747 ("If the provocation was insufficient for a normal man, it could not help the accused that he was conscious of his impotence and therefore liable to be more excited if 'twitted' or attacked on the subject of that particular infirmity.").

56. Even today, for example, Illinois law recognizes only the following types of provocation as reasonable: "substantial physical injury or substantial physical assault, mutual quarrel or combat, illegal arrest, and adultery with the offender's spouse." People v. Garcia, 651 N.E.2d 100, 110 (Ill. 1995).

57. See, e.g., People v. Cooley, 27 Cal. Rptr. 543 (1962); People v. Washington, 187 N.E.2d 739 (Ill. 1963); Sanders v. State, 106 S.E. 314 (Ga. App. 1921).

58. See, e.g., State v. Douglas, 407 P.2d 117 (Ariz. 1965); Green v. State, 25 S.E.2d 502 (Ga. 1943); Cavanaugh v. Commonwealth, 190 S.W. 123 (Ky. 1916); State v. Spears, 300 P.2d 551 (Wyo. 1956).

59. See, e.g., State v. Robinson, 185 S.W.2d 636 (Mo. 1945); In re Fraley, 109 P. 295 (Okla. 1910).

60. For example, commentators have faulted the holding in *Bedder*, see supra n. 55, for basically asking the jury to evaluate Bedder's killing as if it were committed by someone without Bedder's condition, thereby presenting the jury with a hypothetical case divorced from the key elements of the real one. See, e.g., George P.

Fletcher, *Rethinking Criminal Law* 278 (Little, Brown 1978) (arguing that we "can hardly say that the jury passed judgment on Mr. Bedder if they did not consider the most significant facts that influenced his loss of control"); Singer, supra n. 52, at 289 ("[T]he legal issue to be decided by the jury was [in effect] whether a reasonably potent man would have been incensed to the point of killing by taunts regarding his impotence. The question, of course, was silly.").

61. See generally Robinson & Darley, supra n. 6.

62. Model Penal Code § 210.3(1)(b).

63. The commentary states:

> The critical element in the Model Penal Code formulation [offering mitigation for extreme mental or emotional disturbance] is the clause requiring that reasonableness be assessed "from the viewpoint of a person in the actor's situation." The word "situation" is designedly ambiguous. On the one hand, it is clear that personal handicaps and some external circumstances must be taken into account. Thus, blindness, shock from traumatic injury, and grief are all easily read into the term "situation." . . . On the other hand, it is equally clear that idiosyncratic moral values are not part of the actor's situation. . . . In between these two extremes, however, there are [less clear] matters. . . . The proper role of such factors cannot be resolved satisfactorily by abstract definition of what may constitute adequate provocation. The Model Penal Code endorses a formulation that affords sufficient flexibility to differentiate in particular cases between those special aspects of the actor's situation that should be deemed material for purpose of grading and those that should be ignored. There thus will be room for interpretation of the word "situation," and that is precisely the flexibility desired.

Model Penal Code § 210.3, Comment 5(a) at 62–63 (1980). And, in the context of negligence, the drafters explain:

> A further point in the Code's concept of negligence merits attention. The standard for ultimate judgement [sic] invites consideration of the "care that a reasonable person would observe in the actor's situation." There is an inevitable ambiguity in "situation." If the actor were blind or if he had just suffered a blow or experienced a heart attack, these would certainly be facts to be considered in a judgement [sic] involving criminal liability, as they would be under traditional law. But the heredity, intelligence or temperament of the actor would not be held material in judging negligence, and could not be without depriving the criterion of all its objectivity. The Code is not intended to displace discriminations of this kind, but rather to leave the issue to the courts.

Model Penal Code § 2.02, Comment 4, at 242 (1985).

64. See Colo. Rev. Stat. Ann. § 18–3–103(3)(b) (reasonable person); Ga. Code Ann. § 16–5–2(a) (reasonable person); La. Rev. Stat. Ann. § 14:31(1) ("average person"); Mo. Ann. Stat. § 565.002(1) ("person of ordinary temperament"); Nev. Rev. Stat. Ann. § 200.050 (reasonable person); Tenn. Code Ann. § 39–13–211(a) (reasonable person); Tex. Penal Code Ann. § 19.02(a)(1) ("person of ordinary temper"); Wis. Stat. Ann. § 939.44(1)(a) ("ordinarily constituted person"); cf. Utah Code Ann. § 76–5–205(3) ("reasonable explanation or excuse" as "determined from the viewpoint of a reasonable person under the then existing circumstances").

65. See Laurie J. Taylor, Comment, *Provoked Reason in Men and Women: Heat-of-Passion Manslaughter and Imperfect Self-Defense*, 33 UCLA L. Rev. 1679, 1687 n. 48 (1986) (identifying twenty-three states using a reasonable-person formulation for provocation).

66. See Kevin Jon Heller, *Beyond the Reasonable Man? A Sympathetic but Critical Assessment of the Use of Subjective Standards of Reasonableness in Self-Defense and Provocation Cases*, 26 Am. J. Crim. L. 1, 109–20 (1998). The survey examines all fifty states and the District of Columbia, but not the federal jurisdiction. The author concludes that the remaining three jurisdictions—New Jersey, Pennsylvania, and Wisconsin—use generally objective standards but have adjusted them to consider certain particular traits of the defendant. See idem.

67. See idem. Another survey, focusing specifically on states' treatment of Battered Woman Syndrome (BWS) for self-defense purposes, reached a comparable figure. See Holly Maguigan, *Battered Women and Self-Defense: Myths and Misconceptions in Current Reform Proposals*, 140 U. Pa. L. Rev. 379, 461–67 (1991) (listing ten states rejecting BWS evidence based on adherence to purely objective standard; five states with split appellate authority, some of which favored a purely objective standard; and sixteen states that had yet to address the BWS issue at the appellate level).

68. See Heather R. Skinazi, Comment, *Not Just a "Conjured Afterthought": Using Duress as a Defense for Battered Women Who "Fail to Protect,"* 85 Cal. L. Rev. 993, 999–1003, 1011–13 (1997) (contrasting objective approach for duress with more common, modified-objective "hybrid" approach for self-defense).

69. People v. Goetz, 502 N.Y.S.2d 577, 577 (N.Y. Trial Term 1986).

70. The court held as follows:

> Under the self-defense statute, the crucial factors are the defendant's subjective belief that the use of physical force or deadly physical force was necessary under the circumstances and whether that belief was reasonable *to him*, not whether a reasonable prudent man would share the belief. On that basis, . . . an instruction which substitutes an objective for the subjective standard is improper and constitutes reversible error.

People v. Goetz, 501 N.Y.S.2d 326, 329 (N.Y. App. Div. 1986).

71. Idem at 330 (emphasis in original). The dismissal was, however, reversed by the Court of Appeals. See People v. Goetz, 497 N.E.2d 41 (N.Y. 1986).

72. Moosa Hanoukai obtained a mitigation from murder to manslaughter after claiming that his wife's constant ridiculing of him, including making him sleep on the floor, drove him to beat her to death with a wrench. See Margot Slade, *At the Bar: In a Growing Number of Cases, Defendants Are Portraying Themselves as the Victims*, N.Y. Times, May 20, 1994, at B20.

73. This defense was created by William Kunstler and first used, though unsuccessfully, in the trial of Colin Ferguson, a man accused of murdering six passengers on the Long Island Railroad. Kunstler's theory is that anger over racial injustice combined with mental problems to drive Ferguson to commit acts of violence. See Sheryl McCarthy, *A Rage That's Not Violent*, Newsday (N.Y.), Mar. 28, 1994, at A8.

74. Geraldine Richter was acquitted of drunk driving charges after claiming that the hormonal changes that she undergoes each month drove her to commit disruptive and violent acts. See Martin Kasindorf, *Allowing Hormones to Take the Rap: Does the PMS Defense Help or Hinder Women?*, Newsday (N.Y.), June 16, 1991, at 17.

75. This defense was used in the trial of fifteen-year-old Ronney Zamora, who was convicted of murdering an eighty-two-year-old woman despite his claim that violence on television brainwashed him. See Tom Shales, *Zamora Is Guilty, but What about TV?*, Wash. Post, Oct. 9, 1977, at H1.

76. This defense is raised by men who believe that sex should be spontaneous and that a woman who resists at first will eventually give in if pushed hard enough. See Irene Lacher, *The Rape Debate: Is There an Epidemic of Sexual Assaults? or Just a Wave of Politicized Hysteria? From Bedroom to Courtroom, the Rules Are Changing*, L.A. Times, Oct. 17, 1993, at 1; Tom Kuntz, *Word for Word, a Scholarly Debate: Rhett and Scarlett: Rough Sex or Rape? Feminists Give a Damn*, N.Y. Times, Feb. 19, 1995, at 7.

77. This defense was first employed by Daimian Osby, who claimed that violent conditions in his neighborhood induced him to shoot his two cousins, who were demanding the return of $400 he won from them in a dice game. The jury eventually split 11 1 (for conviction), which resulted in the judge dismissing the jury and declaring a mistrial. See Hugh Aynesworth, *Defense Ploy Wins Texas Mistrial*, Wash. Times, Apr. 21, 1994, at A3.

78. Dan White gained a mitigation from murder to involuntary manslaughter after claiming, among other things, that he had become seriously depressed because of overindulgence in junk food. See People v. White, 172 Cal. Rptr. 612 (Cal. App. 1981); see also William J. Winslade & Judith Wilson Ross, *The Insanity Plea* 21–51 (Scribner's 1983); Lisa Stansky, *Court Guts Diminished Capacity Claims: Ruling Limits Downgrade of Murder to Lesser Crime*, Recorder (San Francisco, Cal.), Dec. 13, 1991, at 1; George F. Will, *Shocking Crimes, Astounding Sentences*, Wash. Post, Dec. 11, 1983, at C7; Richard M. Harnett, *"He'll Be Hounded to Hell . . . ,"* UPI, Jan. 6, 1984; Janet Maslin, *"Harvey Milk" Relives Coast Slaying*, N.Y. Times, Oct. 7, 1984, at 86; Jane E. Brody, *Diet Therapy for Behavior Is Criticized as Premature*, N.Y. Times, Dec. 4, 1984, at C1; Maura Dolan, *Killed S.F. Mayor, Supervisor in '78: Parole Ends: White Now Free to Leave L.A. County*, L.A. Times, Jan. 7, 1985, at 1; Jay Mathews, *Dan*

White Commits Suicide; Ex-San Francisco Supervisor Killed 2 City Officials in '78,
Wash. Post, Oct. 22, 1985, at A3.

79. For an empirical research effort to sort out cases of both sorts—those factors
that should and those that should not be allowed to individualize the objective standard—see Robinson & Darley, supra n. 6, at Study 11.

CHAPTER 3

1. See infra nn. 27–28 and accompanying text (discussing evidentiary rationale
for felony-murder rule, which is rooted in reliability concern).

2. Interview by Ryan McLennan with Lauren Kustudick in Glenview, Illinois
(Nov. 28, 2000) (notes on file with authors).

3. The facts of the *Howard* case are derived from the following sources: Cook
County Sheriff's Police Department Report (Mar. 17, 1978); Sheriff's Police Depart-
ment, Supplementary Report (May 18, 1978); interview by Ryan McLennan with
Lauren Kustudick in Glenview, Illinois (Nov. 28, 2000) (notes on file with authors).

4. See Wayne R. LaFave et al., *Criminal Procedure* § 18.5(a) at 876 (4th ed., West
2004) (noting that statutes exist "to ensure a timely commencement of prosecution"
and discussing variations as to "what act will suffice to show such commencement,"
thereby satisfying statute).

5. See *Preliminary Proceedings: Speedy Trial*, 33 Geo. L.J. Ann. Rev. Crim. Proc.
344, 344 (2004) (footnotes omitted) ("The Sixth Amendment's speedy trial guarantee,
the Speedy Trial Act of 1974, other federal statutes, and the *Federal Rules of Criminal Procedure* protect defendants from undue post-accusation delay. . . . Statutes of
limitations are the primary safeguards against prejudicial preaccusation delay."); see
also, e.g., United States v. Marion, 404 U.S. 307 (1971) (speedy-trial right does not at-
tach until arrest or commencement of criminal charge); LaFave et al., supra n. 4, at §
18.1(c) (discussing when speedy-trial right attaches).

6. One modern tactic for avoiding this demand to begin prosecution is to procure
a "John Doe indictment" against an as-yet-unidentified offender—perhaps including
a DNA profile of the offender as a means of identification—and then to prosecute the
case whenever the culprit has been found. See Meredith A. Bieber, Comment, *Meeting the Statute or Beating It: Using "John Doe" Indictments Based on DNA to Meet
the Statute of Limitations*, 150 U. Pa. L. Rev. 1079, 1079 n. 1 (2002) (noting use of
such indictments "in New York, Pennsylvania, California, Florida, and Wisconsin,
among other states"); Frank B. Ulmer, Note, *Using DNA Profiles to Obtain "John
Doe" Arrest Warrants and Indictments*, 58 Wash. & Lee L. Rev. 1585, 1617–20
(2001). For discussion of particular cases involving use of such indictments, see, for
example, Richard Willing, *Police Expand DNA Use, Charge Man with Rape Using
Only Genetic Profile*, USA Today, Oct. 25, 2001, at A1; Michael Luo, *Unnamed Man
Indicted by DNA*, Newsday (N.Y.), Aug. 9, 2000, at A3. Other rules also "toll" the
running of the limitation period, effectively stopping the clock during the time to
which the rule applies.

7. See Limitation Act of 1623, 21 Jac. 1, ch. 16 (imposing time limitations on some civil and criminal actions "[f]or quieting Men's Estates, and avoiding of Suits").

8. For information about advancements in forensic science, see generally Jay A. Siegel et al., *Encyclopedia of Forensic Sciences* (Academic 2000); see, e.g., idem at 1054 ("[A]dvances of the past 20 years or so have been positively breathtaking."). For a somewhat skeptical view of the impact of these advances on truth determination, see Scott Bales, *Turning the Microscope Back on Forensic Scientists*, 26 No. 2 Litigation 51, 58 (2000) ("Forensic science is a powerful tool that will become even more powerful in the years to come. But forensic scientists, like pretty much everyone else, are fallible and sometimes blind to their own shortcomings. Given the power, and sometimes the mystery, of sophisticated forensic science, it is important . . . to evaluate expert testimony critically in criminal cases.").

9. See LaFave et al., supra n. 4, § 18.5(a), at 875 ("[T]hese [limitations] statutes . . . prevent prosecution of those who have been law abiding for some years[.]").

10. Idem.

11. Yair Listokin, *Efficient Time Bars: A New Rationale for the Existence of Statutes of Limitations in Criminal Law*, 31 J. Legal Stud. 99, 99 (2002).

12. See United States v. Lovasco, 431 U.S. 783, 789–90 (1977); see also United States v. Marion, 404 U.S. 307, 324–25 (1971).

13. See Ky. Rev. Stat. § 500.050(1); Greco v. State, 499 A.2d 209 (Md. App. 1985) ("Maryland does not recognize a period of limitations in felony cases."); State v. Hardin, 201 S.E.2d 74 (N.C. App. 1973) ("In North Carolina, there is no statute of limitations barring the prosecution of a felony.").

South Carolina and Wyoming are the only two states with no limitation period for any crime, whether felony or misdemeanor. See Story v. State, 721 P.2d 1020, 1027 (Wyo. 1986) ("Wyoming is one of the two states which has no statute of limitations for any criminal case."); Alan L. Adlestein, *Conflict of the Criminal Statute of Limitations with Lesser Offenses at Trial*, 37 Wm. & Mary L. Rev. 199, 249–50 & n. 223 (1995).

14. See Va. Code Ann. § 19.2–0.

15. W. Va. Code § 61–11–9.

16. See Paul H. Robinson, 2 *Criminal Law Defenses* § 202(a) n. 3 (West 1984 & 2004 supp.) (listing authorities).

17. See, e.g., Ala. Code § 15–3–5(a)(2) (no limitation for any felony "involving the use, attempted use, or threat of, violence to a person"); Idaho Code § 19–402(1) (no limitation for voluntary manslaughter); 720 Ill. Comp. Stat. 5/3–5(a)(1) (no limitation for involuntary manslaughter or reckless homicide); Minn. Stat. § 628.26(a) (no limitation for any offense where victim dies); Mont. Code Ann. § 45–1–205(1)(a) (no limitation for "deliberate, mitigated, or negligent homicide"); N.J. Stat. § 2C:1–6(a) (no limitation for manslaughter); Or. Rev. Stat. § 131.125(1) (no limitation for manslaughter); 42 Pa. Cons. Stat. § 5551(2) (no limitation for voluntary manslaughter); R.I. Gen. Laws § 12–12–17(a) (no limitation for any homicide); Tex. Code Crim. Proc. art. 12.01(1)(A) (no limitation for manslaughter); Utah Code Ann. § 76–1–301 (no limitation for manslaughter).

18. See, e.g., State v. Stillwell, 418 A.2d 267 (N.J. App. 1980) (invalidating conviction for manslaughter based on statute of limitations, where defendant was indicted and tried for murder); *Recent Case*, 105 U. Pa. L. Rev. 1000, 1001 & n. 12 (1957) (noting that "[o]ne cannot be convicted of manslaughter on a murder indictment if the statute of limitations bars an indictment for manslaughter" and citing examples). Cf. Padie v. State, 557 P.2d 1138 (Alaska 1976) (defendant may seek manslaughter instruction without waiving defense to manslaughter conviction based on statute of limitations).

19. Ark. Code Ann. § 5–1–109(b)(1) (extending limitation period for rape from six to fifteen years where prosecution is based on DNA evidence "or other tests which may become available through advances in technology"); Ga. Code Ann. 17–3–1(c.1) (eliminating limitation for kidnapping, armed robbery, rape, and aggravated sexual offenses where DNA used to identify offender); 720 Ill. Comp. Stat. 5/3–5(a)(2) (eliminating limitation for sexual offenses where offender's DNA has been entered into DNA database and where offense was reported within two years); Ind. Code Ann. § 35–41–4–2(b) (extending prosecution for class B or C felony until one year after discovery of, or reasonable ability to discover, offender's identity using DNA evidence); Kan. Stat. Ann. § 21–3106(7) (extending limitation for certain sexual offenses until one year after discovery of offender's identity using DNA evidence); Mich. Comp. Laws Ann. § 767.24(2)(b) (extending limitation for certain sexual offenses until ten years after discovery of offender's identity using DNA evidence); Minn. Stat. § 628.26(e) (eliminating limitation for certain sexual offenses "if physical evidence is collected and preserved that is capable of being tested for its DNA characteristics"); 22 Okla. Stat. § 152(C)(2) (extending limitation for sexual offenses until three years after discovery of offender's identity using DNA evidence); Or. Rev. Stat. § 131.125 (extending period from six to twelve years for rape and sodomy if offender is identified using DNA); Tex. Code Crim. Proc. art. 12.01(1)(B) (eliminating limitation for sexual assault if investigation generates DNA evidence that "does not match the victim or any other person whose identity is readily ascertained"); Utah Code Ann. § 76–1–302(2), (3) (extending limitation for specified "violent felonies" until one year after discovery of offender's identity using DNA evidence). See also N.J. Stat. Ann. 2C:1–6(c) (tolling running of limitation period "until the State is in possession of both the physical evidence and the DNA or fingerprint evidence necessary to establish the identification of the actor by means of comparison to the physical evidence"); 18 U.S.C. § 3282(b) (allowing indictment of as-yet-unidentified offender using offender's DNA profile).

20. See Ark. Code. Ann. § 5–1–109 (three, five, or six years, except for extension to fifteen years for rape prosecution using DNA evidence); D.C. Code § 23–113(a)(2) (six years); Iowa Code §§ 802.1–.3 (three years for any felony other than murder, sexual abuse, or incest); 17 Me. Rev. Stat. § 8 (three or six years for any felony except murder or sexual offense against a minor); N.D. Cent. Code § 29–04–02 (three years); N.H. Rev. Stat. § 628:8 (six years); Nev. Rev. Stat. §§ 171.080, 171.085 (three or four years for any felony other than murder or terrorism); 22 Okla. St. §§ 151, 152 (three, five, or seven years); Or. Rev. Stat. § 131.125 (three or six years for any felony other

than murder, attempted murder, or manslaughter); Utah Code Ann. § 76–1–301, – 302(1)(a) (four years for any felony other than murder, manslaughter, or kidnapping); Wis. Stat. § 939.74 (six years).

21. See, e.g., Conn. Gen. Stat. § 54–193(a) (no limit for class A felonies); 11 Del. Code § 205(a) (no limit for class A felonies); Ind. Code Ann. § 35–41–4–2 (no limit for class A felonies); S.D. Codified Laws § 23A–42–1 (no limit for class A, B, or 1 felonies).

22. See, e.g., Ala. Code §§ 15–3–3, 15–3–5(6), (7) (longer periods for forgery, counterfeiting, and conversion of revenue); Ariz. Rev. Stat. § 13–107 (no limitation on prosecution for misuse of public monies or falsification of records); Colo. Rev. Stat. § 16–5–401(1)(a) (no limitation for forgery); Fla. Stat. § 775.15(2)(e)–(h) (five-year period for Medicaid fraud and other frauds against government, or abuse of public office, as opposed to general four-year period for first-degree felonies); Kan. Rev. Stat. § 21–3106(3) (ten-year period for crime against Kansas public employees' retirement system; two or five years for other felonies).

23. See, e.g., Tenn. Code Ann. § 40–2–101 (imposing varying periods, from no limitation to fifteen, eight, four, or two years, based on grade of offense; also imposing special limits of six years and three years for government fraud and tax offenses).

24. See H.B. 329, 1999 Leg., 91st Gen. Assem. (Ill. 1999).

25. An I.Q. of 70 or lower qualifies a person as mentally retarded, both clinically and (in most places) legally. See Atkins v. Virginia, 536 U.S. 304, 308 n. 3, 309 n. 5, 317 n. 22 (2002).

26. The facts of the *Garnett* case are derived from *Garnett v. State*, 632 A.2d 797, 332 Md. 571 (1993). In October 1992, Garnett is convicted and sentenced to five years in prison. The judge suspends his sentence and, instead, places Garnett on probation for five years and requires him to pay restitution to Erica and her family. Garnett's lawyer appeals, and the Maryland Supreme Court issues a writ of certiorari, thereby skipping over the usual intermediate appellate review. The Supreme Court affirms the conviction and finds that the lower court was correct in barring Garnett's evidence of his belief. See idem.

27. The evidentiary justification we discuss here is just one of several theories supporting imposition of strict liability. See Paul H. Robinson, *Imputed Criminal Liability*, 93 Yale L.J. 609, 619–21 (1984). Two other theories, the *causal* theory and the *equivalency* theory, are directly designed to track desert and therefore need not be addressed. See idem. A fourth theory, the *nonculpability* theory, is most commonly used to defend strict liability. That theory is rooted in a concern with deterrence, and we accordingly address it in our discussion of deterrence-motivated rules, which appears in chapter 8.

28. Model Penal Code § 213.6(1).

29. See Model Penal Code § 210.2 (1985); idem, Comment at 39.

30. In the case of felony murder, laypersons' intuitions of justice reflect this position, but somewhat imperfectly. Lay consensus would appear to support a diluted, "felony manslaughter" version of the rule, rather than its total abolition. See Paul H.

Robinson & John Darley, *Justice, Liability, and Blame: Community Views and the Criminal Law* 169–81 (Westview 1995).

31. This language states the Model Penal Code's test for negligence. See Model Penal Code § 2.02(2)(d); supra chapter 2 n. 63 (discussing the Code's modified objective formulation based on reasonable person "in the actor's situation").

32. See generally Robinson, supra n. 27, at 652–57.

33. See, e.g., Robbins v. People, 350 P.2d 818 (Colo. 1960) (upholding felony-murder conviction of *D* where *D* and *C* robbed *X*, *D* hit *X* over the head with butt of pistol, accidentally discharging pistol and killing *C*); State v. Baker, 607 S.W.2d 153 (Mo. 1980) (upholding felony-murder conviction of *D* where *D* and *C* were disturbed by *Y* while robbing *X*, *D* shot at *Y*, and *Y* returned fire causing *D* to flee, after which *Y* shot and killed *C*).

One might argue that we can rely upon the discretion of prosecutors to forgo prosecution in such cases, but others would claim that such an expectation is unrealistic. More important, such an argument concedes that the law itself fails to make the distinctions necessary for a just result, adopting a position inconsistent with the legality principle and with modern notions of justice. See generally Paul H. Robinson, *Criminal Law* § 2.2 (Aspen L. & Bus. 1997).

34. See infra chapter 7, "Moral Credibility 'versus' Legitimacy: Evaluating the Tradeoffs" (discussing relevance of law's moral credibility to its efficacy in utilitarian terms).

35. See Federal Bureau of Investigation, Uniform Crime Reports, *Crime in the United States: 2002*, at 27 table 2.14, available at http://www.fbi.gov/ucr/02cius.htm (hereinafter *Crime in the U.S. 2002*) (listing data for individual years from 1998 to 2002, with five-year sum of 11,632 "felony type" murders out of 68,535 total murders; also listing a total of 368 "suspected felony type" murders). See also James Alan Fox & Marianne W. Zawitz, Bureau of Justice Statistics, *Homicide Trends in the U.S.: Homicide Circumstances*, available at http://www.ojp.usdoj.gov/bjs/homicide/tables/circumsttab.htm (using similar source data to F.B.I.'s UCR report, but with higher absolute figures based on extrapolations from Supplemental Homicide Reports used by UCR; showing same rates of felony-situation homicides, where "homicide" is defined similarly to UCR's "murder" definition).

Indeed, the F.B.I. report defines "murder" to include only "the willful (nonnegligent) killing of one human being by another," as determined by police investigation, rather than judicial determination. *Crime in the U.S. 2002*, supra, at 19. Even so, it seems likely that police reports would classify nearly any homicide in a felony context as "murder" if the criminal code does the same—for example, 360 of the listed "murders" occurred in the context of arson, in which situation the intentionality of the offender as to the death (rather than as to the arson) may sometimes be in doubt, but for which the police would seem likely to categorize any resulting death as "murder." See idem at 27 table 2.14 (five-year sum of figures from individual years). Also, nonfelony murder situations in the data include brawls arising from the influence of alcohol or narcotics, for which an offender's culpability might also not involve "intent" as defined by the criminal code, even though the act might be "willful" in another sense. See idem at 27 table 2.14.

36. See idem (percentages calculated using five-year sums of figures from individual years).

37. See idem (percentages calculated using five-year sums of figures from individual years).

38. See authorities collected in 1 Robinson, supra n. 16, at § 104 nn. 9–12.

39. Cf. United States v. Balint, 258 U.S. 250, 254 (1922) ("Congress weighed the possible injustice of subjecting an innocent seller [of drugs] to a penalty against the evil of exposing innocent purchasers to danger from the drug, and concluded that the latter was the result preferably to be avoided."); United States v. Halper, 490 U.S. 435, 447 n. 8 (1989) (noting that "strict liability crimes are principally directed at social betterment rather than punishment of culpable individuals"). For a general source about the history of and justifications for strict liability (which is critical of the "risk the innocent to get the guilty" view), see Richard G. Singer, *The Resurgence of Mens Rea: III: The Rise and Fall of Strict Criminal Liability*, 30 B.C. L. Rev. 337 (1989).

40. Significantly, expansion or retraction of a rule of imputation is not the only possible reform that society can undertake to advance the evidentiary rationale. If the need for effective prosecution is substantial—as in instances of food adulteration, for example—it may be better to tolerate more intrusive investigative procedures, rather than to tolerate more erroneous convictions arising under a strict-liability rule. See generally Wayne LaFave, 5 *Search and Seizure: A Treatise on the Fourth Amendment* § 10.2(d) (4th ed., West 2004) (discussing relaxed requirements for legal searches of heavily regulated industries).

41. "At the outset . . . the primary (and perhaps the exclusive) basis for excluding confessions . . . was the 'untrustworthiness' rationale, the view that the confession rule was designed merely to protect the integrity of the fact-finding process." Yale Kamisar et al., *Modern Criminal Procedure: Cases, Comments and Questions* 440 (10th ed., West 2002), see also, e.g., LaFave et al., supra n. 4, § 6.2(a); John Henry Wigmore, 3 *Evidence in Trials at Common Law* §§ 820–22 (James H. Chadbourn, ed., rev. ed., Little, Brown 1970).

This is not the only basis for the privilege today, however. It was also thought unseemly or unfair to require a defendant to be the agent of his own demise. See, e.g., 8 idem § 2251(11)(c), (d) (John T. McNaughten, ed., rev. ed., Little, Brown 1961) (collecting sources). This concern is similar to the "fundamental fairness" issues we discuss infra chapter 7 and further supports granting the privilege. The important point, though, is that no further support for the privilege is needed: the unreliability of compelled self-incrimination is reason enough, even under pure desert principles, to justify the privilege.

42. See, e.g., Haynes v. Washington, 373 U.S. 503 (1963); Spano v. New York, 360 U.S. 315 (1959); Payne v. Arkansas, 356 U.S. 560 (1958); Brown v. Mississippi, 297 U.S. 278 (1936).

43. Lynumn v. Illinois, 372 U.S. 528, 534 (1963).

44. Idem (quoting Blackburn v. Alabama, 361 U.S. 199, 208 (1960)).

45. See, e.g., Fed. R. Evid. 403 ("Although relevant, evidence may be excluded if its probative value is substantially outweighed by the danger of unfair prejudice, confusion of the issues, or misleading the jury[.]").

46. See e-mail from Eugene Volokh to "crimprof" list, June 19, 2002.

47. See e-mail from Richard McAdams to "crimprof" list, June 19, 2002.

48. See United States v. Wade, 388 U.S. 218, 237–39 (1967) (excluding identification because absence of counsel at lineup violated right to counsel).

49. Even in those cases, though, the rule may be based on an underlying skepticism about any evidence offered to show the accuracy or reliability of such a lineup, since without the presence of defense counsel, later descriptions of the situation are likely to tell only one side of the story or ignore salient facts. (Of course, as with other assumptions we discuss in this part, whether that skepticism has merit is an empirical question regarding which further research may be warranted.) Further, a lineup identification is a form of evidence over whose acquisition law-enforcement officials can exercise control; they can arrange to conduct the lineup at a specific time, with defense counsel present, without suffering any costs (other than the defense counsel's ability to prevent misconduct). Additionally, from the police perspective, there is no exigency requiring immediate action, as the suspect is already in custody.

50. To the extent that the lineup situation also raises concerns about maintaining basic fairness, as opposed to promoting accuracy, see infra chapter 7; the presumption might also require the state to provide a legitimate justification for the absence of defense counsel at the lineup.

CHAPTER 4

1. See John Henry Wigmore, 8 *Evidence in Trials at Common Law* § 2281 n. 11 (John T. McNaughten, ed., rev. ed., 1961 & 1998 supp.) (listing state and federal immunity statutes).

2. See idem at 492 ("[Immunity statutes] have for more than two centuries been the expedients resorted to for the investigation of many offenses, chiefly those whose proof and punishment were otherwise impracticable because of the implication in the offense itself of all who could bear useful testimony."). But cf. Alexander J. Menza, *Witness Immunity: Unconstitutional, Unfair, Unconscionable*, 9 Seton Hall Const. L.J. 505, 544–47 (1999) (arguing that untrammeled prosecutorial discretion leads to corruption and abuse).

3. See George Fisher, *Plea Bargaining's Triumph*, 109 Yale L.J. 857, 1042–43 (2000).

4. As George Fisher explains:

> To the extent that a plea bargain delivers a verdict that onlookers acknowledge to be truthful, it protects the jury and the system that sponsors it from the risk of issuing the wrong verdict—or to be precise, a verdict the public will perceive to be wrong. That is, despite all the criticism heaped upon plea bargaining by those who think it deprives de-

fendants of their trial right or the public of its right to uncompromised punishment, when it comes to the apparent accuracy of outcomes, plea bargaining helps protect the system's legitimacy. . . .

The usefulness of this division of labor between plea bargaining and jury trial, in which the bargaining process handles the easy cases and the jury the hard ones, becomes clear when we reflect on the consequences of the jury's returning a "wrong" verdict in a "clear" case. The system's legitimacy suffers its greatest strain when the public feels sure that the jury has erred. But because defendants who face overwhelming evidence of guilt typically bargain for the best deal they can get, the jury rarely faces a clear case and rarely risks being clearly wrong.

Idem. By increasing the system's "legitimacy," plea bargaining may also indirectly enhance the criminal law's moral force. See supra chapter 1.

Fisher has since developed his article into a full book-length treatment of the history of plea bargaining. See George Fisher, *Plea Bargaining's Triumph: A History of Plea Bargaining in America* (Stanford 2003).

5. Helen Weathers, *I Betrayed Teflon Don; Exclusive: Inside the Mafia; How Sammy Gravano Broke Mafia Silence to Bring Down John Gotti*, Mirror (UK), May 7, 1997.

6. The facts of the *Gravano* case are derived from United States v. Gotti, 644 F. Supp. 370 (E.D.N.Y. 1986); United States v. Gotti, 634 F. Supp. 877 (E.D.N.Y. 1986); United States v. Gotti, 771 F. Supp. 552, 554 (E.D.N.Y. 1991); United States v. Gravano, plea agreement (E.D.N.Y. Nov. 13, 1991) (on file with authors); United States v. Gravano (E.D.N.Y. Sept. 26, 1994) (on file with authors); Superseding Information against Salvatore Gravano from Andrew J. Maloney, U.S. Attorney, Eastern District of New York 4 (undated document); the Government's Sentencing Memorandum from Zachary W. Carter 2 (Aug. 15, 1994) (on file with authors); Letter from Sam Nunn, Chairman, U.S. Senate Permanent Subcommittee on Investigations, and William V. Roth, Jr., Ranking Minority Member, U.S. Senate Permanent Subcommittee on Investigations, to I. Leo Glasser 1 (July 25, 1994); Peter Maas, *Underboss: Sammy the Bull Gravano's Story of Life in the Mafia* (HarperCollins 1997); AP, *Reputed Mafia Boss Indicted in 4 Murders*, Chicago Trib., Dec. 4, 1990; Pete Bowles, *Gravano Could Be Free by Spring*, Newsday (N.Y.), Apr. 27, 1994; Pete Bowles, *Gotti's Got to Spend Some Time in Jail; Judge Denies Bail; Hearing Set Monday*, Newsday (N.Y.), Dec. 13, 1990; Pete Bowles, *Gotti Proclaims, "I'm Still the Boss": FBI Tapes of Reputed Mob Chief*, Newsday (N.Y.), Aug. 3, 1991; Pete Bowles, *Gravano Guilty in Ecstasy Case; Wife, 2 Children also Plead to Ariz. Charges*, Newsday (N.Y.), June 30, 2001; Pete Bowles, *Indictment Includes 5 Murders*, Newsday (N.Y.), Jan. 19, 1992; Jimmy Breslin, *The Main Event: Bull vs. the Mob*, Newsday (N.Y.), Mar. 3, 1992; Leonard Buder, *Gotti Is Acquitted in Conspiracy Case Involving the Mob*, N.Y. Times, Mar. 14, 1987; Julie Cart, *Former Mob Hit Man Pleads Guilty to Role in Ecstasy Ring; Crime: "Sammy the Bull" Gravano Gets 20 Years in Arizona Case Involving 46 Defendants*, L.A. Times, June 30, 2001; Timothy Clifford, *Gotti and Associate Cleared in*

Assault, Conspiracy Case, Newsday (N.Y.), Feb. 10, 1990; Richard Esposito, *"I'm Outta Here," Gotti Says: But Prosecutors Confident of Convicting Reputed Crime Boss,* Newsday (N.Y.), Jan. 25, 1989; Alan Feuer, *Gravano and Son Are to Enter Guilty Pleas in Ecstasy Case,* N.Y. Times, May 25, 2001; Alan Feuer, *Gravano Pleads Guilty to Drug Sales in Arizona,* N.Y. Times, June 30, 2001; Joseph P. Fried, *Judge Clears Gotti of Assault Charges at a Trial in Queens,* N.Y. Times, Mar. 26, 1986; Joseph P. Fried, *Witness in Gotti Trial Fails to Identify Defendants as Attackers in Queens Dispute,* N.Y. Times, Mar. 25, 1986; *Reputed Mob Boss Shot Dead,* Record (Bergen County, N.J.), Dec. 18, 1986; William Glaberson, *Gravano, Ever a Showman, Takes Stand Again,* N.Y. Times, Oct. 18, 2003, at B3; John J. Goldman, *Gotti Accuser Sentenced to Five Years in Plea Deal; Mafia: Salvatore Gravano Is Rewarded for Testifying against the Notorious Gambino Family Boss and Other Organized Crime Figures,* L.A. Times, Sept. 27, 1994; Dennis Hevesi, *Police Hunt Reputed Mob Officer Reported Missing for Past Week,* N.Y. Times, June 14, 1986; Beth Holland & Pete Bowles, *Grieving Mom Tries to Spit on Mob Killer,* Newsday (N.Y.), Mar. 4, 1992; Murray Kempton, *Gotti Always Able to Go Distance,* Newsday (N.Y.), Dec. 13, 1990; Arnold H. Lubasch, *Gotti Confidant Tells Courtroom of Mafia Family's Violent Reign,* N.Y. Times, Mar. 3, 1992; Robert D. McFadden, *Organized-Crime Chief Shot Dead Stepping from Car on E. 46th St.,* N.Y. Times, Dec. 17, 1986; Larry McShane, *Once Again, Sammy the Bull Betrays Friends,* Record (Bergen County, N.J.), June 3, 2001; Larry Neumeister, *Gotti Brother Charged in Plot to Rub Out "Sammy the Bull,"* AP, Aug. 19, 2003; Andy Newman, *Mafia Turncoat Gets 20 Years for Running Ecstasy Ring,* N.Y. Times, Sept. 7, 2002, at B3; Selwyn Raab, *Gotti Accused of Role in Castellano Slaying,* N.Y. Times, Dec. 13, 1990; Selwyn Raab, *Gotti Not Guilty on All 6 Charges in Assault Trial,* N.Y. Times, Feb. 10, 1990; William M. Reilly, *Gotti Jury Hears Testimony on Two Alleged Mob Rubouts,* UPI, Feb. 19, 1992; Michael Specter, *"Dapper Don" Gotti Indicted in N.Y.: Reputed Crime Family Leader Charged in Killing of Predecessor,* Wash. Post, Dec. 13, 1990; David Treadwell, *Gotti Indicted in 1985 Murder of Crime Boss; Mafia: Prosecutors Say Evidence against the Reputed Mob Czar Includes Secretly Taped Conversations,* L.A. Times, Dec. 13, 1990; Raghuram Vadarevu, *Mob Hitman Indicted in Cop Killing,* Record (Bergen County, N.J.), Aug. 29, 2003; Dennis Wagner, *Gravanos Face New Allegations; Plotted Murders, Prosecutors Say,* Ariz. Repub., May 12, 2001; Dennis Wagner, *Gravano Wove Deceptive Web,* Ariz. Repub., Mar. 25, 2001; *Gravano Gets 20 Years for Dealing Ecstasy,* Ariz. Repub., Sept. 7, 2002, at 3B; Dennis Wagner, *Gravano Sentenced to 19-Year Term,* Ariz. Repub., Oct. 31, 2002, at 3B; *Gravano's Son Gets 9 Years,* Orlando Sentinel, Oct. 18, 2002, at A25.

7. See Bureau of Justice Statistics, U.S. Dep't of Justice, *Felony Sentences in State Courts, 2000,* at 8, table 9 (2001) (table showing that in 2000, 879,200 of 924,700 state felony convictions—or 95.1%—were obtained by guilty pleas), available at http://www.ojp.usdoj.gov/bjs/pub/pdf/fsscoo.pdf (downloaded Apr. 6, 2004); U.S. Sentencing Commission, *2001 Sourcebook of Federal Sentencing Statistics,* at table 10 (pleas involved in 96.6% of cases); idem at fig. C (tracking increase in rate of guilty pleas from 93.2% of cases in 1997 to 96.6% in 2001—meaning that percentage of cases going to trial was halved, from 6.8% to 3.4%, in four years). Cf. Markus Dirk Dubber, *Ameri-*

can Plea Bargains, German Lay Judges, and the Crisis of Criminal Procedure, 49 Stan. L. Rev. 547, 551–52 (1997) ("Plea bargaining has long ago replaced the trial as the main process by which the state imposes punishment.").

8. See G. Nicholas Herman, *Plea Bargaining* 1 (Lexis 1997) (noting that an overwhelming number of the approximately 90% of U.S. criminal convictions resulting from guilty pleas are achieved through plea bargains); see also Daniel C. Richman, *Bargaining about Future Jeopardy*, 49 Vand. L. Rev. 1181, 1237 (1996) ("[P]lea bargaining is the dominant mode of adjudication."); Ernest Van den Haag, *Punishing Criminals: Concerning a Very Old and Painful Question* 171 (U. Press of Am. 1991) ("More than 90 percent of all cases are settled by striking a bargain: the defendant is allowed to plead guilty to a lesser charge than the one originally brought so that in exchange for his lower punishment the trial can be avoided."). Cf. Fisher, supra n. 3, at 860 ("[P]lea bargaining has so fast a grip on our institutions of justice that antagonistic institutions cannot survive.").

9. U.S. Sentencing Guidelines § 3E1.1.

10. Federal immunity requests reached their peak in 1986, with prosecutors making 2,550 requests (involving 5,013 witnesses); since then, the number of requests has decreased, with 913 requests (involving 1,613 witnesses) occurring in 2003. See Bureau of Justice Statistics, U.S. Dep't of Justice, *Sourcebook of Criminal Justice Statistics*, at 398, table 5.1 (Kathleen Maguire & Ann L. Pastore, eds.) (hereinafter *Sourcebook*), available at http://www.albany.edu/sourcebook/pdf/t51.pdf (downloaded June 14, 2005). The decrease in immunity requests at the federal level is almost certainly attributable to the rise of the similar but more flexible tools we discuss in the text.

11. See John G. Douglass, *Confronting the Reluctant Accomplice*, 101 Colum. L. Rev. 1797, 1811 (2001). Prosecutors prefer such an arrangement for several practical reasons: "The prosecutor purchases not only the testimony, but also the opportunity to prepare the accomplice to testify. And an accomplice who undergoes hours of pretrial preparation is more predictable, and hence more valuable, than one who is forced to testify under a simple grant of immunity." Idem at 1826–27. In addition, unlike statutory immunity, a promise not to prosecute may be conditioned on the witness providing full cooperation and truthful testimony.

12. U.S. Sentencing Guidelines § 5K1.1.

13. See *Sourcebook*, supra n. 10, at table 5.36, available at http://www.albany.edu/sourcebook/pdf/t536.pdf (downloaded June 14, 2005).

14. John J. Goldman, *Gotti Accuser Sentenced to Five Years in Plea Deal; Mafia: Salvatore Gravano Is Rewarded for Testifying against the Notorious Gambino Family Boss and Other Organized Crime Figures*, L.A. Times, Sept. 27, 1994.

15. The Government's Sentencing Memorandum from Zachary W. Carter 2 (Aug. 15, 1994) (on file with authors).

16. Goldman, supra n. 14.

17. William J. Stuntz, *Plea Bargaining and Criminal Law's Disappearing Shadow*, 117 Harv. L. Rev. 2548, 2564–65 (2004).

18. For a contrary account, asserting that the practices of plea bargaining and witness immunity are inconsistent with any retributivist, as opposed to consequential-

ist, theory of punishment—and concluding that this inconsistency reveals a flaw with retributivism, rather than with bargaining—see Russell L. Christopher, *The Prosecutor's Dilemma: Bargains and Punishments*, 72 Fordham L. Rev. 93 (2003).

19. See Michael S. Moore, *Placing Blame: A Theory of Criminal Law* 156–58 (Clarendon 1997) (arguing that using immunity to punish more, or more serious, offenders rather than fewer, or less serious, ones may advance goal of desert-based punishment). But cf. Christopher, supra n. 18, at 117 (asserting that "[t]he idea that 'half a loaf is better than none' underscores the consequentialist premise of bargain justice") (citation omitted).

20. See Gerard E. Lynch, *Screening versus Plea Bargaining: Exactly What Are We Trading Off?*, 55 Stan. L. Rev. 1399, 1406 (2003) (hereinafter Lynch, *Screening versus Bargaining*) ("We really want the criminal justice system to accomplish the best practicable accommodation between the conflicting goals of promoting public safety and protecting individual rights, not to produce theoretically pure outcomes. 'Bargained' dispositions of cases in which conviction is uncertain may well do a better job of that than all-or-nothing jury trials.").

21. See, e.g., Christopher, supra n. 18, at 131–34 (criticizing bargaining on retributivist grounds as treating equally culpable wrongdoers unequally).

22. See, e.g., Stephen J. Schulhofer, *Plea Bargaining as Disaster*, 101 Yale L.J. 1979, 2009 (1992) (hereinafter Schulhofer, *Disaster*) ("Plea bargaining is a disaster [that] can be, and should be, abolished."); Albert W. Alschuler, *The Changing Plea Bargain Debate*, 69 Cal. L. Rev. 652–56, 668–69 (1981); Marshall J. Hartman & Marianna Koval, *The Immorality of Plea Bargaining*, in *Legality, Morality, and Ethics in Criminal Justice* 70 (Nicholas N. Kittrie & Jackwell Susman, eds., Praeger 1979); Raymond I. Parnas & Riley J. Atkins, *Abolishing Plea Bargaining: A Proposal*, 14 Crim. L. Bull. 101, 101 (1978) (starting with "the premise that there is no legal or wise basis for the retention of" plea bargains) Cf Gerard E. Lynch, *Our Administrative System of Criminal Justice*, 66 Fordham L. Rev. 2117, 2130 (1998) ("[N]o one pictures 'plea bargaining' as a rational way to determine guilt or innocence.").

Even some commentators who agree, or assume, that abandoning plea bargains would be infeasible contend that reforms are necessary. See, e.g., Joseph A. Colquitt, *Ad Hoc Plea Bargaining*, 75 Tul. L. Rev. 695, 698 (2001) (asserting that "the system needs extensive cleansing to extirpate the ill-advised, unauthorized, and thus illegal bargains [that] permeate plea bargaining"); Nancy Jean King, *Priceless Process: Nonnegotiable Features of Criminal Litigation*, 47 UCLA L. Rev. 113 (1999) (proposing framework for determining which rights should be "nonnegotiable" even in bargaining system).

23. For one discussion of the relation between bargaining and desert, see Christopher, supra n. 18 (critiquing bargaining as violation of abstract principles of retributivism).

24. See, e.g., Albert W. Alschuler, *Implementing the Defendant's Right to Trial: Alternatives to the Plea Bargaining System*, 50 U. Chicago L. Rev. 931, 933, 937 (1983) (hereinafter Alschuler, *Alternatives*) (claiming that plea bargaining "has led the Supreme Court to a hypocritical disregard of its usual standards of waiver in

judging the most pervasive waiver that our criminal justice system permits"; suggesting "that a less restrictive form of bargaining could be substituted for plea bargaining—bargaining for waiver of the right to jury trial but not for waiver of the right to trial before a court"); Robert A. Carp & Ronald Stidham, *Judicial Process in America* 159 (5th ed., CQ Press 2001); John H. Langbein, *Torture and Plea Bargaining*, 46 U. Chicago L. Rev. 3, 12–13 (1978) (comparing coercive power of plea bargaining to medieval torture); cf. Daniel P. Blank, *Plea Bargain Waivers Reconsidered: A Legal Pragmatist's Guide to Loss, Abandonment and Alienation*, 68 Fordham L. Rev. 2011, 2016 (2000) ("The most common criticisms of the practice of plea bargaining are that the threat of much harsher penalties after trial is impermissibly coercive upon defendants and causes them to abandon the procedural protections of trial; that it is hypocritical to use 'an elaborate trial process as window dressing, while doing all the real business of the system through the most unelaborate process imaginable;' and that the inequality of relative bargaining strength between the government and the defendant renders the plea bargaining process inaccurate and unfair, especially to poor and unsophisticated defendants.") (citation omitted).

25. See Albert W. Alschuler, *The Defense Attorney's Role in Plea Bargaining*, 84 Yale L.J. 1179 (1975); Stephanos Bibas, *Plea Bargaining outside the Shadow of Trial*, 117 Harv. L. Rev. 2463, 2476–86 (2004); Schulhofer, *Disaster*, supra n. 22, at 1987–91; Stephen J. Schulhofer, *Criminal Justice Discretion as a Regulatory System*, 17 J. Legal Stud. 43, 49–60 (1988); cf. Robert E. Scott & William J. Stuntz, *Plea Bargaining as Contract*, 101 Yale L.J. 1909, 1928 (1992) (noting that "agency problems no doubt exist in the [plea-bargaining] context, particularly in cases of appointed counsel for poor defendants," but arguing that problems would be worse without plea bargaining).

26. See R. A. Duff, *Trials and Punishments* 141 (Cambridge 1986) ("[A] guilty plea should properly express the defendant's recognition, and voluntary admission, of her guilt. . . . But if we obtain a guilty plea by offering her irrelevant and improper inducements or threats, which are meant to provide her with a purely prudential motive for pleading guilty, that plea loses its meaning and its value; and we no longer address or respect her as a rational agent.").

27. See Bibas, supra n. 25, at 2481–86.

28. See idem at 2498 2519. Bibas also notes the problem of "information deficits" in certain cases where defendants lack good information about the state's evidence. See idem at 2493–96.

29. See Hartman & Koval, supra n. 22, at 72 ("Some innocent defendants are persuaded that it is advantageous to plead guilty, despite their innocence."); Albert W. Alschuler, *The Prosecutor's Role in Plea Bargaining*, 36 U. Chicago L. Rev. 50, 65 n. 43 (1968) (asserting that plea bargains "permit situations in which it is to the apparent advantage of innocent men to plead guilty"); Duff, supra n. 26, at 141 (citing "strong evidence" that, in England, many defendants are induced into guilty pleas, even though some "are actually innocent, in whole or in part, of the charges to which they plead guilty").

30. See Hartman & Koval, supra n. 22, at 70, 74 ("The result of [the plea-bargaining] system is that those who do exercise their constitutional rights may re-

ceive a more severe sentence. . . . [Over time,] the sentencing system adjusts [to bargaining,] and defendants who plea bargain and plead guilty get the sentence[s] they ought to get, but defendants who demand trial and are convicted get longer sentences."). Cf. Lynch, *Screening versus Bargaining*, supra n. 20, at 1401–02 ("[T]here is no reason to assume that offenders who receive 'plea bargained' dispositions are receiving any lower a sentence or charge of conviction than the system as a whole regards as appropriate for their case. . . . Given the extreme severity of sentencing in the United States by world standards . . . it is hard to take seriously the notion that ninety percent of those serving our remarkably heavy sentences are the beneficiaries of 'bargains.'").

31. See David D. Friedman, *Law's Order: What Economics Has to Do with Law and Why It Matters* 91–92 (Princeton 2000).

32. See, e.g., Lawrence Baum, *American Courts: Process and Policy* 195 (3d ed., Houghton Mifflin 1994) (stating that the most common criticism of plea bargaining is that defendants are allowed to escape full punishment); Douglas D. Guidorizzi, Comment, *Should We Really "Ban" Plea Bargaining? The Core Concerns of Plea Bargaining Critics*, 47 Emory L.J. 753, 768 (1998) ("[C]riminals benefit from bargaining with the state and avoid what may be seen as the appropriate sanction for their crime."); see also Hartman & Koval, supra n. 22, at 71–72 ("The anomaly of this process is that we sentence defendants who we know are guilty to less severe sentences than those defendants about whose guilt we may be uncertain. . . . To give the admitted criminal a lighter sentence is not only anomalous, it is patently unjust."). But see Lynch, *Screening versus Bargaining*, supra n. 20, at 1402 n. 4 ("[T]he sentences actually meted out to defendants under the plea bargaining regime . . . are certainly not, by any objective standard, unduly lenient.").

33. See Bibas, supra n. 25, at 2470–76; Stuntz, supra n. 17, at 2554; Edward L. Glaeser et al., *What Do Prosecutors Maximize? An Analysis of the Federalization of Drug Crimes*, 2 Am. L. & Econ. Rev. 259 (2000).

34. See Bibas, supra n. 25.

35. See Stuntz, supra n. 17.

36. See Paul H. Robinson & Michael T. Cahill, *The Accelerating Degradation of American Criminal Codes*, 56 Hastings L. J. 633(2005); see also Stuntz, supra n. 17, at 2556–58.

37. See Stuntz, supra n. 17, at 2558 ("It sounds odd, but legislators' incentive is to vote for rules that even the legislators themselves think are too harsh."); see also William J. Stuntz, *The Pathological Politics of Criminal Law*, 100 Mich. L. Rev. 505, 546–57 (2001).

38. See Paul H. Robinson et al., *The Five Worst (and Five Best) American Criminal Codes*, 95 Nw. U. L. Rev. 1, 16 (2000).

39. See Bibas, supra n. 25, at 2530 (acknowledging that numerous identified concerns and biases that may distort actual bargains from theoretical model are "difficult to quantify and measure" and that "this difficulty should spur empirical research to measure these factors"). Cf. Guidorizzi, supra n. 32, at 770–71 ("The benefits of the certainty of conviction and the efficiency of the process outweigh the cost for se-

curing a conviction."). Advocates also argue that the reduced sentences resulting from bargains may be appropriate. See Naomi Aoki, *Plea Bargains Lighten Courts' Loads, Help Cinch Convictions, Experts Say*, Va. Pilot & Ledger-Star, Oct. 20, 1997, at 1 (including quote that prosecutors "can show mercy for a first-time offender or offer treatment instead of incarceration. They can evaluate each case on its merits and use plea agreements to get convictions and sentences that fit the crimes.").

40. See Peter F. Nardulli et al., *The Tenor of Justice: Criminal Courts and the Guilty Plea Process* 207 (U. Ill. 1988) (stating that the criminal-justice system is "highly complex and is composed of largely autonomous units that must cater to a variety of interests while handling large numbers of defendants of varying backgrounds charged with a variety of different acts," making consistency practically impossible).

41. See Bureau of Justice Statistics, U.S. Dep't of Justice, *Sourcebook of Criminal Justice Statistics 1997*, at 427, table 5.56 (Kathleen Maguire & Ann L. Pastore, eds., U.S. Gov't Printing Office 1998) (1994 statistics; see also Bureau of Justice Statistics, U.S. Dep't of Justice, *Sourcebook of Criminal Justice Statistics 1995*, at 505, table 5.56 (Kathleen Maguire & Ann L. Pastore, eds., U.S. Gov't Printing Office 1996) (1992 statistics: following guilty plea, average sentence of 72 months and median of 48 months; following bench trial, average of 88 months and median of 60 months; following jury trial, average of 190 months and median of 108 months). Subsequent editions of the *Sourcebook*, curiously, seem to lack an equivalent table.

42. See supra nn. 3–4 and accompanying text.

43. See, e.g., Michael Gorr, *The Morality of Plea Bargaining*, 26 Soc. Theory & Practice 129, 146 (2000) ("[I]t must be conceded that defenders of the efficiency argument have a strong prima facie case for their view."); Hartman & Koval, supra n. 22, at 73 ("The economic efficiency of plea bargaining is the strongest argument in favor of maintaining the system."); Fred C. Zacharias, *Justice in Plea Bargaining*, 39 Wm. & Mary L. Rev. 1121, 1138 (1998) (stating that plea bargaining may be justified based on "notions of efficiency or resource preservation").

44. See Robert A. Weininger, *The Abolition of Plea Bargaining: A Case Study of El Paso County, Texas*, 35 UCLA L. Rev. 265, 271–313 (1987) (describing slowdown in case processing following abolition of plea bargaining in El Paso).

45. See Stephen J. Schulhofer, *Is Plea Bargaining Inevitable?*, 97 Harv. L. Rev. 1037 (1984) (arguing that plea bargaining could be replaced with bench-trial system without significantly increasing caseload or cost pressures and citing successful experience with bench-trial system in Philadelphia); see also Alschuler, *Alternatives*, supra n. 24, at 1048 ("The impediments to implementation of a plea bargaining prohibition are not worth a fraction of the paralysis that they have prompted."); Schulhofer, *Disaster*, supra n. 22, at 2009 (asserting that plea bargaining "can be, and should be, abolished").

46. See Hartman & Koval, supra n. 22, at 74 ("The guilty-plea process is inefficient in that it generates extensive appellate litigation which results in frequent remands to the trial courts for evidentiary and other kinds of hearings. . . . [P]lea bargaining makes it difficult to use judicial and prosecutorial time effectively. When a trial is cancelled at the last minute because a defendant has agreed to plead guilty, it

is often impossible for the judge and the lawyers to reschedule other trials. The result is wasted time.") (citation omitted).

47. See Ronald Wright & Marc Miller, *The Screening/Bargaining Tradeoff*, 55 Stan. L. Rev. 29 (2002). The proposal is more specifically an alternative to charge bargaining, which is arguably more objectionable than sentence bargaining in that the prosecutor's decisions to alter or dismiss charges are not reviewable and may send confusing signals. See idem at 111–13.

48. See idem at 31–32 (setting out basic terms of proposal).

49. See idem at 58–84.

50. Cf. idem at 33 ("Plea bargaining is dishonest because the offense of conviction does not match either the charges the state filed or the reality of the offender's behavior. . . . The public in general, and victims in particular, lose faith in a system where the primary goal is processing and the secondary goal is justice. The public doubts justice has been done when the sanction in a negotiated plea case does not match the actual behavior."). But cf. Lynch, *Screening versus Bargaining*, supra n. 20, at 1402–03 n. 5 ("[H]owever offensive [charge bargaining] might be to academic seekers of truth (and, indeed, to at least some members of the public), the practical focus of both defendants and law-enforcement officials is much more likely to be on the sentence imposed than on the precise count of conviction. This focus may occasionally deflect attention from the desirability of accurately defining the defendant's wrongdoing, but the costs of such deflection are indirect and hard to quantify when compared to the more pressing question of the appropriate level of punishment."); idem at 1405 ("To the mugging victim, and to the general public, whether the mugger is convicted of attempted robbery, robbery in the first or second degree, or larceny, will rarely matter as much as whether and for how long the offender is jailed.").

51. See Ronald Wright & Marc Miller, *Honesty and Opacity in Charge Bargains*, 55 Stan. L. Rev. 1409, 1410–13 (2003).

52. See Lynch, *Screening versus Bargaining*, supra n. 20, at 1403–04.

53. For a list of the sources upon which this narrative is based, see supra n. 6.

CHAPTER 5

1. One might think that discretion is troubling only to the extent that the judgment or good faith of those exercising it is suspect. Yet who is to decide which figures are trustworthy enough? Any inadequacies in the system for selecting or monitoring those in authority—whose operation will itself typically involve the exercise of discretion—will be reflected in the makeup of those who are given the authority. Further, a person abusing her discretion will never admit it, often will hide it, and sometimes will not realize it. The difficulties of determining who will use discretion wisely, or even whose *past* exercise of discretion was sound or legitimate, argue in favor of applying the legality principle strictly.

2. All too often, discretion is employed arbitrarily or, worse, discriminatorily. The Jacksonville "prowling by auto" and "vagrancy" offenses, for example, were used by

Florida officials in the late 1960s to harass interracial couples. See Papachristou v. City of Jacksonville, 405 U.S. 156 (1972) (invalidating Jacksonville statutes as unconstitutionally vague).

3. Authority to create common-law offenses is not the only way for courts to make substantive criminalization decisions. Vague or ambiguous statutes are de facto delegations of the criminalization authority to the judges, who must determine the contours of the offense ex post.

4. To a certain extent, it must be noted, some of these justifications overlap with the goal of desert, with the deterrence objective discussed in chapter 6, or with the "fairness" principles discussed in chapter 7. For example, it may be thought unjust (i.e., antithetical to desert) to punish one who lacked reasonable notice as to the law's commands. Also, some violations of legality may be seen as more fundamental than others and therefore more likely to warrant deviation from desert, while other, less problematic cases (from the standpoint of legality) should give way to the desert interest. For example, one might contend that the legality principle should give way to criminal liability in cases involving a subjective belief of illegality or where there is "constructive" or "moral" notice, albeit not actual notice. Cf. Dan M. Kahan, *Ignorance of the Law Is an Excuse—But Only for the Virtuous*, 96 Mich. L. Rev. 127 (1997) (suggesting, in analogous but converse context, that ignorance or mistake should excuse only in morally neutral situations).

We have two comments about these issues. First, to tackle the question of which violations of legality are more "serious" and which ought to defer to desert is to engage in precisely the sort of debate on the merits about the abstract validity of legality vis-à-vis desert that, however interesting, is not part of our immediate project. We posit the validity of a principled commitment to legality, rather than taking any normative position (here, at least) as to whether that commitment should be strong or weak.

Second, as to the overlap between legality and other concerns we discuss elsewhere, we acknowledge the potential for legality concerns to duplicate or spill over into other concerns. Yet to limit the scope of the legality interest to those concerns, viewed in isolation, may take an overly reductive view. Legality derives its basis not only from fairness concerns but also (as the text notes) from a complex, interrelated set of interests that, taken together, seem rather powerful. The multiplicity of underlying justifications would also complicate any potential project, noted in the previous paragraph, to identify certain violations of legality as more or less serious than others.

5. Procrustes was a "legendary robber of ancient Greece who forced his victims to fit a certain bed by stretching or lopping off their legs." *Webster's Third New International Dictionary* 1809 (3d ed., Merriam-Webster 1993).

6. Erin McClam, *The Living Remain Strangers in a Town of Uncremated Dead*, Record (Bergen County, N.J.), Mar. 3, 2002.

7. Angela Couloumbis, *Loophole in Law Allowed Crematory to Go Unchecked*, Philadelphia Inquirer, Feb. 20, 2002.

8. Andrew Buncombe, *Police Start Grim Task of Putting Name to Piles of Bodies Found at Crematorium*, The Independent (London), Feb. 19, 2002.

9. Dareh Gregorian, *Corpses Piling Up—Crematorium Left Hundreds to Rot for Decades*, N.Y. Post, Feb. 18, 2002.

10. Gary Tanner, *Hurt Continues 3 Months Later*, Chattanooga Times, May 15, 2002.

11. Sara Rimer, *Dazed by the Crematory Scandal, Undertakers' Trust Is Shaken*, N.Y. Times, Mar. 5, 2002.

12. U.S. Const. art. I, § 9, cl. 3 ("No bill of attainder or *ex post facto* law shall be passed[.]"); U.S. Const. art. I, § 10, cl. 1 ("No State shall   pass any bill of attainder, *ex post facto* law . . .").

13. The vagueness prohibition is rooted in the Due Process Clauses of the Fifth and Fourteenth Amendments. The prohibition requires that the statute give "sufficient warning that men may conform their conduct so as to avoid that which is forbidden." Rose v. Locke, 423 U.S. 48, 50 (1975) (holding that the statutory phrase "crime against nature" gave adequate notice that forced cunnilingus was prohibited).

14. The rule of lenity—which is a common-law, rather than a constitutional, rule—directs that an ambiguity in a penal statute be resolved against the state and in favor of the defendant. See Rewis v. United States, 401 U.S. 808 (1971) (ambiguity in statute prohibiting interstate travel with intent to "promote, manage, establish . . . certain kinds of illegal activity" could not be construed to extend to operation of illegal establishment frequented by out-of-state customers).

15. Under Model Penal Code § 1.05(1), for example: "No conduct constitutes an offense unless it is a crime or violation under this Code or another statute of this State."

16. See idem.

17. See generally Paul H. Robinson, *Criminal Law* § 2.2 (Aspen L. & Bus. 1997).

18. Most state constitutions also include prohibitions against ex post facto laws. See Model Penal Code § 1.02, Comment at 3 n. 2 (1985).

19. See Model Penal Code § 1.02(3); idem, Comment at 33 nn. 76, 78 (listing twenty-four states adopting "fair import" or similar rule).

20. Looking only at the five largest states—California, Florida, Illinois, New York, and Texas—and only at one legality-based rule (the ex post facto prohibition), there have been a number of reversals of convictions or sentences over the last decade. See People v. Davis, 872 P.2d 591 (Cal. 1994) (denying retroactive application of judicial reading of statute); Gwong v. Singletary, 683 So.2d 109 (Fla. 1996) (regulation regarding administration of sentence); State v. Snyder, 673 So.2d 9 (Fla. 1996) (denying retroactive application of a judicial enlargement); Downs v. Crosby, 2004 WL 868212 (Fla. App. Apr. 23, 2004) (certiorari granted to consider ex post facto claim in habeas petition); Williams v. State, 873 So.2d 444 (Fla. App. 2004) (mandatory minimum sentence); Jones v. State, 872 So.2d 938 (Fla. App. 2004) (mandatory minimum sentence); Shelton v. State, 739 So.2d 1235 (Fla. App. 1999) (invalidating sentencing departure on ex post facto grounds); Lepak v. State, 707 So.2d 805, 806 (Fla. App. 1998) (reversing conviction); People v. Ramsey, 192 Ill. 2d 154 (Ill. 2000) (ruling earlier statute invalid; refusing on ex post facto grounds to apply new statute); In re F.G.,

318 Ill. App. 3d 709 (Ill. App. 2000) (juvenile case); People ex rel. Smith v. Greiner, 674 N.Y.S.2d 588 (N.Y. Sup. 1998) (sustaining writ of habeas corpus); Munoz v. State, 133 S.W.3d 836 (Tex. App. 2004) (sentence); Nolan v. State, 102 S.W.3d 231 (Tex. App. 2003) (sentence); Goodman v. State, 935 S.W.2d 184 (Tex. App. 1996) (reversing conviction); Johnson v. State, 930 S.W.2d 589 (Tex. Crim. App. 1996) (sentence); Ieppert v. State, 908 S.W.2d 217 (Tex. Crim. App. 1995) (reversing conviction).

21. Cf. Lawrence Solan, *Statutory Inflation and Institutional Choice*, 44 Wm. & Mary L. Rev. 2209 (2003) (discussing potential for broad readings of statutes imposing both civil and criminal sanctions to facilitate improper prosecutions in criminal context and role of lenity considerations in combating "statutory inflation").

22. See William J. Stuntz, *The Pathological Politics of Criminal Law*, 100 Mich. L. Rev. 505, 576–79 (2001); see also Paul H. Robinson & Michael T. Cahill, *The Accelerating Degradation of American Criminal Codes*, 56 Hastings L.J. 633(2005) (discussing trend of expanding criminal rules and prohibitions).

23. See Stuntz, supra n. 22, at 578–79 (discussing overcriminalization); idem at 588–91 (asserting need to reinvigorate notice requirements given increasing scope and complexity of criminal law).

24. Idem at 579; see also William J. Stuntz, *Reply: Criminal Law's Pathology*, 101 Mich. L. Rev. 828, 829 (2002) ("The irony is thick: we have a deeply lawless criminal justice system in part because that system is deeply committed to legality.").

25. See generally Stuntz, supra n. 22, at 519–23.

26. For example, the standing Law Commission for England and Wales regularly reviews all existing laws, including criminal laws, and recommends appropriate reforms. See http://www.lawcom.gov.uk (Law Commission Web site); see also, e.g., http://www.alrc.gov.au (Web site for Australian Law Reform Commission); see also Paul H. Robinson & Michael T. Cahill, *Can a Model Penal Code Second Save the States from Themselves?*, 1 Ohio St. J. Crim. L. 169, 176–77 (2003) (proposing ongoing criminal-law review and reform efforts).

27. See, e.g., George P. Fletcher, *Rethinking Criminal Law* § 3.3 at 177 (Little, Brown 1978) ("Of course, one could legislate a new offense that would cover all cases in which people act in the belief that they were violating the law. . . . There is something untoward about hitching criminal liability exclusively to the actor's beliefs about what he is doing. Yet this form of liability would not be different in nature from punishing the act of putting sugar in coffee, if the act is accompanied by a wicked intent.").

28. The facts of the *Marsh* case are derived from the following sources: State of Georgia, Seventh Judicial Administrative District, *Orders/Motions in the Criminal Tri-State Crematory Case*, available at http://www.7jad.com/Criminal%20Orders.htm; Author Unknown, *Cremation Crook Should Stay Jailed for Own Good*, N.Y. Post, Feb. 23, 2002; Author Unknown, *Families Raise Concern over Operation of Crematory*, N.Y. Times, Mar. 11, 2002; Norman Arey, *Charges against Marsh Mount*, Atlanta J. & Const., Feb. 27, 2002; Norman Arey, *Crematory Scandal: Sloppiness behind Piles of Corpses?*, Atlanta J. & Const., Apr. 7, 2002; Norman Arey, *Tri-State Probe Not Any Closer to Explanation*, Atlanta J. & Const., June 2, 2002; Norman Arey, *Crematory*

Trial Costs Escalate: Marsh Pleads Poverty, Wants New Venue, Atlanta J. & Const., Sept. 24, 2003, at 1C; AP, *Examiner Tri-State Situation "Sorriness,"* Chattanooga Times, May 23, 2002; AP, *Officials End Search of Georgia Crematory,* N.Y. Times, Mar. 6, 2002; AP, *Test Shows Machine at Georgia Crematory Works,* N.Y. Times, Mar. 5, 2002; Andrew Buncombe, *Police Start Grim Task of Putting Name to Piles of Bodies Found at Crematorium,* Independent (London), Feb. 19, 2002; Richmond Eustis, *Questions Grow with Body Count,* Fulton County Daily Report, Feb. 19, 2002; David Firestone & Michael Moss, *More Corpses Are Discovered Near Crematory,* N.Y. Times, Feb. 18, 2002; David Firestone & Robert D. McFadden, *Scores of Bodies Strewn at Site of Crematory,* N.Y. Times, Feb. 17, 2002; David Goldberg, *Crematory Scandal Crimps Thinly Spread Budget at Bad Time,* Atlanta J. & Const., Feb. 23, 2002; Dareh Gregorian, *Corpses Piling Up—Crematorium Left Hundreds to Rot for Decades,* N.Y. Post, Feb. 18, 2002; Erin McClam, *The Living Remain Strangers in a Town of Uncremated Dead; Georgia's Community Is Really a Strip of Road,* Record (Bergen County, N.J.), Mar. 3, 2002; Nikki Middlebrook, *Noble Residents Rebuilding, Marsh Family to Help with Community Effort,* Chattanooga Times, May 22, 2002; Michael Pearson, *Body Count Halted as Search Expands,* Atlanta J. & Const., Feb. 18, 2002; Michael Pearson, *Crematory Corpses Discarded Like Trash: Creepy Scene in Rural Georgia,* Atlanta J. & Const., Feb. 17, 2002; Michael Pearson, *Crematory Investigation: Why Didn't Tri-State Just Cremate the Bodies?,* Atlanta J. & Const., Feb. 24, 2002; Bill Poovey, *Cemeteries Forced to Help Find Answers to Crematory Secrets,* AP, Mar. 3, 2002; Bill Poovey, *Crematory Kin Want Answers,* Record (Bergen County, N.J.), Feb. 24, 2002; Bill Poovey, *Search for Dumped Corpses Takes New Turns: Body Count Reached 191,* AP, Feb. 19, 2002; Sue Anne Pressley, *Crematory Questions Stir Anguish: Ga. Town Shaken as Body Count Rises,* Boston Globe, Feb. 24, 2002; Sara Rimer, *Crematory Owners' Family Asks Why,* N.Y. Times, Feb. 24, 2002; Sara Rimer, *Dazed by Crematory Scandal, Undertakers' Trust Is Shaken,* N.Y. Times, Feb. 21, 2002; Duane D. Stanford, *Crematory Crackdown: Why So Late?,* Atlanta J. & Const., Mar. 25, 2002; Duane D. Stanford, *Crematory Probe: Regulators Tried to Close Tri-State,* Atlanta J. & Const., Feb. 22, 2002; Duane D. Stanford & Michael Pearson, *Gruesome Toll Worsens, Funeral Home Licenses in Jeopardy,* Atlanta J. & Const., Feb. 19, 2002; Gary Tanner, *Crematory Judge Issue Goes to State High Court,* Chattanooga Times, June 4, 2002; Gary Tanner, *Hurt Continues 3 Months Later,* Chattanooga Times, May 15, 2002; Kristen Wyatt, *Families Identify Bodies at Georgia Crematory: At Least 200 Corpses Strewn About,* Record (Bergen County, N.J.), Feb. 18, 2002; WXIA-TV Atlanta, *Judge: Crematory Trial Staying Put,* Dec. 3, 2003.

29. Regina v. Dudley & Stephens, 14 Q.B.D. 273, 286–88 (1884).

30. The facts of the *Dudley* case are derived from *Regina v. Dudley & Stephens,* 14 Q.B.D. 273 (1884); two drafts of Tom Dudley's *Account of the Foundering of the Yacht Mignonette,* Public Record Office, Kew, England; A. W. Brian Simpson, *Cannibalism and the Common Law: A Victorian Yachting Tragedy* (Hambledon 1994); Note, *In Warm Blood: Some Historical and Procedural Aspects of* Regina v. Dudley & Stephens, 34 U. Chicago L. Rev. 387 (1967).

31. 14 Q.B.D. 273 (1884).

32. For a discussion of the specific doctrines that serve this purpose—barring liability where the offender admittedly has violated the criminal law's rules of conduct—see Paul H. Robinson, *Structure and Function in Criminal Law* 138–42 (Clarendon 1997). One might make the same argument with regard to acquittals based on the absence of an offense's culpability requirements, although such acquittals may have a less damaging effect on the force of the conduct rules, because the reasons for acquittal are more common to the community's own experience.

Note that this argument is similar to, but distinct from, the fear-of-abuse concern we discussed in chapter 2, which also urges limitation or rejection of excuse defenses. That concern relates in part to the possibility of distortions and manipulations in the courtroom *after* a violation, whereas the *Dudley & Stephens* concern—to the extent it relates to behavior modification—seeks to ensure that the criminal law is clear and prevents potential violators ex ante from thinking that certain improper conduct is acceptable. Moreover, as noted in the text, the *Dudley & Stephens* concern is ultimately grounded in an abstract sense that the criminal law's imperatives must be absolute and certain.

33. See generally idem at 143–56.

34. For a list of the sources upon which this narrative is based, see supra n. 30.

35. See, e.g., Ind. Code Ann. § 35–42–4–1 (removing spousal exemption); 18 Pa. Cons. Stat. Ann. § 3106 (providing that complainant's testimony need not be corroborated); Fed. R. Evid. 412 (codifying "rape-shield" law that commonly bars admission of complainant's sexual history); N.J. Stat. Ann. § 2C:13–5 (broadening coercion definition to include more than force or threat of force). See generally Wayne R. LaFave, *Substantive Criminal Law* § 7.18, at 752–56 (3d ed., West 2000).

36. Reformers believe that in calling for changes to rape laws, they make "a clear statement about which behaviors we citizens consider wrong and criminal." Cassia C. Spohn, *The Rape Reform Movement: The Traditional Common Law and Rape Law Reforms,* 39 Jurimetrics J. 119 (1999) (quoting Ian BenDor, *Justice after Rape: Legal Reform in Michigan,* in *Sexual Assault: The Victim and the Rapist* 149, 152 (Marcia J. Walker & Stanley L. Brodsky, eds., Lexington 1976)). See also Susan Estrich, *Rape,* 95 Yale L.J. 1087, 1093 (1986) (arguing that "there is no 'model statute' solution to rape law, because the problem has never been the words of the statutes as much as our interpretation of them. . . . The difference must come in our understanding of 'consent' and 'will' and 'force.'").

37. See Margaret T. Gordon & Stephanie Riger, *The Female Fear: The Social Cost of Rape* 60–61 (U. Ill. 1991).

38. See, e.g., LaFave, supra n. 35, § 7.20.

39. See generally Paul H. Robinson & John M. Darley, *The Utility of Desert,* 91 Nw. U. L. Rev. 453 (1997).

40. For a discussion of the dangers to the law's moral credibility of a purely objective standard of reasonableness, see generally Robinson, supra n. 17, at 248–56.

41. This is not to say, however, that the concerns noted above are not significant to the lay public. It remains the case that juries are more reluctant to convict, and the general public is troubled by the prospect of substantial punishment, where a DUI of-

fender has caused no harm and seems not to have created a substantial risk of harm. See James B. Jacobs, *Drunk Driving: An American Dilemma* 13, 193–95 (U. Chicago 1989); Rebecca Snyder Bromley, *Jury Leniency in Drinking and Driving Cases: Has It Changed? 1958 versus 1993*, 20 Law & Psych. Rev. 27, 47–48 (1996) (comparing rates of DUI convictions when DUI is accompanied by evidence of unsafe driving, or by an accident, versus cases without these features).

Some academic commentators also consider the concerns noted in the text to be troubling. See, e.g., Douglas N. Husak, *Reasonable Risk Creation and Overinclusive Legislation*, 1 Buff. Crim. L. Rev. 599 (1998). In any case, and significantly, we are neither endorsing nor opposing current DUI schemes, just as we take no position here as to the proper scope of sexual-assault liability. Neither debate involves a clear deviation from desert so much as a dispute about what conduct is properly subject to punishment—which, however interesting, is not the kind of issue this project seeks to address. See supra chapter 1. For present purposes, we are merely pointing to aspects of the anti–drunk-driving movement that have helped enable its success and that seem to suggest potentially effective strategies for rape reformers.

42. See Model Penal Code § 2.08(2); Paul H. Robinson & John M. Darley, *Justice, Liability, and Blame: Community Views and the Criminal Law*, Study 10 (Westview 1995).

43. See, e.g., Jacobs, supra n. 41, at 127–200; Gerald D. Robin, *Waging the Battle against Drunk Driving: Issues, Countermeasures, and Effectiveness* 7–19, 109–18 (Praeger 1991).

44. See idem at 117–18; Johannes Andenaes, *Punishment and Deterrence* 59–60 (U. Mich. 1974); Roger C. Cramton, *Driver Behavior and Legal Sanctions: A Study of Deterrence*, 67 Mich. L. Rev. 421, 453 (1969); John R. Snortum & Dale E. Berger, *Drinking and Driving: Detecting the "Dark Figure" of Compliance*, 14 J. Crim. Just. 475 (1986); John R. Snortum, *Controlling the Alcohol-Impaired Driver in Scandinavia and the United States: Simple Deterrence and Beyond*, 12 J. Crim. Just. 142 (1984).

CHAPTER 6

1. See generally Paul H. Robinson & John M. Darley, *The Role of Deterrence in the Formulation of Criminal Law Rules: At Its Worst When Doing Its Best*, 91 Geo. L.J. 949 (2003) (hereinafter Robinson & Darley, *Role of Deterrence*); see also Paul H. Robinson & John M. Darley, *Does Criminal Law Deter? A Social Science Investigation*, 24 Oxford J. Legal Stud. 173 (2004) (hereinafter Robinson & Darley, *Does Criminal Law Deter?*), appendix available at http://www.law.upenn.edu/fac/phrobins/Oxford DeterrenceAppendix.pdf.

2. See generally Paul H. Robinson, *Punishing Dangerousness: Cloaking Preventive Detention as Criminal Justice*, 114 Harv. L. Rev. 1429 (2001) (arguing that the constraints inherent in the criminal-justice system produce a less effective preventive detention system than would an explicit system of civil preventive detention).

3. See idem.

4. In doing so, the judge deviates from the apparent demand of the controlling Illinois statute, which provides that when a person is convicted of first-degree murder for killing a peace officer, "the court *shall* sentence the defendant to a term of natural life imprisonment [if] the death penalty is not imposed. . . ." See 730 Ill. Comp. Stat. 5/5–8–1(a)(1)(c)(iii) (emphasis added). The judge apparently felt that the life sentence was too harsh for a seventeen-year-old with little criminal history. The state apparently agreed, for no writ of mandamus was sought to enforce the statutory requirement.

5. The facts of the *McCarty* case are derived from Custodial Status Sheet for De-Sean McCarty, Cook County Detention Center, Dec. 27, 1996; Markham Police Department, Supplemental Report on Sean Laura's death, Sept. 20, 1997; Transcript of Communications between Markham Dispatcher and Markham Police Unit 384 during McCarty's police chase, Markham Police Department, Sept. 20, 1997; Markham and Harvey Police Investigation Reports, Markham and Harvey Police Departments, Sept. 20, 1997; Accident Reconstruction Report for accident of Sept. 20, 1997, Harvey Police Department, Supplement to Report #11665a–97; Markham Police Department Offense Incident Report, Markham Police Department, Sept. 20, 1997; Cook County Police Reports—Booking Officer, State v. DeSean McCarty, Sept. 20, 1997; Harvey Police Lineup Report (includes DeSean McCarty's four lineups), Sept. 22, 1997; Statement of DeSean McCarty, Cook County State's Attorney's Office, Sept. 22, 1997; Grand Jury Testimony of Andre Griffin, In Re John Doe Investigation, Sept. 23, 1997; Medical Records of DeSean McCarty, Cermak Health Services of Cook County, Sept. 24, Oct. 9, and Oct. 14, 1997; Statement of Muhammed Williams, Cook County State's Attorney's Office, Sept. 1997; Grand Jury Indictment of DeSean McCarty, Oct. 1997; Cook County Forensics Report on DeSean McCarty and Sean Laura's body, Office of the Medical Examiner, Feb. 5, 1998; Closing Arguments of the Attorneys, State v. McCarty, Sept. 15, 1998; Victim Impact Statement of Patricia Laura, Mother of Sean Laura, Office of the State's Attorney, Cook County, Ill., Oct. 28, 1998; People v DeSean McCarty, Sept. 15, 1998 (on file with authors); Brief for Defense, People v. De-Sean McCarty, Nov. 3, 2000 (on file with authors); Brief for Prosecution, People v. DeSean McCarty (on file with authors); Telephone Interview by C. Todd Inniss, Eve Brensike, and Colette Routel with Frank Rago, public defender, Markham Public Defender's Office, Feb. 1999 (notes on file with authors); Sarah Karp, *Mother Copes with Cop's Death: Markham Officer Struck by Harvey Police Car*, Daily Southtown, Sept. 22, 1997; Karen Mellen, *Reckless Abandon: Families Want Driver Charged with Murder*, Chicago Trib., Oct. 7, 1998; T. Shawn Taylor, *Cops Arrest Teen Linked to Officer's Fatal Chase: Police Want Subject Held Accountable*, Chicago Trib., Sept. 23, 1997; T. Shawn Taylor, *Markham Cop's Death Becomes Murder Case: Bond Hearing Set in Fatal Police Chase*, Chicago Trib., Sept. 24, 1997.

6. The case gained notoriety from its inclusion in a criminal-law coursebook as an illustration of the vagaries of the felony-murder rule. See Paul H. Robinson, *Criminal Law Case Studies* 1–7 (West 2000).

7. See People v. McCarty, 785 N.E.2d 859, 271 Ill. Dec. 665 (Ill. 2003), citing People v. Belk, 203 Ill. 2d 187, 784 N.E.2d 825, 271 Ill. Dec. 271 (Ill. 2003).

8. The felony-murder rule is also sometimes defended on the ground that it operates only where the defendant probably has the requisite culpability for murder, but where this would be hard to prove. We discuss this evidentiary rationale in chapter 3.

9. See Robinson & Darley, *Role of Deterrence*, supra n. 1, at 957–59, 961.

10. See idem at 959–63.

11. See idem at 963–67.

12. See idem at 967–69.

13. Importantly, the evidentiary rationale, mentioned supra n. 8 and discussed in chapter 3, and the deterrence rationale discussed here are not merely alternative justifications for a single doctrine. The two different justifications suggest different formulations of the doctrine itself. The evidentiary rationale supports a formulation of the felony-murder rule that, for example, limits the rule to those instances in which the likelihood of actual recklessness (or at least negligence) as to causing death is high. See Paul H. Robinson, *Imputed Criminal Liability*, 93 Yale L.J. 609, 663–65 (1984). The deterrence rationale suggests no such limitation. See idem. Thus, if empirical evidence indicates that the inference of culpability underlying the evidentiary basis is generally valid, a formulation rooted in that basis would not conflict with, but would further, the goal of desert. A formulation rooted in the deterrence basis can make no such claim.

14. Holmes expressed this view:

> [I]f experience shows, or is deemed by the law-maker to show, that somehow or other deaths which the evidence makes accidental happen disproportionately often in connection with other felonies, or with resistance to officers, or if on any other ground of policy it is deemed desirable to make special efforts for the prevention of such deaths, the law-maker may consistently treat acts which, under the known circumstances, are felonious . . . as having a sufficiently dangerous tendency to be put under a special ban. The law may, therefore, throw on the actor the peril, not only of the consequences foreseen by him, but also of consequences which, although not predicted by common experience, the legislator apprehends.

Oliver Wendell Holmes, *The Common Law* 49 (Little, Brown 1881).

15. "[The] rational function of the felony-murder rule is to furnish added deterrent to the perpetration of felonies which, by their nature or by the attendant circumstances, create a foreseeable risk of death." State v. Goodseal, 553 P.2d 279, 285 (Kan. 1976).

16. James B. Brady, *Strict Liability Offenses: A Justification*, 8 Crim. L. Bull. 217, 222 (1972). Brady uses the example of adulteration of milk. See idem at 223–24.

17. See, e.g., Richard A. Wasserstrom, *Strict Liability in the Criminal Law*, 12 Stan. L. Rev. 731, 736 (1960) (arguing generally that "a person engaged in a certain

kind of activity would be more careful precisely because he knew that this kind of activity was governed by a strict liability statute").

18. See Tom R. Tyler & John M. Darley, *Building a Law-Abiding Society: Taking Public Views about Morality and the Legitimacy of Legal Authorities into Account when Formulating Substantive Law*, 28 Hofstra L. Rev. 707, 713 & nn. 19–23 (2000) ("[R]esearch findings suggest that people's compliance with the law is, at best, weakly linked to the risks associated with law-breaking behavior. As a result, social control strategies based primarily on a deterrence model of human behavior have, at best, had limited success."); see also Paul H. Robinson & John M. Darley, *The Utility of Desert*, 91 Nw. U. L. Rev. 453, 458–64 (1997) (hereinafter Robinson & Darley, *Utility of Desert*) (summarizing reasons that current punishment system has limited deterrent effect and providing supporting empirical data).

19. See idem at 458–60 (providing statistics that show low conviction rates for serious crimes).

20. Many, if not most, offenders may be unrealistically optimistic about the precautions they take to avoid being caught, or the simple likelihood of being caught, and thus may underestimate that probability. See Floyd Feeney, *Robbers as Decision Makers*, in *The Reasoning Criminal: Rational Choice Perspectives on Offending* 53, 65–66 (Derek Cornish & Ronald Clarke, eds., Springer 1986). Feeney's work with robbers suggests that first-time robbers feel a good deal of fear and apprehension, while more experienced robbers are much less tentative and fearful while committing robberies.

At the same time, as a general matter, people notoriously place high discounts on events that exist far in the future. See, e.g., George Anslie & Nick Haslam, *Hyperbolic Discounting*, in *Choice over Time* (George Loewenstein & Jon Elster, eds., Russell Sage 1992). The case for the discount of future pain is less clear than for the discount of future gain. If a future pain, such as an unavoidable electric shock, is certain, people often choose to get it over with quickly, probably to avoid anticipatory dread and anxiety. George Loewenstein, *Anticipation and the Valuation of Delayed Consumption*, 97 Econ. J. 667 (1987). But, of course, prison terms are by no means certain, or even likely. Elster and Loewenstein suggest a relationship between probability and dread that probably fits the present case. "At very low probability levels, below a threshold of conceivability, . . . dread will be nil. Beyond this threshold, we would expect a sudden jump and then low marginal sensitivity over a wide range of probabilities beyond that point[.]" Jon Elster & George Loewenstein, *Utility from Memory and Anticipation*, in *Choice over Time*, supra, at 213–34.

21. See generally Robinson & Darley, *Utility of Desert*, supra n. 18.

22. See idem, at 468–71.

23. See Anup Malani, *Does the Felony-Murder Rule Deter? Evidence from the FBI Crime Data* (unpublished manuscript, Nov. 11, 2002).

24. Idem at 23.

25. See idem at 19.

26. One might argue that in a few instances, such as the felony-murder situation, the potential harm is sufficiently serious that the law ought to do everything within its power to avoid a violation, and strict liability provides that special "super-punch."

But this argument misunderstands the nature of negligence. In judging an actor's negligence, the seriousness of the harm is taken into account. As the potential harm becomes greater, disregarding that harm becomes increasingly unreasonable, so that an actor's ability to avoid negligence liability for his inattentiveness diminishes.

27. See generally Robinson & Darley, *Does Criminal Law Deter?*, supra n. 1; Robinson & Darley, *Role of Deterrence*, supra n. 1.

28. See, e.g., Andrew von Hirsch & Lisa Maher, *Should Penal Rehabilitationism Be Revived?*, in *Principled Sentencing: Readings on Theory & Policy* 26, 27, 32 (Andrew von Hirsch & Andrew Ashworth, eds., 2d ed., Nw. U. Press 1998) (claiming that "[t]he extent of recent treatment successes remains very much in dispute" and concluding that "[r]ehabilitation . . . cannot be the primary basis for deciding the sentence, nor can it be the rationale for supporting less harsh sanctions than we have today"); see generally Douglas Lipton et al., *The Effectiveness of Correctional Treatment: A Survey of Treatment Evaluation Studies* (Praeger 1975).

Studies have also questioned the rehabilitative efficacy of the juvenile justice system specifically. See generally, e.g., Richard J. Lundman, *Prevention and Control of Juvenile Delinquency* (Oxford 1984). Lundman interprets the data to indicate that institutionalization may reduce the incidence of juvenile crime, but through simple incapacitation or deterrence, rather than rehabilitation. See idem at 187–214. Criticism of the juvenile justice system's rehabilitative potential has led to a clear shift away from policies promoting that goal and toward rules more likely to promote retribution, deterrence, or incapacitation. See, e.g., Ira M. Schwartz & Deborah A. Willis, *National Trends in Juvenile Detention*, in *Reforming Juvenile Detention* 13 (Ira M. Schwartz & William H. Barton, eds., Ohio St. U. Press 1994).

29. Such a presumption is an example of the deviating bright-line rules that stem from the refusal to soften rigid, objectively defined culpability standards. We discuss such rules in chapter 2. As with some other such rules, a more flexible rule allowing the defendant to rebut the presumption would make a better tradeoff between the abuse concern and the goal of desert.

30. The potentially erroneous irrebuttable presumptions inherent in current immaturity defenses might be justified by noting that a successful "defense" does not release a defendant, but only transfers jurisdiction to the juvenile court. Therefore, the argument runs, we need not worry that blameworthy offenders are going free under the defense. It is not always true, though, that blameworthy offenders receiving the defense are simply transferred to juvenile court custody for confinement. The criteria for juvenile detention may be unrelated to the issue of blameworthiness. For example, many state statutes focus on an offender's dangerousness. See, e.g., Ala. Code § 12–15–71.1; Ky. Rev. Stat. Ann. § 645.180; N.C. Gen. Stat. § 7A–574; Utah Code Ann. § 78–3a–30. Thus, a blameless juvenile may be confined and a blameworthy juvenile may be released.

31. See Parker v. State, 484 A.2d 1020, 1021 (Md. App. 1984). The court in *Parker* rejected the defendant's claim, holding that the defense should be applied according to the defendant's birth*day* but not his birth *hour*. See 484 A.2d at 1022. Of course, this hardly alters the arbitrariness of the defense or the irrationality of its results.

Under the court's rule, Parker would have been entitled to the defense if he had committed the offense nine hours and forty-six minutes earlier, or if he had been born eleven hours and eleven minutes later.

32. As of 1997, twenty-four states would allow (and three of those would *require*) prosecution as an adult for a *ten*-year-old accused of murder: Alaska (presumption in favor of prosecution as adult), Arizona, Delaware, Florida, Georgia, Hawaii, Idaho, Indiana, Kansas, Maine, Maryland, Nebraska, Nevada (mandatory prosecution as adult), Oklahoma, Oregon, Pennsylvania (mandatory prosecution as adult), Rhode Island, South Carolina, South Dakota, Tennessee, Vermont, Washington, West Virginia, and Wisconsin (mandatory prosecution as adult). See Patrick Griffin et al., *Trying Juveniles as Adults in Criminal Court: An Analysis of State Transfer Provisions* 14–15, appendix (Dep't of Justice, Office of Juvenile Justice and Delinquency Prevention 1998), available online at http://virlib.ncjrs.org/JuvenileJustice.asp.

33. Note that in this situation, a presumption would relate to the defendant's capacity to establish a defense, not to the prosecution's need to prove an element of an offense, and would therefore be constitutionally permissible. See infra chapter 9 nn. 6–7.

34. See, e.g., In re Gault, 387 U.S. 1, 14–15 (1967) (describing the development of the juvenile court system to serve protective and rehabilitative goals); Frederick J. Ludwig, *Rationale of Responsibility for Young Offenders*, 29 Neb. L. Rev. 521, 534 (1950) ("Given a choice between imprisonment or execution of a young offender and his return to society as a useful citizen, the overwhelming preference is obvious. Add the proposition that probability of reform is magnified when offenders are younger and freedom from legislative prescriptions makes possible complete administrative individualization of treatment, and the rationale of juvenile court laws is manifest."); idem at 537 ("Because it is ill-adapted to rehabilitation of actual [juvenile] offenders, punishment for deterrence of potential ones must be confined within justifiable limits.").

35. Almond was charged under 18 U.S.C. § 922(g), which makes it unlawful for certain persons (such as convicted felons, the provision under which Almond was prosecuted) "to ship or transport in interstate or foreign commerce, or possess in or affecting commerce, any firearm or ammunition; or to receive any firearm or ammunition which has been shipped or transported in interstate or foreign commerce." The career-offender sentencing provision for that offense appears in 18 U.S.C. § 924(e), which states:

> (1) In the case of a person who violates section 922(g) of this title and has three previous convictions by any court referred to in section 922(g)(1) of this title for a violent felony or a serious drug offense, or both, committed on occasions different from one another, such person shall be fined under this title and imprisoned not less than fifteen years, and, notwithstanding any other provision of law, the court shall not suspend the sentence of, or grant a probationary sentence to, such person with respect to the conviction under section 922(g).
>
> (2) As used in this subsection— . . .

· · ·

> (B) the term "violent felony" means any crime punishable by im-
> prisonment for a term exceeding one year, or any act of juvenile delin-
> quency involving the use or carrying of a firearm, knife, or destructive
> device that would be punishable by imprisonment for such term if
> committed by an adult, that—
>
> (i) has as an element the use, attempted use, or threatened use of
> physical force against the person of another; or
>
> (ii) is burglary, arson, or extortion, involves use of explosives, or
> otherwise involves conduct that presents a serious potential risk of
> physical injury to another[.]

18 U.S.C. § 924(e)(1), (2)(B). Arnold's convictions in the 1960s for (1) burglary of an unoccupied building, (2) throwing a "missile" (a rock) at a car, and (3) breaking and entering into the office of the Peeler Oil Company were treated as the requisite three prior "violent felonies" under this provision.

36. The facts of the *Almond* case are derived from the following sources: United States v. Almond, Apr. 1, 1992 (on file with authors); Almond v. United States, 854 F. Supp. 439 (W.D. Va. 1994).

37. See, e.g., U.S.S.G. § 4A1.1 et seq.; idem at ch. 5, part A (Sentencing Table) (setting guideline sentence as function of "offense level" and "criminal history category"); Ariz. Stat. § 16-90-801(b)(1); Del. Stat. tit. 11, § 6580(c)(1); Wash. Stat. § 9.94A.010(1).

38. See, e.g., 18 U.S.C. § 3559 (requiring life imprisonment upon a third serious violent felony conviction); Mont. Code Ann. § 46-18-219 (requiring life sentence without possibility of release after second or third felony conviction, depending on the felonies committed); see generally Ewing v. California, 538 U.S. 11, 15 (2003) ("Between 1993 and 1995, 24 States and the Federal Government enacted three strikes laws."); John Clark et al., *"Three Strikes and You're Out": A Review of State Legislation* 9–10 (Nat'l Inst. of Justice: Research in Brief, NJC 165369, 1997) (noting that many states have expanded preexisting repeat-offender statutes); Alex Glashausser, Note, *The Treatment of Foreign Country Convictions as Predicates for Sentence Enhancement Under Recidivist Statutes,* 44 Duke L.J. 134, 134–35 (1994) ("Every state currently authorizes increased punishment for repeat offenders under statutes varying in scope, harshness, and degree of discretion granted to sentencing judges."); Andrea E. Joseph, Note, *What Goes Around Comes Around—Nichols v. United States: Validating the Collateral Use of Uncounseled Misdemeanor Convictions for the Purpose of Sentence Enhancement,* 23 Pepp. L. Rev. 965, 1000 n. 203 (1996) ("At a minimum, every state has adopted some type of legislation that enhances sentences for recidivist behavior.") (citing 24 C.J.S. Criminal Law §§ 1526–28 (West 1989 & supp. 1995)).

39. A twenty-five-year-old offender committing a felony that normally carries a ten-year sentence, for which less time than that normally would be served, can get

mandatory life imprisonment without the possibility of parole, which may mean a sentence of forty-five years or more. See, e.g., Del. Code Ann. tit. 11, § 4214 (third felony conviction carries a life sentence for violations including kidnapping, aggravated robbery, rape, and unlawful discharge of a firearm from a vehicle); 720 Ill. Comp. Stat. Ann. 5/33B-1 (third felony conviction carries a life sentence for violations including manufacture or delivery of controlled substances, indecent solicitation of an adult, possession of metal-piercing bullets, or any armed felony).

Even the less dramatic habitual-offender statutes, which have been in use for some time, can have a substantial effect. For example, the Model Penal Code provision, which is the structural model for such statutes, allows an "extended term of imprisonment" for a repeat offender, which essentially doubles the maximum authorized sentence: the maximum sentence for a third-degree felony is increased from five years to ten; for a second-degree felony, it is increased from ten years to twenty; for a first-degree felony, it is increased from a maximum of twenty years to a requirement of life imprisonment. Model Penal Code § 7.03(3) & (4).

Even in the absence of either three-strikes or habitual-offender statutes, a similar increase in punishment for dangerousness is provided by sentencing guidelines that tie the sentence in large part to the offender's criminal history. Under the U.S. Sentencing Guidelines, for example, a level 10 offense gets six to twelve months in the absence of a criminal record, but twenty-four to thirty months for a significant record; a level 19 offense gets thirty to thirty-seven months, but with a record gets sixty-three to seventy-eight months; a level 37 offense normally gets eighteen to twenty-two years, but with a record gets between thirty years and life imprisonment. See 2 *Federal Sentencing Guidelines Manual* 1151 (West 2004).

40. 1 *Federal Sentencing Guidelines Manual* 349 (West 2004).

41. See, e.g., Nev. Rev. Stat. § 193.168 (enhancing criminal penalties for felonies committed to promote criminal gang activities); Okla. Stat. Ann. tit. 21, § 856(D)–(F) (creating a crime encompassing gang recruitment activities); Cal. Penal Code § 186.22(a) (providing special penalties for facilitating gang crime); see generally Bart H. Rubin, Note, *Hail, Hail, the Gangs Are All Here: Why New York Should Adopt a Comprehensive Anti-Gang Statute*, 66 Fordham L. Rev. 2033 (1998) (discussing the attributes of antigang statutes). The California statute is part of the state's Street Terrorism and Enforcement Prevention Act, which was a response to "a state of crisis which has been caused by violent street gangs whose members threaten, terrorize, and commit a multitude of crimes against the peaceful citizens of their neighborhoods." Cal. Penal Code § 186.21.

42. Between 1992 and 1995, forty-one states passed laws making it easier to try juveniles as adults. Melissa Sickmund et al., *Juvenile Offenders and Victims: 1997 Update on Violence* 30 (Nat'l Ctr. for Juvenile Justice 1997). Twenty-five jurisdictions now allow prosecution as adults for ten-year-olds for at least one offense. See supra n. 32 (listing twenty-four states allowing or requiring prosecution as adult for ten-year-old accused of murder); Griffin et al., supra n. 32, at 14, appendix (noting that District of Columbia allows for adult prosecution at any age for certain weapons offenses, and noting crimes other than murder for which ten-year-olds can be tried as

adults in the twenty-four states previously mentioned). Some of these states require juvenile court judges to agree to the transfer of juveniles to adult court; others leave the decision to transfer to prosecutorial discretion; and still others require the transfer for certain offenses. See idem at 85–89; see generally Eric K. Klein, *Dennis the Menace or Billy the Kid: An Analysis of the Role of Transfer to Criminal Court in Juvenile Justice*, 35 Am. Crim. L. Rev. 371, 401–09 (1998) (discussing the problems that result when children are tried as adults). According to a recent Justice Department report, "every state now has at least one provision to transfer juveniles to adult courts." Kevin J. Strom, *Profile of State Prisoners under Age 18, 1985–97*, at 1 (Bureau of Justice: Special Report, NCJ 176989, 2000). As of 1997, twenty-eight states had statutes that automatically excluded certain types of offenders from juvenile court jurisdiction; fifteen states permitted prosecutors to file some juvenile cases in adult criminal courts directly; and forty-six states allowed juvenile court judges to send cases to adult courts at their discretion. Idem at 2; see also Griffin et al., supra n. 32, at 2. As a result of such changes, the number of minors under age eighteen sent to prison rose from 18 per 1,000 violent crime arrestees in 1985, to 33 per 1,000 arrestees in 1997. Strom, supra, at 5 table 4.

Legislative histories provide further evidence of the incapacitative rationale underlying these reforms. The report for the 1994 California legislation, for example, explains the need for lowering the age of criminal prosecution from sixteen to fourteen by noting that "the public is legitimately concerned that crimes of violence committed by juveniles are increasing in number and in terms of the level of violence" and concluding that the legislation "is a rational response to the legitimate public desire to address what is a serious problem." A.B. 560, 1993–1994 Leg., reg. sess. (Cal. 1994) (enacted). The Congressional Research Service similarly summarizes the rationale for such state legislation: "locking up dangerous kids so that they will not commit further crimes." Cong. Res. Serv., Pub. No. 95 1152 GOV, *Juveniles in the Adult Criminal Justice System: An Overview* 5 (Library of Cong. 1995).

43. See, e.g., Model Penal Code § 5.05(1) (attempt to commit first-degree felony is excepted).

44. See Paul H. Robinson & John M. Darley, *Justice, Liability, and Blame: Community Views and the Criminal Law*, Study 1 at 14–28 and Study 3 at 33–42 (Westview 1995) (hereinafter Robinson & Darley, *Justice, Liability, and Blame*). Moral theorists, on the other hand, are divided on this issue, making this one of the few areas (and perhaps the only major one) we discuss in which some retributivists and desert utilitarians might disagree as to the dictates of desert. See supra chapter 1 nn. 6–7 and accompanying text.

45. As the drafters explain, "The theory of this grading system may be stated simply: To the extent that sentencing depends upon the antisocial disposition of the actor and the demonstrated need for a corrective sanction, there is likely to be little difference in the gravity of the required measures depending on the consummation or the failure of the plan." Model Penal Code § 5.05(1), Comment at 490 (1985). Similarly, the drafters explain, "The primary purpose of punishing attempts is to neutralize dangerous individuals." Model Penal Code § 5.01, Comment at 323 (1985); see also idem at

298, 299, 331. For other examples of the Model Penal Code's concern for dangerousness, see Paul H. Robinson, *Criminal Law* § 12.1 at 647–48 (Aspen L. & Bus. 1997).

46. Model Penal Code § 5.05(2).

47. The HIV-positive son who attempts to kill his long-hated father by spitting on him can escape liability if the killing method turns out to be impossible and he is not otherwise dangerous (if, say, the despised father has since died from natural causes). (For an example of such an HIV-mistaken-effect attack, see State v. Smith, 621 A.2d 493 (N.J. Super. 1993).) But if the son's intention to kill unjustifiably is real, and he has shown his willingness to fulfill it, his blameworthiness is clear.

48. There is considerable disparity among judges in the sentencing purposes that they follow—a prime factor in the introduction of federal sentencing guidelines in the Sentencing Reform Act of 1984. See S. Rep. No. 98–225, at 41 n. 18 (1983), reprinted in 1984 U.S.C.C.A.N. 3182, 3224 n. 18 ("While one-fourth of the judges thought rehabilitation was an extremely important goal of sentencing, 19 percent thought it was no more than 'slightly' important; conversely, about 25 percent thought 'just deserts' was a very important or extremely important purpose of sentencing, while 45 percent thought it was only slightly important or not important at all.").

49. See generally Andrew von Hirsch, *Past or Future Crimes: Deservedness and Dangerousness in the Sentencing of Criminals* 132–38 (Rutgers 1985).

50. See Robinson, supra n. 2, at 1436 & n. 27.

51. See idem at 1450 & n. 79.

52. See Franklin E. Zimring et al., *Punishment and Democracy: Three Strikes and You're Out in California* (Oxford 2001); Mike Males & Dan Macallair, *Striking Out: The Failure of California's "Three Strikes and You're Out" Law*, 11 Stan. L. & Pol'y Rev. 65 (2000); see also Michael Vitiello, *Punishment and Democracy: A Hard Look at Three Strikes' Overblown Promises*, 90 Cal. L. Rev. 257, 268–80 (2002) (reviewing book by Zimring et al., supra, and discussing its data).

53. See Linda S. Beres & Thomas D. Griffith, *Habitual Offender Statutes and Criminal Deterrence*, 34 Conn. L. Rev 55, 69 (2001) ("One survey of parolees showed that at ages seventeen or less more than 75% of parolees were rearrested within three years of their release. By ages twenty-five to twenty-nine, the number dropped to 65% and at ages forty-five and older only 40.3% were rearrested."); Linda S. Beres & Thomas D. Griffith, *Do Three Strikes Laws Make Sense? Habitual Offender Statutes and Criminal Incapacitation*, 87 Geo. L.J. 103, 135 (1998) ("The average career of an active offender is estimated to last between five and ten years. The peak ages for criminal activity are the late teens and early twenties. Only a small portion of offenders continue to commit offenses after the age of forty."); William Spelman, *Criminal Incapacitation* 14 (Plenum 1994) (noting that criminal career lasts between five and ten years); Alfred Blumstein, *Prisons*, in *Crime* 387, 395–98 (James Q. Wilson & Joan Petersilia, eds., ICS Press 1995) (noting that peak criminal activity is during teen years).

54. See Joanna M. Shepherd, *Fear of the First Strike: The Full Deterrent Effect of California's Two- and Three-Strikes Legislation*, 31 J. Legal Stud. 159, 159 (2002) (using county by county data to find greater deterrent effect from three-strikes legislation, claiming that during first two years it deterred approximately eight murders, 3,952

aggravated assaults, 10,672 robberies, and 384,488 burglaries); James A. Ardaiz, *California's Three Strikes Law: History, Expectations, Consequences*, 32 McGeorge L. Rev. 1, 3–7 (2000) (arguing that three strikes deters criminals from committing further crimes and achieves the goals of rehabilitation, retribution, and incapacitation); Brian P. Janiskee & Edward J. Erher, *Crime, Punishment and Romero: An Analysis of the Case against California's Three Strikes Law*, 39 Duq. L. Rev. 43, 53 (2000) (critiquing the Zimring study, supra n. 52, and concluding that the decline in the crime rate was sharper after three-strikes law); see also Bill Jones, *Why the Three Strikes Law Is Working in California*, 11 Stan. L. & Pol'y Rev. 23 (1999) (article by secretary of state of California, who was involved in drafting the three-strikes legislation, concluding law has been effective in deterring crime). Cf. Peter Greenwood et al., *Estimated Benefits and Costs of California's New Mandatory-Sentencing Law*, in *Three Strikes and You're Out: Vengeance as Public Policy* (David Shichor & Dale K. Sechrest, eds., Rand 1996) (projecting that California's three-strikes law would result in 338,000 fewer crimes, at a cost of $16,300 per serious crime prevented).

CHAPTER 7

1. The right to counsel does not fit within this category, as it does not necessitate any known or predictable sacrifices of desert. On the contrary, that right is designed to help enable and ensure accurate decisions on the merits, rather than some other goal unrelated or even opposed to substantive accuracy.

2. See, e.g., Tom R. Tyler & John M. Darley, *Building a Law-Abiding Society: Taking Public Views about Morality and the Legitimacy of Legal Authorities into Account when Formulating Substantive Law*, 28 Hofstra L. Rev. 707, 723–24 & nn. 70–72 (2000) ("[S]tudies suggest that legitimacy is linked to the fairness of the procedures used by authorities to make decisions. Consequently, legal authorities can maintain their legitimacy by making decisions ethically."); see also E. Allen Lind & Tom R. Tyler, *The Social Psychology of Procedural Justice* 65–83 (Plenum 1988); John Thibaut & Laurens Walker, *Procedural Justice: A Psychological Analysis* 67–116 (Erlbaum 1975) (discussing studies linking legitimacy to procedural fairness).

Courts have made the same point:

> Decency, security, and liberty alike demand that government officials shall be subjected to the same rules of conduct that are commands to the citizen. In a government of laws, existence of the government will be imperiled if it fails to observe the law scrupulously. Our Government is the potent, the omnipresent teacher. For good or for ill, it teaches the whole people by its example. Crime is contagious. If the Government becomes a lawbreaker, it breeds contempt for law; it invites every man to become a law unto himself; it invites anarchy. To declare that in the administration of the criminal law the end justifies the means—to declare that the Government may commit crimes in order to secure the

> conviction of a private criminal—would bring terrible retribution.
> Against that pernicious doctrine this Court should resolutely set its face.

Olmstead v. United States, 277 U.S. 438, 485 (1928) (Brandeis, J., dissenting).

3. See Tom R. Tyler, *Why People Obey the Law* 32–37, 64–68 (Yale 1990) (discussing significance of legitimacy in inducing compliance with law); see also infra "Moral Credibility 'versus' Legitimacy: Evaluating the Tradeoffs." Supreme Court proponents of the judicial-integrity view have recognized its relation to the system's public reputation. See, e.g., United States v. Calandra, 414 U.S. 338, 357 (1974) (Brennan, J., dissenting) ("The exclusionary rule, if not perfect, accomplishe[s] the twin goals of enabling the judiciary to avoid the taint of partnership in official lawlessness and of assuring the people—all potential victims of unlawful government conduct— that the government would not profit from its lawless behavior, thus minimizing the risk of seriously undermining popular trust in government.").

4. Of course, the practical tradeoffs involved in weighing a rule's impact on substantive credibility against its impact on procedural legitimacy may also tell us something about the public's view of the relative importance of those goals in the abstract. If we consistently found that improving substantive results, at a corresponding cost to procedural fairness, enhanced the system's public reputation, we might (tentatively) infer that the public cares more about achieving desert than about ensuring fairness. Any increase or decrease in desert or fairness based on specific rule changes, however, would occur at the margin, and it would be a mistake to extrapolate any finding into an overall judgment that people care more about one than the other.

5. Gera-Lind Kolarik, *Freed to Kill: The True Story of Larry Eyler* (Chicago Rev. 1990).

6. Idem.

7. Idem.

8. The facts of the *Eyler* case are derived from the following sources: Eyler v. Babcox, 582 F. Supp. 981 (N.D. Ill. 1983); People v. Eyler, 477 N.E.2d 774 (Ill. App. 1985); Eyler v. Illinois, 498 U.S. 881 (1990); Gera-Lind Kolarik, *Freed to Kill: The True Story of Larry Eyler* (Chicago Rev. 1990), George Anastaplo, *Lawyers, First Principles, and Contemporary Challenges: Explorations,* 19 N. Ill. U. L. Rev. 353 (1999); John O'Brien, *The Eyler Legacy: 21 Deaths; Murderer Admitted Grisly 2-State Spree,* Chicago Trib., Mar. 9, 1994; Sarah Talalay, *Eyler Dies in Prison, Had AIDS: Lawyer to Talk on Confessions,* Chicago Trib., Mar. 7, 1994.

9. See Weeks v. United States, 232 U.S. 383 (1914) (establishing exclusionary rule for federal courts); Mapp v. Ohio, 367 U.S. 643 (1961) (extending *Weeks's* exclusionary rule to state proceedings).

10. 384 U.S. 436 (1966). In fact, as to the similarity between the Fourth Amendment exclusionary rule and the Fifth Amendment rules, it has recently been argued that *Miranda* and its rules are best understood as expressing interests arising under the Fourth Amendment rather than the Fifth Amendment. See Timothy O'Neill, *Rethinking* Miranda: *Custodial Interrogation as a Fourth Amendment Search and Seizure,* 37 UC Davis L. Rev. 1109 (2004).

11. See William J. Stuntz, *The Virtues and Vices of the Exclusionary Rule*, 20 Harv. J. L. & Pub. Pol'y 443, 444 (1997) ("The [Fourth Amendment] exclusionary rule generates a lot of litigation—tens of thousands of contested suppression motions each year. That litigation is displacing something else, and the something else may well have more to do with guilt and innocence. That problem is much more serious than the occasional drug dealer whose Fourth Amendment claim is a ticket to get out of jail: the point is that the exclusionary rule skews the many cases in which drug dealers lose, not just the few that they win."); idem at 451–55.

12. Paul G. Cassell, Miranda's *Social Costs: An Empirical Reassessment*, in *The Miranda Debate* 175, 183, 185 (Richard A. Leo & George C. Thomas III, eds., Northeastern U. 1998). See also Paul G. Cassell & Bret S. Hayman, *Police Interrogation in the 1990s: An Empirical Study of the Effects of* Miranda, in *The* Miranda *Debate*, supra, at 222, 232 (conducting a new empirical study and concluding that "the benefits of *Miranda* seem slim while the costs seem substantial"). But see George C. Thomas III, *Plain Talk about the* Miranda *Empirical Debate: A "Steady-State" Theory of Confessions*, in *The* Miranda *Debate*, supra, at 236, 246 (questioning conclusions of Cassell & Hayman study and concluding that "[w]e do not have enough evidence to accept the hypothesis that *Miranda* has an effect" on confession rates).

13. Stephen J. Schulhofer, Miranda's *Practical Effect: Substantial Benefits and Vanishingly Small Social Costs*, in *The* Miranda *Debate*, supra n. 12, at 191, 192.

14. See United States v. Leon, 468 U.S. 897, 908 n. 6 (1984) (citing, for statistic noted in text, Thomas Y. Davies, *A Hard Look at What We Know (and Still Need to Learn) about the "Costs" of the Exclusionary Rule: The NIJ Study and Other Studies of "Lost" Arrests*, 1983 Am. B. Found. Res. J. 611, 621).

15. See United States v. Leon, 468 U.S. 897, 950–51 n. 11 (1984) (Brennan, J., dissenting) (citing, among other things, Peter F. Nardulli, *The Societal Cost of the Exclusionary Rule: An Empirical Assessment*, 1983 Am. B. Found. Res. J. 585, 596, Floyd Feeney et al., *Arrests without Conviction: How Often They Occur and Why* (Nat'l Inst. of Just. 1983))

16. Stephen G. Valdes, Comment, *Frequency and Success: An Empirical Study of Criminal Law Defenses, Federal Constitutional Evidentiary Claims, and Plea Negotiations*, 153 U. Pa. L. Rev. 1709, 1728–29 (2005). In offering estimates about how often such claims were made in their geographic area more generally, as opposed to how many they saw in their own practices, the respondents offered somewhat lower estimates of about 4.5% for Fourth Amendment claims and about 2.5% for Fifth Amendment claims. See idem. Estimated success rates for the area were also lower, in the range of just 2–5%. See idem.

Beyond the rates at which they explicitly arise in actual litigation, however, the rules may also have significant indirect effects, as by leading prosecutors to decline to pursue cases where an expected assertion of an exclusionary rule would make conviction unlikely. Study respondents estimated that expected Fourth Amendment claims led to nonprosecution in about 7 out of 1,000 cases; estimated rates of nonprosecution due to viable Fifth Amendment claims, on the other hand, were lower than 1 in 1,000. See idem.

17. As to the Fourth Amendment rule, see United States v. Janis, 428 U.S. 433, 446 (1976) ("The 'prime purpose' of the rule, if not the sole one, 'is to deter future unlawful police conduct.'") (quoting United States v. Calandra, 414 U.S. 338, 347 (1974)); Terry v. Ohio, 392 U.S. 1, 12 (1968) (noting that rule's "major thrust is a deterrent one"); Linkletter v. Walker, 381 U.S. 618, 636–37 (1965) ("[A]ll of the cases since Wolf [v. Colorado, 338 U.S. 25 (1949)] requiring the exclusion of illegal evidence have been based on the necessity for an effective deterrent to illegal police action."); Mapp v. Ohio, 367 U.S. 643, 656 (1961) ("[T]he purpose of the exclusionary rule 'is to deter—to compel respect for the constitutional guaranty in the only effectively available way—by removing the incentive to disregard it.'") (quoting Elkins v. United States, 364 U.S. 206, 217 (1960)); see also United States v. Leon, 468 U.S. 897, 906, 916 (1984); Stone v. Powell, 428 U.S. 465, 485 (1976); Joshua Dressler, Understanding Criminal Procedure § 21.02 (2d ed., Lexis 1997) (citing deterrence as central if not sole purpose of rule); Charles H. Whitebread & Christopher Slobogin, Criminal Procedure: An Analysis of Cases and Concepts § 2.01, at 18 (4th ed., West 2000) ("Today . . . the only purpose for the rule . . . is as a method of deterring the police from engaging in unconstitutional searches and seizures.").

18. As to the Fourth Amendment rule, see Arizona v. Evans, 514 U.S. 1, 10 (1995) (noting that "the Fourth Amendment contains no provision expressly precluding the use of evidence obtained in violation of its commands"); United States v. Leon, 468 U.S. 897, 905 (1984) (rejecting "[l]anguage in the opinions of this Court and of individual Justices [that has] sometimes implied that the rule is a necessary corollary of the Fourth Amendment"); United States v. Calandra, 414 U.S. 338, 347 (1974) (exclusionary rule is a "judicially created remedy, rather than a personal constitutional right"). As to the rule for Miranda, see Dickerson v. United States, 530 U.S. 428, 120 S. Ct. 2326 (2000).

19. It has also been argued that these rules, in addition to curtailing abuses of power by the executive branch, maintain the integrity of the judiciary branch. See supra nn. 2–3, infra nn. 32–33, see also Thomas S. Schrock & Robert C. Welsch, Up from Calandra: The Exclusionary Rule as a Constitutional Requirement, 59 Minn. L. Rev. 251, 257–60 (1974); Silas Wasserstrom & William J. Mertens, The Exclusionary Rule on the Scaffold: But Was It a Fair Trial?, 22 Am. Crim. L. Rev. 85, 87–88, 151–52 (1984); cf. Timothy Lynch, In Defense of the Exclusionary Rule, 23 Harv. J. L. & Pub Pol'y 711 (2000) (defending exclusionary rule on separation-of-powers grounds).

It may also be asserted that these rules promote fundamental fairness and prevent the state from exerting too much control over the individual. The integrity argument and the fairness argument each provide some support for the position that these rules are necessary to maintain the system's legitimacy in the public's mind, as discussed below. See infra "Moral Credibility 'versus' Legitimacy: Evaluating the Tradeoffs." But cf. infra nn. 32–34 and accompanying text (questioning utility of rules, as currently formulated, in maintaining or strengthening system's legitimacy).

20. See infra nn. 32–34 and accompanying text.

21. See, e.g., Wong Sun v. United States, 371 U.S. 471 (1963).

22. See generally supra chapter 3.

23. Cf. Akhil Reed Amar & Renee B. Lettow, *Fifth Amendment First Principles: The Self-Incrimination Clause*, 93 Mich. L. Rev. 857, 858 (1995) (arguing that "the Court should . . . declare that a person's (perhaps unreliable) compelled pretrial statements can never be introduced against him in a criminal case but that reliable fruits of such statements virtually always can be"). But cf. New York v. Quarles, 467 U.S. 649, 669–72 (1984) (O'Connor, J., concurring in part) (drawing distinction for poisonous-tree purposes between *Miranda*-violating and "involuntary" confessions, stating that in latter case "a broader exclusionary rule is warranted," apparently because a "core" constitutional right is involved).

24. See supra chapter 6 nn. 18–20 and accompanying text.

25. Some fifteen years after *Mapp v. Ohio*, 367 U.S. 643 (1961), extended the Fourth Amendment exclusionary rule to the states, the Supreme Court itself acknowledged that "[n]o empirical researcher . . . has yet been able to establish with any assurance whether the rule has a deterrent effect." United States v. Janis, 428 U.S. 433, 452 n. 22 (1976). One study provides statistics regarding the number of convictions prevented by the exclusionary rule and suggests that the rule has not been an effective deterrent to police misconduct. See L. Timothy Perrin et al., *If It's Broken, Fix It: Moving beyond the Exclusionary Rule*, 83 Iowa L. Rev. 669, 734–36 (1998).

26. See Wayne R. LaFave, 1 *Search and Seizure: A Treatise on the Fourth Amendment* § 1.2(b), at 33 (4th ed., West 2004) ("The evidence tending to show that the exclusionary rule does deter is, by comparison [with that indicating that it does not], of a 'softer' variety, but most likely this is inevitably so."); Charles Alan Wright, *Must the Criminal Go Free if the Constable Blunders?*, 50 Tex. L. Rev. 736, 739 (1972); Bradley C. Canon, *Ideology and Reality in the Debate over the Exclusionary Rule: A Conservative Argument for Its Retention*, 23 S. Tex. L.J. 559, 560 (1982) (finding that "neither side can satisfy any very demanding standard of proof that the rule does or does not have a deterrent effect"); Arval A. Morris, *The Exclusionary Rule, Deterrence and Posner's Economic Analysis of Law*, 57 Wash. L. Rev. 647, 653 (1982) (contending that "no conclusively sound social science study of the exclusionary rule's deterrent effect will actually be produced").

27. Dallin H. Oaks, *Studying the Exclusionary Rule in Search and Seizure*, 37 U. Chicago L. Rev. 665, 721–22 (1970).

28. Terry v. Ohio, 392 U.S. 1, 14 (1968).

29. For discussion and criticism of the Supreme Court case law recognizing the impeachment exception, see 6 LaFave, supra n. 26, § 11.6(a).

30. See Carmen R. Parcelli, *The Exclusionary Rule*, 88 Geo. L.J. 1043, 1055–56 & nn. 625–32 (2000) (collecting cases).

31. Cf. Stephen J. Markman, *Six Observations on the Exclusionary Rule*, 20 Harv. J. L. & Pub. Pol'y 423, 428 (1997) ("When something less draconian than the exclusionary rule is restored as a remedy for an unreasonable search and seizure, then the judiciary will be less inclined to interpret the Fourth Amendment in the narrowest possible fashion in an effort to avoid the application of the rule.").

32. See, e.g., Mapp v. Ohio, 367 U.S. 643, 659 (1961) (noting the "imperative of judicial integrity" as a basis for the Fourth Amendment exclusionary rule); Elkins v.

United States, 364 U.S. 206, 223 (1960) (stating that admission of illegally obtained evidence would make the courts "accomplices in the willful disobedience of a Constitution they are sworn to uphold"); Weeks v. United States, 232 U.S. 383, 394 (1914) ("To sanction such proceedings would be to affirm by judicial decision a manifest neglect if not an open defiance of the prohibitions of the Constitution, intended for the protection of the people against such unauthorized action.").

33. One case describes the integrity-deterrence relationship as follows:

> Judicial integrity clearly does not mean that the courts must never admit evidence obtained in violation of the Fourth Amendment. The requirement that a defendant must have standing to make a motion to suppress demonstrates as much. . . . The primary meaning of "judicial integrity" in the context of evidentiary rules is that the courts must not commit or encourage violations of the Constitution. In the Fourth Amendment area, however, the evidence is unquestionably accurate, and the violation is complete by the time the evidence is presented to the court. . . . The focus therefore must be on the question whether the admission of the evidence encourages violations of Fourth Amendment rights. As the Court has noted in recent cases, this inquiry is essentially the same as the inquiry into whether exclusion would serve a deterrent purpose.

United States v. Janis, 428 U.S. 433, 458 n. 35 (1976) (citations omitted); see also Stone v. Powell, 428 U.S. 465, 485 (1976) ("While courts, of course, must ever be concerned with preserving the integrity of the judicial process, this concern has limited force as a justification for the exclusion of highly probative evidence."); Michigan v. Tucker, 417 U.S. 433, 451 n. 25 (1974) (noting that in Fifth Amendment context, judicial integrity is not independent basis for exclusion); cf. 1 LaFave, supra n. 26, § 1.1(f), at 23 ("The Court's focus in recent years has been almost exclusively upon the deterrence function[.]").

34. See, e.g., INS v. Lopez-Mendoza, 468 U.S. 1032 (1984) (allowing use of improperly obtained evidence in deportation proceeding); Stone v. Powell, 428 U.S. 465 (1976) (allowing use of improperly obtained evidence in federal habeas corpus proceeding); United States v. Janis, 428 U.S. 433 (1976) (allowing use of improperly obtained evidence in federal civil tax proceeding); idem at 455 n. 31 ("It is well established, of course, that the exclusionary rule, as a deterrent sanction, is not applicable where a private party or a foreign government commits the offending act.").

35. See United States v. Leon, 468 U.S. 897 (1984).

36. See supra n. 30 and accompanying text.

37. See, e.g., Christopher Slobogin, *Toward Taping*, 1 Ohio St. J. Crim. L. 309, 309 & n. 1 (2003) ("Numerous authors, from all points on the political spectrum, have advocated that police interrogations be taped.") (citing Paul G. Cassell, *Miranda's Social Costs: An Empirical Assessment*, 90 Nw. U. L. Rev. 387, 489–92 (1996); Welsh S.

White, *False Confessions and the Constitution: Safeguards against Untrustworthy Confessions*, 32 Harv. C.R.-C.L. L. Rev. 105, 153–55 (1997)).

38. See Craig M. Bradley, *The Emerging International Consensus as to Criminal Procedure Rules*, 14 Mich. J. Int'l L. 171, 183–86 (1993).

39. See William A. Geller, *Videotaping Interrogations and Confessions*, in *The Miranda Debate* 303, 303 (Richard A. Leo & George C. Thomas III, eds., Northeastern U. 1998).

40. See State v. Scales, 518 N.W.2d 587 (Minn. 1994) (mandating that the police videotape all custodial interrogations, including *Miranda* warnings); Stephan v. State, 711 P.2d 1156, 1162 (Alaska 1985); Tex. Code Crim. Proc. art. 38.22 § 3(a)(1) (2002). The Texas law is somewhat more limited in that only the confession, and not the interrogation leading to the confession, must be recorded. See idem.

41. See 20 Ill. Comp. Stat. 3930/7.2.

42. See Margaret Graham Tebo, *ABA Says States Should Decide Who Can Marry*, 3 No. 6 ABA J. E-Report 2 (Feb. 13, 2004).

43. "In all criminal prosecutions, the accused shall enjoy the right to a speedy and public trial[.]" U.S. Const. amend. VI. To determine whether a defendant's speedy-trial right has been violated, courts employ a case-by-case balancing test that considers four elements: (1) the length of the pretrial delay; (2) the reason(s) for the delay; (3) whether, and by what means, the defendant asserted his right to a speedy trial; and (4) the prejudice to the defendant. See Barker v. Wingo, 407 U.S. 514, 530–33 (1972). Unless there has been a presumptively prejudicial delay—i.e., unless the fourth factor is satisfied—the other factors are not considered. See Barker, 407 U.S. at 530. See generally *Preliminary Proceedings: Speedy Trial*, 33 Geo. L.J. Ann. Rev. Crim. Proc. 344, 347 (2004).

44. See generally idem at 350–60 (discussing federal Speedy Trial Act); Wayne R. LaFave et al., *Criminal Procedure* § 18.3(c) (4th ed., West 2004) (noting that "all but a few states have adopted statutes or rules of court on the subject of speedy trial" and offering general discussion of such rules).

45. See 18 U.S.C. § 3161(c)(1) (stating that trial must "commence within seventy days from the filing date (and making public) of the information or indictment, or from the date the defendant has appeared before a judicial officer of the court in which such charge is pending, whichever date last occurs"); 18 U.S.C. § 3161(h) (setting out excusable periods of delay); 18 U.S.C. § 3161(h)(8) (allowing continuance serving "ends of justice").

46. See United States v. Ewell, 383 U.S. 116, 120 (1966) ("This guarantee is an important safeguard to prevent undue and oppressive incarceration prior to trial, to minimize anxiety and concern accompanying public accusation and to limit the possibilities that long delay will impair the ability of an accused to defend himself."); see also LaFave et al., supra n. 44, § 18.1(b).

47. See Barker v. Wingo, 407 U.S. 514, 521–22 (1972); Strunk v. United States, 412 U.S. 434, 439–40 (1973); LaFave et al., supra n. 44, §18.3(c) at 871 ("As for the applicable sanction when a defendant by timely motion has shown that the time specified

by a [state] statute or court rule has run, the prevailing view is that only dismissal with prejudice will suffice, meaning that the defendant may not later be charged with the same offense (or, some of the provisions specify, with any related offense).").

Under the federal Speedy Trial Act, when a violation occurs, dismissal may be with or without prejudice:

> In determining whether to dismiss the case with or without prejudice, the court shall consider, among others, each of the following factors: the seriousness of the offense; the facts and circumstances of the case which led to the dismissal; and the impact of a reprosecution on the administration of this chapter and on the administration of justice.

18 U.S.C. § 3162(a)(1) & (2).

48. See Anthony G. Amsterdam, *Speedy Criminal Trial: Rights and Remedies*, 27 Stan. L. Rev. 525, 525 (1975) (noting that current system "convert[s] the right of every criminal defendant to have a speedy trial into a very different sort of right: the right of a few defendants, most egregiously denied a speedy trial, to have the criminal charges against them dismissed on that account").

On the other hand, one might argue that the stiffness of the penalty provides a strong deterrent, ensuring that violations do not occur in the first place. Cf. supra nn. 16–30 (discussing deterrence argument in exclusionary-rule context).

49. *Strunk*, 412 U.S. at 440.

50. See, e.g., Amsterdam, supra n. 48, at 534–35 (stating that "[o]n its face, [*Strunk's*] proposition is incredible"; citing various cases—including U.S. Supreme Court cases—employing other means of enforcing right; and discussing alternative options such as expediting trial, releasing defendant from pretrial confinement, and dismissing without prejudice).

51. Of course, these alternative remedies are impossible to implement under current law, as Supreme Court precedent has held that dismissal with prejudice is the only constitutional remedy for a speedy-trial violation. See *Barker*, 407 U.S. at 521–22; *Strunk*, 412 U.S. at 439–40.

52. Another way to narrow the rule while preventing prosecutorial misconduct might be to make the prerequisites to establishing a violation more similar to the usual requirements for establishing a violation of constitutional due process based on delay. Under due process, "a defendant must show that the government's delay was an 'intentional device to gain tactical advantage' and that the delay resulted in actual and substantial prejudice." *Preliminary Proceedings: Speedy Trial*, supra n. 43, at 344–45 (quoting United States v. Marion, 404 U.S. 307, 324 (1971)). Speedy-trial law currently establishes a presumption of prejudice once the trial is delayed beyond a certain point. See idem at 347 n. 1226 (collecting cases).

53. See Amsterdam, supra n. 48, at 533 (noting that this was the remedy under the English Habeas Corpus Act of 1679); idem at 535.

54. For a more detailed discussion of this proposal, see infra chapter 10. One could conceive of a system of "reverse bail" whereby the state would have to post a bond

on its guarantee that the defendant will be tried in a timely fashion. If the defendant is not tried within the prescribed period, the state would forfeit the bond, or perhaps a daily increment would be withdrawn for each day by which the trial is delayed beyond the prescribed date.

55. More precisely, the desert-consistent solution would be to give offenders credit against their sentence for time served prior to trial. Of course, numerous jurisdictions already give such credit. See, e.g., 18 U.S.C. § 3585(b) ("A defendant shall be given credit toward the service of a term of imprisonment for any time he has spent in official detention prior to the date the sentence commences[.]"); Charles Alan Wright et al., 3 *Federal Practice and Procedure: Criminal 3d* § 528 n. 23 (West 2004) (briefly noting history of provision); Lynn S. Branham, *The Law of Sentencing, Corrections, and Prisoners' Rights* 95 (West 1998). Even in such jurisdictions, however, "extra" credit could be given where trial is delayed, so that after a certain point, each additional day of pretrial detention would subtract more than one day from any subsequent sentence—perhaps using a staggered timetable and increasing the additional incremental credit as the delay continues.

This solution is more plausible under modern sentencing guidelines that confine trial judges' sentencing discretion, thereby preventing a judge from making an end run around the remedy by imposing an inflated sentence that is then "reduced" to account for pretrial incarceration. Cf. Amsterdam, supra n. 48, at 535–36 n. 81 (arguing against sentence-reduction remedy based on this potential for subversion).

56. See supra n. 47 (noting factors for court to consider when deciding whether to dismiss charges with or without prejudice following violation of Speedy Trial Act); see also LaFave et al., supra n. 44, § 18.3(c) at 871 (noting that dismissal without prejudice is allowed under some state speedy-trial statutes, "while a few other jurisdictions provide for dismissal with prejudice only for lesser offenses").

57. Cf. Amsterdam, supra n. 48, at 537 (rejecting conception of speedy-trial right as "a single, indivisible right: a right that either is or is not violated, for all purposes, by a particular amount of delay under the circumstances of a particular case"); idem at 538 ("[I]t seems apparent that a given delay, in the context of a particular prosecution, may infringe upon one of the defendant's interests but not the others, and may violate the sixth amendment for one purpose but not for all purposes.").

58. Cf. Amsterdam, supra n. 48, at 538 ("To debate the question whether the sixth amendment has been violated in . . . [most] cases that now seem to be coming before the federal courts . . . is itself to make a feeble farce of the amendment. *Of course* the amendment has been violated in these cases.").

59. For sources of facts in the *Eyler* narrative, see supra n. 8.

60. Elinor J. Brecher, *Brenda Schaefer: "That Woman Who Disappeared": How Could This Ordinary Person with No Apparent Enemies—a Doctor's Office Assistant Who Lived with Her Parents—Just Simply Vanish?*, Courier-Journal (Louisville, Ky.), Mar. 5. 1989, at 1A.

61. Idem.

62. Susan Craighead, *Police Focused Investigation on Ignatow from Start, Files Show*, Courier-Journal (Louisville, Ky.), Feb. 13, 1990, at 1B.

63. Brecher, supra n. 60.

64. Leslie Scanlon, *I Did Not Kill Her: Ignatow's Ex-Lover Admits Helping Dig Hole for Victim*, Courier-Journal (Louisville, Ky.), Dec. 18, 1991, at 1A.

65. Susan Craighead, *Attorney's Slip of the Tongue Led to Break in Schaefer Case*, Courier-Journal (Louisville, Ky.), Mar. 1, 1990, at 1A.

66. Bob Hill, *Double Jeopardy: Obsession, Murder, and Justice Denied* 328 (Morrow 1995).

67. The facts of the *Ignatow* case are derived from Bob Hill, *Double Jeopardy: Obsession, Murder, and Justice Denied* (Morrow 1995); Elinor J. Brecher, *Brenda Schaefer: "That Woman Who Disappeared": How Could This Ordinary Person with No Apparent Enemies—a Doctor's Office Assistant Who Lived with Her Parents—Just Simply Vanish?*, Courier-Journal (Louisville, Ky.), Mar. 5, 1989, at 1A; Susan Craighead, *Attorney's Slip of the Tongue Led to Break in Schaefer Case*, Courier-Journal (Louisville, Ky.), Mar. 1, 1990, at 1A; Susan Craighead, *Family Urge[s] Bond Be Set at Affordable Level*, Courier-Journal (Louisville, Ky.), Feb. 1, 1990, at 1B; Susan Craighead, *Police Focused Investigation on Ignatow from Start, Files Show*, Courier-Journal (Louisville, Ky.), Feb. 13, 1990, at 1B; Todd Murphy, *Ignatow Witness Pleads Guilty to Evidence Tampering*, Courier-Journal (Louisville, Ky.), Dec. 3, 1991, at 1B; Mary O'Doherty, *Threatening-Letter Trial Begins for Missing Woman's Boss*, Courier-Journal (Louisville, Ky.), Aug. 9, 1989, at 1B; Clay Ryce, *Schaefer's Boss Is Charged in Threat against Her Fiancé*, Courier-Journal (Louisville, Ky.), Mar. 26, 1989, at 1B; Leslie Scanlon, *Bizarre Murder Case Enters New Stage with Jury Selection*, Courier-Journal (Louisville, Ky.), Dec. 4, 1991, at 1A; Leslie Scanlon, *Schaefer Wasn't Going to Wed Ignatow*, Courier-Journal (Louisville, Ky.), Dec. 14, 1991, at 5A; Leslie Scanlon, *Shore-Inlow to Tell Jury Her Side of Schaefer Case*, Courier-Journal (Louisville, Ky.), Dec. 17, 1991, at 1B; Leslie Scanlon, *I Did Not Kill Her: Ignatow's Ex-Lover Admits Helping Dig Hole for Victim*, Courier-Journal (Louisville, Ky.), Dec. 18, 1991, at 1A; Leslie Scanlon, *Ignatow Confesses to Killing Schaefer*, Courier-Journal (Louisville, Ky.), Oct. 3, 1992, at 1A; Leslie Scanlon, *Ignatow's Defense Rests without His Testimony in Murder Trial*, Courier-Journal (Louisville, Ky.), Dec. 21, 1991, at 11A; Leslie Scanlon, *Ignatow's Lawyer Blames Shore-Inlow: Former Girlfriend Described as Jealous*, Courier-Journal (Louisville, Ky.), Dec. 10, 1991, at 1A; Leslie Scanlon, *Kenton Jury Acquits Ignatow in Death of Fiance Schaefer*, Courier-Journal (Louisville, Ky.), Dec. 22, 1991, at 1A; Leslie Scanlon, *No Evidence Links Ignatow with Murder, Jurors Say*, Courier-Journal (Louisville, Ky.), Dec. 23, 1991, at 1A; Cary B. Willis, *FBI Recorded Murder Suspect in Brenda Schaefer Case*, Courier-Journal (Louisville, Ky.), Feb. 6, 1990, at 1A; Cary B. Willis, *Ignatow Lawyer Says Release of Tape Should Rule Out Death*, Courier-Journal (Louisville, Ky.), Feb. 7, 1990, at 1A; Cary B. Willis, *Top Schaefer-Case Suspect Talks to Federal Grand Jury*, Courier-Journal (Louisville, Ky.), Oct. 17, 1989, at 3B; Andrew Wolfson, *Court Won't Hear Ignatow Perjury Appeal; 2001 Conviction for Lying about Schaefer Stands*, Courier-Journal (Louisville, Ky.), Apr. 21, 2004, at 5B; Andrew Wolfson, *Finding Evidence in Home a Fluke*, Courier-Journal (Louisville, Ky.), Oct. 3, 1992, at 1A; Deborah Yetter, *Federal Grand Jury Indicts Ignatow on Perjury Charge*, Courier-Journal (Louisville, Ky.), Jan.

9, 1992, at 1A; Deborah Yetter, *Textbook Example: Ignatow Fits Profile of Sexual Sadist*, Courier-Journal (Louisville, Ky.), Oct. 11, 1992, at 1A.

68. "[N]or shall any person be subject for the same offense to be twice put in jeopardy of life or limb[.]" U.S. Const. amend. V. See Missouri v. Hunter, 459 U.S. 359 (1983); North Carolina v. Pearce, 395 U.S. 711 (1969). Actually, in addition to the "one crime, multiple prosecutions" situation, the rule also has a "one crime, multiple offenses" ban—it prohibits conviction, whether after a single trial or multiple trials, for two or more offenses each of which punishes the same harm or evil. See *Hunter;* Albernaz v. United States, 450 U.S. 333 (1981); Blockburger v. United States, 284 U.S. 299 (1932). This aspect of the rule seeks to prevent, for example, prosecution of a pickpocket simultaneously for "larceny," "theft," "stealing," and "pickpocketing"— where all of these offenses prohibit the same conduct and harm—for a single instance of pickpocketing. But see Susan R. Klein, *Double Jeopardy's Demise*, 88 Cal. L. Rev. 1001, 1006 (2000) ("[My] interpretation of the Clause places the focus squarely on the number of prosecutions, rather than the total amount of punishment. This is exactly as it should be. The Fifth Amendment does not prohibit, by its own terms, the total quantity of punishment imposed in a single criminal trial for a single offense."); idem at 1008 ("A double jeopardy bar against multiple punishments for the same offense in a single proceeding is entirely unnecessary, because the due process clause already prohibits a judge from imposing a sentence greater than that authorized by the legislature."). The "one crime, multiple offenses" ban, however, is not significant for our purposes, as it is entirely consistent with, and indeed promotes, the goal of desert by preventing inappropriate multiple punishment of the same conduct and harm.

69. Justice Hugo Black expressed these twin goals in *Green v. United States*:

> [T]he State with all its resources and powers should not be allowed to make repeated attempts to convict an individual for an alleged offense, thereby subjecting him to embarrassment, expense and ordeal and compelling him to live in a continuing state of anxiety and insecurity, as well as enhancing the possibility that even though innocent he may be found guilty.

Green v. United States, 355 U.S. 184, 187–88 (1957).

70. See Valdes, supra n. 16, at 1719–20. The survey was patterned after an earlier project that was limited to lawyers and judges in Tennessee. See Neil P. Cohen et al., *The Prevalence and Use of Criminal Defenses: A Preliminary Study*, 60 Tenn. L. Rev. 957 (1993). The Tennessee study did not ask about double jeopardy, however.

71. Klein, supra n. 68, at 1028.

72. Because the tension between double jeopardy and maximization of desert-based outcomes relates to the multiple-prosecution prohibition rather than to the multiple-punishment prohibition, this issue relates more to the meaning of "put in jeopardy" than the meaning of "same offense" under the clause. Even so, the scope of the judicial reading of "same offense" is also highly relevant, as it determines when the Double Jeopardy Clause comes into play in the first place. Cf. Anne Bowen

Poulin, *Double Jeopardy Protection from Successive Prosecution: A Proposed Approach*, 92 Geo. L.J. 1183 (2004) (proposing broad reading of "same offense" to prohibit abusive successive prosecutions, but also suggesting balancing approach to enable successive prosecutions where appropriate).

73. Jeopardy currently attaches in a jury trial when the jury has been impaneled and sworn and in a bench trial when the first witness is sworn. See Crist v. Bretz, 437 U.S. 28, 38 (1978) (jury trial); Finch v. United States, 433 U.S. 676 (1977) (bench trial); cf. Goolsby v. Hutto, 691 F.2d 199 (4th Cir. 1982) (holding that jeopardy attached in bench trial when first witness was sworn, even when prosecutor refused to ask him questions).

74. For a discussion of the current rules governing when reprosecution following a mistrial is allowed under the Double Jeopardy Clause, see generally LaFave et al., supra n. 44, at § 25.2. For rules regarding dismissals, see generally idem §§ 25.2(f), 25.3(a), (d).

75. See Kepner v. United States, 195 U.S. 100, 134 (1904) (Holmes, J., dissenting) ("[L]ogically and rationally a man cannot be said to be more than once in jeopardy in the same cause, however often he may be tried. The jeopardy is one continuing jeopardy from its beginning to the end of the cause."); Akhil Reed Amar, *Double Jeopardy Law Made Simple*, 106 Yale L.J. 1807, 1842–46 (1997) (arguing that prosecutors should be allowed to appeal acquittals resulting from a trial judge's alleged legal error).

76. Cf. Aleman v. Judges of the Circuit Court, 138 F.3d 302 (7th Cir. 1998) (recognizing such an exception, but only for bench trials and only where prosecution can show beyond reasonable doubt that defendant participated in fraud); Anne Bowen Poulin, *Double Jeopardy and Judicial Accountability: When Is an Acquittal Not an Acquittal*, 27 Ariz. St. L.J. 953, 988–91 (1995) (advocating *Aleman*-type exception). See generally David S. Rudstein, *Double Jeopardy and the Fraudulently Obtained Acquittal*, 60 Mo. L. Rev. 607 (1995) (considering case law, theoretical bases, and policy considerations and concluding that likelihood of prosecutorial abuse of exception is too high, warranting retention of finality of acquittal even if obtained by improper means).

77. See Amar, supra n. 75, at 1846–48 (arguing that rules regulating retrial after mistrial are more properly seen as due-process concerns). And "once we see that a judicial award of acquittal is a kind of due process penalty for low blows, it becomes clear that this extreme sanction is only one of a whole set that could be devised." Idem at 1847.

78. See Criminal Justice Act 2003, part 10: Retrial for Serious Offences, available online at http://www.legislation.hmso.gov.uk/acts/acts2003/20030044.htm; see also Robert L. Weinberg, *Try, Try Again: If at First They Don't Succeed, Criminal Prosecutions in England Now Get a Second Chance*, Legal Times, Feb. 16, 2004, at 52; *Delivering Justice for All—Criminal Justice Bill Receives Royal Assent*, M2 Presswire, Nov. 21, 2003.

79. See Criminal Justice Act 2003, supra n. 78, at § 75(8) (defining "qualifying offence" as "an offence listed in Part 1 of Schedule 5").

80. See idem at sch. 5 pt. 1 (listing offenses).

81. See idem at §§ 76, 77(1).

82. See idem at §§ 76(4), 78(1).

83. Idem at §§ 77(1), 78(1), 79(1).

84. Idem at § 79(2).

85. See Clare Dyer, *Police Have a Hit List, Says Former Law Lord*, Guardian (London), Jan. 6, 2004, at 17.

86. See Law Commission, *Report 70: Acquittal following Perversion of the Course of Justice* 16 (2001), available online at http://www.lawcom.govt.nz.

87. See idem.

88. See idem at 16–18.

89. See Diana McCurdy, *Verdict of Public Hits the Courts*, New Zealand Herald, June 26, 2004, at B8; Lesley Deverall, *Changes to the Law to Allow for Majority Verdicts in Court and Changing the Double Jeopardy Rules Have Been Introduced into Parliament; Majority Verdicts Bill Introduced*, IRN News, June 23, 2004. To our knowledge, the law remains pending. See *New Law to Tackle Threats to Juries*, New Zealand Herald, Apr. 17, 2005.

90. For sources of facts in the *Ignatow* narrative, see supra n. 67.

91. See authorities collected at Paul H. Robinson, 2 *Criminal Law Defenses* § 208(b) (West 1984 & 2004 supp.).

92. See idem at §§ 208(e), (f).

93. See, e.g., Ariz. R. Crim. P. 11.1; Idaho Code § 18–210; N.C. Gen. Stat. § 15A.

94. Under the Supreme Court's decision in *Jackson v. Indiana*, 406 U.S. 715 (1972), such commitment until competency may not become a de facto life sentence; the *Jackson* Court held that a defendant may be committed only for "a reasonable period of time" to determine if he would recover in "the foreseeable future." Idem at 738. If, after a reasonable time, the defendant is likely to recover, the Court held that continuing commitment can be justified only by "progress toward that goal." Idem. If he is not likely to recover, he must be discharged. Commitment after discharge can be justified only under the usual standards for civil commitment.

95. See Drope v. Missouri, 420 U.S. 162 (1975); Pate v. Robinson, 383 U.S. 375 (1966); Youtsey v. United States, 97 F. 937, 941 (6th Cir. 1899).

96. See generally Wayne R. LaFave, 1 *Substantive Criminal Law* § 4.4(a) at 568 (2d ed., West 2003).

97. See idem. This justification may share some features with the judicial-integrity justification for exclusionary rules. See supra nn. 2–3, 19, 30–33, and accompanying text. And, like that justification, it also relates to the need to promote the justice system's legitimacy in the eyes of the governed. See generally infra "Moral Credibility 'versus' Legitimacy: Evaluating the Tradeoffs."

98. See, e.g., Pate v. Robinson, 383 U.S. 375, 384 (1966); Taylor v. United States, 282 F.2d 16, 23 (8th Cir. 1960); Seidner v. United States, 260 F.2d 732, 734 (D.C. Cir. 1958).

99. See 1 LaFave, supra n. 96, at 568.

100. See 2 Robinson, supra n. 91, § 208(f) nn. 33, 35 (collecting authorities); Sir Matthew Hale, 1 *Historia Placitorum Coronae* 35 (George Wilson, ed., T. Payne 1778); William Blackstone, 4 *Commentaries on the Law of England* 396 (Repub. 1854).

101. For discussion of other rationales that do not disagree in theory with the goal of desert, see generally supra chapters 2–4.

102. See 1 LaFave, supra n. 96, at 568.

103. Model Penal Code § 4.06(3).

104. Judith Cummings, *DeLorean Is Freed of Cocaine Charge by a Federal Jury*, N.Y. Times, Aug. 17, 1984.

105. Judith Cummings, *DeLorean, in Tape, Tells of Lacking Drug Money*, N.Y. Times, Apr. 21, 1984.

106. Jay Mathews, *The Trials of John DeLorean*, Wash. Post, Mar. 4, 1984.

107. Judith Cummings, *Drug Trial of DeLorean Brings Out Actions Embarrassing to Both Sides*, N.Y. Times, July 12, 1984.

108. Cummings, supra n. 104.

109. The facts of the *DeLorean* case are derived from Associated Press v. U.S. District Ct., 705 F.2d 1143 (9th Cir. 1983); Ivan Fallon & James Srodes, *Dream Maker: The Rise and Fall of John Z. DeLorean* 24 (Smithmark 1983); *DeLorean Arrest Jars Britons*, N.Y. Times, Oct. 22, 1982; *DeLorean Reportedly Stumbled into Drug Probe*, UPI, Oct. 23, 1982; *DeLorean to Build Sports Cars in Belfast Instead of Puerto Rico*, Wash. Post, Aug. 8, 1978; *I.R.A. Denies DeLorean Ties*, N.Y. Times, Dec. 22, 1982; *Three Month Delay in DeLorean Trial*, UPI, Dec. 8, 1982; *Stung by John DeLorean*, N.Y. Times, Aug. 18, 1984, at sec. 1, 22; *Where John DeLorean Is Now*, Daily Telegraph, Apr. 22, 1995; *Untitled*, Wall St. J., Aug. 7, 1980; *Untitled*, N.Y. Times, May 11, 1973; AP, *British to Close Books on DeLorean*, Chicago Trib., Nov. 23, 1997; AP, *DeLorean Plea for Aid Said to Bring Many Calls*, N.Y. Times, Nov. 9, 1984; AP, *Judge Names Examiner for DeLorean Motor*, N.Y. Times, Jan. 6, 1983; James Bates, *Company Town*, L.A. Times, Aug. 18, 1995.; Judith Cummings, *A Film about DeLorean Is Planned*, N.Y. Times, June 11, 1984; Judith Cummings, *A Reporter's Notebook: De Lorean: The Defendant as Celebrity*, N.Y. Times, May 8, 1984; Judith Cummings, *Agent Tells of Plan to Arrest DeLorean with Drug*, N.Y. Times, May 4, 1984; Judith Cummings, *Agent Tells of Report on DeLorean*, N.Y. Times, June 16, 1984; Judith Cummings, *Coast Judge Orders a Trial Delay of DeLorean in Drug Plot Charge*, N.Y. Times, Oct. 4, 1983; Judith Cummings, *DeLorean Automobile Executive Arrested in Drug Smuggling Case*, N.Y. Times, Oct. 20, 1982; Judith Cummings, *DeLorean Facing Drug Trial Alone*, N.Y. Times, June 25, 1983; Judith Cummings, *DeLorean Is Freed of Cocaine Charge by a Federal Jury*, N.Y. Times, Aug. 17, 1984; Judith Cummings, *DeLorean Granted Delay in His Trial*, N.Y. Times, June 24, 1983; Judith Cummings, *DeLorean, in Tape, Tells of Lacking Drug Money*, N.Y. Times, Apr. 21, 1984; Judith Cummings, *DeLorean Link with I.R.A. Not Confirmed or Disproved*, N.Y. Times, Dec. 22, 1982; Judith Cummings, *Drug Trial of DeLorean Brings Out Actions Embarrassing to Both Sides*, N.Y. Times, July 12, 1984; Judith Cummings, *First Candidates Interviewed for Jury to Hear Drug Trial of John DeLorean*, N.Y. Times, Mar. 14,

1984; Judith Cummings, *Flynt Arrested on Refusal to Yield Tapes of DeLorean to Court*, N.Y. Times, Nov. 2, 1983; Judith Cummings, *Jury in Drug Case Indicts De-Lorean*, N.Y. Times, Oct. 30, 1982; Judith Cummings, *Man in the News: DeLorean Trial Judge*, N.Y. Times, June 28, 1984; Judith Cummings, *One of 8 DeLorean Drug Charges Dismissed, but Trial Goes On*, N.Y. Times, July 13, 1984; Judith Cummings, *Prosecution Rests in DeLorean Case*, N.Y. Times, July 11, 1984; Chuck Conconi, *Personalities*, Wash. Post, July 31, 1984; Charlotte Curtis, *Wife Says DeLorean Has Bids for Film Deal*, N.Y. Times, Nov. 5, 1982; James J. Doyle, *Attorneys Allege Break-ins in DeLorean Case*, UPI, July 15, 1983; James J. Doyle, *DeLorean Attorneys Accuse Federal Agent of Illegal Activity*, UPI, July 14, 1983; James J. Doyle, *DeLorean Gets Trial Postponement and New Trial Date*, UPI, June 23, 1983; Jonathan Friendly, *TV News Officials Tell Why They Showed DeLorean Tapes*, N.Y. Times, Oct. 25, 1983; Robin Gaby Fisher & Bev McCarron, *DeLorean Is Now Cruising beneath Radar*, Times-Picayune (New Orleans, La.), Dec. 17, 1995; Lloyd Grove, *Barbara Walters Gets First Interview after Acquittal*, Wash. Post, Aug. 17, 1984; Dan Jedlicka, *Ambitious DeLorean Planning a Come-Back*, Chicago Sun-Times, Oct. 3, 2000; Dan Jedlicka, *Lure and Lore of DeLorean: Flashy Looking Sports Car Never Lived Up to Its Billing*, Chicago Sun-Times, Jan. 5, 1997; William H. Jones, *DeLorean Acknowledges GM Book*, Wash. Post, Nov. 15, 1979; Ken Hoover, *A Trial of Images: Do the Secret Tapes Show the Real John DeLorean?*, Nat'l L.J., July 2, 1984; Robert Lindsey, *Cocaine Trafficking and Its Huge Profits Luring Middle Class*, N.Y. Times, Oct. 24, 1982; Robert Lindsey, *Path that Lead [sic] to DeLorean Began and Ended with Cases of Money*, N.Y. Times, Oct. 21, 1982; Jay Mathews, *DeLorean, Tales out of Court—Wife Reveals Movie Talk during Cocaine Deal Trial*, Wash. Post, June 2, 1984; Jay Mathews, *Letter from the Trial: Covering DeLorean, a Mogul, a Model, and Glittering Banalities*, Wash. Post, Apr. 22, 1984; Jay Mathews, *The Trials of John DeLorean*, Wash. Post, Mar. 4, 1984; Jay Mathews, *US Tape Law Said No Issue on DeLorean*, Wash. Post, Nov. 11, 1983; Jay Mathews, *Vindicated: DeLorean Hopes to Resume Old Life*, Wash. Post, Aug. 16, 1984; Craig Pittman, *Couple Sentenced to Probation in De-Lorean Movie Fraud*, St. Petersburg Times, Apr. 12, 1997; Craig Pittman, *DeLorean and a Broker Sued by Investors*, N.Y. Times, Aug. 25, 1983; Steven Rattner, *Aid Halted, DeLorean Idles 1,100*, N.Y. Times, Jan. 30, 1982; Steven Rattner, *Receivership Declared at DeLorean*, N.Y. Times, Feb. 20, 1982; H. G. Reza, *Lawyer Granted De-Lorean Land for Defense Fee*, L.A. Times, Mar. 29, 1986; Reuters, *1,715 Luxury Autos Recalled to Correct Potential Hazard*, N.Y. Times, Nov. 27, 1981; Reuters, *Around the Nation: Flynt Delivers Fine in Overstuffed Suitcases*, N.Y. Times, Nov. 17, 1983; Reuters, *DeLorean Is Cleared*, N.Y. Times, Oct. 13, 1981; Peter J. Schuyten, *Untitled*, N.Y. Times, Nov. 9, 1979; Jeremy Smith, *An Automobile with a History Attached: The DeLorean DMC-12*, Marion Online, at http://www.cityofmarion.net/features/DMC.php.

110. See Erich Weyand, Comment, *Entrapment: From* Sorrells *to* Jacobson—*The Development Continues*, 20 Ohio N.U. L. Rev. 293 (1993).

111. See Valdes, supra n. 16, at 1715–16.

112. See Cohen et al., supra n. 70, at 960, 963–64. Judges and prosecutors saw less of an influence on nontrial results. See idem. Tennessee uses a subjective formulation of the entrapment defense. Tenn. Code Ann. § 29–11–505.

113. See 2 Robinson, supra n. 91, § 209(a), (b) n. 1 (collecting authorities).

114. Utah Code Ann. § 76–2–303.

115. See, e.g., State v. Taylor, 599 P.2d 496 (Utah 1979). The Model Penal Code adopts a similarly objective formulation. It defines unlawful entrapment as conduct that "creates a substantial risk that such an offense will be committed by persons other than those who are ready to commit it." Model Penal Code § 2.13(1)(b). (Under the Code, an officer also entraps if he "[makes] knowingly false representations designed to induce the belief that such conduct is not prohibited." Idem § 2.13(1)(a).) There is no requirement that the defendant actually be a member of the group of persons "other than those ready to commit it." The Code also requires only that the defendant's offense be "in response to" the police conduct. Model Penal Code § 2.13(2). It does not even require, as Utah does, that the defendant be "induced" by the police conduct.

116. Del. Code Ann. tit. 11, § 432.

117. But compare Harrison v. State, 442 A.2d 1377, 1379–80 (Del. 1982) (denying entrapment defense based on predisposition revealed by offense itself), with Jacobson v. United States, 503 U.S. 540 (1992) (overturning conviction where no preexisting evidence demonstrates predisposition to break the law).

118. U.S. 435, 442 (1932).

119. See, e.g., Hampton v. United States, 425 U.S. 484, 489–90 (1976) (plurality opinion by Rehnquist, J.) (rejecting view of entrapment as tied purely to nature of police conduct; holding that predisposition is sole issue in entrapment and that any unconscionable police conduct amounting to due-process violation should be remedied through direct sanction against police, not through the entrapment defense).

120. See Sorrells, 287 U.S. at 458 (Roberts, J., concurring) ("Whatever may be the demerits of the defendant or his previous infractions of law these will not justify the instigation and creation of a new crime, as a means to reach him and punish him for his past misdemeanors."); Sherman v. United States, 356 U.S. 369, 380 (1958) (Frankfurter, J., concurring) ("The courts refuse to convict an entrapped defendant, not because his conduct falls outside the proscription of the statute, but because . . . the methods employed on behalf of the government to bring about conviction cannot be countenanced."); Hampton, 425 U.S. at 495 (Brennan, J., dissenting).

121. See, e.g., United States v. Twigg, 588 F.2d 373 (3d Cir. 1978) (due-process rights of defendant were violated by government involvement in manufacture of methamphetamine that was indispensable element in commission of crime); cf. Hampton, 425 U.S. at 491 (Powell, J., concurring) (affirming conviction, but refusing to foreclose the possibility of a defense, on due-process grounds, for improper police conduct). But cf. United States v. Russell, 411 U.S. 423 (1976) (undercover agent's participation in manufacturing of methamphetamine did not violate due-process rights of defendant).

122. Russell, 411 U.S. at 432 (quoting Kinsella v. United States ex rel. Singleton, 361 U.S. 234, 246 (1960)).

123. See, e.g., State v. Williams, 623 So.2d 462 (Fla. 1993) (law-enforcement manufacture of "crack" cocaine from ordinary cocaine for use in reverse-sting operation qualified as outrageous conduct; conviction of buyer reversed), corrected reh'g denied, 18 Fla. L. Weekly S491 (Fla. 1993).

124. This seems to be the assumption of many writers. See, e.g., Jonathon C. Carlson, *The Act Requirement and the Foundations of the Entrapment Defense*, 73 Va. L. Rev. 1011, 1037 (1987); Roger Park, *The Entrapment Controversy*, 60 Minn. L. Rev. 163 (1976). But see, e.g., Anthony M. Dillof, *Unraveling Unlawful Entrapment*, 94 J. Crim. L. & Criminology 827 (2004) (advancing argument about entrapment that focuses on status of entrapping party as government agent, rather than on defendant).

125. See Christopher Moore, Comment, *The Elusive Formulation of the Entrapment Defense*, 89 Nw. U. L. Rev. 1151 (1995); 2 Robinson, supra n. 91, § 209(b) at 515–16.

126. See Paul H. Robinson, *Criminal Law* § 9.1 at 487 (Aspen L. & Bus. 1997); idem § 9.4 at 531–32.

127. See, e.g., United States v. Perl, 584 F.2d 1316, 1321 (4th Cir. 1978) ("[A] defendant, in order to assert the defense of entrapment, . . . must produce evidence of government involvement in the scheme to entrap.").

128. See, e.g., Wayne R. LaFave & Jerold H. Israel, *Criminal Procedure* § 5.2 at 418 (West 1984) (noting similarities); National Comm'n on Reform of Federal Criminal Laws, 1 *Working Papers* 318 (U.S. Gov't Printing Office 1970) ("There are pervasive and obvious analogies between the defense of entrapment and those exclusionary rules which spring from violations of the fourth and fifth amendments[.]"); cf. Dillof, supra n. 124, at 860–62 (questioning relation between entrapment defense and Fourth Amendment exclusionary rule, but generally arguing for view of entrapment as unfair law-enforcement practice).

129. Tyler & Darley, supra n. 2, at 725.

130. See sources cited supra n. 2.

131. See, e.g., Tyler & Darley, supra n. 2, at 726 ("If people correctly understand the law, and the law truly reflects public moral values, then the legitimacy of the law and personal morality would converge as forces for law-abidingness.").

132. See, e.g., Tyler & Darley, supra n. 2, at 715; Paul H. Robinson & John M. Darley, *The Utility of Desert*, 91 Nw. U. L. Rev. 453, 471–74 (1997); Martin L. Hoffman, *Moral Internalization: Current Theory and Research*, in 10 *Advances in Experimental Social Psychology* 85, 85–86 (Leonard Berkowitz, ed., Academic 1977).

133. See Tyler & Darley, supra n. 2, at 730–32.

134. For a discussion of the relative strengths and weaknesses of morality versus legitimacy as methods of inducing compliance, see generally Tyler & Darley, supra n. 2, at 724–37.

135. See Linda J. Skitka & David A. Houston, *When Due Process Is of No Consequence: Moral Mandates and Presumed Defendant Guilt or Innocence*, 14 Soc. Just. Res. 305 (2001). Linda Skitka's work generally supports the claim that people give precedence to substantive desert over procedural fairness when the two conflict. See, e.g., Linda J. Skitka, *Do the Means Always Justify the Ends or Do the Ends Sometimes Justify the*

Means? A Value Protection Model of Justice, 28 Personality & Soc. Psychol. Bull. 588 (2002); Linda J. Skitka & Elizabeth Mullen, *Understanding Judgments of Fairness in a Real-World Political Context: A Test of the Value Protection Model of Justice Reasoning,* 28 Personality & Soc. Psychol. Bull. 1419 (2002); Linda J. Skitka & Elizabeth Mullen, *The Dark Side of Moral Conviction,* 2 Analyses of Soc. Issues & Pub. Pol'y 35 (2002).

136.　See works cited supra n. 135; Tyler, supra n. 3, at 59–60 & table 5.1 (study showing that compliance with law has much stronger correlation with its connection to "personal morality" than with its perceived "legitimacy"); idem at 32–37 (comparing past studies finding higher correlation based on law's instantiation of shared normative views than on perception of legitimacy); idem at 60 ("The most important normative influence on compliance with the law is the person's assessment that following the law accords with his or her sense of right and wrong[.]"); idem at 68 ("[P]ersonal morality is clearly a more important influence on compliance than [is] legitimacy."); Harold G. Grasmick & Robert J. Bursik, Jr., *Conscience, Significant Others, and Rational Choice: Extending the Deterrence Model,* 24 L. & Soc'y Rev. 837, 853–54 (1990); Harold G. Grasmick & Donald E. Green, *Legal Punishment, Social Disapproval and Internalization as Inhibitors of Illegal Behavior,* 71 J. Crim. L. & Criminology 325, 334 (1980) (stating that certain variables, including "moral commitment" and "threat of social disapproval," act as factors inhibiting illegal behavior).

137.　See Tyler, supra n. 3, at 63 ("Respondents are almost equally likely to comply with the law because they view it as legitimate . . . whether or not they think their peers would disapprove of law breaking, and whether or not they think law breaking is morally wrong."); Herbert C. Kelman & V. Lee Hamilton, *Crimes of Obedience: Toward a Social Psychology of Authority and Responsibility* 89 (Yale 1989) ("Once a demand is categorized as legitimate, the person to whom it is addressed enters a situation where his personal preferences become more or less irrelevant[.]"); idem at 16 ("Through authorization, the situation becomes so defined that the individual is absolved of the responsibility to make personal moral choices. . . . [A] different kind of morality, linked to the duty to obey superior orders, tends to take over."); David Beetham, *The Legitimation of Power* 4–5 (Prometheus 1991); Mark C. Suchman, *Managing Legitimacy: Strategic and Institutional Approaches,* 20 Acad. Mgmt. Rev. 571, 579 & n. 2 (1995).

138.　This seems more likely to be true for some rules than others. For example, the Fourth Amendment exclusionary rule, as currently formulated, would seem to do a poor job of promoting legitimacy. See supra nn. 33–34 and accompanying text.

139.　See Harvey Wingo, *Rewriting* Mapp *and* Miranda: *A Preference for Due Process,* 31 U. Kan. L. Rev. 219 (1983) (advocating flexible due-process approach to Fourth and Fifth Amendment exclusionary-rule issues); Michael J. Daponde, Comment, *Discretion and the Fourth Amendment Exclusionary Rule: A New Suppression Doctrine Based on Judicial Integrity,* 30 McGeorge L. Rev. 1293, 1315–19 (1999) (proposing new Fourth Amendment rule that would consider totality of circumstances).

140.　See Canadian Charter of Rights and Freedoms § 24(2) (emphasis added); see also James Stribopoulos, *Lessons from the Pupil: A Canadian Solution to the American Exclusionary Rule Debate,* 22 B.C. Int'l & Comp. L. Rev. 77 (1999).

141. See Model Code of Pre-Arraignment Procedure § 290.2(4); see also Philip S. Coe, *The ALI Substantiality Test: A Flexible Approach to the Exclusionary Sanction,* 10 Ga. L. Rev. 1 (1975) (explaining and defending Model Code approach, but also stating that current need for additional alternative sanctions to control police conduct would remain under that approach).

142. See generally Christopher Slobogin, *The World without a Fourth Amendment,* 39 UCLA L. Rev. 1 (1991); Christopher Slobogin & Joseph E. Schumacher, *Rating the Intrusiveness of Law Enforcement Searches and Seizures,* 17 Law & Hum. Behav. 183 (1993).

143. See William J. Stuntz, *O. J. Simpson, Bill Clinton, and the Transsubstantive Fourth Amendment,* 114 Harv. L. Rev. 842, 870 (2001) ("We could have a small number of substantive categories for most searches and seizures—I'd suggest five, though the precise number would not matter much—with more forgiving rules for more serious crimes and tougher rules for less serious crimes.").

CHAPTER 8

1. The facts of the *Lindsey* case are derived from the following sources: United States v. Lindsey, 525 F.2d 5 (9th Cir. 1979); telephone interview by June Y. Kim with Tom Lindsey (June 21, 2001) (notes on file with authors); telephone interview by June Y. Kim with Warren S. Derbidge (June 21, 2001) (notes on file with authors); telephone interview by June Y. Kim with Mike Merkley (June 21, 2001) (notes on file with authors).

2. See John C. Coffee, Jr., *Does "Unlawful" Mean "Criminal"? Reflections on the Disappearing Tort/Crime Distinction in American Law,* 71 B.U. L. Rev. 193, 216 (1991) (hereinafter Coffee, *Does Unlawful Mean Criminal?*).

3. Lindsey was charged with building a camp without a permit (36 C.F.R. 261.52e) and building a campfire without a permit (36 C.F.R. 261.52a). Both of those regulations derive their authority from 16 U.S.C. § 551, 16 U.S.C. § 472, 7 U.S.C. § 1011(f), 16 U.S.C. § 1246(i), 16 U.S.C. § 1133(c)–(d)(1), and 16 U.S.C. § 620(f). Punishment for such violations is a fine of no more than $500, six months in prison, or both, per 36 C.F.R. 261.1b.

4. See Paul H. Robinson & John M. Darley, *The Utility of Desert,* 91 Nw. U. L. Rev. 453, 479–82 (1997). But see Stuart P. Green, *Why It's a Crime to Tear the Tag Off a Mattress: Overcriminalization and the Moral Content of Regulatory Offenses,* 46 Emory L.J. 1533, 1613 (1997) (claiming that "the moral content of regulatory offenses is far more complex and varied than previously recognized").

5. See Bureau of Justice Statistics, U.S. Dep't of Justice, *Sourcebook of Criminal Justice Statistics,* table 5.19 (Kathleen Maguire & Ann L. Pastore, eds.) (Sentences Imposed in Cases Terminated in U.S. District Courts), available at http://www.albany.edu/sourcebook/pdf/t519.pdf (downloaded June 15, 2005).

6. A year after the camping offense, Mike Merkley sets up surveillance cameras around Pittsburgh Landing, an established launch site for rafting and kayaking on the river. Expensive wooden warning signs and permit boxes are erected in this area.

A friend of Tom's is arrested for floating the river without a permit, causing Tom's anger against the Forest Service to resurface. Tom smashes one of the permit boxes and throws the permits into the river. Tom is indicted for destruction of government property, a felony charge later bargained down to a misdemeanor, for which Tom is put on probation and fined $250.

7. For additional commentary, pro and con, on the issue of corporate criminal liability, see the works listed in Joseph F. C. DiMento, Gilbert Geis, & Julia M. Gelfand, *Corporate Criminal Liability: A Bibliography*, 28 W. St. U. L. Rev. 1 (2000).

8. See Coffee, *Does Unlawful Mean Criminal?*, supra n. 2, at 261.

9. See, e.g., Lawrence Friedman, *In Defense of Corporate Criminal Liability*, 23 Harv. J. L. & Pub. Pol'y 833, 855–56 (2000) (arguing that unique moral condemnation accompanying a corporate criminal conviction sends an important retributive message); Dan M. Kahan, *Social Meaning and the Economic Analysis of Crime*, 27 J. Legal Stud. 609, 618–19 (1998) ("Punishing corporations, just like punishing natural persons, is also understood to be the right way for society to repudiate the false valuations that their crimes express. Criminal liability 'sends the message' that people matter more than profits and reaffirms the value of those who were sacrificed to 'corporate greed.' In light of these sensibilities, substituting civil liability for criminal might be expressively irrational. Just as fines fail to express condemnation relative to imprisonment of natural persons, so civil damages fail to express it relative to criminal liability for corporations."). But see Gilbert Geis & Joseph F. C. Dimento, *Empirical Evidence and the Legal Doctrine of Corporate Criminal Liability*, 29 Am. J. Crim. L. 341, 363 (2002) (stating, in response to Friedman's claim, that "we have no reliable information on whether the end [of sending a moral message about corporate misconduct], amorphous as it is, in fact is achieved by criminal charges or whether the criminal law is the suitable method for achieving it").

10. See, e.g., Robert P. Abelson et al., *Perceptions of the Collective Other*, 2 Personality & Soc. Psych. Rev. 243, 246 n. 2 (1998); David L. Hamilton & Steven J. Sherman, *Perceiving Persons and Groups*, 103 Psychological Rev. 336 (1996), Matthew J. O'Laughlin & Bertram F. Malle, *How People Explain Actions Performed by Groups and Individuals*, 82 J. Personality & Soc. Psych. 33 (2002); Jennifer L. Welbourne, *The Impact of Perceived Entitativity on Inconsistency Resolution for Groups and Individuals*, 35 J. Experimental Soc. Psych. 481, 499, 500–01 (1999).

11. See, e.g., Michael E. Bratman, *Faces of Intention: Selected Essays on Intention and Agency* (Cambridge 1999); Margaret Gilbert, *Sociality and Responsibility: New Essays in Plural Subject Theory* (Rowman & Littlefield 2000); Christopher Kurtz, *Complicity: Ethics and Law for a Collective Age* (Cambridge 2000); J. David Velleman, *How to Share an Intention*, 58 Phil. & Phenomenological Res. 29 (1997).

12. See, e.g., Geis & Dimento, supra n. 9, at 362 ("No evidence is offered [in Friedman's recent article; see supra n. 9] that citizens notably desire or demand criminal retribution against corporations or that such criminal retribution particularly satisfies the outrage that allegedly ought to trigger the criminal proceedings.").

13. Cf. Geis & Dimento, supra n. 9, at 369–70 ("If only civil suits were permissible against corporate entities, would prosecutors be more dedicated to locating a guilty

individual and proceeding against that person criminally? If so, what consequences might this have in terms of deterrence, principles of justice, ideas of expressive justice, and similar matters?").

14. John C. Coffee, Jr., *Corporate Criminal Responsibility*, in *Encyclopedia of Crime & Justice* 253, 260 (Sanford Kadish, ed., Gage 1983).

15. See Geis & Dimento, supra n. 9, at 372 ("[E]mpirical resolution [of this assertion] would contribute significantly to the debate on corporate criminal liability. . . . How often and under what circumstances does this scenario [of the corporation aiding the prosecution of individual defendants] come into play? And how often does the opposite occur, that defendants bec[o]me witnesses against the corporation in exchange for leniency for themselves?"); see also idem at 374–75 ("The development of the doctrine of corporate criminal liability has been the result almost exclusively of expediency rather than of empirical information. . . . [T]he holistic perplexity that is corporate criminal liability has suffered from the failure to recognize and, most importantly, to use empirical utensils to shed light on the legal principle of corporate criminal liability.").

16. That current American law allows criminal liability of organizations may indicate how much American criminal law has strayed from its traditional criterion of moral blameworthiness. European countries rarely permit such liability. See V. S. Khanna, *Corporate Criminal Liability: What Purpose Does It Serve?*, 109 Harv. L. Rev. 1477, 1488–91 (1996) (comparing corporate criminal liability in the United States and Western Europe); John C. Coffee, Jr., *"No Soul to Damn, No Body to Kick": An Unscandalized Inquiry into the Problem of Corporate Punishment*, 79 Mich. L. Rev. 386 (1981) (hereinafter Coffee, *No Soul to Damn*). Great Britain traditionally has allowed such liability, but only to a limited extent. See Coffee, *Does Unlawful Mean Criminal?*, supra n. 2, at 230; Celia Wells, *Corporations and Criminal Responsibility* 95–107 (Oxford 1993). There has been an increasing trend in Europe toward allowing corporate criminal liability, however. See infra chapter 10 n. 6.

17. See generally Daniel R. Fischel & Alan O. Sykes, *Corporate Crime*, 25 J. Legal Stud. 319 (1996); Khanna, supra n. 16; see also Albert W. Alschuler, *Ancient Law and the Punishment of Corporations: Of Frankpledge and Deodand*, 71 B.U. L. Rev. 307, 311–12 (1991) ("Our efforts to stigmatize aggregations of people, most of whom are blameless, are unjustified in principle and may be less effective in practice than civil alternatives would be."); *Developments in the Law: Corporate Crime: Regulating Corporate Behavior through Criminal Sanctions*, 92 Harv. L. Rev. 1227, 1365–74 (1979).

18. See Laura J. Kerrigan et al., *Project: The Decriminalization of Administrative Law Penalties: Civil Remedies, Alternatives, Policy, and Constitutional Implications*, 45 Admin. L. Rev. 367, 374–75 (1993). In certain circumstances, however, constitutional criminal protections will apply to an enforcement action notwithstanding that the legislature has labeled it civil rather than criminal. See idem at 397–419.

19. See generally Paul H. Robinson, *Criminal Law* § 4.3 (Aspen L. & Bus. 1997).

20. See Sally S. Simpson, *Corporate Crime, Law, and Social Control* at xi–xii (Cambridge 2002) (noting the "woeful lack of research on corporate deterrence, es-

pecially from a criminological perspective" and that in "the few studies that do exist the evidence [on deterrence] is far from conclusive"); idem at 159 (concluding that corporate crime rules may be "bad policy" rooted in "bad science").

21. See idem at 21 (finding that "state imposition of harsh punishment [on corporations] may, in fact, be counterproductive," based on risk of backlash against regulators and defiance of law); see also Jennifer Arlen, *The Potentially Perverse Effects of Corporate Criminal Liability*, 22 J. Legal Stud. 833 (1994) (suggesting that penalties under the U.S. Sentencing Guidelines do not give corporations proper incentive to locate individual wrongdoers and thereby may increase the amount of wrongful conduct).

22. See Coffee, *No Soul to Damn*, supra n. 16, at 430–32, 454–55.

23. The facts of the Ayree case are derived from the following sources: Chuck Ashman & Pamela Trescott, *Diplomatic Crime: Drugs, Killings, Thefts, Rapes, Slavery and Other Outrageous Crimes!* at 25 (Acropolis 1987); Robert Ferrigno, *There's Also a Short Arm of the Law*, Chicago Trib., Sept. 27, 1987; Jo Ann Moriarty, *Untitled*, States News Service, June 25, 1987; Eric Pianin, *Bounds of Diplomatic Immunity: Victims to Testify in Support of Helms Bill Limiting Exemptions*, Wash. Post, Aug. 5, 1987.

24. 22 U.S.C. §§ 254a–d. Immunity also is granted under the United Nations Charter and Headquarters Agreement, 22 U.S.C. § 288d(b), which is limited to actions in performance of functions. See People v. Leo, 425 N.Y.S.2d 709 (N.Y. Crim. Ct. 1979).

25. Vienna Convention of Diplomatic Relations, Apr. 18, 1961, art. 31, 23 U.S.T. 3227, T.I.A.S. No. 7502, 500 U.N.T.S. 95 (ratified by U.S. Senate, Sept. 14, 1965; ratification deposited, Nov. 13, 1972; entered into force for the United States, Dec. 13, 1972; adopted by the Diplomatic Relations Act of 1978, 22 U.S.C.A. § 254a) (hereinafter Vienna Convention).

26. See Vienna Convention, supra n. 25, at art. 37(1)–(4).

27. These figures were obtained in a telephone conversation on Feb. 10, 2004, between research assistant Joseph Wheatley and Chenobia Calhoun of the U.S. Department of State's Office of Protocol.

28. See Note, *The Diplomatic Relations Act of 1978 and Its Consequences*, 19 Va. J. Int'l L. 131, 142 n. 64 (1978). Perhaps in recognition of this concern, the 1978 Act allows the President to extend either more or less favorable treatment than that provided by the Vienna Convention, if reciprocity demands it. See 22 U.S.C. § 254c. A foreign country may not bring one of its nationals within the scope of the act by a unilateral act. See United States v. Enger, 472 F. Supp. 490 (D.N.J. 1978).

29. See Albert H. Garretson, *The Immunities of Representatives of Foreign States*, 41 N.Y.U. L. Rev. 67, 70 (1966).

30. See Taylor-Carroll de Mueller, *Some Aspects of Diplomatic Immunities in the United States*, 6 Law of the Americas 1, 13 (1974).

31. See Vienna Convention, supra n. 25, at art. 9, §§ 1–2.

32. See Taylor-Carroll de Mueller, supra n. 30, at 16.

33. But cf. Dept. of State, 43 Bulletin No. 1101, 173, 177–78 (Aug. 1, 1960) (suggesting that the statutory authority for such restraint and expulsion is unclear).

34. See Vienna Convention, supra n. 25, at art. 31, § 4; see generally Taylor-Carroll de Mueller, supra n. 30, at 13.

35. See, e.g., United States v. Arizti, 229 F. Supp. 53, 55 (S.D.N.Y. 1964); In re Doe, 860 F.2d 40 (2d Cir. 1988) (Marcos's diplomatic immunity withdrawn by successor Aquino). For a general discussion of waiver of diplomatic immunity, see Garretson, supra n. 29, at 76.

36. With respect to judicial immunity, see authorities collected at Paul H. Robinson, 2 *Criminal Law Defenses* § 204(b) n. 2 (West 1984 & 2004 supp.). With respect to legislative immunity, see authorities collected at idem § 204(c) n. 10. The Speech and Debate Clause of the U.S. Constitution, U.S. Const. art. I, § 6, cl. 1, also protects federal legislators and some legislative employees from civil or criminal liability arising from the performance of legislative duties. Officials of the executive branch generally do not share the broad immunities from criminal prosecution available to members of the judicial and legislative branches. On the issue of executive privilege to withhold information, see generally *Construction and Application, under State Law, of Doctrine of "Executive Privilege,"* 10 A.L.R.4th 355 (1981 & 2004 supp.). The more limited scope of immunity for executive officials is appropriate given the somewhat less sensitive nature of the executive branch decision-making process. See, e.g., United States v. Nixon, 418 U.S. 683, 706 (1974) ("[N]either the doctrine of separation of powers nor the need for confidentiality of high-level communications, without more, can sustain an absolute, unqualified Presidential privilege of immunity from judicial process[.]"). In *Nixon*, the Supreme Court reasoned, "The impediment that an absolute, unqualified privilege would place in the way of the primary constitutional duty of the Judicial Branch to do justice in criminal prosecutions would plainly conflict with the function of the courts under Art. III." Idem at 707. The Court in *Nixon* compelled only the production of papers; it sidestepped the issue of whether the President could be a defendant in a criminal case while still holding office. See idem at 687 n. 2.

37. See, e.g., Bennett v. Ahrens, 57 F.2d 948 (7th Cir. 1932) (construing statute, current version of which is at 725 Ill. Ann. Stat. 5/107–7(d), exempting judges, counselors, attorneys, and similar persons from arrest while attending or going to or from court); People v. Scordo, 231 N.Y.S.2d 456 (N.Y. Crim. Ct. 1962) (officer of court exempt from any arrest during term of court that would prevent him from appearing; traffic citation does not fall within exemption); Zumsteg v. American Food Club, Inc., 143 N.E.2d 701 (Ohio 1957) (construing Ohio Rev. Code Ann. § 2331.11, which exempts parties, attorneys, and certain other officers of court from arrest while going to, attending, and returning from court).

38. Powell v. McCormack, 395 U.S. 486, 505 (1969); 2 Robinson, supra n. 36, § 204(b) at 475 n. 3 (discussing judicial immunity).

CHAPTER 9

1. As to most defenses, it is already the case that the defendant bears the "burden of production," which must be met for the issue to even be considered by the factfinder. Thus the defendant must introduce some evidence that, for example, he acted

in self-defense, even though it usually then becomes the prosecution's duty to disprove the self-defense claim beyond a reasonable doubt.

2. See Clifford S. Fishman, 1 *Jones on Evidence* § 3:12 at 242 (7th ed., Law. Co-op. 1992 & 2004 supp.) (burden on each issue should fall on party who, without proving the issue, is not entitled to relief); idem § 3:26 (burden on defendant to prove "disfavored contentions," such as statute of limitations, laches, contributory negligence, or assumption of risk, that entitle defendant to win although plaintiff has stated a valid claim); idem § 3:28 (burden falls on party seeking to come within exception to general rule); cf. Model Penal Code § 1.12(4)(a) (stating that for facts other than offense elements, "the burden of proving the fact is on the prosecution or defendant, depending on whose interest or contention will be furthered if the finding should be made").

3. In several states, the fact that the defendant is younger than a specified age creates only a rebuttable presumption of immaturity. See Ariz. Rev. Stat. Ann. § 13–501 (under fourteen); Cal. Penal Code § 26 (under fourteen); Nev. Rev. Stat. §§ 194.010(1)–(2), 193.210 (between ages eight and fourteen); Okla. Stat. Ann. tit. 21, § 152(1)–(2) (between ages seven and fourteen); S.D. Codified Laws Ann. § 22–3–1(1)–(2) (between ages ten and fourteen); Wash. Rev. Code Ann. § 9A.04.050 (between ages eight and twelve). This also was the approach of the common-law rule. Children under seven were given a defense; children over seven but under twelve (or fourteen) were entitled to a presumption of immaturity, but the presumption could be rebutted. See William Blackstone, 4 *Commentaries on the Laws of England* 23 (1769); Sir Matthew Hale, 1 *Historia Placitorum Coronae* 22 (George Wilson, ed., T. Payne 1778).

4. See supra chapter 6, "Rehabilitation."

5. See, e.g., United States v. Amos, 803 F.2d 419, 420 (8th Cir. 1986) (describing this federal rule and its modification by the Insanity Defense Reform Act of 1984).

6. See, e.g., 18 U.S.C. § 17(b) (providing that "defendant has the burden of proving the defense of insanity by clear and convincing evidence"); authorities listed at Paul H. Robinson, 2 *Criminal Law Defenses* § 173(a) n. 7 (West 1984 & 2004 supp.).

7. See Patterson v. New York, 432 U.S. 197 (1977) (allowing burden shifting for mitigating issue of extreme emotional disturbance); Rivera v. Delaware, 429 U.S. 877 (1976) (dismissing, for want of substantial federal question, appeal seeking review of statute shifting burden for insanity defense); Leland v. Oregon, 343 U.S. 790 (1952) (upholding statute shifting burden to defendant to prove insanity beyond a reasonable doubt).

8. See Laurie L. Levenson, *Good Faith Defenses: Reshaping Strict Liability Crimes*, 78 Cornell L. Rev. 401 (1993) (proposing good-faith defense to strict liability where defendant can prove, beyond a reasonable doubt, honest effort to comply with law).

9. See Reference re Section 94(2) of the Motor Vehicle Act, 2 S.C.R. 486 (Can. 1985) (rejecting absolute liability for offenses involving mandatory incarceration); Regina v. City of Sault Ste. Marie, 2 S.C.R. 1299, 1315–16 (Can. 1978) (recognizing good-faith defense to strict liability); Eric Colvin, *Principles of Criminal Law* 22 (2d ed., Thomson 1991); Levenson, supra n. 8, at 442–45; G. L. Peiris, *Strict Liability in Commonwealth Criminal Law*, 3 Legal Stud. 117, 124–25, 129–30 (1983).

10. See Levenson, supra n. 8, at 435–42 (discussing history of British approach); Joseph Yahuda, *Mens Rea in Statutory Offences*, 118 New L.J. 330, 330–31 (1968).

11. See Levenson, supra n. 8, at 445–48. New Zealand, unlike Australia, requires only that the defendant introduce a reasonable basis for the offense conduct, at which point the burden shifts back to the state to prove the absence of a mistake. Idem at 447.

12. 397 U.S. 358, 364 (1970) (in juvenile delinquency proceeding for twelve-year-old charged with stealing, the child is entitled, as matter of due process, to have case against him proven beyond reasonable doubt).

13. 421 U.S. 684 (1975).

14. 432 U.S. 197 (1977).

15. See *Patterson*, 432 U.S. at 229–30 & n. 14 (Powell, J., joined by Brennan & Marshall, JJ., dissenting) (offering interpretation of *Winship* and *Mullaney* leaving states free to enact "[n]ew ameliorative affirmative defenses" and providing example of "defense" increasing culpability as to victim's age for statutory-rape offense from strict liability to negligence, but shifting burden to defendant).

16. See *Patterson*, 432 U.S. at 214 n. 15 ("There is some language in *Mullaney* that has been understood as perhaps construing the Due Process Clause to require the prosecution to prove beyond a reasonable doubt any fact affecting 'the degree of criminal culpability.' . . . Carried to its logical extreme, such a reading of *Mullaney* might also, for example, discourage Congress from enacting pending legislation to change the felony-murder rule by permitting the accused to prove by a preponderance of the evidence the affirmative defense that the homicide committed was neither a necessary nor a reasonably foreseeable consequence of the underlying felony. . . . The Court did not intend *Mullaney* to have such far-reaching effect.").

17. See, e.g., Mullaney v. Wilbur, 421 U.S. 684 (1975) (forbidding burden shifting for issue of provocation); Sandstrom v. Montana, 442 U.S. 510 (1979) (forbidding burden shifting for issue of intent).

18. See Martin v. Ohio, 480 U.S. 228 (1987) (allowing burden shifting for issue of self-defense); Patterson v. New York, 432 U.S. 197 (1977) (allowing burden shifting for issue of extreme emotional disturbance).

19. See *Patterson*, 432 U.S. at 210 (noting that Court's "view may seem to permit state legislatures to reallocate burdens of proof by labeling as affirmative defenses at least some elements of the crimes now defined in their statutes," but adding vague qualification that "there are obviously constitutional limits beyond which the States may not go in this regard"); idem at 211 n. 12 (noting that "[t]he applicability of the reasonable-doubt standard . . . has always been dependent on how a State defines the offense that is charged in any given case").

20. For a more thorough treatment of this proposal, see Paul H. Robinson et al., *Making Criminal Codes Functional: A Code of Conduct and a Code of Adjudication*, 86 J. Crim. L. & Criminology 304, 327–32 (1996); Paul H. Robinson, *Structure and Function in Criminal Law* 145–46, 204–7 (Clarendon 1997).

21. See supra chapter 5, "Cannibalism at Sea."

22. See supra chapter 8, "Diplomatic and Official Immunity."

23. In the 1990s, a California state senator introduced a bill to replace the verdict of "not guilty" with "not proven guilty," the purpose being to "defuse any public outrage in future controversial court cases" based on "the confusion [that] comes from the mistaken assumption of untrained people that 'not guilty' means 'innocent.'" Jon Matthews, *We the Jury Render a Verdict of—"Not Proven"?* Sacramento Bee, Jan. 24, 1996, at A3. But see Andrew D. Leipold, *The Problem of the Innocent, Acquitted Defendant,* 94 Nw. U. L. Rev. 1297, 1305 n. 25 (2000) (questioning assertion that laypeople commonly equate acquittal with finding of innocence).

24. See, e.g., Fed. R. Evid. 609 (permitting impeachment by prior conviction even though defendant is subsequently pardoned); State v. Clark, 402 So.2d 684 (La. 1981) (same); cf. Hozer v. State Dep't of Treasury, 230 A.2d 508, 511–12 (N.J. Super. App. Div. 1967) (holding pardoned policeman not entitled to pension for "honorable service," as pardon did not erase moral stain of offense).

25. See, e.g., Mo. Stat. Ann. §§ 561.016–.026; Minn. Stat. Ann. § 609.165; N.D. Cent. Code § 12.1–33–01; see generally Eric E. Younger, *Not Completely Dead—but Seriously Injured: Collateral Consequences of Misdemeanor Arrest and Conviction,* 52 L.A. Bar J. 50 (1976).

26. See, e.g., Ariz. Rev. Stat. Ann. § 13–3410 (authorizing licensing authority to revoke professional license on conviction of certain drug offenses); Schanuel v. Anderson, 708 F.2d 316 (7th Cir. 1983) (upholding as constitutional a statute prohibiting an ex-felon from obtaining employment as a detective).

27. See, e.g., N.J. Stat. Ann. § 2C:13–12.1; N.D. Cent. Code §§ 12.1–33–01 to –02.1; see generally Special Project, *The Collateral Consequences of a Criminal Conviction,* 23 Vand. L. Rev. 929 (1970); President's Commission on Law Enforcement and Administration of Justice, *Task Force Report: Corrections* 88–92 (U.S. Gov't Printing Office 1967); Model Penal Code §§ 6.04, 6.13.

28. See, e.g., Fed. R. Evid. 404, 609.

29. For habitual or persistent offender statutes, see, for example, Conn. Gen. Stat. Ann. § 53a–40, Del. Code Ann. tit. 11, § 4214; N.C. Gen. Stat. § 14–7.1; N.J. Stat. Ann. 2C:44–3(a). For statutes authorizing aggravation of penalties for recidivists, see, for example, Haw. Rev. Stat. § 706–606.5. See also 1 Robinson, supra n 6, § 38(a) at 100–01.

30. See Paul H. Robinson, *Hybrid Principles for the Distribution of Criminal Sanctions,* 82 Nw. U. L. Rev. 19, 22–28 (1987).

31. See Paul H. Robinson, *The Virtues of Restorative Processes, the Vices of Restorative Justice,* 2003 Utah L. Rev. 375.

32. See Matti Huuhtanen, *A $103,000 Speeding Ticket? Finnish Millionaire Proves It: The More You Earn, the More You Pay,* Phila. Inquirer, Apr. 21, 2002. The fine was later reduced to less than $5,300—because the executive successfully argued on appeal that the court had used the wrong year's income to calculate the fine—but other high fines have been imposed, such as a fine of more than $40,000 on hockey player Teemu Selanne for reckless driving in 2000. See idem.

Germany, Austria, Sweden, and Denmark all employ similar "day-fine" systems that relate the size of a fine to both the gravity of the offense and the offender's income. See Judith A. Greene & Sally T. Hillsman, *Tailoring Criminal Fines to the Financial Needs of the Offender*, 72 Judicature 38, 39 (1988); see generally Moshe Bar Niv (Burnovski) & Zvi Safra, *On the Social Desirability of Wealth-Dependent Fine Policies*, 22 Int'l Rev. L. & Econ. 53 (2002).

33. See generally *Developments in the Law: Alternatives to Incarceration*, 111 Harv. L. Rev. 1863 (1998) (discussing various alternative sanctions, including shaming mechanisms, and assessing their potential efficacy).

34. See generally Paul H. Robinson, *Desert, Crime Control, Disparity, and Units of Punishment*, in *Penal Theory and Practice: Tradition and Innovation in Criminal Justice* 93–107 (Antony Duff et al., eds., St. Martin's 1994).

35. See Robert E. Harlow et al., *The Severity of Intermediate Penal Sanctions: A Psychophysical Scaling Approach for Obtaining Community Perceptions*, 11 J. Quantitative Criminology 71 (1995); see also Maynard L. Erickson & Jack P. Gibbs, *On the Perceived Severity of Legal Penalties*, 70 J. Crim. L. & Criminology 102 (1979); Leslie Sebba, *Some Explorations in the Scaling of Penalties*, 15 J. Res. in Crime & Delinquency 247 (1978); Leslie Sebba & Gad Nathan, *Further Exploration in the Scaling of Penalties*, 22 British J. Criminology 221 (1984).

36. See Rev. Code. Wash. § 9.94A.680; David Boerner, *Sentencing in Washington* § 6.17 (Butterworth 1985).

37. See Or. Admin. Rules §§ 213–005–0011 & –0012; Kathleen Bogan, *Oregon's Sanction Units Exchange System for Felony Sentencing Guidelines*, 4 Fed. Sent. Rep. 36 (1991).

38. See, e.g., Michael Tonry, *Intermediate Sanctions in Sentencing Reform*, 2 U. Chicago L. Sch. Roundtable 391, 406–08 (1995) (discussing limitations of Oregon and Washington approaches and questioning viability of units method based on difficulty of translating significant incarceration periods into alternative sanctions).

39. See Bureau of Justice Statistics, U.S. Dep't of Justice, *Sourcebook of Criminal Justice Statistics* table 5.47 (Kathleen Maguire & Ann L. Pastore, eds.) (summary table showing that 32% of all state felony sentences, and 22% for violent offenses, were to probation), available at http://www.albany.edu/sourcebook/pdf/t547.pdf (downloaded June 15, 2005).

40. See, e.g., James P. Gray, *Why Our Drug Laws Have Failed and What We Can Do about It: A Judicial Indictment of the War on Drugs* 29–30 (Temple 2001); R. H. Peters, *Drug Treatment in Jails and Detention Settings*, in *Drug Treatment and Criminal Justice* (J. A. Inciardi, ed., Sage 1993); David B. Kopel, *Prison Blues: How America's Foolish Sentencing Policies Endanger Public Safety*, May 17, 1994, available at http://www.cato.org/pubs/pas/pa-208.html; Joe Tyrrell, *No Room for Mercy in 1998 Drug Case: Man Sold Marijuana in Bar near a School*, Newark Star-Ledger, Mar. 4, 2002 ("'This is part of the absurdity of drug laws in America,' said Lewis Katz, a criminal justice professor at Case Western Reserve University in Ohio. In some states, Katz said, 'violent offenders are released early to make room for drug offenders who must serve mandatory sentences.'"); Nancy Gibbs, *Truth, Justice and the Reno Way*, Time, July 12, 1993, at 20, 26.

41. See 142 Cong. Rec. S3703, 3704 (Apr. 19, 1996) (statement of Sen. Abraham).

42. Philip Brickman and Donald T. Campbell, *Hedonic Relativism and Planning the Good Society*, in *Adaptation-Level Theory: A Symposium* 287–302 (M. H. Appley, ed., Academic 1971).

43. Shelly Taylor, *Adjustment to Threatening Life Events: A Theory of Cognitive Adaptation*, 38 Amer. Psych. 1161 (1983); Ronnie Janoff-Bulman & Camille Wortman, *Attributions of Blame and Coping in the "Real World": Severe Accident Victims React to Their Lot*, 35 J. Personality & Soc. Psych. 351 (1977).

44. Shane Frederick & George Loewenstein, *Hedonic Adaptation*, in *Well-Being: The Foundations of Hedonic Psychology* 302–29 (Daniel Kahneman et al., eds., Russell Sage Found. 1999).

45. Daniel Kahneman, *Objective Happiness*, in *Well-Being: The Foundations of Hedonic Psychology* 4 (Daniel Kahneman et al., eds., Russell Sage Found. 1999).

46. D. Redelmeier and Daniel Kahneman, *Patients' Memories of Painful Medical Treatments: Real Time and Retrospective Evaluations of Two Minimally Invasive Procedures*, 116 Pain 3 (1996). Kahneman summarizes the effect of increasing the duration of, for instance, a painful medical procedure, on the later reported aversiveness of that event:

> A consistent finding of these experiments was that duration always combined additively with other determinants of global evaluation and participants appeared to use it as a minor extra feature (used to evaluate the painfulness) of each trial, as if they were telling themselves "this episode is painful and is also rather long," or "this episode is painful but it is short."

Daniel Kahneman, *Evaluation by Moments, Past and Future*, in *Choices, Values and Frames* 698 (Daniel Kahneman & Amos Tversky, eds., Russell Sage Found. 2000).

47. See Paul H. Robinson & John M. Darley, *Does Criminal Law Deter? A Social Science Investigation*, 24 Oxford J. Legal Stud. 173 (2004), appendix available at http://www.law.upenn.edu/fac/phrobins/OxfordDeterrenceAppendix.pdf.

CHAPTER 10

1. See Guy Stessens, *Corporate Criminal Liability: A Comparative Perspective*, 43 Int'l & Comp. L.Q. 493, 503 (1994); Gunter Heine, *New Developments in Corporate Criminal Liability in Europe: Can Europeans Learn from the American Experience—or Vice Versa?*, 1998 St. Louis-Warsaw Transatl. L.J. 173, 174.

2. Idem at 174–75. As to the potential for Germany's forfeiture rules to exceed the usual limit, Stessens notes that "*Süddeutsche Zementindustrie* seems to hold the record in this respect: on a charge of price fixing it has been fined DM 224 million." Stessens, supra n. 1, at 516.

3. See Stessens, supra n. 1, at 503.

4. See idem at 504.

5. Heine, supra n. 1, at 174; see also Stessens, supra n. 1, at 503 ("The imposition of an administrative fine under [the German] system does not imply any kind of moral judgment stigma and this consideration seems to have been the most important for the German legislature in opting for administrative sanctions rather than leaving the matter under the aegis of the criminal law.").

6. Unfortunately, there has lately also been a disturbing trend in Europe to follow the American model toward criminal liability for regulatory offenses and corporations. See Heine, supra n. 1, at 175; see also Eli Lederman, *Models for Imposing Corporate Criminal Liability: From Adaptation and Imitation toward Aggregation and the Search for Self-Identity*, 4 Buff. Crim. L. Rev. 641, 645 (2000) (noting changes in France and Netherlands). (Perhaps the oddest such initiative, from the perspective of the traditional goals of criminal liability, is the Belgian rule "requiring each company that commences business activity to designate a responsible person. If a criminal act results from the business activity, that person bears automatic criminal liability, without the necessity of proving any illegal activity on his part." Heine, supra n. 1, at 177–78.) Even so, this trend has been controversial: "From the standpoint of many European countries . . . an important feature of the criminal law is jeopardized, when the state uses its repressive apparatus too frequently. The more a criminal sanction is divorced from certain principles of blameworthiness, the more it loses its punitive character." Idem at 185–86.

7. Stessens, supra n. 1, at 504 & n. 50.

8. Richard S. Frase & Thomas Weigend, *German Criminal Justice as a Guide to American Law Reform: Similar Problems, Better Solutions?*, 18 B.C. Int'l & Comp. L. Rev. 317, 320–21 (1995).

9. See Stessens, supra n. 1, at 502.

10. See John C. Coffee, Jr., *Corporate Criminal Responsibility*, in 1 *Encyclopedia of Crime and Justice* 253 (Sanford H. Kadish, ed., Gale 1983); Steven Walt & William S. Laufer, *Why Personhood Doesn't Matter: Corporate Criminal Liability and Sanctions*, 18 Am. J. Crim. L. 263, 266 (1991).

11. See United States v. Bank of New England, N.A., 821 F.2d 844 (1st Cir. 1987).

12. See United States v. Beusch, 596 F.2d 871 (9th Cir. 1979); see generally Walt & Laufer, supra n. 10, at 266.

13. See generally Kenneth Mann, *Punitive Civil Sanctions: The Middleground between Criminal and Civil Law*, 101 Yale L.J. 1795 (1992).

14. See generally Laura J. Kerrigan et al., *Project: The Decriminalization of Administrative Law Penalties: Civil Remedies, Alternatives, Policy, and Constitutional Implications*, 45 Admin. L. Rev. 367, 387–95 (1993).

15. Idem at 377–78 (footnotes omitted).

16. See generally Kenneth Culp Davis & Richard J. Pierce, Jr., 1 *Administrative Law Treatise* § 4.3 (3d ed., Aspen 1994).

17. See Kerrigan et al., supra n. 14, at 374–77.

18. Cf. Mann, supra n. 13, at 1865 (arguing that a middle-ground approach would provide the optimal enforcement level and "more proportionate punitive sanction-

ing . . . increasing overall sanctioning while reducing reliance on both criminal sanctions and merely remedial sanctions").

19. Such a reform could well give defendants greater protections, because they are currently denied standard criminal rights when agencies initiate civil proceedings against them. For a discussion of when constitutional protections apply to civil regulatory enforcement proceedings, see Kerrigan et al., supra n. 14, at 397–419.

20. See, e.g., L. Timothy Perrin et al., *If It's Broken, Fix It: Moving beyond the Exclusionary Rule,* 83 Iowa L. Rev. 669, 743–53 (1998) (proposing and defending an administrative process through which victims recover monetary penalties against officials); Christopher Slobogin, *Why Liberals Should Chuck the Exclusionary Rule,* 1999 U. Ill. L. Rev. 363; Akhil Reed Amar, *Fourth Amendment First Principles,* 107 Harv. L. Rev. 757, 811–16 (1995); Stephen J. Markman, *Six Observations on the Exclusionary Rule,* 20 Harv. J. L. & Pub. Pol'y 423, 427–29 (1997); Donald Dripps, *The Case for the Contingent Exclusionary Rule,* 38 Am. Crim. L. Rev. 1 (2001) (proposing system where exclusionary rule is available, but contingent on government's failure to pay alternative fine remedy). For a debate about one such proposal, see *Symposium on Reform of the Exclusionary Rule,* 26 Pepp. L. Rev. 789 (1999). For an exhaustive review of Fourth Amendment exclusionary rule criticisms and reform proposals, see generally Wayne R. LaFave, 1 *Search and Seizure: A Treatise on the Fourth Amendment* § 1.2 (4th ed., West 2004).

21. See S. 3, 104th Cong. 507(b) (1995).

22. See Harry M. Caldwell & Carol A. Chase, *The Unruly Exclusionary Rule: Heeding Justice Blackmun's Call to Examine the Rule in Light of Changing Judicial Understanding about Its Effects outside the Courtroom,* 78 Marq. U. L. Rev. 45 (1994).

23. See Minn. Stat. § 481.10; see also Peter Erlinder, *Getting Serious about Miranda in Minnesota: Criminal and Civil Sanctions for Failure to Respond to Requests for Counsel,* 27 Wm. Mitchell L. Rev. 941 (2000). It appears, however, that the statutory civil remedy in Minnesota, although it pre-dated *Miranda* by nearly ninety years, has led to recovery for a private plaintiff in only one case in its history—and that award was later overturned on appeal. See Mullins v. Churchill, 616 N.W.2d 764 (Minn. App. 2000); see also Erlinder, idem at 952–60 (discussing *Mullins*).

24. For just a few discussions of the subject, which themselves cite numerous other efforts, see works cited supra nn. 20–23 and in chapter 7 nn. 11–19, 25–28, 139–43.

25. See supra chapter 7, "Released to Kill."

26. See supra chapter 7, "A Winged Car Powered by Cocaine."

27. See, e.g., 1 LaFave, supra n. 20, § 1.2(a) at 30–31.

28. See United States v. Leon, 468 U.S. 897 (1984) (creating "good-faith" exception). But see William A. Schroeder, *Restoring the Status Quo Ante: The Fourth Amendment Exclusionary Rule as a Compensating Device,* 51 Geo. Wash. L. Rev. 633, 636 (1983) (arguing that "the principal role of the exclusionary rule should be to restore victims of those unconstitutional searches and seizures that yield incriminating evidence to the position they were in before the illegality occurred"); Jerry E. Norton, *The Exclusionary Rule Reconsidered: Restoring the Status Quo Ante,* 33 Wake Forest L. Rev. 261 (1998).

29. See supra chapter 7 nn. 16–30 and accompanying text.

30. See, e.g., Perrin et al., supra n. 20, at 732 n. 452 (citing police officers' own responses to proposal of direct sanctions, including claim that police "would be too scared to search" if they were subject to such sanctions); William C. Heffernan & Richard W. Lovely, *Evaluating the Fourth Amendment Exclusionary Rule: The Problem of Police Compliance with the Law*, 24 U. Mich. J. L. Reform 311, 361 (1991) (citing concerns about efficacy of law enforcement if direct sanctions exist; arguing that officers subject to direct sanctions may choose inaction when, as is frequently the case, they are uncertain about legality of search).

31. See, e.g., 1 LaFave, supra n. 20, § 1.2(f) (discussing proposal to lift exclusionary sanction where police department can show soundness of its procedures to train and discipline officers and finding that "[t]his proposal deserves serious attention").

32. See, e.g., Perrin et al., supra n. 20, at 728–29 (discussing results of survey in which officers correctly answered search-and-seizure hypotheticals just over half the time and interrogation hypotheticals less than three-quarters of the time); Heffernan & Lovely, supra n. 30, at 333–34 (reporting results of survey in which officers reached correct conclusions about lawfulness in search-and-seizure hypotheticals 56.7% of the time and correctly answered multiple-choice questions less than half the time).

33. See supra chapter 6, "Incapacitation"; see also Paul H. Robinson, *Punishing Dangerousness: Cloaking Preventive Detention as Criminal Justice*, 114 Harv. L. Rev. 1429, 1438–42 (2001); Christopher Slobogin, *A Jurisprudence of Dangerousness*, 98 Nw. U. L. Rev. 1 (2003) (hereinafter Slobogin, *Jurisprudence of Dangerousness*); cf. Christopher Slobogin, *The Civilization of Criminal Law*, 58 Vand. L. Rev. (forthcoming 2005) (arguing for system of preventive detention as replacement for, instead of supplement to, criminal-justice system).

34. For statutes authorizing detention of dangerously mentally ill persons, see, e.g., Conn. Gen. Stat. Ann. § 17a–498; Idaho Code § 66–329; La. Rev. Stat. Ann. § 28:55; Mass. Ann. Laws ch. 123, § 12; Minn. Stat. § 253B.02, subd. 13, 17; Mo. Rev. Stat. § 552.040; N.H. Rev. Stat. Ann. § 135–C:34; N.J. Stat. Ann. § 30:4–27.1; N.Y. Mental Hyg. Law § 9.37; Utah Code Ann. § 62A–5–312; Wash. Rev. Code § 71.05.280; Wis. Stat. § 51.20; Wyo. Stat. Ann. § 25–10–101. For statutes authorizing detention of persons with a communicable disease, see, e.g., Ala. Code § 22-11A-10 (tuberculosis), -14 & -18 (sexually transmitted diseases), -24 (notifiable diseases); Colo. Rev. Stat. § 25-1-650 (communicable diseases); Del. Code Ann. tit. 16, § 505 (communicable diseases); Fla. Stat. ch. 384.28 (sexually transmitted diseases); Haw. Rev. Stat. § 325-8 (infectious, communicable, or other diseases dangerous to public health); Iowa Code Ann. § 139.3 (communicable diseases); Kan. Stat. Ann. § 65-128 (infectious or communicable diseases); Minn. Stat. § 144.4180 (communicable diseases); N.H. Rev. Stat. Ann. § 141-C:11 (communicable diseases); N.C. Gen. Stat. § 130A-145 (communicable diseases); Ohio Rev. Code Ann. § 3707.08 (communicable diseases); R.I. Gen. Laws § 23-8-4 (communicable diseases); Tenn. Code Ann. § 68-5-104 (communicable or contagious diseases); Wis. Stat. Ann. § 143.05 (communicable diseases). For statutes authorizing detention of persons with a chemical dependency, see, e.g., Cal. Welf. & Inst. Code §§ 3000–3111; D.C. Code Ann. §§ 24-601 to -611 (1992); Minn. Stat.

§ 253B.02, subd. 14 (1990); S.C. Code Ann. §§ 44-52-50 to -210. For statutes authorizing detention of persons with a drug dependency, see authorities cited at Paul H. Robinson, *The Criminal-Civil Distinction and Dangerous Blameless Offenders*, 83 J. Crim. L. & Criminology 693, 712 n. 59 (1993).

35. The first statute of this kind was Wash. Rev. Code § 71.09 (1991). Other states have since enacted similar laws. See, e.g., Iowa Stat. § 709C.2(4); Kan. Stat. Ann. § 59–29a01; Minn. Stat. § 253B.02(18b); Wis. Stat. § 980. The constitutionality of the Kansas statute was challenged in December 1996. At that time, five other states had such statutes—Arizona, California, Minnesota, Washington, and Wisconsin—and thirty-eight states, including New Jersey and New York, filed amicus briefs urging the Supreme Court to uphold the law, which it did. See Kansas v. Hendricks, 521 U.S. 346, 371 (1997). The Kansas statute was enacted after a finding that the existing civil involuntary commitment procedure was inadequate to deal with the risk that some sex offenders pose to society: "[S]exually violent predators generally have anti-social personality features which are unamenable to existing mental illness treatment modalities[,] and those features render them likely to engage in sexually violent behavior. [S]exually violent predators' likelihood of engaging in repeat acts of predatory sexual violence is high." Kan. Stat. Ann. § 59–29a01 (as enacted by L. 1994, ch. 316, § 1).

36. See Kansas v. Hendricks, 521 U.S. 346, 358 (1997) (citing Heller v. Doe, 509 U.S. 312, 314–15 (1993); Allen v. Illinois, 478 U.S. 364, 366 (1986); Minnesota ex rel. Pearson v. Probate Court, 309 U.S. 270, 271–72 (1940)).

37. See Rummel v. Estelle, 445 U.S. 263 (1980).

38. See, e.g., John Monahan et al., *Rethinking Risk Assessment: The MacArthur Study of Violence and Disorder* (Oxford 2001); Slobogin, *Jurisprudence of Dangerousness*, supra n. 33, at 9 ("Due to a number of methodological difficulties in measuring prediction validity, we may never know precisely how accurate the various modes of prediction are. But we can say that prediction science—in particular, methods that utilize actuarial tables or structured interviews has improved to the point where clear and convincing evidence of dangerousness, if not proof beyond a reasonable doubt, is available for certain categories of individuals."); idem n. 32 (listing empirical studies).

39. See generally Robinson, supra n. 33.

40. See Rummel v. Estelle, 445 U.S. 263 (1980).

CONCLUSION

1. See William J. Stuntz, *Race, Class, and Drugs*, 98 Colum. L. Rev. 1795, 1819–20 (1998).

2. See idem at 1820–21.

3. Cf. idem at 1821 (noting that drug-enforcement tactics in poor neighborhoods impose costs on residents, rather than police); idem at 1822–23 (discussing how Fourth Amendment rules encourage street encounters in poor areas rather than home searches in more upscale areas).

4. Kevin Reitz, American Law Institute, *Model Penal Code: Sentencing: Plan for Revision*, 6 Buff. Crim. L. Rev. 525, 596 (2002).

5. For an argument that current drug penalties cannot be supported by any desert-based, retributivist explanation but can only be defended on utilitarian grounds, see Paul Butler, *Retribution, for Liberals*, 46 UCLA L. Rev. 1873, 1884–88 (1999). See also Paul Butler, *Much Respect: Toward a Hip-Hop Theory of Punishment*, 56 Stan. L. Rev. 983, 1003–04 & nn. 117–19 (2004).

6. See Stuntz, supra n. 1, at 1826–27 & nn. 73–75.

7. As William Stuntz has put it:

> [E]nforcement bias is undermining the normative force of the drug laws, and perhaps undermining the normative force of the criminal law as a whole. . . . [G]iven the sheer volume of incarceration, the declines [in crime] have been surprisingly small. That may be because greater tangible punishment is serving mostly to compensate for a decline in the intangible kind.

Idem at 1829, 1831–32.

8. See generally idem at 1825–32.

INDEX

Abuse of legal rules, 27–51, 203, 205–6
  affecting ex ante behavior, 33, 34
  legality concerns contrasted with, 109
    n.32
  post-offense efforts to "game the
    system," 27, 33, 34–35
  revised verdict system as means of
    addressing, 210–12
Administrative enforcement of "viola
    tions," 194, 204, 218–21
  American models for, 220–21
  European systems of, 219
Almond, Charles, 132–33
Alternative sanctions, 210 17. See also
    Fines; Units of punishment
American Law Institute, 41, 184
Andrade, Leandro, 3–4
Attempt, 19–20, 125. See also Resulting
    harm, significance of
"Attempting to commit a crime" as
    distinct offense, 99
Attorney, right to. See Right to counsel
Ayree, Manuel, 195–99, 210

Bench trials, 82–83
"Black rage" defense, 50
Bright-line rules. See also Abuse of legal
    rules; Legality principle
  generally, 33–34, 87–88, 89–116, 130
    n.29
  abuse concerns and, 109 n.32

  benefits of, 89–90
  case-by-case bargains contrasted with, 84
  desert and, 90 n.4
  deterrence and, 90 n.4
  evidentiary standards contrasted with,
    69, 206–07
  misconduct concerns and, 90 n.4
  revised verdict system as alternative
    to, 210–12
  rejection of exceptions to maintain
    clarity of, 107–9
  strengthening cultural norms with,
    111–16
British law, 33 n.11, 47 n.55, 58, 98 n.26,
    155, 168–69, 193 n.16, 208. See also
    Foreign law
Burden of persuasion, 9, 43, 49, 203,
    205–09. See also Evidentiary
    burdens; Presumptions

Canadian law, 184, 208. See also Foreign
    law
Carson, Johnny, 174
Civil commitment, 9–10, 42 nn.34&36,
    119, 136, 171, 204, 225–28. See also
    Incapacitation
Civil sanctions, 9–10, 204, 218–28
  for corporations, 193–94, 218–21
  for law-enforcement violations of
    rights, 204, 222–24
  for regulatory offenses, 191, 218–21

Clarity of prohibitions. *See* Bright-line rules

Colombo crime "family," 74–75

Common-law offenses, prohibition of, 89–90 & n.3, 96. *See also* Legality principle

Confessions. *See* Exclusionary rules; Fifth Amendment; *Miranda* warnings; Self-incrimination, privilege against

Cooperation agreements, 79 & n.11. *See also* Witness immunity

Corporate criminal liability, 186, 192–94, 204
    desert and, 192–93
    difficulty of applying standard culpability rules to, 192–93, 220
    European approaches to, 193 n.16, 219 & n.6
    using administrative sanctions to address, 193–94, 218–21

Cosa Nostra, 74–78

Counsel, right to. *See* Right to counsel

Culpability. *See also* Negligence; Reasonableness standards; Strict liability
    corporate criminal liability and, 192–93, 220
    difficulty of proving, 52, 207–8
    individualized definitions of, 48–51
    objective definitions of, 28, 46–48
    resulting harm and, 19–20
    revising evidentiary rules for proving, 207–9
    strict liability as contrary to usual requirement of, 65, 66
    strict liability as evidentiary substitute for requirement of, 65–69

Davis, Sammy Jr., 173

"Day fines," 213 n.32

Defenses. *See* Excuse defenses; Justification defenses; Nonexculpatory defenses

DeLorean, John, 172–80, 223

Desert. *See also* Moral credibility; Utilitarian goals
    generally, 3–11, 13–23, 206, 229–31
    debates regarding meaning of, 14–15
    definition of, 13–14, 18–21
    existing legal rules' relation to, 16–17
    goals competing with, 5–6, 15–16, 18, 87–88, 212, 229–31

growing acceptance as basis of criminal law, 10, 16–18
    procedural rights' relation to, 69–71, 81, 183–85
    relation between retributivist and community-view models of, 19–20
    retributivist model of, 17, 19–20, 21
    role of community views in establishing, 19–21
    significance for laypeople, 3, 16
    utilitarian goals' relation to, 11, 17–18, 21–23, 74, 128, 212, 229–31

Deterrence. *See also* Felony murder; Strict liability; Utilitarian goals
    generally, 4, 117–30, 190, 192–94, 215–16, 231
    alternative strategies for achieving, 129–30, 212–17
    desert and, 126–27
    impediments to, 127–28
    of police misconduct via exclusionary rules, 151–55, 222–24
    skepticism regarding, 126–30
    as ubiquitous justification for criminal rules, 125–26

Diplomatic immunity, 88, 186–87, 194–201, 210. *See also* Nonexculpatory defenses

Diplomatic Relations Act of 1978, 199–200

Discretion. *See also* Misconduct of government agents
    generally, 89 & nn.1–2, 97, 111, 191
    motivations of prosecutors and, 82
    plea bargaining and, 82
    reliance on to avoid injustices, 67 n.33

DNA evidence, 58

Double Jeopardy Clause, 137, 156, 159–70, 211
    British version of, 168–69
    desert and, 166–67
    due-process requirements compared with, 168
    frequency of application of, 166–67
    interpreting scope of, 167–68
    lack of alternative remedies for violations of, 167
    meaning of "same offense" for purposes of, 167 n.72
    New Zealand version of, 169
    prohibition of multiple overlapping convictions by, 166 n.68
    promotion of accurate outcomes by, 166

purposes of, 166 & n.69
when jeopardy "attaches" for purposes
    of, 167–68
Drug offenses, 68, 229–31
Drunk driving laws, 115–16, 126
Dudley, Thomas, 101–11, 207
Dudley & Stephens, Regina v., 107–09
Due process, 60, 96 n.13, 156 n.52, 168,
    181–82, 184 n.139, 208–09
Duress defense, 49. *See also* Excuse
    defenses
Driving under the influence, 115–16

English law. *See* British law
Entrapment defense. *See also* Misconduct
    by government agents; Nonexculpa-
    tory defenses
    generally, 138, 172–83, 211
    alternatives to, 183, 222–24
    desert and, 182
    deterrence of police misconduct by,
        183
    due-process requirements compared to,
        181–82
    exclusionary rules compared to, 183,
        222–23
    frequency of, 180
    objective formulations of, 180–81
    subjective formulations of, 181
Evidentiary burdens, 43, 49, 52, 206 &
    n.1, 219–21. *See also* Burden of per-
    suasion; Presumptions
Exclusionary rules. *See also* Fifth
    Amendment; Fourth Amendment;
    Miranda warnings
    generally, 149–55, 172, 183, 184–85,
        211, 222–24, 230
    alternative remedies to, 155, 157,
        222–24
    Canadian version of, 184
    desert and, 149–50, 154
    deterrence of police misconduct by,
        151–55
    exceptions to, 153, 154
    frequency of application of, 150
    "fruits" of confession or search and,
        151–52
    indirectly affecting prosecutions, 150
        n.16
    indirectly causing deviations from
        desert, 150
    relation to underlying constitutional
        rights, 150–51, 154–55, 223

Excuse defenses. *See also* Abuse of legal
    rules; Duress defense; Immaturity;
    Insanity defense; Mistake-of-law
    defense
    generally, 27–28, 109, 182, 206–7
    abuse concerns and, 31–35, 41–44, 109
        n.32
    clarity of law and, 109
    definition of, 28 n.1
    deterrence and, 125
    evidentiary concerns and, 206–7, 209
Executive immunity. *See* Official im-
    munity
Ex post facto laws, 96. *See also* Legality
    principle
Eyler, Larry, 139–49, 157–59, 223

Fair import, rule of, 96. *See also* Legality
    principle
Fairness. *See also* Legitimacy; Miscon-
    duct by government agents; Proce-
    dural rules
    generally, 88, 151 n.19, 155
    lineups and, 70 n.50
Felony murder. *See also* Deterrence;
    Strict liability
    generally, 65–69, 118–30, 207
    frequency of, 68 & n.35
    Model Penal Code formulation of, 66
    public attitudes toward, 66 n.30
    questionable deterrent effect of, 128–29
Ferguson, Colin, 50 n.73
Fifth Amendment, 69–71, 137, 149–55,
    159, 222. *See also* Double Jeopardy
    Clause; Exclusionary rules; *Miranda*
    warnings; Self-incrimination, privi-
    lege against
Fines, 32, 126, 191, 194, 212–13 & n.32,
    219–20
Fingerprinting, 58
Foreign law, 193 n.16, 208, 213 n.32, 219.
    See also British law; Canadian law;
    German law; New Zealand law
Fourth Amendment, 137, 149–55, 159,
    184–85, 222–24. *See also* Exclusion-
    ary rules
Frazier, Erica, 63–65
"Fruits" of confession or search, 70,
    151–52

Gambino crime "family," 75–78
Gamesmanship. *See* Abuse of legal rules;
    Misconduct by government agents

Garnett, Raymond, 53, 62–65, 67, 207
General defenses. *See* Excuse defenses;
    Justification defenses; Nonexculpa-
    tory defenses
German law, 213 n.32, 219
Glasser, I. Leo, 78, 80
Goetz, Bernhard, 49
Goldstein, Andrew, 28, 35–41
"Gone With the Wind" syndrome, 50
Gotti, John, 75–78, 85–86
Gounagias, John, 28, 44–48
Gravano, Sammy "the Bull," 74–78,
    79–80, 84–86
"Guilty but mentally ill," 28, 41–44

Heat of passion. *See* Manslaughter miti-
    gation
Hells Canyon Recreation Act, 187–88
Hinckley, John, 43, 207
Howard, Herbert, 53–57, 62

Ignatow, Melvin, 159–66, 169–70
Immaturity, 33–34, 130–31, 206–07 &
    n.3. *See also* Excuse defenses
Immunity. *See* Diplomatic immunity;
    Official immunity; Witness immu-
    nity
Incapacitation. *See also* Civil commitment;
    "Three strikes" laws; Utilitarian goals
    generally, 4, 42 n.34, 117–19, 131–36;
        225–28, 231
    costs of, 4, 136, 214–15
    desert and, 135
    punitive effects of, 215–16
    skepticism regarding, 135–36
    using civil commitment to achieve,
        225–28
Incarceration. *See* Incapacitation
Incompetency defense, 138, 156, 170–72,
    211
    desert and, 171–72
    purposes of, 171
    relation to constitutional rights, 171
    scope of, 170–71
Insanity defense. *See also* Excuse defenses
    generally, 28, 35–44, 125, 207
    formulations of, 41
    public misconceptions regarding, 43–44
    shifting burden of persuasion for, 43,
        207
Integrity, judicial, 138 n.2, 139, 151 n.19,
    154 & n.33, 171, 181. *See also* Legit-
    imacy

Interrogation. *See* Exclusionary rules;
    Fifth Amendment; *Miranda* warn-
    ings; Misconduct by government
    agents; Self-incrimination, privilege
    against
Investigation procedures, 66, 69 n.40. *See
    also* Exclusionary rules; Fifth
    Amendment; Fourth Amendment;
    Misconduct by government agents

"John Doe" indictment, 50 n.6
Judicial immunity. *See* Official immunity
Judicial integrity. *See* Integrity, judicial
Jury
    as representative of community
        norms, 33
    potential of GBMI verdict to con-
        fuse, 42
    role of, 42
    sentences following trial before, 82–83
Justification defenses. *See also* Lesser
    evils defense; Self-defense
    generally, 32–33, 201
    definition of, 28 n.1
    rationale, 32
Juvenile courts, 33–34, 130–31, 133–34,
    206–7

"Kendra's Law," 40
Kunstler, William, 50 n.73
Kustudick, Lauren (Lori), 53–57, 58,
    59, 62

Legality principle. *See also* Bright-line
    rules
    generally, 87–88, 89–101
    desert and, 90, 97–99
    frequency of application to prevent
        conviction, 96–97
    prosecutorial power and, 96–97
    rules based on, 96
Legislative immunity. *See* Official
    immunity
Legitimacy, 83, 138–39, 151 n.19, 154,
    157, 169, 183–85, 231
    relation to moral credibility, 138–39,
        183–85
Lenity, rule of, 96. *See also* Legality
    principle
Lesser-evils defense, 32–33, 107–09. *See
    also* Justification defenses
Limitation Act of 1623, 58
Lindsey, Tom, 187–90, 192

Lineups, requirement of counsel for, 70–71
  benefits in terms of promoting accuracy, 70 n.49

Malum prohibitum offenses, 32 n.7, 190.
  See also Regulatory offenses
Manipulation. *See* Abuse of legal rules
Manslaughter mitigation. *See also*
  Reasonableness standards
  generally, 28, 44–49, 125, 208
  criticism of objective standard for, 48
  formulations of, 48–49
  use of objective standard for, 47–48
Marrero, Julio, 28–31, 32, 34
Marsh, Ray Brent, 90–96, 99–101
McCarty, DeSean, 119–24
"Meek-mate" syndrome, 50
Miranda warnings. *See also* Exclusionary rules; Fifth Amendment; Self-
  incrimination, privilege against
  generally, 70–71, 149–55
  coerced confessions and, 70–71
  frequency of lost convictions due to
  lack of, 150
  videotaping and, 155
Misconduct by government agents. *See*
  also Double Jeopardy Clause;
  Entrapment defense; Exclusionary
  rules; Incompetency defense; Self-
  incrimination, privilege against;
  Speedy-trial right
  generally, 88, 137–85, 191, 204
  deterring via civil sanctions, 204,
  222–24
  double jeopardy and, 159, 166–69
  entrapment defense and, 180–83
  exclusionary rules as deterring, 149–55
  incompetency defense and, 170–72
  legality concerns and, 90 n.4
  self-incrimination privilege and, 69
  speedy-trial right and, 155–57
Mistake-of-law defense, 28–32, 125,
  206–7. *See also* Excuse defenses
Model Code of Pre-Arraignment Procedure, 184
Model Penal Code, 33 n.16, 48–49, 65, 66,
  68, 96, 134, 172, 181 n.115
Moral credibility, 7, 22–23, 67, 113–16,
  128, 138–39, 157, 183–85, 190–91,
  193–94, 201, 210, 221, 231
  plea bargaining's potential to protect,
  74 n.4
  relation to legitimacy, 138–39, 183–85

Narcotics. *See* Drug offenses
Necessity defense. *See* Lesser-evils de-
  fense
Negligence, 28, 46, 65–67, 129, 194, 207.
  See also Culpability; Reasonableness
  standards; Strict liability
New Zealand law, 169, 208
Nonexculpatory defenses, 182–83, 201,
  210–12. *See also* Diplomatic immu-
  nity; Entrapment defense; Incompe-
  tency defense; Official immunity;
  Statutes of limitation
Notice of legal rules, 89–90, 99. *See also*
  Bright-line rules; Legality principle

Official immunity, 186–87, 194–95,
  200–201, 210–11. *See also* Nonexculpatory defenses
Overcriminalization. *See also* Regulatory
  offenses
  generally, 6, 190–91
  legality and, 97
  mistakes of law and, 32
  plea bargaining and, 82
Overzealous enforcement. *See* Misconduct by government agents

Pataki, George, 36, 40–41
Plea bargaining. *See also* Resource constraints; Witness immunity
  generally, 72–86
  alternatives to, 83–84
  as screen for "easy" cases, 73–74, 83
  "charge bargaining" versus "sentence
  bargaining," 79, 83 n.47
  concerns with excessive punishment
  from, 81
  concerns with insufficient punishment
  from, 81–82
  desert and, 80, 82
  frequency of, 79
  law's relation to, 82
  possible reputational benefits to justice
  system from, 74 n.4
  right to counsel and, 81
  right to trial and, 81
  system's dependency on, 83
Police interrogation. *See* Exclusionary
  rules; Fifth Amendment; *Miranda*
  warnings; Misconduct by government agents; Self-incrimination,
  privilege against
"Premenstrual stress syndrome," 50

Presumptions. *See also* Burden of persuasion; Evidentiary burdens
  generally, 34, 68, 70, 131, 206–09
  Model Penal Code's use of, 66, 68
  strict liability as irrebuttable presumption of culpability, 65–69
Prison. *See* Incapacitation
Privacy. *See* Exclusionary rules; Fourth Amendment; Misconduct by government agents
Procedural rules, 137–39, 184–85, 194, 211–12, 219–20. *See also* Double Jeopardy Clause; Exclusionary rules; Fairness; Legitimacy; Misconduct by government agents; Speedy-trial right
Prosecutorial discretion. *See* Discretion
Prosecutorial immunity. *See* Official immunity
Prosecutorial screening, 83–84. *See also* Discretion; Plea bargaining
Provocation. *See* Manslaughter mitigation
Public attitudes. *See also* Legitimacy; Moral credibility
  limits of law's power to shape, 114–16
  toward crime rate, 4
  toward desert, 3–5, 14, 16
  toward drunk driving, 115–16 & n.41
  toward insanity defense, 43–44
  toward legitimacy versus moral credibility, 139 & n.4, 169, 183–85
  toward liability for corporations and other groups, 192–93
  use of legal reforms to shape, 111–16

Rape. *See* Sexual assault offenses; Statutory rape
Reasonableness standards. *See also* Manslaughter mitigation; Negligence
  generally, 28, 46–51, 114, 125
  difficulty of defining, 51
  individualized, 49–50
  Model Penal Code approach to, 48 n.63, 66
  objective, 46–48
Recidivism, 133–36. *See also* Incapacitation; "Three strikes" laws
Regulatory offenses, 11, 32, 186, 190–91, 204
  sanctions imposed for, 191
  using administrative sanctions to address, 218–21

Rehabilitation, 117–19, 130–31. *See also* Deterrence; Immaturity; Incapacitation; Utilitarian goals
Reliability concerns, 52–71
  "fruit of poisonous tree" doctrine as rooted in, 151–52
  incompetency defense and, 171
  potential overinclusiveness of rules based on, 69
Reputation of criminal-justice system, 7, 22, 138–39, 151. *See also* Legitimacy; Moral credibility
Resource constraints, *see also* Plea bargaining
  generally, 25–26, 72–86, 151, 193
  desert and, 66, 73, 80
Resulting harm, significance of, 19–20, 134. *See also* Attempt
Retributivism, 17, 19–20, 21. *See also* Desert
Right to counsel, 5, 70–71, 81, 137 n.1, 171, 222
Ryan, George, 62

Searches and seizures. *See* Fourth Amendment
Self-defense, 49–50. *See also* Justification defenses
Self-incrimination, privilege against. *See also* Fifth Amendment; *Miranda* warnings
  generally, 69–71
  as rule of evidence, 69–70
  bases for, 69 & n.41
  "fruits" of confession and, 70
  reliability concerns and, 69–70
Sentencing rules, 79, 82, 126, 134, 212–17. *See also* "Three strikes" laws; Units of punishment
Sexual assault offenses, 111–16. *See also* Statutory rape
Sixth Amendment. *See* Right to counsel; Speedy-trial right
Speedy-trial right, 58, 137, 149, 155–57
  alternative remedies for, 156–57 & nn.54–55, 222–24
  balancing test for violations of, 155 n.43
  as deterrent of prosecutorial delay, 156 n.48
  due-process requirements compared with, 156 n.52
  purposes of, 155–56
  remedy for violation of, 156–57

Speedy-trial statutes, 155–56
Statutes of limitation. *See also* Nonexculpatory defenses
  generally, 53–62
  desert-related costs of, 60
  exclusion of murder from, 61
  justifications for, 58–60
  speedy-trial rights and, 58, 155
  technological advances and, 58
  variation across jurisdictions, 60–61
Statutory rape, 62–66, 207. *See also* Sexual assault offenses; Strict liability
Stephens, Edwin, 101–11
Strict liability. *See also* Deterrence; Felony murder
  generally, 62–69, 119–30
  causal theory of, 65 n.27
  deterrence-based theory of, 65 n.27, 124–30
  equivalency theory of, 65 n.27
  evidentiary presumptions as alternative to, 207–09
  evidentiary theory of, 52–53, 65–69, 125 n.8, 127 n.13
  frequency of imposition of, 67–68
  overbreadth concerns with, 67–69
  as promoting clarity, 112–13
  tension with desert, 113, 126–27

"Television intoxication," 50
Terry stops, 146–47
Thatcher, Margaret, 174
"Three strikes" laws, 4, 11, 133, 225, 228. *See also* Civil commitment; Deterrence; Incapacitation
Trivial offenses. *See* Regulatory offenses
"Twinkie defense," 50

United States Sentencing Guidelines, 79
Units of punishment, 9, 203, 212–17
  available sanctions for system of, 212–13
  feasibility of system of, 214
"Urban survival syndrome," 50
Utilitarian goals. *See also* Desert; Deterrence; Incapacitation; Rehabilitation
  generally, 16–18, 42 n.34, 88, 117–36
  desert-based system's potential to achieve, 17–18, 21–23, 118–19, 128
  skepticism about, 10, 17–18, 118–19
  using "units of punishment" to facilitate, 9, 203, 212–17

Vagueness, 90 n.3, 96. *See also* Legality principle
Verdict system, 9, 98–99, 109, 111, 114, 200–01, 203, 205, 210–12
  collateral effects of conviction verdict, 210–11
  confusion of "not guilty" verdict with finding of innocence, 210 & n.23
  options in cases involving insanity claims, 41–44
Videotaping of interrogations, 155
Vienna Convention of Diplomatic Relations, 199

Witness immunity. *See also* Nonexculpatory defenses; Plea bargaining; Resource constraints
  generally, 72–86
  frequency of, 79 & n.10
  relation to desert, 73, 80
Witness Protection Program, 84–85